NR   2/6

KITCHEN ENCYCLOPEDIA

NELLA WHITFIELD

KITCHEN ENCYCLOPEDIA

SPRING BOOKS • LONDON

Published by

SPRING BOOKS

SPRING HOUSE . SPRING PLACE . LONDON NW5

Printed in Czechoslovakia

T 458

PART I

A DICTIONARY OF
COOKING TERMS AND METHODS

ABAISSE. A thin pastry used for lining tarts, soufflés, croustades.

ABATIS, AUX. Clear or thickened soup made with giblets or poultry.

ABERNETHY BISCUIT. A crisp biscuit named after the small town in Scotland where it was first made. It always contains caraway seeds.

ABRASIVES. Salt, scouring powders and pastes for cleaning saucepans and oven-ware. Great care must be taken to rinse the utensils after use.

ABRICOTE. A cake or pudding masked with apricot marmalade.

ABSINTHE. An aromatic herb from which a liqueur, an apéritif and a flavouring are made. The apéritif used to be drunk in large quantities in France. It is said to be extremely bad for the liver.

ACID CURD. In cheese-making a curd produced by coagulation of casein by acids, normally lactic acid.

ACIDIMETER. A method of measuring the acidity in milk for cheese-making by using phenolphthalein and caustic soda.

ACID ICE. A mixture of whisked egg-whites, sugar and lemon juice, after the style of meringue, for use on puddings and pies.

ADAM & EVE PUDDING. Cooked apples, covered with a cake mixture spread over the top, and baked.   (See recipe)

ADMIRAL. A hot punch made with claret, sugar and spices. Sometimes moistened with egg yolk.

ADVOCAAT. A famous Dutch liqueur made with brandy and fresh egg-yolks.

AERATED BREAD. A machine-made bread, made without yeast, but with carbon dioxide mechanically introduced. It is said to be more easily digested than yeast or balm bread.

AERATED FLOUR. Another name for self-raising flour.

AERATED WATER. Water either naturally or artificially charged with carbonic acid gas. Water aerated naturally springs from the soil and may be drunk or bottled on the spot. Other types of aerated or mineral waters are those artificially carbonated; they are less expensive, but contain none of the valuable mineral salts found in the natural waters. The commonest of artificially carbonated waters are soda, potash and lithia.

AFRICAINE. Rice soup with a curry flavour.

AGAR-AGAR. One of a number of red Oriental gelatinous seaweeds. They are rich in carbohydrates and make good soups and jellies.

AGNES SOREL. A cream of poultry soup flavoured with mushrooms.

AGRIMONY. A common weed which grows in waste places in many parts of Great Britain. It bears a spike of small yellow flowers. The stems, leaves and flowers are used to make agrimony tea, an infusion of which is said to clear the blood. Used also for making a home-made wine.

AGUAXIMA. A variety of Brazilian black pepper.

AIGRETTES, CHEESE. Cheese straws.

AIGUILLE A BRIDER. A larding needle.

AIGUILLETTES. Needles. Thin strips of cooked fish or meat.

AILERONS. Stuffed chickens' wings.

AILLADE. A veal dish flavoured with garlic.   (See recipe)

AILLOLI. A rich garlic sauce of the South of France.   (See recipe)

AITCH BONE OR EDGE BONE. The cut of beef lying over the rump and known as 'Poor Man's Sirloin'.

AJOUTEES. Mixed, or added; for example, small garnishes or side dishes added to or served with the main dish.

A LA CARTE. A list of dishes for hotel or restaurant meals which shows the price against each dish and from which a meal may be composed at choice, whereas a Table d'Hôte menu restricts the choice and usually bears a fixed inclusive price.

A LA MODE DE . . . In the style or fashion of: for example, *à la Russe, à la Française* — in Russian or French style.

ALBACORE. A species of tunny-fish.

ALBERT. A rich cream sauce with chopped shallots cooked in tarragon vinegar, horse-radish and parsley.

ALBONI. A brown sauce seldom served with any other food but venison. It has red currant jelly and roasted beech nuts added and is of delicious flavour.

ALBUMEN AND GLOBULIN. Albuminous proteins, coagulated by heat, in cheese-making.

ALBUMEN WATER. A drink for invalids made by whisking one egg-white with 1/2 pint of water and a teaspoonful of lemon juice. The liquid is left to stand until the egg-white has dissolved.

ALCOHOL. Produced by fermented sugar. Gives to wines, spirits and beers their intoxicating quality. It is highly inflammable.

ALEBERRY. Fine oatmeal mixed with weak ale and left to soak for a couple of hours, then strained, boiled and sweetened.

ALEVIN. The first stage of a salmon.

ALEWIFE. A member of the herring family very abundant off the Atlantic coasts of North America.

ALFALFA. A leguminous plant grown for cattle food in normal times, but a valuable food for man in times of scarcity.

ALICANTE. One of the best known wines of Levante. The Alicante vineyards are responsible for producing about 10 million gallons of wine a year. It is a red dessert wine, rather sweet.

ALICOT. A famous French country dish made with pieces of left-over goose, bacon, onions, tomatoes and a bouquet garni (q. v.).

ALLEMANDE. A white velouté sauce well reduced.

ALLSPICE. The common name for Jamaica pepper; the dried unripe berry of the pimento or allspice tree. Not to be confused with mixed spice.

ALLUMETTES. Fried potatoes cut as finely as match-sticks.

ALMONDS. The fruit of two main trees which produce sweet almonds or bitter almonds. The sweet almonds are roughly divided into 5 classes, the Common, Large, Sultan, Jordan and Pistache.
Almonds are used in many kinds of confectionery and sweet making, as well as in a few savoury dishes. The flavour of the bitter almond is due to a benzaldehyde which develops with minute quantities of prussic acid when the almond is moistened and crushed.   (See recipe)

ALSACIENNE. A soup of finely chopped sauerkraut thickened with a little flour and served with small potato balls.

ALUM. A white transparent astringent mineral salt. Sometimes used to whiten flour.

ALUMINIUM SAUCEPANS. To remove discolouration, boil apple-peelings or rhubarb in them. Tartaric acid does equally well.

AMANDINE. A dish containing, or prepared with, almonds.

AMEAUX. A pastry made of puff paste and eggs.

AMER PICON. A popular brand of French apéritif, with a slight flavour of burnt orange. Sometimes served straight, but usually with a little Grenadine and one to two parts of iced water.

AMIRALE. A garnish consisting of fried oysters, slices of lobster, and brown sauce, usually used for fish. The term is also applied to meat dishes.

AMMONIA. Use a few drops in warm water for cleaning kitchen tiles, sinks, washing up cloths and mops.

AMONTILLADO. One of the most popular types of sherry, with a fairly dry finish. It is one of the sherries to serve, very slightly chilled, before a meal.

AMOURETTES. The French name for the marrow from calves' and sheep's bones, poached and seasoned and served as a garnish.

AMULET. The old name for omelette, especially a sweet one made with flour, sugar, egg-yolks and orange-flower water and egg-whites separately.

ANCHOVY. A small herring-like fish caught in the Mediterranean and the English Channel. Very good when fresh, and of a unique flavour when cured; used for making the anchovy sauce so much employed in cooking, also as a relish and appetiser for hors-d'œuvres and snacks.

ANDALOUSE. A cold sauce of mayonnaise with tomato pulp and finely shredded red pepper, served with eggs, fish and macedoine of cold vegetables.

ANDOUILLE. A large cooked pork sausage usually served as part of an hors-d'oeuvre. It is made in several parts of France, notably Normandy.

ANDOUILLETTE. A small Andouille.

ANGEL CAKE. A light sweet cake which originated in America. It is made with the whites of the eggs only, with a high proportion of sugar, and is almost always baked in a specially shaped sloping mould with a hole in the centre.

ANGELICA. A native of northerly parts of Russia and Germany, this sweet and aromatic flavoured plant was brought to England in the 16th century. It has been cultivated and has flourished ever since. The thick hollow stems are crystallised for sweetbreads and cakes. Old tales connect it with angelic powers against evil spirits and witchcraft.

ANGELS ON HORSEBACK. An appetiser consisting of plump oysters wrapped in pieces of back rasher of bacon, fastened with small wooden toothpicks and pushed on skewers in threes. It is dipped in batter and fried, or else grilled without being dipped in batter.

ANGELS' PIE. Made with young tender pigeons, madeira wine, cayenne pepper, lemon juice, hard cooked plovers' or pigeons' eggs, forcemeat and gravy, covered with flakey pastry and cooked very gently for a long time.

ANGEL TIPS. A glass of the liqueur Crème de Cacao with a layer of sweet cream floating on the top.

ANGLAISE. Coating of beaten egg and fine breadcrumbs for fish or meat, rissoles, fish-cakes, or croquettes, to give a golden crusty surface with an appetising flavour.

ANGLAISE, A L'. To cook in plain salted water and finish with plain melted butter.

ANGLER. A large ugly fish found in the Atlantic off some European countries and America. Sometimes known as devil-fish or frog-fish.

ANGOSTURA. The bitter and aromatic bark of the *galipea cusparis* tree, a native of Venezuela. Made into a liquid which is used for flavouring gin, cocktails and fruits or fruit salads.

ANGUILLE DE MER. The French name for conger eel.

ANIS. The Spanish name for an aniseed-flavoured cordial usually drunk as a long drink with iced water.

ANISETTE. A French liqueur, of a licorice flavour, made with aniseeds.

ANNATTO. A colouring made from the seeds of an evergreen tree, used sometimes to give a yellow tinge to butter and to colour cheeses.

ANTIBIOTIC. A chemical substance derived from a mould, which inhibits the growth or activity of micro-organisms.

ANTIPASTO. A collection of small appetising snacks. The same as hors-d'œuvres.

APERITIF. A short drink taken before a meal, not necessarily alcoholic. Seasoned tomato juice, passion-fruit juice or grapefruit juice is sometimes served.

APFELSTRUDEL. A dessert popular in Vienna and in Hungary. The chief characteristic feature of the sweet is that the dough with which it is made must be stretched out over a large table, covered with a clean cloth, until it is as thin as tissue paper and almost transparent.
(See recipe)

APPAREIL A MOUSSE. A mixture of ice-cream and whipped cream, used in making ice cream bombes.

APPETISERS. The name given to rich little tit-bits of fish, egg, sausage, mushrooms, etc., served with cocktails or before a meal. These morsels are smaller than hors-d'œuvres.

APPLE. The fruit of any member of the genus *malus,* of which there are many different species. In Great Britain there is a difference between eating- and cooking-apples. The cooking variety is large, green and acid, and their qualities allow such apples to be cooked to a pulp. The dessert apples are generally sweet and of excellent flavour.
Varieties include Beauty of Bath, Worcester Pearmain, Blenheim Orange, Cox's Orange Pippin, Ribston Pippin, Ellison's Orange and Laxton's Superb.
The best cookers are Bramley Seedling, Newton Wonder and Lane's **Prince Albert.** (See recipe)

APPLE AMBER. A dish made of apple purée, lemon, eggs and puff pastry.
(See recipe)

APPLE CHARLOTTE. A sweet made with sponge fingers and apple purée,
piped with cream.   (See recipe)

APPLE JACK (APPLE BRANDY). Two names for the same kind of
colourless spirit distilled from cider at a high alcoholic strength. The
most famous is that made in Normandy and called Calvados.

APPLES IN NIGHT-GOWNS. A form of Apple Dumpling. Apples,
peeled, cored, filled with orange conserve or thick marmalade, wrapped
in rich crust, sugared and baked.

APRICOT. A soft, juicy stone-fruit extensively cultivated in China originally, now grown in all temperate countries.
    A fruit which lends itself to successful drying; hence large quantities
are imported from California. Australia and the Cape. In France the
apricots are crystallised and make a delicious sweetmeat or dessert.
(See recipe)

AQUA VITAE. The Latin name for Brandy.

AQUAVIT (AKVAVIT). The Scandinavian form of aqua vitae, a highly-
rectified, practically neutral spirit, distilled mostly from grain or potatoes
and flavoured with caraway seeds. It is neither sweetened nor coloured
nor aged. It is usually swallowed at a gulp, like vodka, as a cocktail.

'ARF AND 'ARF. The old Cockney name for a blend of porter and pale
ale. Another Cockney name is 'Mother-in-law'.

ARLESIENNE. An elaborate garnish for small pieces of grilled steak, for
little lamb cutlets, or for pieces of grilled veal fillet. It consists of slices
of aubergine or egg-plant, rings of onion and slices of tomato fried in
olive oil with a tiny morsel of crushed garlic in the oil, and is sprinkled
with parsley.

ARMAGNAC. A brandy distilled from wine of the Gers Department in
France.

AROMATES. Aromatic herbs used for flavouring, such as thyme, marjoram,
tarragon, chervil, bayleaves, parsley, etc.

ARRACK. A spirit produced by fermenting the juice of the cocoa and
other palms. Used extensively in the East, but little known in Europe.
(See recipe for arrack liqueur)

ARROPE. Unfermented grape juice boiled to the thickness of syrup and
used for sweetening sherry and some other Spanish wines.

ARROWROOT. A dry powdery starch made from the pith of plants of
the *maranta* type. It is gelatinous when boiled with water or any other
liquid and can be used to make sauces and thicken stews. With milk
it is an excellent item of food for invalids.   (See recipe)

ARTICHOKE.

Globe. Actually a form of thistle. The heads are composed of many layers of pointed leaves folded round a hairy core. Usually served boiled, hot or cold, the leaves are pulled off one by one and dipped into melted butter and salt or a Sauce Vinaigrette or mayonnaise and eaten in the fingers. The artichokes are also cooked in many a rich fashion.

Jerusalem. The Jerusalem artichoke is a tuber-like vegetable resembling in appearance a knobbly potato. Should be soaked in water for 30 min., scraped and boiled with lemon juice or vinegar in the water to prevent it from turning black. May also be eaten raw in salads with mayonnaise.

ASPARAGUS. A plant which grows in light sandy soil, cultivated and highly prized for its delicious flavour. It is rich in mineral salts, Vitamins A and B. The fleshy white stalk, which is not eaten, is much tougher than the delicate green tip and the asparagus should therefore be tied in small bundles and stood upright in the saucepan to cook.

ASPIC (IN ASPIC). A savoury piquant jelly used either to make a complete jellied dish, or, chopped, to garnish a cold dish. Fish, poultry, meats, vegetables and salads are frequently set in aspic.

ASSIETTE ANGLAISE. The name given in French restaurants to a salad of different kinds of cold meat, usually including underdone roast beef, ham, ox tongue and sausage.

ASSIETTES VOLANTES. Small savoury soufflés and other small dishes, which should be served very hot and taken quickly round to the guests.

ASTRACHAN. A name of one kind of caviar.

ATELETES (SOMETIMES KNOWN AS HATELETS). Skewers for decorating joints and entrées, usually of silver and with decorative heads.

ATHOL BROSE. A Scotch drink — looked upon as a certain cure for colds and chills — made by pouring water over oatmeal, sweetening with honey and lacing well with whisky. Occasionally a well-beaten egg is stirred into the mixture.

AUBERGINES. See *Egg-plant.*

AU BEURRE. Cooked in butter.

AU BLANC. Cooked in White Sauce.

AU BLEU. A term applied to fish cooked in salted water seasoned with vinegar, herbs and thinly sliced vegetables.

AU FOUR. Baked in the oven.

AU GRAS. Dishes containing meat dressed with rich gravy and sauces.

AU GRATIN. Dishes finished with a crust or sprinkling of crisped crumbs and browned beneath the grill or in a hot oven. The terms now usually means with crumbs and grated cheese mixed, which makes a far more appetising finish than plain crumbs.

AU JUS. Meat or poultry served with its own gravy.

AU MAIGRE. Any dish prepared without meat or gravy or sauce but made from meat or bones. Usually food served during Lent or on Fridays.

AU NATUREL. Food cooked very simply without garnish; for example, plain boiled potatoes.

AURORE. Rice soup coloured with tomato puree.

AVOCADO PEAR. The fruit of a tree which is a native of tropical Africa, but is now grown extensively in the U. S. A. and many sub-tropical countries. There are several varieties, the fruits varying in size and from about 6 oz. to 4 lbs. in weight. The best weight is that of about $1/2$ lb. The skins are hard and green and shiny. The flesh is rich in oil, proteins and Vitamin B. It is usually scooped out with a spoon and eaten as it is, but it may also be dressed with mayonnaise, or salt and lemon juice. It has wrongly been called the alligator pear.

AVOCET. A scarce migrant bird which formerly bred between the Humber and Sussex. It is not usually eaten, but was used during the War.

AYOLI. See *Ailloli*.

BABA. A light yeast cake, originating in France. It is usually soaked in apricot syrup and rum and served with whipped cream.   (See recipe)

BABY. A quarter bottle of wine or spirits.

BACARDI. A brand of rum distilled in Cuba and much used for cocktails; an American cocktail is named after the rum.

BACON. The flesh of the pig salted, dried and usually smoked. If salted and dried and not smoked, it is known as green bacon.
                                (See recipes for curing and salting bacon)

BAGNES. A hard Swiss cheese known as fromage à la Raclette. The orthodox method of eating this cheese is to cut it in thick slices, toast it before a wood fire till the surface softens, scrape it off with a knife and spread it on thick bread, preferably a rye bread. The modern way is to toast the cheese before an electric fire.

BAG PUDDING. A pudding boiled in a cloth instead of a basin. A well-floured cloth is laid in a bowl or colander and filled with the suet crust and meat; then the crust is sealed over and the cloth knotted. The pudding is then dropped into boiling water and boiled gently for 2—3 hrs.

BAGRATION. A cold sauce of mayonnaise with anchovy purée and caviar.

BAIN-MARIE. A vessel containing hot water over which another pan or dish containing food is placed, to keep it hot without burning it or drying it up.

BAKE BLIND. To bake tart or tartlet cases of pastry without filling, in order that they may be used later as required.

To keep the pastry flat without bubbles and uneven rising, greaseproof paper is laid on the uncooked pastry, covered with bread crusts, dried peas or haricot beans and baked until the pastry is done. The paper and its contents are then removed, leaving a flat surface upon which to spread jam, fruit or custard.

BAKEWELL TART. A rich tart of pastry, jam and custard, sometimes almonds, originally made in Derbyshire. (See recipe)

BAKING POWDER. A mixture of chemicals used for aerating bread, buns or cake mixtures. (See recipe)

BALM. A sweet-smelling herb used to flavour soup, salads and drinks, or to make an infusion to drink as tea. Known as lemon or sweet balm. Also another name for yeast (q. v.).

BALMORAL. A cream soup with breast of mutton and herbs.

BALORINE. A hash of finely minced meat with beetroot, spring onions and caraway seeds. Of Russian origin.

BAMBOO. Young bamboo shoots are used extensively in Eastern cooking. They may be bought in tins or jars in Oriental delicatessen shops.

BANANAS. The fruit of the banana palm. The fruit grows in large bunches. For export the bunches are picked green in order that they may ripen as they travel. Bananas may be dried. (See recipes)

BANBURY CAKES. A cake of puff pastry and mincemeat, owing its name to the town of Banbury in Oxfordshire, which has been famous for the cake for many years. (See recipe)

BANNOCKS. Scottish cakes made with oatmeal mixed with egg and milk. In olden times different kinds of Bannocks were baked for different occasions, especially for the four quarter-days and for Hallowe'en.
(See recipe)

BAR. A white-fleshed sea fish with good flavour, commonly known as dog-fish. Served with any sauces or in any recipes used for salmon it is good.

BARBECUE. This used to mean roasting a large animal whole in the open air, usually at winter fêtes or skating carnivals. Americans used the term later for out-door sports parties, where smaller joints, steaks, chops and hamburgers are cooked on small built-up ranges. An important part of the barbecue dish is the rich piquant sauce served with the meats.

BARLEY. A cereal which is used a great deal for malting. Pearl barley is ripe barley with the husks removed, steamed, rounded and polished. Used in stews and for making cooling drinks for invalids and for soups or puddings.   (See recipe)

BARLEY SUGAR. A simple sweetmeat made with sugar, water and lemon juice. It does not contain barley.   (See recipe)

BARLEY WINE. Very strong beer of good quality.

BARON (OF BEEF). A double sirloin joined together at the backbone.
                                                    (See *Sirloin*)

BARQUETTES. Short pastry, sweet or savoury, baked empty in small boat-shaped patty tins and filled with savoury mixtures as required, or with whipped cream, strawberries or chopped glacé fruits in liqueur or jelly.

BARREL. A liquid measure of 36 gallons.

BASIL. Two kinds of this seasoning herb are grown, sweet basil and bush basil. They are used in stuffings and soups and the flavour goes particularly well with tomatoes.

BASIL SHERRY. A flavouring much favoured for enriching soups especially mock turtle or real turtle soup.   (See recipe)

BATARDE. Butter sauce made with melted butter seasoned with lemon juice and salt.

BATHBUN. A yeast cake or bun or irregular shape containing candied peel, with a sugar-crusted top. It takes its name from the city of Bath where it originated.

BATH CHAPS. Pigs' cheeks, cured, salted and rolled into horn-shaped cylinders. The meat is very fat, but very tender and appetising. Usually sold cooked and skinned and rolled in browned crumbs.

BATTER. A thin cream made with eggs, flour, milk and seasoning, prepared according to what kind of food is to be coated.
                                                    (See recipes)

BATTERED TROTTERS. Pigs' or sheep's trotters or calves' feet stewed with vegetables, boned, covered with thick batter and deep-fried.

BAY LAUREL. An evergreen with bright shiny leaves which have a pleasant almond flavouring; used for custards, milk puddings, soups and stews; also in making rollmops and soused herrings.

BEANS. A vegetable of which there is a great number of varieties, including scarlet runners, which are dark green and grow sometimes to a foot in length; French beans, long, slender, pale green, usually cooked whole; and broad beans, the seeds only of which are eaten; which seeds, when small and young, are very much like marrowfat peas, though later they become coarse, when the outer skins must be removed. Usually boiled and served with hot ham and parsley sauce.

Apart from the fresh beans, there are many dried beans including haricot and butter beans.   (See recipes)

BECHAMEL. A creamy white sauce which forms the basis for many other cream sauces.   (See recipes)

BEDFORDSHIRE CLANGER. A meal of two courses cooked together, originally made by the Luton straw-weavers and hat-makers.

This very robust meal consisted of suet pastry, minced meat and onions, salt and pepper and jam.

The pastry was rolled out, one end spread with the meat and onion, a strip of pastry placed down the centre of the oblong of paste, the other end spread with jam or treacle, the whole rolled tightly, the ends pressed firmly and turned over to keep in the contents of the roll, the whole tied in a floured cloth and boiled.

The meaty half was eaten first, the jammy half afterwards.

BEDSTRAW. A delicate wild herb, yellow and white. The stems and leaves can be used like rennet, for curdling milk. The flowers are often used for colouring cheese and butter.

BEEF. The flesh of the bullock and the cow. There are at least 18 different cuts, not including the tail, tongue, liver and cheeks.

BEEF OLIVES. Very thin slices of cold beef filled with savoury stuffing, rolled and tied with fine twine, browned in a little fat, then simmered in thick gravy until very hot.   (See recipe)

BEEF TEA. Essence of beef.   (See recipe)

BEETROOT. There are red and white beetroots, but by far the better known are the red ones, of rich crimson colour. In spring small globe beets are at their best; during the rest of the year the parsnip-shaped roots are used extensively in salads, or as a hot vegetable, or as a garnish.

Cooked and served like spinach the young leaves are good.   (See recipe)

BEIGNETS (CREPES SUZETTE). Small puffed fritters filled with little pieces of savoury food, or served with sugar and liqueur sauces or fruit-juice sauces.   (See recipe)

BEISTYN (FIRSTLINGS). The first milk given by the cow after calving.

BEL PAESE. A favourite Italian cheese, soft and creamy. The round cheeses wrapped in gaily coloured foils are well-known in Italian restaurants and grocery stores.

BENEDICTINE. A very sweet liqueur made at Fécamp in Normandy by the Benedictine monks and one of the oldest known liqueurs in the world.

The distinctive bottles in which it is sold bear the letters D. O. M. meaning Deo Optimo Maximo (To God Most Good, Most Great). Many people prefer to drink it as B. and B., meaning a blend of brandy and Benedictine.

BENOITON. An eel boned, twisted in a spiral, coated with flour, deep-fried and served with a sauce of red wine, shallots, chopped parsley root, butter and seasoning.

BERCY. A white cream sauce with seasonings.   (See recipe)

BERGERE. Clear tapioca soup with chopped mushrooms and asparagus heads.

BERLINOISE. An eel cooked in pale German beer thickened with grated rye bread.

BEARNAISE. The same as Hollandaise sauce, but made with tarragon vinegar instead of plain malt vinegar.

BEURRE MANIEE. Butter and flour kneaded together to be used as thickening for sauces or soups.

BEURRE NOIR. Literally 'black butter'; invariably served with skate or sole, it is not black, but butter melted and cooked to a light golden colour and immediately poured over the fish. A few drops of lemon juice may be added and whipped into the butter if liked.

BIBLE CAKE. A cake of which the ingredients are all to be found alluded to in verses in books of the Bible. (Also known as 'Scripture cake').
                                                              (See recipe)

BI-CARBONATE OF SODA. A white crystalline substance, used in cooking. As a raising agent it is mixed with twice its volume of cream of tartar. A pinch is often used in cooking vegetables to preserve their colour and to tenderise them.

A pinch also helps to overcome the acidity of rhubarb and gooseberries, when less sugar in needed in the cooking.

BIFFINS. Peeled and partly baked apples, dried and pressed flat.

BIGARADE (COLD). An orange sauce made with wine and currant jelly added.   (See recipe)

BILBERRY (BLAEBERRY). An English berry, found in woods and on hillsides and downs, small and blue-black in colour and taking much patience to pick. The berries are very juicy and are used alone for tarts or with apples. They are known in different parts of Great Britain as whortleberries, worts, hurts, whinberries and blaeberries.

BILTONG. A form of dried meat peculiar to South Africa. It dries so hard that it has to be grated. It has been known to last for 10 years.

BIRCH WINE. A home-made wine fermented, especially in Sussex, from the sap of birch trees with yeast and sugar.

BIRD'S NEST SOUP. A Chinese delicacy. The so-called bird's nest is actually the predigested protein from a seaweed gathered from the sea along the cliffs of the Pacific islands by a particular kind of petrel. The seawed is digested by the alkaline of the mouths of the birds and used for building their nests. It possesses a delicate flavour when cooked in beef stock and is rich in protein, and is said to be particularly good for those suffering from an ulcerated stomach.   (See recipe)

BISMARCK HERRING. Lightly salted and smoked whole herrings used as hors-d'œuvre.

BISQUE. A rich, thick soup made from one of the kinds of shell fish, such as bisque of lobster, of prawns, of crabs, or crayfish.

BLACK BUN (SCOTCH BUN). A rich fruity mixture, well spiced, encased in short crust. Usually made in the shape of a large dumpling, but sometimes made in flat tins.   (See recipe)

BLACK MAN. A rich toffee made with dark treacle and traditionally served on Bonfire nights.

BLACK PUDDING. A mixture of oatmeal, blood from a freshly killed pig with minced liver and chopped white fat and seasoning. Made up in large sausage-shaped bladders brushed over with blood before being baked, which turns them black and gives them the name. The black puddings are traditionally from the North and Midlands.   (See recipe)

BLACK STRIPE. Made with rum and molasses, and so called because the dark treacle lies on the rum in a stripe before it is stirred. In summer ice is added to the drink; in winter, boiling water.

BLANCH. To drop vegetables and nuts or meat into rapidly boiling water for a few minutes, before placing them in cold water in order that the skins of the vegetables or nuts may be removed easily and the membranes or veins of the meat.

BLANCMANGE. Originally a white creamy pudding set in a mould, made of arrowroot or cornflour. Now made with ready-made powders to be mixed with milk, and in various flavours.   (See recipes)

BLEENY. Russian pancakes made with buck-wheat or rye flour. Eaten, prior to the Revolution, in carnival time before Lent, but still served. Favourite method of serving is with butter and sour cream, sometimes with caviar.

BLOATER. Herrings caught near enough to the shore to be taken in and cured without being salted. The best bloaters come from Yarmouth.

BLUE VINNY. Another name for Blue Dorset cheese. 'Vinny' is a corruption of a very old West Country word, 'vinew', meaning mould. The cheese is chalk white with a bright blue streak running through it. The special blue colour of this mould is produced by a different process from that in other cheese.

BOBOTEE. The name given in South Africa to a dish of minced meat and seasonings, very much like our shepherd's pie or rissoles.
(See recipe)

BOLETUS (CEPE). One of the edible fungi. A thick white fleshy mushroom with tubes instead of gills. These should be removed before cooking. May be sliced and dried or cooked, especially in the famous dish, *Cèpes à la Bordelaise.*
(See recipe)

BOLOGNESE SAUSAGE. The most famous of sausages from Bologna and known best as *mortadella.* A large sausage of spiced pork delicately speckled with white fat.

BOMBAY DUCK. Cured raw fish with a very strong odour. It becomes appetising when cooked in fat or baked in the oven. Served with Indian curries or crumbled over rice.

BONDON. French whole milk cheese made in small cylinder shapes and wrapped in soft white paper. A very small quantity of sugar is added to the milk while the cheese is being made. It comes chiefly from Normandy and is now a comparative luxury, having risen in price.

BONNE FEMME (COUNTRY-STYLE). Leek and potato soup. (See recipe; see also *Sole Bonne Femme*).

BORAGE. A herb with greyish-green leaves and stems covered with fine prickly hairs and blue flowers. The young leaves, which have a faint cucumber flavour, can be used in salads; leaves and flowers are used to flavour wine, cider and fruit cups.

BORSHCH. A Polish or Russian soup coloured red with beetroot.
(See recipe)

BOTTOMLESS CASK. A type of mixed fruit cider made by the Circassians. Fruits used are ripe medlars, quinces, apples, pears, with cherry leaves, sugar and cold water. The mixture is left to mature for about 10 days. As the liquid is drawn off, more water is added to the cask to replenish the residue, hence its name.

BOUCHEES. Literally 'mouthfuls'. Small puff paste patties filled with sweet or savoury mixtures and only large enough for one or two bites. Served with cocktails.

BOUCHERE. Strong meat broth, with shredded cabbage and shredded marrow, parsley and chervil.

BOUGH CAKE. A very old cake of German origin, in which dried figs and any other dried fruit and almonds are threaded on a piece of twine and hung and basted with a batter mixture, being turned on a spit so that the batter cooks and sticks to the fruit. When the bough is sufficiently thick with coatings of batter, it is taken down and eaten in slices with sugar. In high-class bakers' establishments and confectioners' a modern version is now made over an electric stove, a much lighter sponge cake mixture being poured over a revolving wooden cylinder in the gentle heat, to produce a long, light, smooth cake with a hole down the centre for filling with flavoured cream, glacé cherries, nuts and shredded peel.

BOUILLABAISSE. A fish soup made with a mixture of small fish, with lobsters, crawfish, saffron, garlic, olive oil, tomato, wine and seasonings. It can be made in England, but the best comes from Marseilles and the Riviera coast, where many small fish suitable for the soup are found.
(See recipe)

BOUILLON. Strong stock, carefully cleared, used for making soups, stews and sauces.

BOUQUET GARNI. A little bunch of herbs such as bayleaf, thyme, parsley, tarragon, sage, piece of celery as required, tied together and cooked with stews, casseroles, braised foods or soups, and removed before finishing touches are added.

BOURBON. An American whisky distilled from a fermented mash of over half, or chiefly, maize. It was first distilled in Kentucky.

BOURGEOISE, A LA. A name given to dishes to show that they are prepared in a simple and homely but tasty and wholesome manner.

BOURGUIGNONNE. A highly seasoned wine sauce.
(See recipe under *Sauces*)

BOXTY. An Irish dish made with scallions and grated raw potatoes, and cooked in milk to a mash, seasoned, and put into a large bowl and covered with melted butter.

BRACKEN. The fronds of young bracken may be tied in bundles, cooked like asparagus and served with melted butter. The fronds should not be more than about 4 inches long and they are only good to eat when the stalks snap easily, otherwise they are stringy.

BRADENHAM HAM. A ham which is distinguished by its black rind, due to the method of curing. These hams, the finest Wiltshire hams, are cured by the Bradenham Ham Company of Wiltshire by a special recipe which has been used since 1781.

BRAISE.

To braise beef or mutton: fry quickly and lightly all over to seal it and hold the juices. The meat is then placed on a bed of mixed sliced vegetables, which have been coloured in a little dripping or butter with a pinch of salt and a teaspoonful of sugar and chosen seasonings. A very little stock is then added, the saucepans closely covered and the contents are allowed to simmer very slowly for about 3—4 hr. according to the kind of meat.

To braise white meat: lightly stiffen on either side but do not brown. Put into a saucepan upon the seasonings and uncoloured vegetables with just enough white stock to moisten. Cover closely. Cook on moderate heat until the stock is reduced. To test whether the meat is done, prick deeply; when colourless juice is exuded, the meat is perfectly cooked.

BRAN. The husks of ground corn, used in making some brown breads, muffins and a nourishing drink.   (See recipe)

BRANDADE DE MORUE. A famous Provençal dish of dried and salted cod.   (See recipe)

BRANDY SNAPS (JUMBLES). Brittle toffee-like sweet cakes, made with syrup, butter, sugar, ginger, and only enough flour to make a thin batter.
(See recipe)

BRAWN. Meat and fat diced and set in a thick jelly with seasonings. Usually made with pig's or calf's head, or with hand and spring of pork or leg of veal, because these meats, when boiled make a solid jelly. Brawn is served cold with piquant sauces.   (See recipe)

BRAZILS. The large globular fruit of a South American tree, with a hard woody husk containing from 18—24 closely packed three-sided nuts. The nuts are very hard to crack, the process being helped a little by heating them or putting them into very hot water for a few minutes. They are highly nutritious and much used in confectionery.

BREAD. The item of food eaten most generally all over the world in different forms according to the kind of grain peculiar to the country.
The breads vary from the very fine white bread made with best wheaten flour to coarse black bread made with rye flour.
(See recipes)

BREAD CUBE TEST. This is a simple household test for the temperature of hot fats. Cut a slice of bread into small cubes about ⅓ in. square. Drop a cube into the fat. (a) For uncooked foods, such as chips, doughnuts, cheese aigrettes, etc., the fat should be hot enough to brown the cube a golden brown colour in one minute. (b) For cooked foods such as potato croquettes, fish and potato cakes, etc., the fat should be hot enough to brown the cube a golden brown colour in ½ min.

BREADFRUIT. Formerly a native fruit of the South Sea Islands, now cultivated in all tropical countries, where it provides one of the most important foods of the natives. It is similar in size and shape to a melon. It can be baked and eaten as bread, sliced and baked, or fried, in oil, stuffed with savoury mixture, or sliced, baked and eaten with sugar, milk or treacle.

BREAD JELLY. A very old invalid delicacy favoured as highly as calf's foot jelly for being 'strengthening'.

Made by boiling the crumb of a fresh small loaf in water, with lemon rind or cinnamon, until thick. The liquid is strained through muslin and put into a basin to set. The rather liquid jelly is served with cream and sugar, or heated with milk or wine.

BREAD ROAST. A sandwich loaf with the top removed and the crumb cut out in one piece, leaving a shell of crust about 1 inch thick. This case is then filled with a savoury mixture of minced meat, vegetables and sauce, the top crust put back as a lid, and the whole thing 'roasted' in a moderate oven until hot through. This very old farmhouse dish was revived during World War II by the Ministry of Food.

BREAD SAUCE. A sauce of white crumbs, milk, onion and seasonings.

(See recipes)

BREAD WINE. A simple country wine made with brown bread, sugar and water, kept in a warm place until it ferments. It is very much like the Russian Kvass.

BRIE. A French whole-milk cheese named after the province La Brie, where it was first made. There are two kinds, the rich creamy one known as *gras* or fat, and the less rich one known as *maigre* or thin.

BRIGHTON. A clear consommé flavoured with sherry.

BRILL. A flat fish found mainly in the Baltic and off the French Atlantic coast. Resembles the turbot but its meat is not as good as that of turbot or sole.

BRILLAT-SAVARIN. Chicken consommé with quenelles of poultry or calves' sweetbreads.

BRINE. 1. A simple brine made with a mixture of salt and water used for preserving meat or for preparing vegetables for pickles, or for keeping the colour of apples and pears while they are being prepared for cooking or bottling.

Vegetables are sometimes brined by being arranged in layers with salt sprinkled between them, without water.

2. A mixture of salt, saltpetre, sugar and water for salting meat to preserve and keep it. Meat being brined is usually subsequently smoked.

BRIOCHE. A French breakfast bun, semi-sweet and light.   (See recipe)

BRISTOL CREAM. The name given to a special brand of sherry sold exclusively by a well-known wine-merchant in Bristol.

BRISTOL MILK. The name given by some Bristol wine merchants to a fine quality of sherry which they ship and blend.

BROAD BEANS. A delicate bean of pale greenish-grey colour, enclosed in large plump pods lined with soft white lining. The beans are delicious when young and fresh and are invariably served in the country with hot boiled bacon and parsley sauce. The ancient Greeks, however, thought that the beans dulled the wits and caused bad dreams.

BROCHE, A LA. Roasted in front of the fire, but usually meaning small pieces of meat, kidney, liver, bacon, etc., arranged alternately with pieces of mushroom on skewers and grilled. The skewers are special long ones, very thin and often of silver.

BROOM. The ordinary yellow broom universally found in England. In olden times the buds were pickled in vinegar and used in the same manner as we now use capers.

BRUNOISE. Vegetables cut into very small squares for garnishing soups or grilled dishes.

BRUSSELS SPROUTS. A popular variety of cabbage, which develops small heads (or sprouts) along its thick stem. First sold in the Belgian markets, hence the name.

BUBBLE-AND-SQUEAK. The name now given to a mixture of left-over vegetables and potatoes fried to a cake, lightly browned to a delicate crispness on the underside and browned on the top. It has been known in England for about 160 years, and originally had fine strips of salt or roast beef included. The meat, or broken up cold sausages, are sometimes added to the vegetables to-day.

BUCKLING. Lightly smoked and salted herrings.

BUCK RABBIT. A poached egg on a slice of good Welsh Rarebit.

BUISSON. Shrimps, prawns or crayfish tails arranged in a bunch or cluster, or lobsters or crabs arranged in pyramid form.

BULL'S BLOOD. A Hungarian wine of a very dark red colour, mellow, aromatic and with a good proportion of tannin.

BULLY BEEF. The name given in England to what Americans call corned beef. The name 'corned' is the old English word meaning cured and was taken to America by the early settlers. Corned beef and cabbage is a famous American dish.

BUMPO. A sailor's drink made with rum, sugar, a little water and nutmeg.

BURNET. A herb with a flavour suggesting cucumber, used in certain soups and salads.

BUTTER, SAVOURY. Fresh butter beaten to a soft cream with various seasonings, flavourings and colourings, to serve with different dishes and to make sandwiches and garnishes for hors-d'œuvres.　　　(See recipe)

BYRON. Demiglace sauce reduced with wine, with fine shreds of truffles.

CABBAGE. Term applied to an extensive variety of vegetables, including white and red cabbages, savoy, Brussels sprouts, broccoli, cauliflower and kales.　　　(See recipe)

CAFE VIERGE. Coffee made with whole roasted coffee beans.

CAFFEINE. A bitter substance with stimulating qualities found in coffee.

CAKE. A mixture of flour, butter, or other fat, eggs, sugar and many variations and additions.　　　(See cake recipes)

CALABRESE. A variety of sprouting broccoli, sometimes called asparagus broccoli because the side shoots grow quite long and are very good cut and cooked as asparagus. The flower heads are green instead of white like the cauliflower, or purplish green like purple sprouting broccoli.

CALAMINT. Alpine catmint; the leaves are used for an infused drink, also in medicines.

CALCIUM. A substance extracted from bones, also found in egg shells and milk and some vegetables. Essential in diet for good teeth and bones.

CALENDULA. The petals of pot marigold, used to flavour and colour some cheeses, soups and stews.

CALF. The meat of a calf is called veal.

CALF'S FOOT. Valued for making jellies and enriching soups, stews, etc., or, if cleaned and skinned, for sweet jellies.　　　(See recipe)

CALORIES. A calorie is a unit of heat used in measuring the fuel (energy) value of food, or technically the amount of heat required to raise 1 kilogram of water 1^0 C.

　　Every adult needs so many calories daily to maintain strength.

　　The following are approximate calorie requirements:

　　An adult man engaged on sedentary work, 2,400 calories; moderate work, 3,200 calories; hard work, 3,200—4,000 calories; and very hard work, 4,000 calories upwards.

　　An adult woman from 2,400 to 2,800, according to the type of work done.

CAMBRIDGE SAUCE. A thick sauce consisting of mashed yolks of hard-boiled eggs, mashed anchovies, capers, cayenne pepper, oil and vinegar.

CAMOMILE. An aromatic bitter plant the daisy-like blooms of which are dried to make a mild tonic tea.

CANAPE. Literally, 'sofa', but has now come to mean pieces of bread, biscuit or toast which 'support', or upon which 'sit', a large variety of savoury tit-bits to serve with cocktail.

Smoked salmon, sliced hard-boiled egg and anchovy fillets, sardine pastes, pieces of lobster, tiny grilled mushrooms, hot mussels and savoury cheese pastes are some of the good mouthfuls used to make canapés.

CANDIED (CRYSTALLISED) FRUITS. Fruits, fresh or preserved, boiled in sugar until saturated with the syrup, then dried.

CANDLING EGGS. To hold to the light to see if the eggs are transparent or, having black spots, addled.

CANDY. Boiled sugar with various flavourings. The American name for any sweetmeat.

CANNELLE. The French name for cinnamon.

CANNELONI. Small rolls of pastry filled with savoury meat or jam.

CANNING. A mode of preserving fruits, meats, fish and vegetables.

CANTERBURY PUDDING. A plain sponge pudding, light as a Madeira cake, served with a sauce made with port wine. A number of cathedral towns had their own puddings, rich or not so rich. The other puddings follow the same recipe more or less.

CANVASBACK DUCK. A species of duck, very appetising and good to eat.

CAPE GOOSEBERRY. An edible berry enclosed in a lantern-shaped calyx. The berry makes excellent jam. The plant, called 'Chinese lanterns', is used for winter decorations.

CAPERCAILZIE. Game bird sometimes called wood-grouse, ocasionally found on Scottish moors. Cooked like a turkey.

CAPERS. Unopened flower buds of a plant cultivated in Spain, Italy and the South of France. Pickled in vinegar, they are used for garnishes, sauces and mayonnaise.

CAPON. Young male castrated fowls, fattened to improve the flavour of the flesh.

CAPSICUMS. Of the same family as chillis, but larger and not so hot. Used generally for decorations in dishes hot and cold. Usually grown in the Bombay area of India.

CARAMEL. Sugar cooked until it is dark brown and sticky, used to coat moulds for puddings and custards, or to form the base of vanilla custards. A favourite French dessert. The common name for caramelised sugar is 'Black Jack'.

CARAWAY SEEDS. The seeds from a small plant chiefly grown in Holland. They are small and half-moon shaped and are chiefly used in this country for making Seedy Cake and biscuits, but more extensively in European countries in cooking potato and cabbage dishes and to flavour liqueurs.

CARBOHYDRATES. A group of foods essential to a balanced diet, including starches, sugars and cellulose, and containing carbon, hydrogen and oxygen.

CARDOONS. A kind of thistle grown in Europe and America, and a close relation of the globe artichoke.

Its root is thick and fleshy and is excellent served cold as hors-d'œuvres with a vinaigrette dressing or thick mayonnaise. The stalks and inner ribs of the leaves may be eaten like celery. If you see the name 'chard' in an American recipe, you will know that it means cardoons.

CARMINE. Crimson colouring used in confectionery.

CARP. One of the largest fresh-water fish, often weighing 40 pounds. They live to a great age and are used in ornamental ponds, where they become very tame. They are found in almost all European countries, but are not eaten in Britain very much, except in Jewish cooking.

CARROTS. A root vegetable, long and tapering in shape, or shorter with rounded ends: some are pale yellow, others reddish-yellow. Introduced into England from Flanders, in the reign of Queen Elizabeth 1.

A very useful vegetable, greatly used in stews of all kinds, or as a separate dish. Carrots are rich in Vitamin A, which helps to keep eyes healthy.　　　　　　　　　　　　　　　　　　　　(See recipes)

CARTE DU JOUR. The bill of fare for the day.

CARVING. The art of cutting up joints of meat, poultry, game and fish into attractive portions for serving. Cutting them in the best and most economical manner.

CASHEW NUTS. Nuts shaped like small new moons, with a sweet almond-like flavour. They come chiefly from America and are much used in vegetarian cookery. A creamy butter, of a much pleasanter flavour than that of peanut butter, is made from the nuts.

CASSAVA. The sweet and bitter cassava grown in West Indies and Brazil. Tapioca is obtained from the roots of the bitter plant. The juices are fermented with molasses into an intoxicating drink.

CASSEROLE. A vessel made of fireproof earthenware, glass, copper, enamelled steel, etc., in which stews of meat, vegetables or poultry with cereals are cooked slowly for a long period.　　(See individual recipes)

CASSIA. The bark of a tree similar to cinnamon, ground in the same manner, but with a less fragrant flavour.

CASSIS. The French name for a cordial prepared from black currants, brandy and sugar. The best known cassis comes from Dijon. Another good make comes from Riga. Cassis and a bitter flavouring, such as angostura, make an excellent mixture.

CASSOULET. A famous Toulouse dish made with pieces of preserved goose, pieces of shoulder of mutton, pork rinds, salt pork, white beans, white wine, onions, garlic, Toulouse sausage, and seasonings, cooked until very tender. A poor imitation is sometimes made in England with mutton, beans, onions, seasonings and sliced sausage.

CAUDLE. A type of punch made with hot wine or hot ale, some with spirits and some with a base of tea.
    A white caudle is made by mixing fine oatmeal with the drink, straining it, boiling it and sweetening it with sugar. In olden days it was given to women in childbirth and for preventing bad or feverish colds.

CAULIFLOWER. A variety of cabbage cultivated and prized for its delicate-flavoured flowery head.
    It is said to have originated in Cyprus and been taken to Italy, where it was described as a cole flower.

CAVIAR. Prepared roe from various members of the fish family, including sturgeon, beluga and steret. The fish are caught in the Caspian sea tributaries and in the Danube Estuary. The best caviar is sturgeon's roe, which is small and black, or greyish, in colour, has a better flavour than other varieties and is mostly exported in tins. It is very expensive.

CELERIAC. A turnip-like rooted celery with a delicious flavour. May be peeled, sliced and boiled in salted water and served with Hollandaise Sauce, or shredded and eaten raw in salads.

CELERY. A plant with many long white stems folded round one another, each topped with green leaves. The sweet, crisp, aromatic stems, which have to be earthed up high to grow to perfection, are cooked as a vegetable in many ways, but they are best braised. Chiefly eaten in England raw with cheese after a meal.   (See recipe)

CELESTINE. A garnish for clear soups, made with a fried pancake cut into fine strips.

CEPE. See *Boletus.*

CHAMBORD. A famous French garnish for fish, consisting of fish quenelles, mushrooms, soft roes, prawns, pieces of truffles and fleurons.

CHANTILLY. A mayonnaise sauce flavoured with lemon, to which whipped cream is added just before serving. The hot Chantilly consists of a Béchamel to which cream is added. The confectionery Chantilly consists of fresh cream whipped and sweetened, as used for filling meringues, etc.

CHAPPATTIS. Very large Indian pancakes made with wholemeal flour and water. Cooked in an ungreased frying pan, lightly buttered, fried to a light brown and eaten with curry. May also be bought ready made.
(See recipe)

CHARCUTERIE. The name seen over French butchers' shops denoting that here are sold all kinds of good things made with pork or parts of the pig, prepared in many different ways. Examples are trotters with truffles, black puddings, various pâtés, etc.

CHARLOTTE RUSSE. A creamy mixture in a case which is usually made of finger-biscuits set closely together.
(See recipe)

CHARTREUSE. There are three kinds, the Green Chartreuse, of very high alcoholic content, and the Yellow, also of delicious flavour, but not so potent as the Green liqueur. This world-famous liqueur was made by the Carthusian Monks at Grenoble for nearly 300 years, until the monks were forced to leave France in 1901 to go to Spain. After the Second World War, the monks were allowed to return to France, where they now make the liqueur again.
The third variety of the liqueur is pure white and is known as Elixir des Pères Chartreux.

CHATEAUBRIAND. A steak cut from the centre of a fillet and often three times the size of an ordinary fillet.

CHAUDFROID. A cold entrée, usually masked with a cream sauce containing aspic jelly.

CHEESE. A palatable and nutritious food, which is made by coagulating or curdling milk, stirring and heating the curd, draining off the whey and collecting and pressing the curd. The desired flavour and texture is obtained partly by control of the acidity of the curd, and also by the curing and ripening process.
There are known to be at least 800 different varieties of cheese. Until the middle of the 19th century cheese-making was a local farm industry, and the methods of making varied according to local custom, but nowadays it is largely a factory process; but high quality milk and a skilful cheese-maker are still essentials to a well-made cheese.
The composition of many cheeses is approximately $\frac{1}{3}$ protein, $\frac{1}{3}$ fat, and $\frac{1}{3}$ water, and all except cream cheese have a high protein value.
Cheese is an excellent source of calcium, supplying 230 mg per ounce. Calcium is essential to the formation of strong bones and good teeth.
Cheese is useful as a protective food; it is a good source of vitamin A, contains traces of vitamin D, and among everyday foods is one of the best sources of riboflavin.

CHELSEA BUNS. A yeast dough that is rolled out, spread with butter, and sprinkled with currants, sugar and peel. It is then rolled up and cut in slices which are baked closely together on a greased baking tin. When pulled apart they are the traditional squarish shapes. (See recipe)

CHERRY. A small stone fruit of which there are many varieties. Morello is considered best for cooking. The whiteheart is favoured most for dessert.

CHERVIL. A delicate fern-like herb with fine seeds that scatter and germinate at all times of the year. Has a flavour like aniseed and is used in soups, salads and stuffings.

CHESTER PUDDING. An egg custard with almonds, lemon rind and butter, spread in a pastry case and topped with a stiffly beaten egg-white. The American lemon meringue pie derives from this pudding.

CHESTNUTS. Large nuts with a floury texture, chiefly grown on the Continent. The English nuts are very few in comparison. The flour of chestnuts is used for making some of the macaroni and other pastes on the Continent, but many good sweets and sweetmeats may be made with the nuts, especially the famous French marrons glacés.   (See recipes)

CHICHESTER PUDDING. A surprise baked pudding made with fine crumbs stirred into milk and egg-yolks, sweetened with castor sugar, flavoured with vanilla or almond flavouring, with stiffly whisked egg-white folded in irregularly and not thoroughly blended.
  When the baked pudding is served, it has a marble pattern. A wine sauce, or a vanilla-flavoured custard, is served with the pudding.

CHICKEN IN HALF MOURNING. The traditional name for a fine chicken cooked in a casserole with stock and seasonings and served with a mushroom sauce and slices of truffle simmered in Madeira wine. The greyish black colour of the mushroom sauce and the slices of black truffle give the dish its name.

CHICLE. The milky juice of the Sapodilla, the basis of chewing gum.

CHICORY. Known also as Belgian Endive. A long white-fingered vegetable with pale green tips, served raw in salads, boiled, drained and served with melted butter, or braised.

CHILLIS. These are grown on shrubs in Japan, Nigeria and Zanzibar. They are very hot, and, when dried and ground, are known as Cayenne pepper. They are brilliant red and full of seeds.   (See also *Peppers*)

CHIPOLATA. The name given to very small sausages, from the Italian meaning 'little fingers'.

CHITTERLINGS (FRAISE OR CROW). Names given to the small intestines of a calf.   (See recipe)

CHIVES. A small purple-flowered onion, green blades of which are used considerably in salads and sauces.

CHOW-CHOW. A pickle consisting of a mixture of vegetables preserved in a highly seasoned and aromatic mustard sauce.

CHOWDER. An American dish consisting of fried onions, pieces of fish, pieces of pickled pork and mashed potatoes, seasoned with spices and ketchup and simmered in a saucepan.

CHRINE. A piquant mixture of grated horse-radish and raw beetroot mixed with sugar, salt and white vinegar. Eaten during the Feast of the Passover by Jewish people, with cold chicken or meat and baked potatoes, but also at all seasons by others.

CHRISTMAS CAKE. A rich fruit cake usually covered with almond paste, then coated and decorated with a hand icing (known as Royal Icing).

CHUB. A fresh water fish of the carp family. Isaac Walton said of the chub: 'He is objected to not only because he is full of forked bones dispersed throughout his body, but eats waterish.'

CHURCH-AND-CHAPEL. Loaf made with enaugh dough to allow it is rise high in the tin and deeply slashed down the centre so that the crust rises and overlaps the sides of the tin like large over-hanging eaves.

CHUTNEY. Originally an Indian condiment made with fruits, spices, vinegar and sugar, and always served with the many different kinds of Indian curries. Mango fruits were considered the best for chutney. In England, all kinds of fruit and vegetables are used for home-made chutneys.   (See recipes)

CIDER SAUCE. A favourite American sauce made with cider, melted butter, flour, liquid in which a piece of ham or bacon has been boiled, pepper and a pinch of sugar; served with hot ham.

CINDER TOFFEE (HONEYCOMB TOFFEE). Boil sugar with a very small amount of water until a little will set when tested in cold water. At this point stir in bi-carbonate of soda. The toffee will then boil and froth. When poured into a shallow tin to cool, it will set full of little holes and crunch like cinders.   (See recipes)

CINNAMON. Has been cultivated in Ceylon for centuries, but came into European favour about 1500 A. D. It is the inner bark carefully removed from the branches of shrubs of about 8 feet in height. The bark, ground to a pale brown colour, is used for flavouring cakes and sauces and the essential oil in medicines.

CITRIC ACID. Known as acid of lemons, obtained from the juice of acid fruits. Used in confectionery, aerated water, and in helping to make jams and jellies set.

CITRONNE. Any dish or drink that has the flavour of lemon.

CLAM. A bivalve found on the Atlantic coast of North America. The two best known varieties are the round or hard clam and the long or soft clam.
Clams may now be bought in tins in this country.

CLARIFY. To clean fat by boiling it in water, leaving it to get cold, then removing the layer of solid fat from the liquid and scraping off impurities from underneath the layer.

CLARY WINE. One of the old home-made variety, made with raisins, clary blossoms, and water, and kept in a cask for 6 months.

CLEMENTINE. A sweet and juicy small fruit like a tangerine, but practically seedless.

CLOD. The upper part of a bullock's shoulder. Suitable for stewing or making into puddings.

CLOVE. The clove has been known and used for over a thousand years. It is the unopened flower bud of an evergreen tree which sometimes grows to a height of 40 feet. The buds are picked when green and dried in the sun until brown in colour. Cloves from Penang are considered better than those from Zanzibar and Madagascar.

COCHINEAL. A red liquid used for colouring sweets, sauces, creams, icing, etc. Originally made from certain small beetles, now often manufactured chemically.

COCKALEEKIE. A soup of ancient Scottish origin, made with an elderly fowl, leeks, barley, seasonings and water.

COCKLE CAKES. Before elaborately-shaped patty-pans and paper cake-cases came into fashion the folk of fishing towns used well-washed cockle and scallop shells in which to bake their cakes. The cakes when turned out and dusted with sugar had the pretty fluted pattern of the shells.

COCKLES. Small shell fish of the bivalve family. They are eaten plain with vinegar, pepper and bread-and-butter, or used in sauces and fish soups.

COCOA BEAN. A variety of French bean, but of a deep purple colour, which changes to green when cooked. It is a climbing bean with a small purple flower, the bean having a more delicate flavour than French or runner beans. When mature, the seeds may be taken from the pods and cooked as haricot beans.

COCONUT. The fruit of the Coconut Palm and one of the most important products of the Tropics. The thick, hard husk is covered with an outer fibrous husk, the pulp being thick and sweet and, when fresh, of almost a jelly consistency. Fresh coconuts may be easily distinguished from stale ones by the sweet milky fluid with which they are filled.
Coconut is eaten raw, dried or desiccated, and used in puddings, cakes and sweetmeats, while to those who make orthodox curries, coconut milk, or an infusion of dried coconut to give a milky fluid, is considered essential to the making of a good curry.   (See recipes)

COD. One of the most important fish foods in the world. It comes from the cold Atlantic waters, much of it being caught off the Dogger Bank. It is salted and dried like ling.

CODDLE. To cook an egg in the shell in very hot water until it is delicately set, without boiling it. Usually served to invalids and children.

COD'S LIVER. Rich in oil and Vitamin B which is extracted and used medicinally.
    Used for making rich forcemeat with breadcrumbs, parsley and seasoning, for stuffing other fish.

COD'S ROE. The roes are very good dried and cured and used for sandwiches, canapés or spread on hot toast.
    When fresh, they are boiled or baked and served in various ways.
                                                            (See recipes)

COLCHESTER PYEFLEETS A variety of oyster found in Essex and particularly in the Colne Valley. They are said to have been exported to Rome in the days of the Roman occupation of Britain.

COLD WATER WILLIES. A plain hard biscuit made in Northumberland in hard times. They were made only of flour, water and salt, and mixed to a stiff dough, the dough being formed into small cakes and baked. They were eaten sometimes with a smear of lard, or dipped into the liquid in which a little piece of bacon or salt pork had been boiled.

COLE SLAW. A type of salad. It is made from the raw heart of cabbage, cut into shreds. Usually eaten with vinegar and seasonings but sometimes it is served cooked, similarly dressed.

COLLARED BEEF. A large joint of the thin end of flank of beef, marinaded in spices and salt for about 10 days, then boned, rolled and tightly bound with tape, and boiled or cooked in a casserole in the oven for up to 6 hr.

COLLIERS' FOOT. The 'smacks' or 'snappin' taken by miners for 'elevenses'. They were made — in long oval shapes like the sole of a boot — of dripping or other fat crust and filled with any mixture of minced meat or bacon, onion and sometimes slices of cheese over the onion.

COLLOPS. The Scottish name given to a much richer and more savoury form of shepherd's pie. Usually made with beef or mutton, with breadcrumbs, onion, parsley, butter and thick sauce.

COMMENDARIA. A sweet dessert wine from Cyprus.

COMPARATIVE TEMPERATURES OF OVENS.

Electric Degrees F.	Gas Mark	Description
250	1/4	Very cool
260	1/2	Very cool
275	3/4	Very cool

Electric Degrees F.	Gas Mark	Description
290	1	Cool
300	2	Cool
325	2	Cool
350	3	Moderate
375	4	Moderate
400	5	Moderate
425	6	Moderately hot
450	7	Hot
475	8	Hot
500	9	Very hot
525	10	Very hot
550	11 & 12	Very hot

On the hot plate, boiling is reached at 212° F., quick simmering at 190° F., slow simmering at approximately 150°, while a tepid or blood heat is 98.4°.

COMPOTE. A stew of small birds, usually pigeons, or fruit or vegetables.

CONDE. Soups or desserts named after a famous and ancient French family and always containing rice. The best known Condé dish is of rice covered with stewed pears and raspberry syrup.

CONDIMENTS. The name given to seasonings to serve with dishes hot or cold and with salads.
They include the four most general on most tables — salt, pepper, mustard and vinegar — and also those of various flavours such as chilli, garlic, tarragon and mint vinegars and bottled sauces.

CONFIT D'OIE. A method of keeping goose for several months, much favoured in the French countryside. The bird is cut up and sprinkled with salt, put into a large jar with a weighted board or dish on top and left for about a fortnight.
The meat is then wiped of excess salt and cooked very slowly with the goose fat. When done the pieces are put into earthenware jars and the hot fat is poured in to cover the meat entirely. The jars are then sealed and set in the coldest place in the house or farm.

CONFITURE. Fruit jams, fruit pastes or sweetmeats, or fruit stewed in thick syrup.

CONGER EEL. Eels found chiefly around the Channel Isles and off the Brittany Coast. In some cases they reach the girth of a man's thigh and are extremely difficult to catch.

CONGER EEL ST. MALO. A dish famous in the restaurants of the French sea port, St. Malo. It is made with sections of a small conger eel, egged and bread-crumbed and fried. It is served with a thick sauce of onion soup, mustard, anchovy essence, chopped parsley and a little white wine.

CONSOMME. The name given to a thin, clear soup made with meat and vegetables as a basis, but there are dozens of different consommés, according to the various additions to the finished stock. (See recipes)

CORDON BLEU. An ancient distinction given to skilful female cooks since the time of Louis XV. It consists of a rosette made of dark blue ribbon, and was, and is, still much prized, as it shows that the cook is in the chef class.

CORNISH FAIR MAIDS. Smoked pilchards, so called from the Spanish word fumade or smoked.

CORNISH HEAVY CAKE. A fruit cake of Cornish origin which belies its name. It is baked in a shallow tin and usually cut in squares for serving.

CORNISH SLY CAKES. Flat pastry cakes with the dried fruit filling showing through as a result of being pressed with a rolling pin. Similar to Eccles Cakes.   (See recipe)

CORNISH (OR DEVON) SPLITS. The name given to some small light scones, much the same in many counties.

CORIANDER. An Eastern condiment. The seeds are strongly flavoured and impart a savoury taste to any stew or soup. A few are often added to a semolina pudding, which, together with a little cream and sugar, makes the semolina a very pleasant dessert. The Romans introduced the coriander to Britain.

COTE. A rib slice of beef or veal.

COTELETTES. Cutlets, small slices of meat, usually cut from the best end of neck of the meat.

COTTAGE PIE. See *Shepherd's Pie.*

COULIBRIAC. A type of Russian fish cake made of a savoury fish mixture folded in puff pastry and baked. The best known of these mixtures is made with fresh salmon.

COULIS (CULLIS). The old name for a good stock or broth used in making other dishes. An 18th century recipe contains bacon, veal, ham, carrots, onions, celery butter, flour and parsley, cooked in a pot until almost dry, then water added and cooked again until a fine yellowish colour, and strained'.

COUPE JACQUES. Vanilla ice cream, halved fresh peaches, sweetened whipped cream.

COURT BOUILLON. A highly seasoned fish stock used for making other fish dishes and fish sauces.   (See fish recipes)

COVENTRY GOD CAKES. A very ancient cake made with rough puff pastry and mincemeat. The cakes were triangular in shape, brushed with white of egg, sprinkled with sugar and baked golden brown and puffy. They were always made at Coventry and given to children by their godparents on New Year's Day, when the children called specially to receive them.

COVER. 'Water or stock to cover'. Just enough liquid to submerge the food to be cooked, e. g. vegetables, meat, poultry, fish or fruit.

COW-HEEL. The foot of a cow, hoof removed and cleaned, can be stewed with onions or leeks and seasonings until clear, cut into small pieces, eaten with parsley sauce or made into a rich jellied brawn. (See recipe)

CRAB. A shell fish of the crustacean order *decapoda*. Usually served dressed, the white meat from the claws flaked round the soft pale-fawn meat, which is mixed with crumbs and seasonings placed in the emptied body shell.

CRAB APPLE. The tree originally came from Siberia, hence the name given to the fruit — 'Siberian Crabs'. It is a very hardy tree and will grow in most soils. While it is chiefly grown for its lovely blossom in the spring, the pretty rosy pink fruit makes excellent preserves.

CRAMBAMBULI. A fine punch to serve on a cold night, but the drink may also be iced in hot weather. It is made by boiling a quart of ale until bubbling, adding sugar and $1/2$ pint of rum. Half a dozen well-whisked eggs are thoroughly stirred into the hot mixture after it is taken from the heat. It is then poured into a large bowl and served in generous portions.

CRANBERRY. A bright-red but very acid small fruit the size of a large currant. It is chiefly grown in America, but it is also grown in some parts of the British Isles. Used for making pies, tarts and jellies. Cranberry sauce is served with turkey in America and the custom is growing in this country.

CREAM. The fat part of fresh milk which rises to the top. Allowed to stand for 12 or 24 hours, at an even temperature, it is then separated by hand or by a mechanical separator. The 12-hour cream is known as Single, the 24-hour as Double Cream.
   Special creams are Cornish and Devonshire Creams made by heating the separated cream at a very low temperature until it is almost solid.

CREAM CHANTILLY. Vanilla-flavoured cream used in pastries.
                                                      (See recipes)

CREAM OF TARTAR. Potassium bitartrate, used as a raising agent in cookery, or as an ingredient in baking-powder and self-raising flour.
   To make baking-powder, mix 2 teaspoonfuls of cream of tartar and 1 teaspoonful of bi-carbonate of soda and use to 1 lb. plain flour.

CRECY. Dishes named 'à la Crécy' usually have carrots or carrot purée in them. It is also a soup made of carrots.

CREME DE CACAO. A liqueur made from the best cocoa, often flavoured with vanilla. It is a strong and potent drink.

DAB. Small plaice.

DACE. A small fresh-water fish.

DAHL. A mixture of lentils, butter and curry powder served as a thick soup. (See recipe)

DAISIES. Long iced drinks, served in large goblets and decorated with floating flowers or aromatic leaves. Plenty of spirit is used in making the various daisies.

DAMASCENES. Small damsons, sometimes, known as Shropshire or Black Jack damsons.

DAME JEANNE. The French name given to a wicker-covered glass bottle used for spirits. Known in England as a Demijohn.

DAMSON. Small round plums of deep purple colour, suitable for preserves, puddings, and tarts, also for making a rich liqueur. (See recipes)

DAMSON CHEESE. Damsons cooked slowly (until the juice runs and the stones rise and can be removed) and rubbed through a sieve, the purée boiled with sugar to a firm set.
Best kept from year to year; sliced, decorated with split almonds and served with a little port wine.

DAMSON GUM. Sago and damsons cooked together until the damsons are tender enough to break and the stones can be skimmed up. Sweeten the mixture well, put it into a large baking- or pie-dish and bake it in a very slow oven until the sago has completely 'melted' and the mixture resembles a thick, firm jelly. Serve hot with sugar and milk, or cold with cream.

DANDELION. A weed which grows in poor soils. The bitter toothed leaves are cooked and eaten as spinach. They are often bleached beneath flower pots and used uncooked in salads.
In the country an old-fashioned home-made brew is made with the flowers. The roots are washed, scraped, dried and ground and used as coffee by devotees of health foods.

DANDELION GREENS. A favourite dish in the country in springtime, when the dandelion leaves are very young and tender and have scarcely any bitter flavour. Large bowls of the leaves are washed, put into a saucepan with scarcely any water, and with pepper and salt. When they are boiled, they are pressed, moistened with a piece of butter or a little bacon fat, and served with the liquid thickened with flour.

DANISH TOAST. Slices of brown bread spread with horseradish sauce and finished with strips of smoked salmon and filleted herring.

DARIOLE. A very old English word originally meaning a small rich cheesecake. Now often used to mean a small high mould.

DARTOIS. Small pieces of light crisp pastry, baked and used as a base upon which to serve small pieces of fish, poultry, etc., as garnishes or as hors-d'œuvres.

DASH. A rule-of-thumb measurement, such as 'a pinch', 'a splash' or 'a spot'.

DATE. The fruit of a palm-tree largely cultivated in Northern Africa, Western Asia and Southern California.
     The best dates are those exported on the stem in the traditional oval-shaped boxes. Good for cakes, puddings, confectionery or desserts.
                                                                        (See recipes)

DAUBE. Meat or poultry larded and stewed, or stewed without being larded, with mixed vegetables and bouquet garni.   (See recipe)

DECANT. To pour wine carefully and gently into glass containers known as decanters, in order to leave sediment behind. Spirits are also decanted, but this is chiefly for the pleasant appearance of the coloured liquids in the decorative glass containers.

DEEP FRYING. To put food, either egg-and-breadcrumbed or dipped in batter, into a deep pan with sufficient hot fat to cover it completely. The fat, when hot, should give off faint blue smoke. The food is cooked to a golden brown and then well-drained.

DEHYDRATED. Freed from water. A method of preserving eggs, milk, herbs, fruits, and vegetables, also some meats.
     Such items have to be reconstituted by mixing with liquid, or in the instance of fruits, vegetables and meats, by soaking for periods in water to restore them to their original form.

DEMI-GLACE. Half-glaze. A sauce reduced until it is almost thick enough for glazing.

DEMI-SEL. A soft whole-milk creamy French cheese only slightly salted.

DEVIL. A very hot, highly spiced sauce served with various food-stuffs. Devilled bones have always been a favourite dish with men. Turkey bones, marrow or mutton bones are devilled. Vegetables, eggs, cutlets and pork chops are also served in this way.
     A devil is made with a combination of such ingredients as chilli sauce, Worcester or other piquant sauces, garlic, mustard, vinegar, paprika, cayenne, black pepper, salt, red wine, chopped onions, etc., according to the chef's taste.

DEVILLED CHICKEN LEGS. Legs of chicken or other poultry treated with a hot relish.   (See recipe)

DEVIL'S FOOD CAKE. The opposite of angels' food cake, being made with the egg yolks and given a dark brown texture with chocolate powder and black treacle. Made in the same kind of mould and usually covered with thick chocolate icing.   (See recipe)

DEXTROSE. Grape sugar.

DIABLOTINS. Small poached gnocchi, sprinkled with grated cheese, flavoured with cayenne, then browned just before serving.

DIET. Diet means the food eaten by everyone in order to live.

Correct diet means good health and freedom from undue fatigue, a good resistance to infections and illness. A bad, unbalanced diet can produce a low state of health, tiredness and lassitude, proneness to catching cold and any ailment of which there may be an epidemic, while, in children, diet deficiencies will give rise to rickets, bad teeth, skin troubles and poor eyesight.

Diets are also sub-divided into special forms suitable for people suffering from certain ailments, such as stomach ulcers, diabetes, nervous disorders, etc.

Finally there are diets followed by those who wish to reduce weight or to add weight. The basic foods are divided into groups containing the essential elements for maintaining full health and some of these foods should be taken every day, or at least every other day.

The continued lack of any of the foods contained in the diet may cause serious illness in due course.

DIGESTIVE BISCUITS. Crisp wheatmeal biscuits.   (See recipe)

DIGBY CHICK. Name given to a small herring or pilchard, after the seaport of Digby in Nova Scotia, near where they are caught.

DILL. Biennial plant with a strong aromatic flavour. The seeds are very much like caraway seeds, with a sweetish flavour. Highly beneficial in digestive troubles and given as a syrup to soothe babies. Dill sauce and pickle are much favoured to serve with fish and cold meats.

DINDONNEAU. A young turkey. Served in the same manner as the large birds, but sometimes boiled.

DIPPER. A ladle used for dipping stock or soups from cooking vessels.

DISJOINT. To cut into pieces at the joints.

DISSOLVE. To mix dry ingredients into a liquid until they melt.

DISTILLATION. The art of separating the alcohol contained in any alcoholic liquid by the application of heat. It is based on the fact that alcohol is vaporised at a temperature of 78° C. instead of 100° C. as is water.

The receptacle in which the distillation takes place is called a still.

DITALINI. A type of Italian macaroni made in thick pipes cut into pieces about 2—3 inches long.

DJUVETCH. A Yugoslavian dish of onions, chopped meat or fish, with tomatoes, rice, oil or butter and stock.

DOLMAS. Stuffed vine leaves.

DORMERS. The old English name given to croquettes of minced meat and rice, egg, seasonings and gravy.

DORURE. Beaten yolks of eggs used for brushing pastry, scones, etc.

DOT. Scatter small pieces of butter, crumbs, cheese or other ingredients over the surface of a dish.

DOUBLE CONSOMME. Consommé cooked until reduced by half, or, alternatively, strengthened by the addition of bouillon cubes.

DOUCETTES. Small fancy cakes and marzipan fancies served with dessert, introduced into England by French chefs in or about the 18th century.

DOUCH. A west-country dish of fresh haddock, fried onions, saffron, cider or ale, and bread to thicken the gravy made with the frying fat and the ale or cider.

DOUGH. A soft mixture of flour or other meal moistened to a consistency firm enough to knead or roll out; fat and sugar is added as required. The dough is used for cakes, biscuits, bread, rolls, or pie or pudding crusts.   (See recipes for dough cake, etc.)

DOUGH DUMPLINGS. In the olden days when bread was made at home, northcountry housewives, especially in Yorkshire, used to save a portion of the risen dough, form it into small balls and cook it with boiled beef, dropping the dough balls into the liquid about 10 minutes before the end of the cooking time. The dumplings swelled up and were beautifully light.

DOUGHNUTS. Cakes made of light dough and fried in deep fat.
(See recipe)

DOVER SOLES. Name given to the choicest soles, to distinguish them from Torbay or lemon soles.   (See recipes)

DOVER SPLITS. Small plain scones to be eaten hot with butter.
(See recipes)

DRAIN. To strain off all liquid from any food cooked in liquid, or to put fried or grilled food on absorbent paper to remove excess fat.

DRAMBUIE. A Scottish liqueur whisky flavoured with heather honey. The name Drambuie, translated from the Gaelic, means 'the drink that satisfies'.

DRAW. To remove the entrails from poultry or game and to clean it.

DRAWN BUTTER. Butter melted and mixed with flour, water, wine and either salt and nutmeg or sugar, and cooked until thickened and smooth. To serve with vegetables or steamed puddings.

DREDGE. To sprinkle with flour or with sugar, or to draw meat or other food through plain or seasoned flour.

DRESS. May mean 'prepare for cooking', or to baste with butter or dripping, or to mix a salad with a dressing.

DRESSED WEIGHT. Weight of poultry or game when plucked but not drawn.

DRESSINGS. Liquids used to moisten salads. The favourite simple dressing consists of two parts of olive oil to one part wine vinegar, seasoned according to taste with salt, pepper, garlic or finely chopped herbs. Cream or lemon juice may be introduced.

More elaborate salad dressings are also used.   (See recipes)

DRINK. A guide to what apéritifs, wines and liqueurs are good to serve before, during and after meals. Individual taste, of course, plays an important part.

Apéritifs before a meal. French vermouth, plain with ice and a piece of lemon, or with an equal proportion of Italian vermouth, or with gin; dry or medium dry sherry, such as Fino, Amontillado or Montilla; dry iced champagne. Iced port wine of the lighter type is becoming a favourite apéritif.

With oysters. A cool but not iced Chablis.

With cold hors-d'œuvres. A lightly chilled dry white wine, such as Moselle, Alsace, Graves or a good *vin rosé.*

With hot hors-d'œuvres, which are now favoured. A light red wine, one of the lighter chianti type.

With the soup. A dry Madeira or a medium dry sherry.

With fish. A richer white wine, like Liebfraumilch, white Burgundy, a hock, or a chilled dry champagne.

With any light entrée, veal or poultry. The same as with fish.

With lamb, mutton, beef. Medoc, Beaujolais, or light red wine served at room temperature (known as 'chambrée').

With rich meats such as pork, goose, duck and dishes made with hare or venison. Any full red wine is suitable: a red Burgundy, a St. Emilion, or a Rhône wine, served at room temperature.

With the sweet. A light wine such as a Sauternes, or Anjou, or a light German white wine.

With cheese or dessert. Port wine, Madeira, Marsala or a rich brown sherry.

With coffee. Brandy or liqueurs.

It has long been the habit to serve brandy in a heated glass. This is not a good practice: it spoils the aroma entirely by bringing out the alcoholic fumes too much. On the contrary, liqueurs are usually served in chilled glasses. This too is bad, since the distinctive flavours of the various liqueurs are killed by being chilled. They should be served in glasses at room temperature to get the richest flavour and aroma.

Sizes of bottles larger than standard.

Magnum	2 bottles	⅓ gallon
Jeroboam	4 bottles	
Rehoboam	6 bottles	1 gallon
Methuselah	8 bottles	
Salmanazar	12 bottles	2 gallons
Balthazar	16 bottles	
Nebuchadnezzar	20 bottles	

Racking
Drawing or syphoning off a clear wine from the deposit.
Viticulturist
Vine grower.

DRIPPING. The fat from roasted meat, or pieces of fat or suet melted and strained from skin and membranes. Used for basting meat, deep frying or spreading on toast.

Also used for making crust for meat, puddings or pies, or schoolboys' cake.

DRUPE. All fleshy foods with stones containing kernels, such as all varieties of plums, apricots, peaches and cherries.

DRYING. Evaporating moisture from herbs and foods by means of warmth.

DUBARRY. Cauliflower served with sauce Mornay.

DUBLIN BAY PRAWNS. The largest of all the prawns. The Italian prawns are better known as scampi.

DUCHESSE. Potatoes finely mashed with butter, milk and egg, and piped through a forcing-bag in whirl shapes, then lightly browned in the oven. Served as a garnish for roast meat and poultry, grills or fish.

DUCK. A domestic poultry bird with rich flesh. The best were formerly from Aylesbury. Wild ducks are also edible, but are tougher and sometimes have a fishy flavour.

There are a great many methods of serving ducks, the favourite being to roast and serve with sage-and-onion stuffing and apple sauce, or orange sauce.   (See recipe)

DULSE. An edible sea weed simmered till tender and eaten with butter, pepper and salt, or made into a nourishing jelly.

DUMPLINGS. Small or large balls of different types of dough, savoury or sweet, boiled in plain water or stock.

Fruit dumplings are made of various fruits encased in pastry dough and baked.   (See recipe for *Sussex Hard Dumplings*)

DUNELIN. A dish of braised mutton.

DUST. To sprinkle lightly with plain or seasoned flour or with fine sugar.

DUTCH CRACKLINGS. Small ginger-flavoured biscuits.

(See recipe)

DUTCH OVEN. A box-like utensil made of stout tin, with one open side and with hooks to attach the contrivance to the bars of a fire grate. Used for cooking small joints or birds.

DUXELLES. A sauce or stuffing containing mushrooms, shallots and parsley finely chopped. Cooked until fairly dry.

EAU D'ARQUEBUSE. An ancient French liqueur that for centuries had the reputation of curing all ills. It used to be made at Lyons, but it is seldom heard of to-day.

EAU-DE-VIE. 'Water of life' — brandy.

EASTER CAKES. Large round flat biscuits made with flour, eggs, currants and peel. Often put into packets tied with yellow ribbons and presented as Easter gifts.   (See recipe)

EBULUM. A very rich liqueur type of home-made wine with a basis of strong ale instead of water, a plentiful quantity of elderberries, some juniper berries, hops and a great many spices. Left to mature in a cask, then served by being poured out over knobs of sugar.

ECCLES CAKES. Made at Eccles. Very much like the Coventry (or Banbury) cakes, but with a richer, spicier filling. Round in shape with slits on the surface.   (See recipe)

ECHAUDER. To scald.

ECLAIR. A French pastry made with choux paste and filled with cream.   (See recipe)

ECOSSAISE. Soup or stew made of mutton with barley and vegetables.

EDAM. A ball-shaped Dutch cheese with a red rind.

EDINBURGH ROCK. A soft brittle sweetmeat which originated in Edinburgh.   (See recipe)

EELS. Serpent-like fish caught in the Thames and other estuaries, and also imported from Holland. In England eels are at their best from August to May. Once very cheap, they are now a luxury fish. They are chiefly served in pies or jellied. Smoked eels are very popular.   (See recipes)

EEL PIE. A rich pie of eels made famous at a restaurant on the Thames island known as Eel Pie Island.   (See recipe)

EGG. Eggs laid by most birds are edible, but chiefly so those of domestic poultry, plovers, gulls and guinea fowl. They all constitute a valuable food. The average weight of a hen's egg is about 2 oz.

The best eggs are those 12 hours old. To test eggs for freshness hold to the light. They should be semi-transparent and have no dark specks.

The yolk is rich in fat; the white consists of albumen and this can be whisked to a stiff froth several times its volume.

Eggs can be served in a great many different ways, the best known of which are the omelette, the breakfast dish of fried egg and bacon, poached egg on toast, spinach or chipped potatoes. They are also used for making mayonnaise and other sauces, for custards and in cakes and puddings.   (See recipes)

EGG-AND-BREADCRUMB. To dip food in fine dry breadcrumbs, then into beaten egg and again in crumbs before frying. Use for fish, cutlets, veal escalops, rissoles, fish cakes, etc., to give a crisp appetising crust and prevent fat soaking into the food.

EGG NOGG. A rich custard-like drink made with eggs, brandy, boiling milk, nutmeg, and sugar.

A very old English drink, but still served by many hostesses instead of punch at midnight on New Year's Eve.

EGG-PLANT (AUBERGINE). A truncheon-shaped vegetable with a deep purple shiny skin and pale greenish pulpy flesh. Originally grown in the West Indies, now extensively grown in France and imported to this country, where they are gaining favour.   (See recipes)

EGG PLUM. Large fleshy plums of good flavour, one variety with a reddish skin, one with yellow skin. Excellent for preserving, halved to fit neatly into the preserving jars; or halved, stoned and thickly dredged with sugar as a dessert.

EGYPTIENNE. Soup with leeks, onions and rice.

ELDER. A tree very commonly found growing wild. The small white flowers have a pleasant perfume and are used to make a white wine-type drink or to flavour certain jams and jellies.

The ripe berries are glossy black and very juicy. Used for making a cordial, jams, jellies and sauces. The tender new stems, peeled, are often pickled.   (See recipes)

ELDERFLOWER. The white flower of the elder tree, which has a fragrant perfume. Used for flavouring jams and jellies or wines.

ELVERS. Freshly spawned eels, so small as to be almost transparent. When boiled they turn to a jelly and are eaten with bread and butter or salad.

EMBROCHER. To impale on a spit or skewer.   (See *Kebabs*)

EMINCER. To cut any food into very thin slices.

EMMENTHAL. A Swiss cheese of Gruyère type.

EMULSION. A combination of oil and water, or milk and margarine or butter, beaten together until thoroughly blended to a cream.

EN BROCHETTE. Small pieces of food fried or grilled and served on skewers. Usually kidney, bacon, mushrooms or mutton.

ENDIVE. Like a lettuce with lace-like leaves, and better known as bataria; sometimes confused with chicory because the French call endive what we call chicory.

ENGLISH BAMBOO. The young shoots of the elder tree peeled and pickled.

ENGLISH FRONTIGNAC. A delicious home-made wine, made with fresh elderflowers, lemons, sugar, yeast and chopped raisins. When properly made and well matured, it is said to resemble, and to be as good as, the French white wine after which it is named.　　　　　　　(See recipe)

EN PAPILLOTE. Food wrapped in paper bags and baked or sometimes grilled. Only the tenderest parts of meat such as veal cutlets, small lamb chops or chicken breasts are used, or delicate fish like mullet.
　　Formerly greaseproof paper bags were used, the food buttered and seasoned and sealed into the bags to prevent loss of juices. Now the modern method is to use aluminium foil.

ENTRECOTE. A cut of steak from the middle part of the loin or sometimes from the rib.

ENTREES. Dishes served between fish and main meat course at dinners, or as a main dish at small luncheons.

ENTREMETS. Hot or cold sweets or pastry, confectionery, fruits, ices and creams, or a dainty dish of vegetables.

EPAULE DE . . . 'Shoulder of' (lamb, mutton, veal or pork).

EPIGRAMMES. The name given in restaurant language to choice small round pieces of mutton, lamb, venison or hare, braised, cooled, all fat removed, egg-and-breadcrumbed and deep-fried.
　　Sometimes the pieces are cut into triangular shapes.

EPINARDS. French for spinach.

EPLUCHER. To peel.

ERYNGO. The name for sea holly. An English seaside plant with thistle-blue flowers and soft grey-green leaves and stems. The fleshy roots and stems can be candied like angelica. It grows prolifically in Brittany.

ESAU. Lentil soup.

ESCALOPE. A thin slice of meat, usually of veal, egg-and-breadcrumbed and fried, preferably in oil.

ESCARGOT. The large edible snail that feeds on vine leaves, which give this snail a special flavour. The best snails are those which come from the Burgundy vines. They are served as hors-d'œuvre with garlic and parsley butter.

ESPAGNOLE. Brown soup made with beef or mutton, thickened with onion purée.

ESPRESSO. Making coffee by passing live steam through well-roasted and ground coffee, producing rapid filtration and a strong brew.

ESSENCE. Highly concentrated flavours of fruit or flowers, or of beef and chicken, used to flavour cakes, puddings, confectionery, or stews and soups, gravies and sauces.

ESSENTIAL FOODS. See *Foods Essential to Health.*

ESTERHAZY. A meat dish in which julienne of vegetables and sour cream are used.

ESTRAGON. A fragrant herb for flavouring, usually known as tarragon.

ETOUFFER. To braise, steam or stew very slowly with a little liquid in a covered pan.

EXETER PUDDING. Known as one of the Cathedral Puddings. Made with plenty of eggs, fine crumbs, sugar, finely grated suet, lemon and rum to taste. Put into a basin well buttered and lined with split raisins and tiny almond biscuits, it is steamed or baked, then served with red or black currant jelly well laced with wine.

EXTRACT. To simmer or bake in a casserole slowly for a long time, to extract goodness. The usual method of making beef tea. Commercial extracts of meat and vegetable juices are now readily available, as well as flavouring ingredients such as vanilla and all the fruit flavourings.

FADGE. Irish potato bread.   (See recipe)

FAGGOTS. A substantial dish of liver, crumbs and seasoning. (See recipe)

FAIRE REVENIR. To partially fry meat or vegetables until slightly browned, without cooking them, in preparation for making various dishes.

FARCE. Forcemeat or stuffing.

FARCIE. Anything stuffed with forcemeat, usually vegetables.

FARINA. The name for a number of different articles of food such as fine meal or flour of any grain, starchy root or nut, the starchy powder or meal made from potatoes, or the purified middlings of hard wheat.

FARINA DOLCE. An Italian sweet flour made from dried and ground chestnuts.

FARLS (FARLES). Oatmeal bannocks divided into four quarters.
                        (See recipe for *Oatmeal biscuits or farls)*

FAT RASCALS. A rich type of scone.   (See recipe)

FAVE DEI MORTI. An Italian pastry made in various parts of Italy. It is called 'Beans of the Dead' because it is specially made on All Souls' Day.
(See recipe)

FECULE. A fine flour obtained from potatoes, tapioca, semolina, etc., and used to thicken soup and sauces.

FENNEL. A light feathery plant that grows wild in some parts of the country.
It is chiefly used, very finely chopped, to make sauces for fish, especially for salmon or mackerel.
In very early days it was believed that it could help restore sight when eaten in leaf form and used as a lotion for bathing the eyes.

FENUGREEK. A spice which comes from Morocco and India. It has a pleasant smell and slightly bitter flavour. The small brown seeds are chiefly used in curry powder and for cattle medicine.

FERMIERE. In farmhouse style. A garnish consisting of carrots, cauliflower, small fried potatoes and lettuce.

FEUILLETAGE. Leafy, flaky puff pastry.

FEVERFEW. A perennial herb which was once grown specially for curing headaches and fevers. Its leaves and flowers are still dried to make a soothing infusion or tea.

FIDELINI. A type of vermicelli paste.

FILBERTS. A nut cultivated in England, especially in Kent, with a sweet crisp texture; they are small, oblong, dark brown and bluntly pointed.
The name is a corruption of St. Philibert, whose feast day is on the 22nd August, the day upon which filberts are said to be ready for picking.
Kentish cobs are classed among the filbert varieties.

FILET (FILLET). The word used for the undercut of beef, but can also mean a long flat piece of meat or boned fish or poultry.

FILET MIGNON. Very small fillet of beef.

FINES HERBES. Parsley, tarragon, chives, and sometimes a very little thyme all finely minced and used for flavouring sauces, omelettes, grilled steaks and some egg dishes. Fresh herbs should be used where possible.

FINNAN HADDIES. Small haddocks smoked over wood smoke, or as in the olden days, over the smoke of seaweed. Originally from the village of Findon, Aberdeenshire.

FIRKIN. A quarter of a barrel of beer, that is, 9 gallons.

FISH, AVERAGE TIME FOR COOKING.
Boiling: 10 min. per lb.
Baking: 12 min. per lb.
Frying: 10—15 min. for a cutlet or fillet.
Grilling: 15 min. or according to size.

FISH POT. A fish soup which is akin to the Mediterranean bouillabaisse. It was, and in some fishing ports still is, made from any discarded fish such as throw-outs from hauls.   (See recipes)

FIZZES. Long drinks, very popular in America, made with syrups, spirits, plenty of ice and a fizzy mineral.

FLAGEOLETS. Small, pale-green haricot beans, cooked in the same way as haricots and often served as an hors-d'œuvre item with oil and vinegar dressing.

FLAMANDE. In Flemish style. A garnish of braised cabbage and mixed vegetables.

FLAMBER. To singe poultry or game after plucking, or to pour spirit over an omelette or pudding and set it alight.

FLAMRI. A sweet dish made with semolina and white wine.   (See recipe)

FLAN. An open fruit tart. Usually made in a special tin from which the rim can be removed. Savoury flans are also made with vegetables and meat or sausages.

FLAP JACKS. Crisp cakes made with rolled oats, fat and sugar.
                                                          (See recipe)

FLEAD CAKES. Made with the inner skin of a pig's inside. The flead has much fat in it and is beaten to break up the fat. It is then cut finely into some flour, with sugar and currants and with water to make a dough, then cut into squares, crusted with sugar and water and baked.

FLEURONS. Scraps of puff pastry rolled thinly, cut into small crescents or 'butterflies' or tied in little knots, fried or baked until golden and crisp and served with soups, entrées or creamed dishes.

FLITCH. A side of bacon with the leg cut off and the bone taken out.

FLORENTINE. The name given to a dish in which spinach is used. Also a thin cake coated on one side with chocolate.   (See recipe)

FLOUNDER. A flat sea-fish with a pleasant flavour not unlike sole. Sometimes known as witch.

FLOUR. Commercial wheaten flour. When the flour has been milled in such a way as to include the whole or a proportion of the bran, it is called wholemeal, whole-wheat, pure whole-wheat, or entire whole-wheat.
   Flour obtained from grinding other cereals or vegetables must be qualified by the name of the grain or plant.

FLUKE. Another name for the witch or flounder.

FLUMMERY. Oatmeal boiled with honey, wine or beer and strained through a sieve, flavoured with orange-flower water and sugar, and set in a dish.
Flummery was the fore-runner of our prepared blancmanges and jellies and was a delicacy for invalids.

FLUTE. The French name of the very long rolls of crusty bread.

FOIE DE VEAU. Calf's liver.

FOIE GRAS. A paste of fat goose liver. The best comes from Strasbourg.

FOLD. To blend together two mixtures, one light and containing air (such as creamed fat, sugar and eggs, or stiffly whisked egg-white) and a heavier mixture. A metal spoon or a palette knife is used to lift and fold the two mixtures over and over one another until thoroughly blended.

FONCER. To line the bottom of a pan or ovenware casserole with thin slices of ham or bacon.

FONDANT. A soft kind of icing, or dessert bon-bons.   (See recipe)

FONDUE. A preparation of melted cheese which originated in Switzerland. Sometimes mixed with white wine and eaten with cubes of bread dipped into the hot mixture.   (See recipe)

FOODS ESSENTIAL TO HEALTH. Food contains the following essential elements for full health: Proteins, Vitamins, Carbohydrates and Minerals.
Some foods rich in each of these elements should be eaten every day to provide a good balanced diet.

Proteins.

Meats, poultry, fish, eggs, nuts, lentils, peas and pulses of all kinds. Animal proteins are the most important, fish, eggs and pulses are secondary proteins.
These are body-builders and energy-producers.

Vitamin A

Principally found in liver, kidney, green vegetables, especially spinach, carrots, tomatoes, eggs, milk, butter and margarine.
Essential for adequate growth and to ensure health of the eyes and mucous membranes.

Vitamin B

An important vitamin of the B group is found in yeast, wholemeal flour and bread, pork, bacon, offal (heart, liver, kidney, brains) cabbage, lettuce, potatoes, leeks, milk, black treacle, meat extracts.
Important for growth and for prevention of fatigue and nervous disorders.

Vitamin C

Found especially in fruits and green vegetables, such as oranges, lemons, grapefruit, black currants, strawberries, rosehips, Brussels sprouts, cauliflower, potatoes (especially when cooked in their jackets), green and red peppers, parsley.

Needed for growth, to promote quick healing of wounds and abrasions, to give firm and healthy gums, clear unblemished skins, increased resistance to disease, especially circulatory troubles and the common cold.

Vitamin D

Rich sources are mackerel, sardines, egg yolks, liver, beef, butter, margarine, cheese (especially Cheddar) cod's liver and roe, milk, and the outer leaves of cabbages and lettuces and other green vegetables.

Essential for strong healthy teeth and bones, and in conjunction with sunshine, to help ensure healthy skins.

Vitamin E

Whole wheat, wheat germ, lettuce, black treacle.

Looks after the heart and muscles.

Carbohydrates

In cereals, breads, both white and wholemeal, sugar, jams, honey, raisins, dates, currants and dried apricots, potatoes, bananas, baked beans. These foods provide one of the cheapest forms of energy.

Minerals

There are about 10 mineral elements to be derived from daily food. The chief are:

Calcium: for building bones and teeth, for ensuring the healthy clotting of blood and healthy finger- and toe-nails, and hair. *Sources:* Cheese, sardines, herrings, watercress, cabbage, turnip, cauliflower and eggs.

Phosphorus: Essential for good bones and teeth, and works in conjunction with the calcium in food. *Sources:* Sweetbreads, cheese, fish, meat, eggs, bread and milk.

Iron: Required to give rich healthy blood, marrow in the bones, and for repairing tissue when abrasions or bleeding occur. *Sources:* Kidney, liver, corned beef, fresh beef, mutton, herrings, watercress, spinach, celery, cabbage, raisins.

Suggested List of Essential Daily Foods

Meat: Choose from beef, pork (any part), corned beef, liver, hearts, heads.

Fish: Herrings, mackerel, sardines, cod's roe, kippers, fresh haddock.

Vegetables: Cabbage, potatoes, leeks, lettuce, cauliflower, carrots, swedes, parsley.

Fruit: Oranges, lemons, grapes, tomatoes, bananas, apples, plums, gooseberries.

Cereals: Sago, tapioca, oatmeal, breakfast cereals, rice.

Additions: Wholemeal and white breads, butter, margarine, dried fruits, dark treacle, sugar, honey, jams, meat-extracts for soups, gravy and sandwiches, milk.

FOODS, FROZEN. See *Frozen Foods*.

FOODS: HOW LONG THEY WILL KEEP WITHOUT SPOILING.

Food	At room temperature	In refrigerator
Milk (covered and placed near evaporator)	4—5 hr.	3—6 days
Butter (wrapped, placed near evaporator)	7 days	1—2 months
Margarine (wrapped, placed near evaporator)	7 days	1—3 months
Lard and Dripping (covered)	1—2 weeks	up to 3 months
Fruit Juice or Tomato Juice. (In cans do not require refrigerator storage for long periods, will keep on shelf 6—8 months. Chill before serving. If cans are opened, pour contents into jug, cover and put in refrigerator)	1—7 days	2—3 weeks
Fresh meat (wrapped or placed in special container provided)	24 hr.	6—8 days
Fish (wrapped or placed in special container provided)	10—12 hr.	1—3 days
Ice cubes	Refill trays when de-frosting	
Frozen vegetables and fruits	Use immediately	2—3 days in evaporator only
Ice cream	Use immediately	1—4 days in evaporator only
Bacon (wrapped)	5—7 days	3—4 weeks
Cheese (wrapped)	1—3 days	2—4 weeks
Soft cheese, Dutch or Cream (wrapped)	1—3 days	1—2 months
Refrigerator biscuit dough (wrapped)	2—3 days	2—3 weeks
Prepared short pastry crumbs (in clean screwtop jars)	2—3 weeks	2—3 days
Dessert-custard containing milk (cover) can be chilled uncovered for 1/2 hour before serving	4—6 hr.	2—3 days
Cooked meat (wrap or place in special container)	2 days	5—6 days
Eggs in shell (covered)	7 days	2—3 weeks
Stock (stored in covered jug)	1—2 days	7—10 days
Melba Sauce (in clean screwtop jar)	4—30 days	1—6 months
Chocolate sauce (stored in clean screwtop jar)	1—2 days	7—10 days

Food	At room temperature	In refrigerator
Short pastry crumbs (in clean screwtop jar)	2—3 days	3 weeks
Dried fruits (in clean screwtop jar)	1—3 months	up to 6 months
Paprika (in clean screwtop jar)	2—3 weeks	2—3 months
Dry cereals (in original packet or screwtop jar)	1—2 months	4—6 months
Salad plants and fresh herbs (wrapped or in special container)	2—6 hr.	7—10 days
Cauliflower (in special container)	1—3 days	3—8 days
Root vegetables and hard apples (in special container)	1—2 weeks	1—4 months
Citrus fruit (in special container)	1—7 days	2—4 weeks
Left-over vegetables (in special container or covered)	1 day	5—7 days

N. B. All vegetables should be trimmed, washed and dried before storing in refrigerator. This keeps the refrigerator clean, takes less space and saves time.

FORBIDDEN FRUIT. An American liqueur made with brandy and grape-fruit.

FORCEMEAT. Finely minced meat and seasonings used for stuffing birds, meat or vegetables; also a mixture of crumbs, herbs, seasonings, suet and egg used for stuffing any other food.

FORCING BAG. A bag made of strong calico, linen, greaseproof paper or, more recently, of polythene, fitted with variously shaped nozzles. The bags are filled with cream, icing or vegetable purées which are forced through the nozzles into fancy shapes. Also used for almond or short-bread pastes to make small biscuits.

FORESTIERE. A garnish of wild mushrooms, diced lean bacon and noisette potatoes.

FOURRE. Coated with sugar or cream.

FRANCHONETTES. Small custard tarts masked with meringue.

FRANGIPANE. A sweet almond cream flavoured with vanilla and a flower essence.

FRANGIPANE TART. Almond mixture as above, in a pastry case.

(See recipe)

FRAPPER. To ice; usually used in connection with cooling champagne.

FRICANDINES. Small patties filled with mince and crisply fried.

FRICASSEE. A white stew of veal or chicken.
(See recipes under *Veal, Fricassée of; Chicken, Fricassée of)*

FRITTERS. Fritters are made by dipping pieces of fresh fruit or well-drained preserved fruit in a light batter and frying in deep fat. The batters are made in various ways, some with egg, milk and flour, as for pancakes; others with whisked egg-white, flour, egg-yolk separately, and with oiled butter, rum or other liqueur flavouring.

The most generally made fritters are apple, banana, pineapple and halved peaches. The fritters are sent to the table dusted with sugar and sometimes with a little powdered cinnamon.

FRITURE. A word used for oil, lard, dripping or butter in which food is fried, or for the food thus fried. Sometimes for a mixture of pieces of different fish or vegetables coated in batter.

FROMAGE DE PORC. French name for a brawn made from a pig's head and trotters.   (See recipes)

FROSTING. Various types of icing used for cakes and puddings. Also, covering with meringue.

FROZEN FOODS. The modern scientific method of quick-freezing food is the latest aid to the housewife.

Quick-frozen foods are those in primest condition, chosen at the places where they grow if fruits and vegetables, where they are caught if fish, or where slaughtered if meat. They are immediately processed and hurried into deep-freezers and stored at temperatures that stop deterioration. This means that the flavour and quality are unchanged from the moment the food is frozen until it is sold. It is kept in refrigerated ships, trains and lorries at a temperature of 0^0 F., whatever the outside temperature may be, until it is placed in the freezing cabinets in the shops.

Foods so treated are nutritionally equivalent to the freshest foods and retain a high proportion of their original vitamins and mineral salts.

The long list of foods from the deep-freeze cabinets include poultry, cooked fillet of chicken, filleted fish — both uncooked and ready for re-heating — shrimps, prawns and scampi, cooked chipped potatoes and potato balls, a large number of vegetables, chicken pies, pastry cases ready for filling, frozen tomato puree for soups, frozen fruits and mousse of various flavours.

All quick-frozen foods should be kept in their packages in a cool place until the time for cooking or serving. If there is no refrigerator, the food, kept in a cool place wrapped in several layers of paper, should be used the same day.

To cook, vegetables should be plunged in their frozen state into boiling water to thaw as they cook. Fruit should be thawed slowly at room temperature. Fish can be cooked in a frozen or semi-frozen state, but more time must be allowed than for fresh fish.

Poultry should be slowly thawed in the refrigerator or a cool place in its unopened packet.

To defrost fish, meat or poultry quickly, put into cold water for 40 minutes and change the water once or twice. Otherwise the food takes 3 hr. to defrost at room temperature.

FRUCTOSE. Natural sugar found in fruit.

FRUIT BUTTERS. Preserves made by cooking fruit until greatly reduced in volume and moisture content. Less sugar is required than when making jam.

FRUIT CHEESE. As above, but the 'cheese' is cooked until it is literally a solid mass, and is usually served, with cream, as a dessert, rather than as a preserve.

FRUIT PRESERVATION. Various methods are used for preserving fresh fruit. These include sterilising fruit in water or sugar syrups in glass jars in the oven or in a sterilising kettle, canning in tins by sterilising, the use of synthetic skins after sterilising in the oven, the use of Campden tablets, containing the chemical sulphur-dioxide, or the old-fashioned method of pouring clarified fat or paraffin wax on top of the fruit to exclude air.   (See recipe for *Fruit Bottling*)

FRUMENTY. A dish of crushed whole wheat, sugar, spice and raisins and skimmed and new milk, simmered in a jar in the oven, or at the back of the stove for 12 hr., then eaten hot or cold.
An old farmhouse dish often served at Christmas-time for breakfast.

FUDGE. A sweetmeat of boiled sugar, milk and butter and various flavourings.   (See recipes)

FUMET. A concentrated liquid of fish or vegetables stewed in wine stock or water until greatly reduced.

GALANTINE. The real galantine is made with boned poultry, veal or pork stuffed with savoury stuffing and hard-boiled eggs, simmered in a strong broth of veal or chicken, and, when cold, coated with aspic jelly. It is sometimes decorated with truffles, sliced gherkins, split almonds and other pretty items in the shapes of flowers and leaves.
The more common kind of galantine is made with any kind of minced meat mixed with sausage meat, crumbs and seasonings, pressed into a mould or basin and steamed or baked, turned out and coated with jelly or merely with crushed browned breadcrumbs.

GALETTE. The French name for thin round cakes made of different kinds of flour.

GALIMAFREE. A dish made with meat cut from a shoulder of mutton, minced, mixed with herbs, chopped bacon, cooked with stock, put back on the bone, covered with the skin and roasted in the usual way.

GALL. The contents of the gall bladder (attached to the liver) in poultry. If the gall is broken, the bitter flavour completely ruins the whole bird.

GALLON. A liquid measure equalling 4 quarts or 8 pints.

GAME. A term including pheasants, partridges, grouse, snipe, black-cock, bustards, quail, capercailzie, woodcock, wild geese, wild duck, ptarmigan, etc., and venison. The important kinds are in season as follows:

Partridges	September to February
Pheasants	October to February
Plovers	October to February
Ptarmigan	September to April
Quail	September to February
Woodcock	August to March

GAMMON. The lower part of a side of bacon cured and prepared in the same way as ham. Thick rashers are cut from the gammon and grilled, fried or baked in the oven.

GAPER. A bivalve which is found in the sand at low-water mark, usually in estuaries. Cooked and eaten like cockles.

GARFISH. Resembling a mackerel, with a long mouth like the bill of a snipe. Caught chiefly off the Channel Isles. Any mackerel recipes can be used for garfish.

GARLIC. A bulb with a pungent and aromatic flavour. The bulb is made up of a number of sections called cloves, encased in layers of thin skin.

It is used extensively in a great many savoury dishes on the Continent and is beginning to be liked here.

A favourite method of flavouring a salad is to make a 'chapon' by cutting a thin crust, rubbing each side with garlic and placing it in the bottom of the salad bowl.   (See recipe for *Garlic bread*)

GARLIC BUTTER. Butter blended with a crushed clove of garlic and rubbed through a sieve.

GARLIC VINEGAR. Several crushed cloves of garlic infused in white vinegar and used for sauces or stews.

GARNISHES. Appetising and attractive additions to main dishes; some are simple, such as a few sprigs of parsley or watercress, others are very elaborate such as mushrooms, scallops, shrimps, asparagus-tips and potato-olives, green or black olives, sweetbreads, chipolata sausages, lobster coral, macedoine of vegetables, etc.

GATEAU. A rich cake made usually with a butter sponge or Genoese sponge foundation and decorated with icing, cream, jam, nuts or butter cream.

GELATINE. The jelly obtained from the tendons, bones and ligaments of animals after long boiling.

Isinglass, a refined gelatine, is from fish skins and bones, whereas inferior gelatine, as well as glue, is made from animal skins and hoofs. Isinglass and some gelatines are sold in sheet form, or in finely granulated form. Isinglass has a great many uses in sweet and savoury cooking and is used for all commercially made sweet jellies and savoury aspic jellies.

GENOA CAKE. A rich fruit cake.   (See recipe)

GENOESE. A rich sponge cake mixture and also a sauce.   (See recipe)

GHERKINS. A very small type of cucumber used extensively for pickling. Gherkins are sliced or shredded for decorating cold meat salads and galantines.   (See recipe)

GIBLETS. The liver, heart, gizzard, gall bladder, neck and feet of birds. Giblets are used for gravy, or for making a good pie.   (See recipe)

GIGOT. French or Scottish for a leg of lamb or mutton.

GILD. To brush a cake or pastry over with beaten egg-yolk to give a golden sheen when baked.

GILL. Measure equal to $1/4$ pint.

GINGER. The root of the ginger plant is the part used. When the stems and flowers have died down, the roots are lifted, freed from soil and dried. The tender parts of the roots are boiled in sugar and water until soft, then packed into jars with heavy syrup. The best ginger comes from Jamaica, Africa and Cochin.

GINGER BEER. A carbonised ginger-flavoured drink much drunk in the summer-time. A pleasant way is to stir a tablespoonful of ice-cream into a glassful.   (See recipe)

GINGERBREAD. A moist cake made with syrup or dark treacle, strongly flavoured with ginger, and sometimes containing chopped ginger and fruit. Usually made in baking-tins or small loaf-tins.
There are many kinds, varying just a little one from another. In olden days, the gingerbread was gilded, especially that made to sell at fairs.
                                                                          (See recipe)

GINGER CAKE. The same mixture as for gingerbread. Baked in a cake tin, with sultanas and shredded peel or with chopped crystallised ginger added. Sometimes the top of the cake is covered with white fondant icing and decorated with strips of ginger.

GINGER NUTS. Crisp, buttery ginger-flavoured biscuits of ancient origin.
                                                                          (See recipe)

GINGER SNAPS. A ginger-flavoured biscuit, more brittle than ginger nuts.

GINGER WINE. A sweet non-alcoholic ginger-flavoured drink. The ingredients for making it can be bought from a chemist, or in a ready-to-use form to which sugar and water are added.   (See recipe)

GIN SLING, COLD. Made with water, gin, ice and sugar.

GIN SLING, HOT. The hot sling should be made with Hollands gin, hot water, grated nutmeg and a slice of lemon.

GIPSY BREAD. A fruit bread containing black treacle. So called because of its dark gipsy-like colour.

GIRDLE (GRIDDLE) CAKES. Cakes or scones cooked on top of the stove or cooker on a special thick circular piece of iron with a handle. The plate is well-heated and greased or floured and the scones or pancakes are cooked straight on it. (See recipe)

GIROLE. A type of fungi very seldom used in England. It is tastiest tossed quickly in butter.

GITANA. A garnish of which Spanish onions forms the greater part. Also means cooked gipsy fashion with a lot of onions in the cooking-pot.

GLASGOW TRIPE. Tripe cooked with a knuckle of veal, salt and pepper, eaten either cold or heated with onion sauce.

GLAZE. A rich stock stiffened with gelatine, used to mask cold dishes.

GLUCOSE. A grape sugar contained in most fruit juice and in honey. It is also obtained by boiling potato or maize starch with dilute acids and refining. Concentrated glucose is the granular form. Although much used in confectionery and medicine it is not as sweet as sugar.

GLUTEN. An albuminous substance obtained from the flour of wheat. It is insoluble in water. Much used in diabetic cookery.

GLYCERINE. A syrupy colourless liquid with a very sweet taste, obtained from vegetable oils and animal fat.
   Glycerine is used medicinally, but also in making cake icings to prevent the icing becoming hard and brittle.

GNOCCHI. Tiny dumplings or little sausages about the size of a thumb, or diamond-shaped pieces made sometimes with a very light dough, with a dry potato purée bound with egg, or with a semolina mixture. All are boiled quickly in stock and served with grated parmesan cheese and tomato sauce, or dropped into white stews or blanquettes.
(See recipe)

GOAT'S MILK. Goat's milk is considered extremely nourishing for children. Not used extensively for cheese-making in this country as the strong flavour is not appreciated. Some doctors consider the milk a cure for eczema.

GODIVEAU. A forcemeat of minced veal, suet, herbs and egg, used for making small balls for garnishes.

GOLDEN POCKETS. The large bright yellow flowers of vegetable marrows, stuffed with savoury forcemeat, often flavoured with garlic, tied together with cotton, dipped in batter and fried; or the pockets may be packed closely in a shallow dish, moistened with olive oil and baked in the oven. A favourite dish in Southern France and Italy.

GOLDEN SAUCE. A sweet sauce served with light steamed puddings.
(See recipe)

GOLDWASSER. A very potent German liqueur with tiny specks of gold leaf floating in it.

GOOSE, BARNACLE. A wild goose which visits the Hebrides and Ireland in winter.

GOOSEBERRY. The fruit of a very prickly shrub which grows chiefly in England. There are many varieties, from the small green ones to the large and luscious pale yellow-green. Used for desserts, pies, jam and chutney.
(See recipe)

GOOSE GREASE. The fat of geese is one of the country-woman's most prized medicaments, being used for chapped hands and faces, in poultices for weak chests, for bronchitis and mixed with gorse flowers and watercress juice for making ointments. It is also used, mixed with mustard and turpentine, in embrocations for rheumatism.

GOSLING. A young goose.

GOULASH. A rich stew flavoured with paprika. Of Hungarian origin.
(See recipe)

GOURDS. A large variety of wine fruits, which include marrows, pumpkins, cucumbers, melons and squashes.
The flesh of all gourds is palatable and can be cooked and served in many ways.

GRAHAM-FLOUR. Flour which has not been passed through a refining sieve after grinding. Another name for wholemeal flour. Used principally for making bread or scones.

GRAINING. A term used in sugar boiling for confectionery, when the sugar turns to crystals, thus spoiling the texture of the sweetmeat. Particularly likely to happen when making fudge.

GRAINS OF PARADISE. The poetical name of the seeds of an East Indian plant which we know as cardamom seeds. They have a strong but attractive flavour, are always used in curry and sometimes form the centres of certain small brightly-coloured sweets.

GRANADILLA. The fruit of the Passion Flower. There are several varieties. The fruit is bottled, eaten with cream and the juice is used with other ingredients for flavouring cocktails or ices.

GRAPE. Fruit of the vines. There are a great many varieties, according to the country and the soil on which they are cultivated.
Grapes seldom ripen out-of-doors in England. Small homegrown grapes may be used for jam, little tarts and a home-made wine.

GRAPEFRUIT. A large citrus fruit with a pale-yellow skin and firm, tart, acid pulp. It makes an excellent marmalade, but is too often served as an hors-d'œuvre.

GRAPPA. An Italian spirit distilled from skins, pips and stalks of the grapes after the grapes have been pressed for wine.

GRAS-DOUBLE. French name for belly of beef, which is used in England for tripe.

GRASS LAMB. Lamb born after 25th June.

GRATE. To rub on a fine or a coarse grater to reduce food to tiny morsels. Cheese, bread and vegetables and some fruits are grated for soups, salads and stuffings.

GRATIN, AU. Dishes which have a rich sauce on which a layer of crumbs is scattered, and which is browned in the oven or beneath the grill. Most au gratin dishes now have grated cheese mixed with the crumbs and are therefore much more appetising.

GRAVY. The name given to meat juice, also to stocks thickened with flour or gravy browning used as gravy.

GRAVY SALT (BROWNING). A dark fluid used to colour gravies, soups, etc. The chief ingredient is burnt sugar.

GRAYLING. A trout-like fish usually found in cold streams. Very pleasant when cooked like trout.

GREASE. To rub any cooking vessel with fat to prevent food sticking during the cooking.

GREENGAGE. A stone fruit of the plum variety of great sweetness, juiceness and good flavour. Known in France as Reine Claude. It bottles well, makes excellent pies and good jam.   (See recipe)

GREEN GOOSE. A young goose, so called until 6 months old. It is a country name for gosling.
  These geese are usually served without the customary sage and onions, a sharp sauce of small green gooseberries being served instead.

GREENING. A green vegetable colour, commonly made with spinach juice and used for coloured confectionery and garnishes of piped potatoes, etc.

GREEN ONIONS. See *Scallion.*

GREEN PEA SPROUTS. Made by germinating dried green peas with water.
  The Chinese people have always used this method of producing the small green sprouts they use so much in their cooking. During the War when all foods containing Vitamin C, and the mineral salts important to health, were so scarce, the Ministry of Health experimented with the method of germinating the sprouts and the results were very satisfactory.

Chinese method of producing the sprouts.

Soak a breakfastcupful of dried green peas in cold water for 2—3 days. As soon as the shells break and a tiny sprout shows, put the peas into a little tub or earthenware flower-pot with a small hole in it. The hole should be covered with a piece of muslin so that the water may drain out, but no peas may fall through. Cover the vessel with a damp cloth, put in a dark place with a temperature of 70—75⁰ and water about 6 times a day, but only very sparingly. In about a week the crop of sprouts will be ready to turn out on a muslin-covered wire tray. Keep the crop in a cool place and use as required.

The sprouts may be cooked alone, or with celery, with meat, or eaten raw in salads.

The orthodox manner of cooking is to fry in oil with small pieces of meat, celery, chicken, pork. The sprouts must be crisp, not soft, when served.

English method of germinating.

Soak the peas as before. Spread them thickly on pieces of damp flannel. Keep the flannel damp until the sprouts are ready to use.

GREEN PEPPERS. The green variety of capsicum. A bell-shaped, dark-green shiny vegetable with many very hot small white seeds. Used for salads and risottos; excellent stuffed.   (See recipe)

GREENS. The general term for any kind of green vegetable plainly boiled in salted water.

GREEN SAUCE. A rich mayonnaise coloured with the juice of pounded parsley, chervil and tarragon leaves, and sometimes a little spinach.

GRENADIN. A fricassée of meat.

GRIG. A small fresh-water eel.

GRILLADE. French for grilled food.

GRILSE. A young salmon when it leaves the sea and begins its travels to go up to the fresh-water streams.

GRISKIN. The spine or backbone left when the sides of bacon have been cut away. It may also be a poor quality piece of loin of pork.

GRISTLE. The cartilage found in meat.

GROG. A mixture of spirits, hot water and lemon. Formerly a sailor's drink, but much used to help cure bad colds, especially that made with rum.

GROSERT FOOL. Scottish name for Gooseberry Fool. Made of sieved sweetened berries mixed with cream.   (See recipe)

GROUNDNUT. Another name for peanut, a native plant of Brazil, but extensively cultivated in sub-tropical countries.

The extracted oil is used for making peanut butter. Peanut brittle is a very good toffee which originated in America.

GROUND RICE. Rice ground to a fine powder, used for milk puddings and to add to steamed puddings, biscuits or shortbreads and petit fours and other cakes.

GROUSE. A small game bird found chiefly in Scotland. Shooting of grouse begins on the 12th August in the British Isles. The grouse has a very fine flavour and served cold was formerly considered a good breakfast dish.

GUARDS PUDDING. A very well-known steamed light pudding made partly with breadcrumbs.   (See recipe)

GUAVA. An American tropical fruit which is now grown in many sub-tropical countries. The fruit is used to make very sweet and delicious jelly, while the pulp from which the juice has drained is made into a firm preserve called guava cheese.

GUDGEON. A fresh-water fish of good flavour. At its best when stuffed with veal stuffing, baked and served with parsley butter.

GUINEA FOWL. A small game bird with a firm flesh that has more flavour than that of a fowl, but less than that of a pheasant. The breasts are very meaty, but there is little flesh elsewhere on the carcase. Served with the same accompaniments as fowl or pheasant.

GULYAS. Hungarian for goulash.

GUMBO (OKRA). The pods of a herbaceous plant. They resemble small cucumbers and are rich in a nourishing mucilage. Used to give a gelatinous texture to soup in South America, the West Indies and U. S. A. Now obtainable here in tins from some good grocers.

GURNET (GURNARD). A fresh-water fish which has a tough membrane running through the flesh which makes it unsuitable for grilling or frying. Not much used in Britain, but in France it is often used in stews like meat, with the usual meat sauces and seasonings.

HADDOCK. A fish allied to cod, with a dark line down the body and having a dark spot behind the gills.
Haddocks are very delicate in flavour when quite fresh. They are dried and smoked more frequently than most fish.
The Findon haddock is considered the best. The favourite British method of using it is by simply poaching it in milk and water, then serving it with a large piece of butter melted on it.

HADDOCKS, SMOKED. The fresh fish are cleaned, slit, and, with heads removed, are left in salt for about 12 hours. They are then hung in the open air to dry and finally smoked in special chimneys over peat, hardwood sawdust, or fir-cones. Small haddocks smoked without being split, chiefly from Arbroath and Auchmittie, are called smokies.

HADDYANEGG. Steamed haddock cooked in milk with a knob of butter; poached eggs on portions of haddock and the milk and butter slightly thickened with flour and poured round the fish.
Large slices of good home-made bread are sopped in the gravy or sauce.

HAGGIS. A famous Scottish dish. It is made with a sheep's pluck and
paunch, beef suet, oatmeal, onions, salt and pepper, nutmeg and stock.
The contents are sewn up in the paunch and boiled. It is served with
great ceremony and the playing of bagpipes at Hogmanay and on the
celebration of Burns Night. Plenty of good whisky is always served
with the haggis.

HAKE. A favourite West Country fish with a very good flavour. It has tender
flesh which is the better for lying in slightly salted water for about
10 minutes before it is cooked. Known as the nursery fish because of its
freedom from small bones.

HALF-GLAZE. A sauce mixed with a jellied liquid or glaze, used for
masking savoury dishes.

HALIBUT. This fish can vary much in size from big fish weighing over
200 pounds to small ones weighing about 2 pounds. The small fish are
known as Chicken Halibut. The largest come from Greenland and have
a wonderful flavour and succulence.

HAM. The hind legs of a pig salted and cured and smoked; the hams are
frequently cured with the whole side of bacon. Shoulders, cushions,
collars and other parts thus cured are also called ham, although they
are really bacon.
   The best-known British ham is York ham.

HAMBURG PARSLEY. A hardy kind of parsley grown for its fleshy root
which can be eaten raw or cooked.

HAMBURGERS. Freshly minced beef made into round cakes and grilled
or fried. The original hamburger has only salt and pepper as seasonings,
and the cakes are usually served with rounds of finely sliced onion on
top. Other varieties may have Worcester sauce, beer, or other seasonings.
   The Americans serve the hamburgers on lightly toasted large plain
buns with a tomato sauce.

HAND OF PORK. The fore leg, also called hand and spring. As it is very
fat, it is usually salted and boiled, although it is good roasted.

HANDY MEASURES WHEN NO SCALES ARE AVAILABLE.
   1 well heaped tablespoonful of light ingredients such as flour, cornflour,
   or blancmange powder or breadcrumbs   = 1 oz.
   1 level tablespoonful of these ingredients   = 1/2 oz.
   1 heaped tablespoonful of sugar, rice, dried fruit   = 1 1/2—2 oz.
   1 tablespoonful of treacle, syrup or jam   = 2 oz.
   1 dessertspoonful of treacle, syrup or jam   = 1 oz.
   A cup which holds 1/2 pint and will, when twice filled, fill a pint
   milk-bottle is equal to 6 oz. of flour packed down.
   Half that cup is equal to 3 oz. of flour.
   A quarter of a pint cup will hold 4 oz. of rice, sugar, sago or heavy
   ingredients.
   A cup which will hold 1/2 pint of water will hold approximately 15 oz.
   of treacle or syrup.

It is very important to use the same measuring cup always, if relying on handy measures, or equal results will never be obtained.
1 average-sized egg in the shell weighs approximately 2 oz.

HARD BAKE. A toffee-sweet with a great many almonds.

HARD SAUCE. A sauce of sugar, butter, spirits and spice put in a cold place until it can be cut into squares and served with hot puddings, especially Christmas Pudding.

HARD-SHELLED CRAB. A crustacean obtainable all the year round, but best from May to August.

HARE. Animal larger than a rabbit, with dark gamey flesh. The most usual method of serving is as jugged hare.　　　　　　(See recipe)

HARICOT BEAN. The fully grown or partly ripe seeds of various kinds of dwarf or climbing beans. There are white ones, large and small, green, flageolets, purple and brown. They are all highly nutritious and are used extensively in stews and casseroles. The best known dried bean dish is Boston baked beans.　　　　　　　　　　　(See recipe)

HARSLET. A pig's fry (i. e. liver, sweetbreads, heart, etc.), sliced, seasoned, mixed with oatmeal or crumbs, rolled in the skin surrounding the suet and baked.

HARTSHORN. Fine shavings from a stag's horn which in olden days were boiled to make jellies.

HASH. Any meat finely minced and re-cooked as a stew.

HASTY PUDDING. The old version of this pudding was a paste of flour and milk rather like a roux, or beginning of a white sauce. It was cooked until it was like a thick paste, then spiced with mace, flavoured with the favourite orange or rose water (for want of the modern synthetic essences), enriched by a knob of butter well blended with the paste, then poured into a dish and served with sugar and powdered cinnamon or grated nutmeg. A more appetising pudding is made in Worcestershire with alternate layers of hasty mixture and sweetened and partly cooked sliced apples, with a thick crust of sugar and cinnamon on top, cooked for about 20—25 min. in a moderate oven.

HATELETS. Small skewers used, garnished, for ornamenting fish dishes.

HATTED KIT. The curds of curdled milk with the whey strained off. Covered with thick cream. Served alone or with fruit, especially black-berries, in season.

HAVER BREAD. A special very thin oat cake made, in the West Riding of Yorkshire, with fine oatmeal, water and yeast and left to rise, when more coarse oatmeal was added. The batter was so thin that it bubbled when poured over the griddle plate. The large lacey pieces were lifted from the griddle with a broad knife and turned for a minute, then hung over a line to dry and become quite brittle. Pieces were broken off and buttered or cooked with bacon fat as required.

HAY BOX COOKERY. Food, partially cooked, put into a vessel that can be closely covered, and the vessel placed in a box insulated by pads filled with hay or chaff, then covered with a thick blanket padding before the lid of the box is closed. The food, boiling when placed in the box, continues to cook gently and slowly for as long as it is left enclosed. A very economical method of cooking stews, root vegetables, dried vegetables or cereals.

HAZELNUTS. Hazelnuts come from Spain, Asia Minor and Italy. Those from the Levant and Naples are considered the best for making confectionery. There are some found in the hedgerows of this country, but not in sufficient quantity to be of commercial value.

Hazels must be dried as soon as possible after they are picked. These nuts are more liable to go rancid or mouldy than other nuts, the rot beginning at the centres. If they are lightly roasted, it not only helps to prevent deterioration but improves the flavour. Hazelnut paste is known as praline mixture.

HEDGEHOG PUDDING. A sponge cake baked in an oval mould, soaked in wine, covered with custard and 'porcupined' closely with blanched and split almonds.

HERBS. The word is now used in a limited sense and has come to mean plants which are used in medicine or cookery. Herbs used in cookery are those with a sweet pungent or aromatic flavour without which our cooking would be dull and tasteless.

Herbs are at their best when used fresh from the garden, but may be well dried and packaged at home or bought from a good herbalist.

Herbs most used in everyday cooking include mint, parsley, thyme, marjoram, sage, rosemary, bayleaf and basil.

HERBS, TO DRY. Herbs for drying are at their best just before they begin to flower and should be gathered on a dry morning after the dew has dried up.

The drying should be carried out with as little heat and crushing as possible. Tie the herbs together in bunches and shake free of dust or any tiny insects, then leave the bunches to dry naturally and gradually in a warm room out of the sun. The bunches may be tied in muslin to keep them free from dust. The leaves are usually dry after about three weeks.

When crisp, rub between the hands to separate from the stems. If powdered herbs are required crush the dried leaves with a rolling-pin.

Keep crushed or powdered herbs in small bottles with good stoppers and store in the dark.

Bay leaves are left whole, or branches of the leaves are tied in muslin and hung in a dry place.

Parsley will continue to grow in the ground through the year, but if dried needs a little artificial heat. Tie in bunches and hang in a warm oven. On no account allow it to scorch. When dry, crush, sieve and store in small stoppered jars.

HERB TEAS. Hot drinks made with different herbs, flowers or seeds, all of which are supposed to be beneficial for various complaints.

The French use herb teas far more than we do, the favourite tea being that infused from dried lime-flowers. This tea is very pleasant and said to be tranquillising at night. Other teas are infused from sage, mint, marigold flowers, balm, rosemary, camomile, etc.

HERRINGS. Known as the 'poor man's fish', this is one of the most nutritious and delicate fish there are. They are in season all the year, but at their best from July to December.

Herrings are caught in great shoals which appear off the different parts of the coast at different times of the year.

There are many ways of cooking herrings.   (See recipes)

HIGHBALL. A long drink of spirits usually diluted with Italian or French vermouth and served with cracked ice or sometimes aerated water.

HIGH TEA. A meal that in some households takes the place of the late dinner.

It is usually made up of the usual bread and butter, jam, scones and cakes, with a hot dish of fish or of meat rissoles, or in summer a cold meat salad with fruit or a tart.

HILSA. A fish which resembles mackerel and which is cooked in the same ways.

HINDLE WAKES. This name is believed to be derived from 'Hen de la Wake' and brought by Flemish spinners when they came over and settled in Lancashire.

For certain feasts they prepared a specially stuffed chicken, and the custom spread to our own Lancashire people, who have stuffed chicken during the Wakes Week.

HIPS. The fruit of the dog rose and other roses. When ripe, they may be made into rosehip syrup or jam. Rosehip syrup is very rich in Vitamin C.   (See recipe)

HODGE-PODGE (HOT-POT). An old-fashioned stew of neck of mutton, potatoes, onions and seasonings.   (See recipe)

HOE CAKES. Another name for Johnny Cakes.

HOG. The male pig.

HOGSHEAD. A hogshead of beer is 72 gallons, a hogshead of claret is 46 gallons.

HOLLANDAISE SAUCE. One of the most popular sauces served with fish, vegetables and salads. A type of well-seasoned mayonnaise.

     (See recipe)

HOLLANDS. The name of a very fine gin made in Holland. Once it was distilled from crushed juniper berries, but now it is made from a mash of barley or oats mixed with ground juniper as a flavouring agent.

HOMARD. French for lobster.

HOMINY. Coarsely ground maize. Used as a breakfast food and also for scones and milk puddings. Not easily obtainable in this country, but some large stores stock it.

HONEY. The sweet substance obtained by bees from the nectar of flowers. It is a natural form of invert sugar. Strained honey is liquid honey drained from the comb.
    Honey is used for all purposes of sweetening and also for making the ancient drink of mead.

HONEY BEANS. A bean of golden honey colour, a dual purpose vegetable. When young the whole pods can be cooked and eaten like young runner beans, or the beans may grow until the seeds are well developed, when they are shelled and dried for using in stews like haricot beans.

HONEYCOMB TOFFEE. See *Cinder toffee.*

HONEYWARE (HENWARE). A form of seaweed which is very good boiled or pickled.

HONGROISE. A garnish of cauliflower sprigs, in a Mornay sauce flavoured with paprika, and plain boiled potatoes.

HOP BEER. A drink made with hops, sugar, water and yeast, which can be made and is ready to drink within a few days.   (See recipe)

HOPS. The vines bearing the papery flowers with which beers are brewed. Hop shoots when young are cooked and served like asparagus.

HOREHOUND. A wild herb from which a medicinal tea and flavouring for cough-sweets is made.

HORS-D'OEUVRES. Small appetising dishes served before the main part of the meal. Usually of fish, such as smoked salmon, oysters, or a mixture of salted herring and sardines. Sometimes of sliced hard-boiled eggs with asparagus tips in mayonnaise. There is a very great number of these dishes, and it is now the custom to serve hot appetisers, such as tiny vol-au-vent cases filled with savoury creamed mixtures.

HORSE BEAN. Another name for broad bean.

HORSE MUSHROOMS. Large field mushrooms whose flesh turns brown when bruised or cut up for cooking.

HORSERADISH. A root with a very hot flavour. Used mainly for sauces, for hot meats and fish, or to flavour cold fish salads.   (See recipes)

HORSE'S NECK. A cocktail so-called because the peel of a lemon in a continuous strip is anchored in the glass with a lump of ice, while the other end of the peel hangs over the edge of the glass. Brandy and ginger ale, with a very little lemon juice, are then poured into the glass.

HOT CROSS BUNS. Spiced buns that have been made for Good Friday for many centuries. The cross on them is said to be older than that of Christian origin.

HOT-POT. See *Hodge-Podge.*

HOT WATER CRUST (PASTRY). A paste made with boiled water and fat, for raised pies.   (See recipe)

HUCKLE-MY-BUFF. The Sussex name for a mixture of beer, brandy and eggs—actually a strong punch.

HUFF CRUST. A crust made with flour, water and salt, rolled thick and used to wrap up an elderly fowl or other bird; the wrapped bird was then gently baked; when done, the crust, full of rich fat and juices, was cut apart, and pieces were served with the bird, which would be very tender.

HUMBLES (UMBLES). The internal organs of deer.

HUNG BEEF. Beef first hung for about 3 weeks until it becomes dry, then salted and rolled tightly. Sometimes smoked, when it will keep for a very long time. If grated, it makes good stews.

HUNGRY GAP. A name given to Kale because it is hardy enough to survive frosts and is therefore available as a vegetable when others have been killed off.

HUSSARDE. A garnish of hollowed tomatoes filled with a purée of onions flavoured with grated horseradish.

HYDROMEL. A very ancient name for a type of unfermented mead made with honey, water and spices.

HYSSOP. A herb with evergreen leaves and deep-blue, white, or pink flowers. Known in olden days as a holy herb because it was used in purification ceremonies. The dried flowers are infused as a tea for coughs and colds; the oil distilled from the leaves is used in the preparation of liqueurs.

ICES. Cream ices are various mixtures of creams, egg-whites, sugar, evaporated milk, custard and flavouring. Cream ices can be served alone or with sauces or mixtures of fruit. Water ices are made from fruit purées.
                                                       (See recipes)

ICING SUGAR. Very finely powdered sugar made specially for icings and some confectionery. It is the most expensive sugar; owing to its fine texture it easily forms into lumps and must be sieved before use.
                                                       (See recipes)

ILES FLOTTANTES. A sweet much favoured in France, made with custard and egg whites.   (See recipe)

IMPERIALE. 1. An out-size green glass bottle made in France for bottling long-keeping Clarets. It usually holds about 8 ordinary bottles of wine.
2. A garnish consisting of foie gras, truffles, mushrooms and quenelles of sweetbread.

IMPERIAL POP. A harmless beverage made with sugar, cream of tartar, etc.
(See recipe)

IMPERIAL WATER. A refreshing non-alcoholic drink named after Napoleon Bonaparte, who is said to have had it made to drink during his campaigns, as it left him with a clear head and did not 'fuddle his brain with the fumes of wine'.
It is made of water, cream of tartar, lemon juice and grated lemon rind. When made now, a little ginger is added. It can be made to drink within a day or two.

INDIAN CHUTNEY. A hot, smooth chutney made with apples.
(See recipe)

INDIAN CORN. A name for sweet maize, of which there are many varieties.
The corn is eaten fresh; a large quantity is canned on or off the cob; also the corn is dried and ground as flour or meal for cakes, scones or puddings. A very large proportion of the crops of the various corns or maizes is used for cattle and poultry feeding.

INDIAN CRESS. The nasturtium, which is of the cress family. The leaves and the brilliant flowers are used in salads and sandwiches; the seeds can be used in the same ways as capers, or added for piquancy to vinegar pickles.

INDIAN RICE. The name given in the British Isles to Patna and other Indian-grown rices. Known as wild rice in the U. S. A.

INFUSE. To steep in hot liquid, without boiling, to extract flavour, as in spicing vinegar.

INK-FISH. Another name for cuttle-fish, or squid. Found in the Mediterranean and Adriatic. Usually cut up and fried in oil with a little garlic. In Spain chocolate is cooked with ink-fish.

INKY-PINKY. A Scottish dish made with sliced cold beef, sliced carrots, onion and gravy seasoned with vinegar and thickened with butter and flour, served on toast.

INVALID COOKERY. Food prepared for people who are suffering from different illnesses and who are on special diets. Such food as eggs, fish, chicken, milk, jellies, and custards are the chief items, but other foods are needed for specific diseases.

IRISH MOSS. A dark purple or green branching translucent sea weed, growing round our own coasts and in Northern Europe and America. It is dried, bleached, and used for making jellies and aspics, after having been soaked in fresh water. It is considered very nourishing. (See recipe)

IRISH STEW. A stew of neck of mutton, sliced potatoes, and onions, with seasonings and water, cooked until tender. Very much like Lancashire Hodge-Podge or Hot-Pot (q. v.) but the Lancashire dish sometimes has kidneys and mushrooms added. (See recipe)

IRLANDAISE. In Irish style, usually applied to dishes, especially stews, containing potatoes.

IRON. One of the minerals necessary to the body to keep the blood healthy and prevent anaemia. It is chiefly found in green vegetables, green salads, cheese, eggs, dried pulse, dried fruit — especially prunes, dates and raisins — whole cereals, liver and beef.

ISABELITA. The Spanish name given to angel fish. Known in America as monkfish, butterfly fish and black angel fish.

ISINGLASS. Fish glue. A white solid mass prepared from fish bladders. The chief constituent of gelatine.
Used in various food preparations and in the fining of beers and wines. Has strong adhesive properties.

ITALIAN PASTES. The over-all name for a number of wheaten or chestnut flour pastes which used to be made exclusively in Italy. The flour kneaded to a stiff dough is forced through perforated cylinders of different styles to produce flat ribbons, large tubes, or very thin sticks. There are well over a hundred different shapes of pastes.

ITALIAN SAUCE. A rich sauce of tomato, mushrooms and ham.

ITALIENNE. Usually denotes that macaroni is with the dish as for instance, a garnish.

IVORY SAUCE. A smooth well-seasoned cream sauce with a third part of meat glaze added to give the creamy tint. Served with boiled or steamed poultry, sweetbreads or veal, or other white stews.

JACK. An old-fashioned spit that turned round by clockwork, bringing all parts of the joint or bird to roast evenly before the heat of the open fire.
Also another name for a large pike.

JACQUES. A garnish for pancakes. Thinly sliced bananas sprinkled with sugar, simmered in butter and sprinkled with Grand Marnier or Chartreuse.

JACQUES, COUPE. A macedoine of fruit in Kirsch with strawberry or lemon ice-cream. A poor imitation is sometimes served of vanilla ice with fruit salad in syrup.

JAM. A preserve made by boiling any fruit with sugar, until it sets and can be potted. Some fruits such as cherries and strawberries are poor in pectin and must have a commercial pectin or a juice from a pectin-rich fruit added. (See recipes)

JAMAICA PEPPER. Another name for allspice.

JAMAICA RUM. Rum distilled from molasses in Jamaica. The fact that it is distilled at comparatively low strength gives it a very pungent flavour. It can vary in colour from a pale gold to a dark brown.

JAMBALAYAH. An American dish of Creole origin, often served for breakfast.   (See recipe)

JAPANESE (JAP) CAKES. Brittle cakes of sugar, egg-whites and almonds.

JAPANESE MEDLAR. The same as Loquat, which see.

JAPANESE PERSIMMON (KAKI). A fruit which has been cultivated in Japan and China for centuries and is now grown in America and in Provence, where it is made into preserves. The sizes vary from that of a plum to a small tomato. The colour is bright pinky red, the pulp extremely juicy.

JAPANESE QUINCE. The berries of an ornamental Japanese shrub which are too hard to eat, but which contain an aromatic juice used for making jellies and preserves.

JARDINIERE. 'Gardener's Style'. A mixture of spring vegetables; anything served with the vegetables is 'à la Jardinière'.

JARRET. Knuckle of veal or mutton.

JARRETS OF PORK. Pickled pigs' trotters boiled and served with sauerkraut.

JAUNE-MANGE. A thick custard made with eggs, to set as a mould, as distinct from blanc-mange made with cornflour.
    Literally, 'yellow eating'.

JELLY. Concentrated essence of fruits and meats assisted by the inclusion of various glutinous substances obtained by boiling them down. Fish and meat bones, meat gristle and various portions of the calf and pig produce good jelly, especially the feet and heads.   (See recipes)

JELLY BAG. A bag made of thin, fine flannel into which cooked fruit is poured, to retain the pulp and allow the juice which is to be 'jellied' to escape clear and unclouded.

JEROBOAM. Name given to a double magnum of Champagne.

JERUSALEM ARTICHOKE. A tuber-vegetable that came to England from America, via France and Italy; the name Girasole was its Italian name and Jerusalem is said to be a corruption of this. It is said to be good for diabetics, and can be cooked in a number of appetizing ways.
                                                    (See recipes)

JEWISH DISHES. The Jewish Laws require that foods must be specially prepared in accordance with Orthodox Jewish requirements. The rules for preparation and for the utensils used are very strict. The most important rule is that meats, poultry and fish must be koshered, that is, freed from blood.

JIGGER. The American name for a measure of spirits of about 1¹/₂ liquid oz.

JINGLE. A mixture of hot ale poured over raisin cake, roasted apples with sugar and nutmeg.

JOCKEY CLUB. A method of cooking fillet of beef. The beef is larded, soaked in Madeira, braised and served garnished with truffles, chicken quenelles, stuffed tomatoes, flat potato croquettes and Madeira sauce.

JOHN COLLINS. A long drink made with gin.   (See recipes)

JOHN DORY. A fish of delicate flavour caught principally off the South and West Coasts. It is best filleted and treated in the same manner as soles.   (See recipes)

JOHNNY CAKES. Buns made of flour, yeast, sugar, butter and eggs, and candied peel. Johnny is a corruption of 'journey cakes', so-called because the buns were baked for men riding on long journeys on horse-back.

JOINT. To cut into pieces, or with poultry, to sever at the joints.

JOINTS. The pieces into which a whole carcase of an animal is cut, i. e. shoulder, leg, loin or saddle of mutton or lamb; leg, loin, hand and spring of pork; breast, neck, loin of veal; sirloin, ribs, top-side, etc., of beef.

JORAM. A ¹/₂ pint measure which owes its name to the Joram, who (Bible, 2nd Samuel, VIII, 10) 'brought with him vessels of silver, and vessels of gold, and vessels of brass'.

JORDAN ALMOND. The best type of almond. Almost the most expensive from Malaga and Almeira.

JUG. To cook very slowly in a casserole or earthenware jug or jar, with seasoning, forcemeat balls and often port wine added, as in the case of jugged hare.

JUJUBE. The fruit of the Chinese date, which grows in tropical countries and in California. May be eaten raw, but is usually candied. Also, the name given to tough jellied sweets liked by children in this country.

JULEP. The name of a sweet drink, between a cocktail and a cup, better known in America than here. The name comes from the Persian Julap, meaning a sweetened draught.

JULIENNE. A clear vegetable soup; also vegetables cut into fine shreds to put into Julienne soups and consommés.

JUMBLES. Small lemon-flavoured cakes.

(See recipe)

JUNIPER. A shrub bearing small blue berries which are mainly used for flavouring gin, but which are also used very sparingly in savoury seasonings for chicken or veal.

JUNKET. Milk artificially thickened with rennet.
     It is considered to be very beneficial to all who suffer from digestive troubles, but, as a pleasant sweet for normal digestions, it is flavoured with rum and served with sugar.

JUICE. The unthickened juice of cooked meats.

JUS LIE. Thickened and seasoned meat juice.

KAFFIR CORN. An African grass; grown for bread-making and for cattle-food in Africa.

KAGNE. A type of vermicelli.

KAISERFLEISCH. Smoked ribs of pork served with sauerkraut and pease-pudding.

KALE. This coarse dark cabbage-like plant with curling leaves and a strong flavour should only be used very young. Much eaten in Scotland and known as Scotch kale, cottage kale or winter greens. It is cooked like cabbage or eaten raw in salads.

KARLSBAD. A beignet made by mixing stoned red cherries with choux paste and frying in deep fat.

KATTERN CAKES. Cakes made with bread dough, caraway seeds and eggs for St. Catherine's Day but really called after Queen Catherine of Aragon.

KEBABS. Tasty little pieces of meat, kidney or bacon run on long thin skewers with mushrooms, then grilled. Originally small pieces of mutton only, with pieces of the mutton fat, as served in Turkey.   (See recipe)

KEDGEREE. A mixture of cooked fish, rice, sliced hard-boiled egg, butter and seasoning. Served as a breakfast dish before a day's hunting or fishing.   (See recipe)

KENTISH HUFFKINS. Flat round dough cakes with a hole in the middle and a very soft crust.   (See recipe)

KENTISH OAST CAKES. When hop-picking was in full swing in the Kentish hop gardens, the women used to make oast cakes to eat with the small beer or light ale that, with some cheese, formed the snack taken in a short break during the morning. The cakes were made with flour, salt and a little dripping and water, and were cooked on iron plates over emergency ovens.

KENTISH PUDDING PIE. So called because it is partly boiled and partly baked. A pudding is first made with ground rice, milk, sugar and lemon rind; when smooth and creamy, currants are mixed with it, the whole is poured into a large pie dish lined with a rich short crust, grated nutmeg is scattered over the top, and the pie baked in the oven. This pie is also known as Kentish Easter Pie, because it was served on Easter Sunday.

KERNELS. Bean-like Indian nuts sold under the name of kernels, which, being cheaper than almonds or hazels, are therefore often used for stretching the better nuts, but are never used alone.

KERN MILK. Scottish name for buttermilk.

KETCHUP (CATCHUP OR CATSUP). A liquor extracted from mushrooms, walnuts or tomatoes, or made with anchovies. Seasoned and used as sauce or flavouring.

KEUFTES. Same as Kioftedes, with the addition of a little white bread soaked in stock, using mutton instead of beef and moulding into finger-shaped rolls. Fried in mutton fat.

KICKSHAWS. Originally denoted delicate little luxury dishes (French *quelque chose* — something). Still used as a term of contempt for little oddments that would not feed a hungry man.

KID. A young goat. Considered a great delicacy. Can be roasted or stewed. The meat is inclined to be dry and needs frequent basting when roasted.

KIDNEY BEANS. This term includes the French, dwarf and runner beans.

KIDNEYS. The kidneys of beef, veal, lamb, mutton or pork are all excellent food and very nutritious. They should, when possible, be bought in their surrounding fat and as fresh as possible.
There are countless methods of cooking and serving them, apart from teaming them with steak.   (See recipes)

KIOFTEDES. A Greek dish made of finely minced beef mixed thoroughly with half its weight in duchesse potato mixture, then seasoned, shaped into flat cakes and fried.

KIPPERS. Split and smoked fish, chiefly herring. Salmon is sometimes 'kippered'.   (See recipe)

KIRSCH. A colourless liqueur made of wild cherries.

KITCHEN PEPPER. A mixture of ground spices, including ginger, kept for seasoning; rather indiscriminate because so many strong flavours are mixed together.

KLIP-FISH. A type of dried cod imported from Norway. Treated in the same manner as dried cod generally.

KNEAD. To press and mould dough with the base of the palms to make the dough smooth and to blend it well.

KNEADED BUTTER. Butter which has absorbed its own weight when kneaded with flour. Small portions of this mixture are used for thickening stews and soups.

KNOBS. Small shellfish like whelks.

KNOT. Small birds rather like the snipe which come to Britain in large numbers from the arctic regions.
　　Once eaten extensively, they are no longer much considered as a food.

KNOTTED MARJORAM. The sweetest and most fragrant of the several varieties of marjoram.

KNUCKLE. The part of the leg of an animal between the 'ham', or shoulder and the foot.
　　The meat is excellent for stews or pies, while the bone with its sinews makes good soup.

KOHL RABI. A species of turnip whose characteristic is that the globe-like root forms above the ground; it has leaves like kale, is very hardy and will last longer than other root vegetables.

KOOFTHAS. An Indian meat ball made of meat or chicken flavoured with curry, then fried.

KOSHER. A special method of preparing food for Jewish cooking. The word means 'fit' or 'proper'.

KRINGLES. Rich short biscuits.   (See recipe)

KROMESKIES. A kind of Russian rissole, made with rolled slices of bacon filled with seasoned minced meat, then dipped in batter and fried in deep fat.

KRONA PEPPER. A mild red pepper.

KÜMMEL. A strong white liqueur with a basis of highly distilled or neutral spirit, of grain or potatoes, flavoured with caraway seeds and sweetened.

KUMQUAT. Small bitter-sweet fruit of Japanese shrubs which will also grow in the open in Florida and California or under glass in this country. Chiefly used for preserves.

KVASS. A Russian beverage prepared regularly in Russian households from fresh dough made with rye flour and malt, boiling water, sugar, yeast and mint leaves.
　　In some households it is made simply with a rye bread, sugar and water.

LACE. To add a dash of spirits, wine or strong sauce to a beverage or a soup.

LADIES' DELIGHT. A home-made pickle of apples, onions, chillis and white vinegar, which can be used a few days after it is made. So called because it took so little time to make at a period when most pickles needed a great deal of preparation.

LAD'S LOVE. Another name for southernwood, a herb allied to tarragon. It may be cooked as spinach or added to salads.

LADY'S SMOCK. Another name for meadow cress, a weed which grows in moist meadows. The rather hot leaves when young may be used in salads or to flavour soups.

LAMB. The young of ewes. English and Scottish lamb is best in early spring, when the flesh is juicy and the fat of delicate flavour.
  A great quantity of New Zealand and Australian lamb is imported during most of the year. The best joints are saddle and shoulder.

LAMB'S LETTUCE. Also known as corn salad. Once a European 'weed', it has been extensively cultivated and used in salads. There are two varieties, one with round leaves and one with longer tooth-edged leaves. Excellent mixed with beetroot and celery.

LAMB'S TAIL PIE. A great delicacy made at lambing time when the lambs' tails are docked for hygienic reasons. The tails are cleaned and freed from scraps of wool, scalded, cut into pieces, put into a pie dish with a little piece of mint, salt and pepper, and covered with a good crust which is usually made with mutton fat.

LAMB'S WOOL. A very old type of Punch made with hot strong ale, apple pulp and spices. The wool was of course represented by the soft apple pulp which floated on top of the punch.

LANCASHIRE CHRISTMAS PUDDING CAKE. Any cold remains of Christmas pudding are used as a rich mincemeat in Lancashire. The cold pudding is broken small and mashed smoothly with a nut of butter and a little brandy or rum, and spread on short or rough puff pastry. The top is brushed with milk or egg and well sugared, and the pie or cake is served very hot for high tea. Sometimes the cake or pie is made in a flat tin and cut into fingers, sometimes separate small cakes are made resembling little mince pies.

LANGOUSTINES. French name for Dublin Bay Prawns.

LAPEREAU. A young rabbit.

LAPIN. A buck rabbit.

LARD. The white fat from the inside of a pig melted and clarified. Considered the best fat for pastry making.

LARDER. To thread lean meat with thin strips of fat. (French: pronounced *lar-day*).

LARDON. Long thin strips of bacon fat or fat bacon, used for 'larding' or threading into dry meat or game. A special larding needle is used and care must be taken not to break the lardons.

LARDY CAKES. A cake originally made in Sussex. Fresh bread dough is saved after bread-making, or a pound or so bought from the baker. The dough is rolled out, spread with lard, sugar and currants, folded and re-rolled three or four times, then cut into small squares, brushed with milk, lightly sprinkled with sugar and baked until risen and golden brown.   (See recipe)

LAURIER. French for bay leaves.

LAVER. A smooth sea-weed which grows on rocks. It is washed and boiled and served either plain or with butter. It is said to contain health-giving minerals, especially iodine. Sailors ate it to prevent scurvy.

LAVER SAUCE. Sauce made with the fine smooth sea-weed that grows round the West Coast of England and Ireland. It is washed, boiled for a long time, then packed into jars. Sauce made with boiled laver and butter used always to be served with mutton.

LEAVEN. Any substance used to lighten dough of bread, buns, cakes; the term includes yeast, balm, baking powder, bi-carbonate of soda or any commercial raising powders.

LEEKS. A long white onion-type vegetable with stiff green leaves. It has a very delicate and distinctive onion flavour and is very good cooked in stews or made into a rich soup.   (See recipes)

LEMON. A citrous fruit, the juice of which is rich in citric acid and the rind in oil of lemon. Grown chiefly in Mediterranean and sub-tropical countries.
   Lemons are used in every kind of cookery, but particularly in cakes, confectionery and preserves. The juice is often added to fruits with a low pectin content to help them set.

LEMON BALM. A lemon-flavoured member of the mint family. The leaves are sometimes used in salads; one or two may be combined with mint in mint sauce, and also in fruit, wine or cider cups.

LEMON CURD. A preserve for tarts made with lemons, eggs and sugar.
                                                                (See recipe)

LEMON SOLE. A small flat fish which looks like a sole, but has not such a good flavour and texture and is much cheaper. It may be treated, however, in exactly the same way as sole.

LEMON SQUASH. A refreshing drink made by squeezing into a receptacle the juice from a lemon, adding sugar to taste and filling with water. A pinch of bi-carbonate of soda is sometimes added.

LENTILS. A small plant native to Southern Europe and parts of Asia and India. The round flat seeds, of which there are two kinds most commonly known — the red and the brown lentils — are used for soups or purées. Well seasoned, the purée makes a savoury sandwich filling.

LETTUCE. The best-known of all salad greens. There are several varieties, those best known being the cabbage or 'round' lettuce and the cos or 'long' lettuce.

There is also a lettuce which does not form a heart but produces leaves throughout the summer, provided that the leaves be cut regularly.

While lettuce is mostly used in salads, it may also be boiled or braised.

LEVERET. A young hare.

LEVULOSE. A sugar found in fruits.

LEVURE. A firm paste made of flour and water and used for sealing the lids of casseroles or ovenproof dishes in which game, poultry or highly seasoned pâtés are being cooked. (The sealing prevents some of the rich flavour escaping with the steam.) First used by French cooks.

LIAISON. A term for the agent used to bind ingredients together, e. g. for binding forcemeat ingredients together the liaison would usually be egg-yolks.

LIFT. To turn a mixture of dry ingredients over and over from the bottom in order to blend them thoroughly.

LIGHTS. The lungs of an animal. Generally used for food for dogs and cats.

LIMA BEAN. A bean native to South America, cultivated for its flat kidney-shaped seeds; there are the white, the green and the mottled varieties, all very nutritious. The large white Madagascar butter beans imported to this country are sold in tins under the name of Lima beans.

LIME. A greenish-yellow fruit much the same shape as a lemon. Used in the same ways as lemons, and much prized as an addition to cool drinks in the West Indies and in sub-tropical countries.

LIME BLOSSOM TEA. An infusion of dried lime flowers. These should be gathered and dried in July and stored in paper bags. A handful of the flowers should be infused in a small teapot full of boiling water. The tea is drunk with a slice of lemon. Said to be sleep-inducing and an aid to digestion.

LIMPETS. Shell-fish which cling to rocks. They look very unattractive, but have such a good flavour that they could be substituted for oysters in dishes which require an oyster garnish.

LINE. To line cake tins with fitted pieces of greaseproof paper or aluminium foil; to cover the inside of pie dishes and pudding basins with dough; or to make a thin coating of sweet or savoury jelly on the inside of a mould before filling with other ingredients.

LING. The largest member of the cod family. It is usually salted and dried. The salted and dried fish is soaked in several relays of cold water, then cooked in milk with butter and garlic or onions until creamy. Black pepper is added, but no more salt.

LINGER TORTE. A famous Austrian Cake.   (See recipe)

LINSEED. The seed of flax. It is very glutinous and much used in making linseed tea for easing bad coughs and chest or bronchial troubles.

LIQUEUR. A name used for flavoured and sweetened spirits; many have aromatic herbs and colouring and may have flavourings from fruits, flowers, roots or seeds or a combination.
    Some famous liqueurs are Chartreuse, Benedictine, Curaçao, Crème de Menthe, Kirsch, Kümmel, and the only Scottish liqueur, Drambuie.

LIQUID MEASURE.

Four gills	=	One pint.
Two pints	=	One quart.
Four quarts	=	One gallon.

LIQUORICE. A plant which grows in sub-tropical climates. The root is dried and either powdered or boiled to obtain an extract.
    It is much used in the making of cough-sweets and cough-mixtures, or for cheaper confectionery in the form of ribbons or pipes. Also used medicinally.

LITRE. A metric measure of capacity equivalent to 1.76 English pints.

LIVE FOODS. Fermented foods such as whole-grain bread, yeast, rennet, sour milk, wine, bean shoots, sauerkraut.

LIVER. The largest of all the viscera of animals.

LIVOURNAISE. Method of cooking a pheasant by braising it with mushrooms and lean bacon.

LOAF SUGAR. Sugar used to be sold in cone-shaped pieces that were broken up with sharp pincers. Now the loaves of sugar are no longer made, but the sugar mechanically broken into small pieces is still called loaf sugar and is best for preserving. That in cubes of equal size is known as lump sugar.

LOBSCOUSE. A dish made by sailors, of stewed salted meat, any vegetable left over during the voyage, and the whole thickened with ship's biscuit.

LOBSTER. A crustacean with large claws and several feelers. When the lobster is caught, the shells are blue-black; they turn brilliant red when cooked. The lobsters are caught during most of the year, but are at their best and most abundant during the summer.

The flesh of the lobster is highly esteemed; it may be served plain boiled with salad and mayonnaise, or made into rich dishes.

(See recipes)

LOGANBERRY. A soft fruit, larger than a raspberry, with a sharper flavour. Introduced into this country in the last century. Used for very good pies and tarts and jams.

LOIN. Portion of an animal between neck and tail.

LONDON BUNS. Plain buns made in the shape of long fingers, covered with white icing. They have been made by London bakers for a great many years.

LONDON EGGS. Old name for eggs that are not new-laid.

LONDON MIXED GRILL. Once a typical City man's luncheon dish consisting of mutton chops or cutlets, fillet of beef, grilled bacon, sausage, fried potatoes, grilled tomatoes, horse-radish sauce and water-cress garnish. Sometimes for the beef a veal cutlet was substituted.

Special sauces made by the various City restaurants to their own recipes were served with the grills.

LONGAN. A pulpy fruit of the same genus as the lychee, grown chiefly in East India.

LONG POTATO. Another name for sweet potato.

LOQUAT (JAPANESE MEDLAR). A small plumtree-like form of an Eastern tree which grows in the Mediterranean, as well as in Florida and California. The fruit has not much flavour alone, but is used with other fruits to make preserves.

LOSANGE. Any food cut or moulded into diamond shapes for garnishing.

LOTTE. A type of fresh-water whiting caught in French lakes and in some English lakes. It has very white flesh, but it is rather tasteless and should be accompanied by appetising sauces.

LOVAGE. Wild angelica, used for flavouring or for candying. The stalks and leaves have a strong flavour of celery. Used in sausage-making and soups.

LOVE-IN-DISGUISE. Calf's heart stuffed with savoury stuffing, wrapped in bacon, then in paper and baked. The paper is removed and the heart 'disguised' by rolling in plenty of crumbs, then browned in the oven and served with red currant jelly.

LOVING CUP. A large receptacle for a ceremonial toast. Usually of fine workmanship in silver or Sheffield plate or china. The drink it contains may be a blend of wines and fruit, but is usually a strong spirit punch. Drunk at weddings, hunt breakfasts, etc.

LUTE. To seal joints with a dough of flour and water. Hams and old fowls are often cooked in this way to seal in the juices and make the flesh tender. Also applies to sealing casseroles and pâté dishes.

LYCHEE (LICHEE or LITCHI). A small round Chinese fruit that will grow in sub-tropical countries. It has a rough reddish outer covering and translucent fruit with a flavour of grapes.

LYONNAISE. When this word is seen in a recipe, it means that finely shredded onion is used in the dish; for example, Lyonnaise potatoes: thin slices of cooked potato fried in butter or dripping with a little finely shredded onion, drained, then sprinkled with a little salt and finely chopped parsley.

LYONNAISE SAUCE. An onion sauce flavoured with white wine.

MACARONI. A paste of flour and water, forced through tubes to make long slender hollow 'pipes'. Invented by the Italians. The best type of macaroni is made with chestnut flour. Although macaroni cheese is the favourite dish made with it, it can be used in a great number of savoury and sweet dishes.   (See recipes)

MACAROONS. Sweet biscuits made with ground almonds, castor sugar and white of eggs.   (See recipe)

MACE. This is the lacy, net-like brownish-red covering of the nutmegs, which are, in turn, the kernels of an apricot-like fruit.
    This lacy covering is pressed flat and dried and used for flavouring stews, sauces, fish and savoury dishes.

MACEDOINE. This can mean a mixture of vegetables or of fruit, all cut into even-sized dice; the vegetables are usually masked with cold meats or fish, the fruit is served in syrup as a salad. The name may also mean a mixture of fruits set in jelly and served with cream. The jelly is often flavoured with a good liqueur such as Kirsch, Curaçao, or Maraschino.

MACKEREL. A beautiful blue-and-silver fish which can be grilled, baked or soused.
    When the Sabbath was observed far more strictly than it is to-day, there was a special law allowing fishmongers to sell mackerel on Sundays because, once caught, it spoils more quickly than any other fish.
    Once it was called 'the scavenger of the sea' because it was said to feed on drowned sailors, but this is now discounted.   (See recipe)

MADEIRA. A rich sweet wine or a light plain cake.   (See recipe)

MADELEINE. Small cakes of crisp sponge in France, but in England of soft sponge coated with jam and coconut and decorated with a cherry.
(See recipe)

MADERE. A dish cooked with Madeira wine.

MADRAS. The name given to Indian curry dishes.

MAGNUM. A bottle holding 2 reputed quarts, usually of champagne.

MAIDS OF HONOUR. Little cakes made for Anne Boleyn, of light puff pastry, an egg, and ground almond and lemon filling.
These were made in Richmond for centuries, but are now so commercialised that they are spoiled. It is best to make them at home.
(See recipe)

MAIGRE, AU. Any dish made without meat. Literally a thin dish, served during Lent and on Fridays and days of abstinence.
Some of the maigre dishes made with eggs and fish are far more appetising than meat dishes.

MAINTENON. 'A la Maintenon' means fish or meat grilled in a paper case.

MAITRE D'HOTEL. Name of a sauce served on grilled meats quickly and plainly presented. Usually made of melted butter and finely chopped parsley. (See recipe)

MALT. Sugar converted from the starch of various grains. It is used in beer-making, in invalid foods and bread-making.

MALT BREAD. A close sweet bread with malt and raisins. (See recipe)

MALT WINE. Another name for stout.

MANCHETS. Bread made of fine wheaten flour and shaped into flat cakes with the hands.

MANDARIN. A small sweet fruit resembling an orange; the rind has an aromatic flavour.

MANGO. A native fruit of Malaya and the West Indies. There are several varieties. The fruit at its choicest has no fibre and is said to rival in flavour any fruit in the world.
When ripe, it is placed on shelves to mature for a few days. Ripe mangos are used to make some of the best chutney. When green they are pickled or salted and eaten with fish curries. Exported here chiefly in tins or as a purée. Obtainable from grocers dealing in Oriental produce.

MANGOLD WURZEL. A large turnip-like root vegetable. It is grown chiefly for cattle food, but, cut into small pieces, it can be boiled and mashed with butter, pepper and salt as a winter vegetable.

MANIOC. A tropical plant from which tapioca and cassava are made.

MARASCHINO. A delicately flavoured white liqueur distilled from a specially grown cherry.

MARBLE CAKE. A cake made of three different-coloured mixtures cooked together in the same tin so that they run together to produce a marbled effect.   (See recipe)

MARGARINE. A fat which looks like butter, but which is made with emulsified vegetable oils and pasturised milk. Since the war it has been fortified with vitamins A and D.

MARIGOLD PIE. A very old country pudding made with short crust, savoury egg custard and handfuls of marigold petals, baked until the custard is set. Served with large wedges of cheese.

MARINADE. A mixture of oil and vinegar or oil and wine, with herbs, and with condiments in which fish, meat, game or poultry is laid to soak in the flavours before being cooked. The liquid is used later in the cooking, usually to make a sauce to go with the dish.

MARJORAM. A bushy annual herb which grows in almost any soil. The leaves have a strong spicey aroma which is not lost when the herb is dried. Used for seasoning stuffings and sausages.

MARMALADE. Conserves of various fruits such as oranges, lemons, quinces, grapefruit or tangerines, but usually meaning orange marmalade.   (See recipes)

MARMITE. An earthenware pot or a stock pot in which food is slowly cooked. Now also a pure vegetable extract much used in vegetarian cookery.

MARRONS GLACES. Chestnuts boiled in sugar. A famous French confection.   (See recipe for *Chestnuts*)

MARROW, VEGETABLE. A gourd, the vine of which grows along the ground. The marrows grow to a large size, when the flesh is coarse, the skin very tough and the seeds hard.
    The vegetables are at their best when between 6—8 inches long, when they can be sliced and fried, unpeeled; larger ones, stuffed and baked, are good and the more mature ones can be made into a jam or chutney.   (See recipes)

MARROW BONES. The large bones of the legs of beef animals. They are filled with a soft easily melted fat which has long been considered a great delicacy, marrow bones having been served to the Lords of the Star Chamber as far back as the 16th century. The fat is extracted from the boiled or roasted bones, spread on toast and seasoned with pepper and salt.

MARROW BUTTER. Made with the centre fat extracted from beef marrow bones by melting; strained and beaten until creamy. It was considered very nourishing for children and was spread on bread instead of butter.

MARSH-MALLOW. A plant with pale pink flowers and downy leaves. The thick fleshy roots are boiled and the liquid is mixed with honey for sore throats and bronchitis. Also the name of a light, fluffy sweetmeat.   (See recipe)

MARZIPAN. This confection has been known since medieval times and first appears in cookery books as almond crème, then as Marchpane. It is made of ground almonds, sugar and flavourings, coloured with vegetable or chemical colourings, as required.

No Christmas, wedding or christening cake is considered complete without marzipan or almond paste. It is also formed into many pretty shapes, especially of fruits, and is much used to decorate small cakes.

Other nut pastes are of ground hazelnuts. This paste is called *noxipan* and is mostly used for chocolate fillings.   (See recipes)

MATE (YERBA MATE TEA). The dried leaves of a South American shrub, chiefly used in the Argentine, Uruguay and Paraguay to make a refreshing tea. The native way of drinking the tea is to put the leaves into a hollowed gourd, dried until it resembles wood, with a silver tube inserted into it. Boiling water is poured on the tea and when cool enough, it is sucked through the tube. The inhabitants of the Latin American countries believe that it has great invigorating and sustaining powers.

MAY CORDIAL. A fragrant liqueur made by infusing freshly opened hawthorn blossoms in brandy with a little sugar. The liqueur is strained and bottled after 3 months. It is seldom drunk alone but is usually added to other drinks as a flavouring.

It was originally made in Germany, but it is found in other countries where the hawthorn flourishes.

MAYONNAISE. A salad dressing made by combining egg yolks and olive oil to a smooth thick cream. Especially important in the making of shellfish salads.   (See recipe)

MAZARINES. Forcemeat ornaments of fish, meat or game made in moulds, used as garnishes for large dishes. Also entrées made of fillets of meat and forcemeat.

MEAD. An alcoholic drink fermented from honey and water and a choice of various herbs. It is one of the oldest drinks known and has been made for centuries. It went out of favour for a long time when Continental cheap wines were freely imported, but it has come back into favour of late years. Good mead should mature for a year. Excellent used as wine for cooking purposes.   (See recipe)

MEAT PIE. A pie made with any kind of meat, poultry or game cooked in a pie dish and covered with a short, rough puff or puff pastry covering; the meat may also be enclosed in a hot water crust. The most common covered pies are of steak or veal and the raised pies of pork or veal and ham.

MEDLAR. The fruit of a hardy tree. It is allowed to get soft and wrinkled before it is eaten. Very few people care for medlars, but a good jelly, said to be indistinguishable from guava jelly in flavour, may be made with them. In Rome they are eaten when freshly picked and are called *nespoli.*

MEGRIM. A flat fish, also known as a witch. The flavour and texture is like that of lemon sole.

MELBA SAUCE. A sweet sauce made with raspberry or strawberry purée and sugar. A make-shift is often made with sieved jam and sugar.

MELBA TOAST. Very thin slices of white bread, cut across in triangles and crusts removed, and baked in a very slow oven until slightly curled and quite crisp.
   Originally made for Dame Nellie Melba, the singer. Served with hors-d'œuvres and with fish.

MELON. Round gourd-shaped fruits of which there are several varieties. The Honeydew and the Cantaloupe are the sweetest and have the best flavour.
   The water melon is the most common and there is also another smaller fruit with a green and yellow-striped rind known as the tiger melon. All are very pleasant to eat in hot weather iced and served with sugar, lemon or ground ginger.
   Very often the flesh is cut out with a small round potato scoop and the balls served as a fruit cocktail.

MELTON MOWBRAY PIE. A rich case of raised pastry crust filled with diced pork, very savoury seasoning and strong stock that jellies round the meat when cold, glazed and baked. A delicacy made at Melton Mowbray in Leicestershire.

MENU. A bill of fare detailing the courses.

MENUS DROITS. Pig's ears cooked and served as an entrée.

MERINGUES. Light cakes made of egg-whites and sugar, filled and sandwiched together with cream or ice-cream.   (See recipe)

MERLUCHE. French name for stockfish or haddock dried or smoked.

MERRYTHOUGHT. The fanciful name given to the 'wish-bone' or part of the breast bone of poultry.

METHEGLIN. The English version of the old Welsh name for honey drinks, meddyglyn.

MIDDLINGS. The coarse part of ground flour which is left after the flour is sifted. It is considered the best and most nutritive part of flour.

MIGNONETTE PEPPER. Coarsely ground pepper corns which resemble mignonette seed.

MILLE FANTI. A thick soup peculiar to the district round Nice. Made with meat stock, thickened with a mixture of fine bread crumbs, grated gruyère cheese and beaten egg, seasoned with grated nutmeg.

MINCE. To cut into very small pieces with knife, food chopper or scissors, or to put through a mincer.

MINCEMEAT. A mixture of dried fruits, candied peel, suet, apple, almonds and spirits with spices, used for tarts and pies chiefly at Christmas time.
(See recipe)

MINESTRONE. A favourite Italian soup.   (See recipe)

MINT SAUCE. Finely chopped mint with lemon juice or vinegar, salt and a little sugar, served with lamb. Eaten by some people with curry.
(See recipes)

MINUTE. A name given to dishes which have been cooked very quickly. The commonest of these is minute steak, which is naturally very under-done.

MIRABELLE. A sweet juicy yellow plum, not much bigger than a cherry. Used for making jam or compotes. Stewed in thick syrup.

MIREPOIX. Vegetables finely chopped and cooked in fat with the necessary herbs and seasonings to form the foundation of soups, sauces and braised meats, poultry or game.

MIRLITONS. French pastries; tartlets of puff pastry filled with a creamy custard mixture.

MIX. To combine ingredients with a circular motion in a bowl or a saucepan. It is a gentle movement, and, unlike beating, is not intended for introducing air into the mixture.

MIXED GRILL. A dish consisting of small lamb cutlets, sausage, bacon, kidney, tomato and mushrooms. Always served with a piquant bottled sauce.

MIXED PICKLES. A mixture of vegetables cut into small pieces and preserved in clear spiced vinegar.   (See recipes)

MOCHA (MOKA). A type of coffee with a fragrant flavour, often blended with chocolate to make a drink or a confectionery flavouring.

MOCK TURTLE SOUP. A soup made with lean beef, calf's head (to give the authentic glutinous consistency), seasonings and sherry. (See recipe)

MOLASSES. A dark thick syrup which is obtained from the sugar cane while the sugar is being refined. It has a slightly bitter flavour, but is rich in vitamins and iron and is much recommended by many dieticians. Some types of rum are distilled from it.

MONKEY NUT. Another name for peanut.

MONT BLANC, CHESTNUT. A rich sweet made with chestnuts, cream, sugar, egg whites and wine, etc.   (See recipe)

MONOSODIUM GLUTAMATE (M. S. G.). A white powder which has no flavour but has the effect of bringing out the flavour of any food into which it is introduced. It may be rubbed into meat before cooking or stirred into soups, stews or sauces. Approximate quantities required: 1/2 teaspoonful to 1 lb. of meat, 1/4 teaspoonful to a pint of liquid.

MOTHERING SUNDAY (SIMNEL) CAKE. A rich fruit cake made for and eaten on the fourth Sunday in Lent, when it was customary for the sons and daughters in service on farms or in big families to have time off to go and visit their homes.

Tradition says that mothers made the cakes for the children, or that the daughters carried the cakes home to their mothers.

Of late years the cakes have become elaborately decorated with almond paste and fancy decorations to commemorate Easter, but this is quite out of keeping with the intention behind the original Mothering Sunday cake.   (See recipe for *Simnel cake*)

MOUILLER. To moisten, to add water, stock or other suitable juice during the cooking of meat.

MOUSSE. A light ice cream or foamy whipped dessert. 'Mossy' because of its soft, spongy texture.   (See recipes)

MUFFINS AND CRUMPETS. Light white cakes of fine yeast batter, cooked on griddles or hot plates in muffin or crumpet rings. These vary in size in different parts of the country, but in the South, and especially in London, they are small, the muffins plump, the crumpets thin. They should be toasted golden brown and buttered until the little holes are filled with butter. Crumpets are buttered on the surface, muffins should be snipped round the crisp edges and torn apart and buttered.   (See recipes)

MUGWORT. Grows in small bushes, wild or cultivated. Has a slightly bitter taste and smell.

MULBERRY. A fruit like a very large loganberry, but deeper red in colour. It has an exquisite flavour and is very juicy. It originally came from China, where it was cultivated for the leaves upon which silk worms are fed. Large numbers of the trees in England were grown for the same purpose, but few survive now, though the trees live to a great age.

MULL, TO. To make any drink, such as wine, spirits or beers, hot, spicey and sweet.

MULLED WINE. See recipe.

MULLET. Red mullet are found round the English and Mediterranean coasts. They are very red, short and firm of flesh. One of the famous methods of cooking is to put the well-cleaned fish on pieces of greaseproof paper well buttered, sprinkle with finely chopped fennel and wrap up like small parcels, then bake for 20 minutes in a moderate oven.

The grey mullet may be cooked in the same way as the red mullet, but it is a coarser fish and not highly esteemed.

MULLIGATAWNY. A meat soup highly flavoured with curry.

(See recipes)

MURAT. An ancient preserve made when mulberry trees flourished in England. Only one part of sugar was used to three parts of honey for making the mulberry jam or conserve, as honey was more common than sugar.

MUSCADE. Nutmeg or mace.

MUSCAT (MUSCARDINE). A variety of grape, and the wine produced from it.

MUSHROOMS. The name given to nearly all edible fungi. Among the best known mushrooms found in England are the beefsteak, so called because it is large and of close texture and when sliced and fried is said to resemble steak, the bluett (blewitt), fairy ring, shaggy cap, horse mushroom, morel and puffball, as well as the one most frequently found in open fields and generally called the common mushroom.

Puffballs sometimes grow as large as footballs and are excellent sliced, coated with egg and breadcrumbs and fried.

Dried Mushrooms.

When mushrooms dotted the fields like daisies every dawn, housewives dried large quantities for the winter stews and soups. Sometimes branches of thorny shrubs were made into bushes in tubs and the stalked mushrooms spiked all over the branches. Sometimes they were stalked and laid with the stalks in the cooling kitchen-range oven until dry and shrivelled, then packed into paper bags and hung in a cool but dry place.

MUSHROOM KETCHUP. A piquant sauce made with mushrooms and spices. (See recipe)

MUSSEL BROSE. Mussels cooked with milk, water and oatmeal.

MUST. The technical term for new wine pressed from grapes or other fruits before it has fermented. Most people would call it fruit juice or parsnip, etc., liquid.

MUSTARD. Powdered seeds of the mustard plant. Mixed to a smooth paste with water, spiced vinegar or warm milk as a condiment. Used with sauces and cheese dishes to give extra flavour and to give piquancy to devilled dishes.

MUTTON. The flesh of a sheep from one to five years old, the best being that from animals of about 3 years. Mutton is commonly cut into joints such as leg, shoulder, loin, saddle, breast, neck, chops, cutlets.

(See recipes)

NAPOLEON BISCUTS. Short almond biscuits sandwiched together with jam.
(See recipe)

NAPPER. To cover a dish with a thick layer of sauce, jam or jelly. If the 'napkin' is a cold one of sauce, it is sometimes decorated with slices of truffles, leaves of chervil or parsley, carrot, cucumber or other pretty coloured scraps.

NASTURTIUM. Originally known as Indian cress, now a popular garden flower, with very gay blooms shading from golden to dark brown. Leaves, flowers and seeds have a hot pungent flavour. Flowers and leaves are used in salads, the seeds when small are pickled in spiced vinegar and used as capers in sauce.
(See recipe)

NATIVES. The name given to oysters spawned and bred in Kentish and Essex beds.

NAVARIN. A brown French mutton stew with herbs, turnips, tomatoes, onions and potatoes.

NAVETS. French for turnips. A garnish *aux navets* — a half shoulder of mutton finished with browned turnips and onions.

NAVY BEANS. See haricot beans, for which 'navy' is another name.

NEAT. Old English name for an ox-neat's tongue; the same as an ox tongue.

NEAT'S FOOT. The old name for the foot of an ox, or cow heel. Usually sold prepared and boiled ready for final cooking.

NECK. The part of the animal between head and shoulders. Neck of mutton and lamb make good stews; neck chops are used for Irish stews and Lancashire hot-pot.

NECTAR. The Greek name for the 'drink of the gods'. Any drink sweet and delicious in flavour. Some French liqueurs have been given the name.

NECTARINE. A fruit like a peach, with a delicate smooth skin and very delicious flavour.

NEGUS. A 'genteel' drink, once favoured by ladies of the 18th and 19th century, made with home-made wines (preferably cowslip wine), lemon juice, calves' foot jelly, sugar and water. The water was added according to the taste of the hostess.
A far more potent negus is made to-day with a good white wine or port wine as the basis.

NELSON. Method of cooking fillet of steak by placing it between sliced onions and sliced potatoes and cooking slowly in a casserole.

NEPAL PEPPER. A yellowish-red pepper of the same type as cayenne; a species of capsicum of a sweet and pungent flavour.

NESSELRODE. A vanilla ice cream with chestnuts and whipped cream.
(See recipe)

NETTLES. A weed which stings painfully when the plant is old. When
young, it can be cooked as spinach. The resulting liquid drunk hot is
considered by country people to be an efficient blood purifier.

NIGHTCAPS. The idea of nightcaps, or soothing hot drinks with which to
finish the evening, seems to be quite an English one and probably
originated from the fact that our bedrooms were once so cold that it
was necessary to take a warming last drink to induce sleep — otherwise
one might lie awake and cold for a long time.

The 'caps' varied from the ordinary hot toddy of rum and water,
or home-made cordial and hot water, to the more elaborate drinks we
usually call punch. Several of these drinks still have ecclesiastical
names.

Bishop is made with port wine, an orange stuck with cloves and roasted
until the skin is brown and shrivelled (giving a lovely perfume), with
other spices and with a little hot water, the whole brought almost to
boiling point, but never allowed to boil.

Lawn Sleeves is another version of bishop, made with sherry, a lemon
and calves' foot jelly, rich enough for an invalid as well as a bishop!

Cardinal is the same, but a rich red claret is used instead of port or
sherry.

Pope is luxurious, but not as heartening, since champagne and no calves'
foot jelly is used.

NIP. A quarter bottle of wine or spirits.

NIPPLEWORT. A weed of the dandelion order which can be used
uncooked in salads or cooked as a vegetable. It has a bitter flavour and
is best cooked with other vegetables.

NOGGIN. A small measure of liquid, equivalent to $1/4$ pint.

NOISETTES. Meat cut from loin fillet in slices of equal size. Slices can
be of lamb, veal, beef or pork. Veal and pork are often egg-and-
breadcrumbed and served with spaghettti, lamb and beef with different
sauces and garnishes.

Also a paste of ground almonds, sugar and egg yolks.

NONPAREILS. Small seeds of confetti-like coloured sugar, or hundreds-
and-thousands. Used for scattering on iced cakes as a decoration.

NOODLES. A flat form of the Italian pastes such as spaghetti or macaroni,
but of a flat ribbon shape which originated in Germany. Noodles are
made of wheat flour and figure a great deal in Chinese cookery.

NORFOLK SPOON DUMPLINGS. A firm batter made with milk, flour
and eggs dropped in boiling water by spoonfuls. When firm, the
dumplings are skimmed out and served with gravy, or as a sweet with
butter and sugar, or syrup.   (See recipe)

NORMANDY PIPPINS. Peeled, par-cooked and dried apples. (See *Biffins*)

NORTH COUNTRY SWEET PIE. A pie made with fat mutton chops, currants, raisins and sultanas, seasoned with salt, pepper, mace and nutmeg, with sugar, lemon juice and a tablespoonful or so of gravy and topped with puff pastry. Once a favourite farmhouse dish when a sheep was killed.

NOUGAT. A sweetmeat made with egg-whites, honey, sugar, pistachio nuts, almonds, and sometimes glacé cherries.
     The most famous is made at Montelimar in France, in Provence. It is even sold on the railway station platforms.   (See recipes)

NOXIPAN. A marzipan made with hazel nuts, used for gâteaux and chocolate fillings.

NOYAU. Fruit stones the kernels of which, with spirit, provide strongly flavoured liqueurs used to flavour puddings, creams and punches.

NUTS. The fruit, consisting of kernels enclosed in a hard casing, of certain trees and shrubs.

NUT BUTTER. A rich paste made from crushed nuts and used for confectionery or as a spread for bread — particularly by vegetarians.
     The best known nut butter is peanut, but cashew nut butter is richer and has a creamier flavour.

NUT FATS AND OILS. Nuts produce rich oils and fats which are valuable in the making of various foods. Nut oils are largely used in vegetarian cookery.

NUTMEG. The kernel of the fruit of an East Indian tree. The thick outer shell is covered with a lacy covering known as mace, which has the same aromatic flavour as the hard nutmeg. Grated nutmeg is used for flavouring both sweet and savoury dishes.

OATMEAL. The grain of oats, husked and dried and ground into three grades, fine, coarse and groats (or unground oats). Oatmeal is very rich in fat and very nutritious. There are now several types of commercially prepared oats which can be cooked as a breakfast food very quickly.
     Oatmeal is used for thickening soups and for making various types of cakes and scones.   (See recipe)

OATMEAL DUMPLINGS. These dumplings have been used to fill hungry children and men since the 14th century.
     Soak coarse oatmeal with meat stock or vegetable water, pour enough into a floured cloth to allow for swelling, tie up the cloth securely and boil in stock with vegetables.
     In good times a little fat bacon is chopped and added. And, for a luxury dumpling, sometimes an onion.

OBLETJES (OUBLIES). Now a South African dish, but originally brought from England. Another name for wafers or waffles.   (See recipe)

OFFAL. This word signifies the parts of animals which are not joints. Once despised and very cheap, now in great demand and expensive. Liver is much used in the diet of diabetic patients.

Offal consists of: Head, tongue, brains, sweetbreads, liver, heart, kidneys, feet, tails and pluck (which is the liver, heart and lights of an animal).

Calf's offal is considered best, with pig's offal as second choice.

To use heads

Soak, blanch, boil and bone, after having removed the brains. Serve the meat and the tongue skinned and sliced with a piquant sauce. They can also be made into soup and brawn.

Brains

Soak, remove membranes, tie in a piece of muslin, bring to the boil in water with a little salt and a spoonful of vinegar. This is to set them and make them easy to use.

Cool, slice, egg-and-breadcrumb and fry in deep fat; serve with fried parsley and tomato sauce or diced in cream sauce on buttered toast.

Heart

Sheep's or lambs' hearts are well washed, stuffed with savoury stuffing, and braised on a bed of vegetables, or roasted. Bullock's heart is stuffed and roasted, or sliced and braised and served with Madeira sauce.

Kidneys

Grilled, after having been removed from the surrounding fat, skinned and split open; cooked on skewers with pieces of mushroom and bacon; sliced and simmered until tender in thick gravy with mushrooms; or sliced in steak-and-kidney pie or pudding.

Feet

Blanched and boiled and generally used for making soups or jellied pies; pigs' trotters are blanched, split, egg-and-breadcrumbed and fried; so are calves' feet.

Cowheel is a popular dish, cooked until jelly-like and served with parsley or mustard sauce.

Sweetbreads

Soak, blanch, remove membranes, poach in slightly salted water, cut in slices, egg-and-breadcrumb and fry, or dice and cook in cream sauce, usually with mushrooms and green peas in the sauce.

A favourite filling for vol-au-vent.

Liver

Grilled, braised or made into a pâté, or, as faggots, cooked with onions, crumbs and savoury seasonings.

Tails

Oxtails make a delicious and nourishing stew with onions, haricot beans, carrots and seasonings. The stock is usually used for soup. Pigs' tails are small and gelatinous and make good soup stock. Lambs' tails are made into pies (q. v.).

OIL. A fluid grease extracted from animals, vegetables and minerals. Animal and vegetable oils are both used in making margarines, vegetable oils in making many cooking fats and for frying. Tea-seed oil is a well known vegetable cooking oil, but olive oil is considered the best of all.

OKA. A richly flavoured Canadian cheese. Also a tuber known as occa or oxalis. The vegetable is the size of walnut and of irregular shape. In this country it is usually parboiled in salted water, then tossed and cooked in butter.

In France it is generally made into a purée with cream.

OKRA (GUMBO). A mucilaginous bean, grown in West Indies and Southern States of America. The young pods are used as vegetables and in soups. They are often obtainable in this country in tins.

OLIO. A Spanish pot-au-feu, consisting of beef, mutton or veal, with pigeons and partridges, spices and vegetables and split peas, all cooked together until tender. The liquor is served as soup, the meats separately.

OLIVES. The fruit of trees extensively grown in Mediterranean countries. Olives resemble small unripe plums. Olive oil is pressed from the ripe olives. Before they are quite ripe, they are pickled in brine and eaten as appetisers, plain or stuffed. They are also used in cooking.

Ripe black olives brined are also eaten as appetisers.

OLLA PODRIDA. This is a mixed stew of meats and vegetables and spices stewed in an earthenware pot called an olla. A national dish of Andalusia.

OMBLE CHEVALIER. A fine fish which is peculiar to the lakes of the Savoia and Switzerland, but not met with elsewhere.

OMELETTE. Eggs beaten lightly, seasoned with a very little salt and pepper, poured into a stout frying pan (kept specially for the purpose), in which a small piece of butter is made sizzling hot. The pan is then tilted gently from side to side, the egg mixture being moved about the pan so that the loose egg may run under the cooked egg. When the omelette is evenly cooked, the top being still moist, fold in half to a half-moon shape. Turn on to a hot plate and serve immediately.   (See recipes)

OMERS. A shell fish found on the rocks of the Channel Islands and commonly called the sea-ear because the shell resembles the shape of an ear. They are highly esteemed locally and usually served in the same ways as scallops.

ONION. A bulbous root of the same family as the lily; it is a native of Asia, now become universal as a flavouring or a vegetable.

There are several varieties.

The spring onions are those that are thinned out when quite small; pickling onions are the very small ones, used not only for pickling but also for garnishing and hors-d'œuvres. Spanish onions are large and of very mild flavour, but are not necessarily from Spain. The Egyptian onion produces smaller onions on the stalks.   (See recipes)

OPEN TART. A tart base of short or rough puff pastry spread with jam and cooked without a top layer of pastry. The tart is often baked 'blind', that is, without filling, and afterwards filled with fresh or cooked fruit.

ORANGE. A rich juicy citrus fruit cultivated in California and in Israel and other Mediterranean countries.

There are several varieties: the blood orange, with a deep red pulp, the navel orange, which is large and almost seedless and very fine, cultivated a great deal in California and the seville orange, or bigarrade, with a sharp bitter flavour, used for marmalade and for sauces with duck or goose. (See recipes)

ORANGEADE. A cool non-alcoholic drink made with orange juice, grated orange rind, sugar and water, and served with ice.

OREGANO. A herb with a flavour between marjoram and sage, much used in Italian dishes.

ORTOLAN. A small European bird also known as the bunting. It is highly prized for its delicate flavour, and is usually cooked wrapped in vine leaves and bacon, basted with butter and served on toast with watercress.

OSMAZOME. The aqueous extract of meat which is soluble in alcohol and contains those constituents of the flesh which determine its taste and smell. Regarded as the purest essence of meat.

OURSINS. Sea-urchins: prickly shell fish with a delicate pulp-like flesh. They are cut in halves and the flesh is eaten at once with a spoon.

OX-CHEEK. The flesh on the sides of an ox's head. (See recipe)

OX-HEART. The heart of an ox. (See recipe)

OX-PALATE. The thick white linings of the upper jaw of the roof of the ox's mouth. (See recipe)

OX-TAIL. The tail of an ox, used for rich soups or stews. (See recipe)

OX-TONGUE. Smoked or freshly pickled. (See recipe)

OYSTER. A marine bivalve mollusc clamped in a tightly closed upper and lower shell, the inside of which is pearly white.

The Native oyster, bred at Colchester, Whitstable and in other Essex or Kent beds, are considered the best in the world and should be eaten from the shell immediately they are opened. The usual accompaniment is thin brown bread-and-butter and stout or dry white wine.

American oysters are the largest, while Portuguese and French ones are small and often of a greenish colour.

Brittany oysters are those most frequently used for restocking depleted beds elsewhere, as they quickly take on the flavour of the ground upon which they are deposited.

The best oysters should never be cooked, but oysters are often used in puddings and savouries, notably in angels on horseback. (See recipe)

OYSTER OF CHICKEN. Two oyster-shaped pieces of meat on the back of a fowl in the cavities of the bone on the lower part of the carcase. The only useful meat on a fowl's back.

OYSTER PLANT. Another name for salsify (q. v.).

PAELLA. A popular Spanish dish composed of rice, chicken, shellfish, etc. (See recipe)

PAIN. French for bread.

PAIN ROTI. Toasted bread.

PALATE. Roof of mouth. See *Ox-palate.*

PALESTINE SOUP. Description given to a soup composed chiefly of Jerusalem artichokes.

PALETTE KNIVES. Flexible wide-bladed knives of different sizes for various purposes. Culinary purposes include that of spreading of icing on cakes, etc.

PALM KERNEL OIL. An oil obtained from the kernels of nuts from the oil palm in West Africa. Used in the preparation of many savoury dishes. Also used in the making of margarine. Similar to coconut oil.

PAMPLEMOUSSE. Grapefruit.

PANADA. A thick paste of flour and liquid used to bind together ingredients which otherwise have no adhesive properties. The term is also sometimes used to indicate soaked bread well squeezed, then pounded and used as a base for forcemeat.

PANCAKES. Very thin flat pliable cakes made from a batter (flour, eggs and milk mixture), cooked in an omelette pan. The French have adopted the word 'crêpes' to describe this delicacy.   (See recipe)

PANCREAS. Sweetbread or thymus gland of sheep or calf, used as a food and easily digestible.

PANDORAS. Fingers of toasted or fried bread spread with a savoury mixture, then dipped in fritter batter and fried in hot fat.

PANDOWDY. A dish of baked sliced apples with crisp bread topping. (See recipe)

PANOCHA. A type of Persian sweetmeat.   (See recipe)

PAP. Soft food, such as is fed to infants.

PAPAW (PAPAYA). A South American fruit, with flesh resembling that of a musk melon. From the sap of the tree, leaves and fruit juice has been prepared a marketable commodity — in both liquid and crystal form — possessing the unique property of making tough meat tender. The crystal form known as Papain is becoming well-known, but it is dangerous used in excess and should *never* be given to children.

PAPILLOTES. A term used to describe a method of cooking small pieces of food — for example small whole fish (trout, mullet, etc.), fillets of fish, small birds, etc. — by wrapping in moisture-proof paper, usually buttered greaseproof paper, with joins sealed or double-folded over firmly to preserve flavour and juices whilst being cooked. The cooking is usually done in the oven, but sometimes by steaming.

PAPRIKA. A mild red pepper. There are two varieties — one produced by drying and grinding the Hungarian capsicum, and a milder, more generally used kind, from the Spanish capsicum. Often included in stews — goulash etc. — and sprinkled over cooked food as a colourful garnish.

PAR-BOIL. To boil until partly cooked.

PARE. To peel thinly.

PARFAIT. A rich ice-cream mixture, usually decorated with a fruit sauce, chopped nuts or fruit.

PARKIN. A type of ginger cake in which oatmeal, treacle or golden syrup are used. (See recipe)

PARMESAN. A hard cheese made in Italy from goat's milk. May also be bought ready-grated. Used extensively for cooking purposes.

PARR. The name given to a young salmon up to the end of its second year.

PARSLEY. Popular kitchen herb of a fresh green colour. Esteemed as a garnish both fresh and fried. (To fry, dip sprays in hot fat until crisp — a few moments only. Eaten with fish dishes, etc.) There are two varieties — the curly-leaved and the straight-leaved (better known as chervil) — and both contain a high percentage of vitamins A and C and are rich in iron.

PARSLEY SAUCE. A basic white sauce to which chopped parsley is added. (See recipe)

PARSNIP. A spindle-shaped root vegetable. (See recipes)

PARSON'S NOSE. The extreme end portion of the tail of a fowl. Also referred to as Pope's Nose.

PARTRIDGE. Edible bird found in most countries. Partridge-shooting season opens 1st September, continuing until end of January. The English partridge is considered to have a finer flavour than the continental species.

PASSION FRUIT. A fruit of exquisite flavour grown in Australia, New Zealand and Central America. It is the size of a large Victoria plum and has a tough purplish skin enclosing orange-coloured pulp with seeds. Sometimes seen in high-class fruiterers — also obtainable canned.

PASSOVER BREAD. Also Matzoth or Matzos. A form of unleavened bread generally shaped into large thin round biscuits.

PASTA. An Italian word in general use for macaroni, spaghetti, and suchlike, but not applied to noodles.

PASTEURIZE. To sterilise partially a liquid at a temperature of 140⁰—180⁰ in order to destroy certain pathogenic organisms and check fermentation.

PASTICCERIA. Italian word for bakeries and their products.

PASTILLES. Small gum lozenges flavoured with concentrated fruit juices.

PASTINA. The small variety of Italian macaroni used in soups.

PASTRY. A dough made with flour, fat, etc. Usually made up under one of various headings — short pastry; rich short pastry (or biscuit crust); puff pastry; hot water pastry (or raised pastry); choux pastry or paste; suet pastry or suet crust. See individual recipes. A savoury pastry can be any one of the above, but for making 'croûtes' (fancy shapes of pastry flavoured with cheese, celery salt, etc.), it is usually short or flaky.
(See recipes)

PASTY. Usually a savoury mixture with pastry top and bottom, often taking the form of a saucer-size round of pastry, folded over with edges pinched together to seal in filling.   (See recipes)

PATE. A firm cold shape of cooked meat, minced finely.   (See recipe)

PATE DE FOIE GRAS. A paste prepared from livers of scientifically fattened geese — the best being made at Strasbourg.

PATE MAISON. A special pâté of the house (hotel, restaurant, etc.).

PATISSERIE. Pastry-cook's shop.

PATTIES. Small round tins are lined with short or puff pastry and filled with savoury fillings of any kind. The tins should be very small. Fillings recommended for buffet and cocktail parties are: creamed chicken, grilled mushroom, oysters, thick cheese sauce, creamed sweetbread.
Another type of patty is made by cutting short crust into small rounds, putting a savoury filling on one half of the round, then closing the other half over in the shape of a half moon.
Brush with egg and bake till golden brown.
Large patties of this shape may be made for main dishes or for luncheon baskets and picnics.

PAUNCH. To remove stomach and intestines of rabbit or hare.

PAUPIETTES. Thin sliced meat (usually veal) rolled round a sausage-shaped piece of forcemeat, e. g. paupiettes de veau. In America these are called veal birds as, when cooked, they bear some resemblance to small headless birds.

PAYSANNE. A dish in which bacon as well as onions is used. Food prepared in a simple way — peasant style.

PEACH. One of the earliest known fruits, at one time known as the Persian apple. There are two types of this juicy, delicately flavoured and easily bruised fruit — the yellow firm-fleshed Californian variety, sometimes called clingstone, and the white more juicy fondant peach. Usually clingstone peaches are canned, but both varieties are excellent dessert fruit. Used also for cooking and preserving.

PEACH BITTERS. Extract of peach kernels.

PEACH MELBA. A dessert named after the well-known opera singer Dame Nellie Melba. (See recipes)

PEACOCK. Once esteemed for the table, but no longer in favour. The young peahen is usually preferred, as its flesh is more delicate and less dry than that of the cock bird. During the Middle Ages the peacock frequently graced the banqueting tables cooked whole and adorned with its own beautiful plumage.

PEA-FLOUR. Ripe peas, dried and milled for use as a thickener for soups and sauces.

PEAHEN. At its best from February to May. When young it tastes not unlike pheasant.

PEANUT. Seeds of a plant that is low-growing. When the flowers fade and droop the seeds that form grow just beneath the soil. Hence the other names for them — groundnuts or earth nuts.

PEANUT BRITTLE. A brittle toffee containing roasted peanuts. (See recipe)

PEANUT BUTTER. A product obtained from roasted, skinned, de-germed and ground peanuts which, with their oil, combine to make a nutritious and pleasantly flavoured paste.

PEARS. A popular fruit but perishable. Some varieties, such as the William, Louis Bonne, Comice, Bartlett, etc., are among the best for dessert — the last-mentioned being a very suitable type for canning, owing to its excellent flavour. There are, however, dozens of varieties equally good for the purpose of preserving. (See recipes)

PEARS, AVOCADO. See *Avocado pears.*

PEAR JAM. See *Preserves.*

PEAS, GREEN. A valuable and nutritious vegetable. To be enjoyed at their best they should be eaten within a few hours of picking. Dried peas when soaked and cooked (without salt) are high in food value.

PEAS, PROCESSED. These are peas which have been thrashed and dried by a process of dehydration and are then soaked to restore the lost moisture. They are usually tinned out of season. The fact of processing must be disclosed on the tins of all peas of this kind which are canned, to distinguish them from fresh garden peas canned in season.

PEAS, SPLIT. Ripe peas dried and the outer skin removed, making them easier to cook.

PEAS, SUGAR. The pods of these peas have not got the tough film peculiar to other pea pods. The peas can be left in their pods for cooking, or cut and cooked like French beans.

PEASE PUDDING. A savoury pudding made by boiling split-peas, tied loosely in a muslin bag, until soft and mushy.   (See recipe)

PECAN NUT. A species of hickory nut, somewhat resembling a small-shelled walnut, but rather more oval in outline. Good flavour with high fat content.

PECTIN. A substance extracted from various fruits (also from some leaves, stalks and roots of plants), available in syrup-like form in bottles, for adding to boiled fruits and sugar to make these set firmly like jam or jelly. Fruits such as lemons, apples, blackcurrants and gooseberries are rich in pectin.

PEKOE TEA. Under the name pekoe fall almost all the fancy China teas — orange pekoe, flowery pekoe, etc. These fancy teas are generally fragrant through contact, after manufacture, with chulan blossoms, which have an odour similar to that of jasmine.

PEMMICAN. Dried meat of the buffalo or deer, ground to a powder and blended with oil or fat, acid berries or currants, and used as a food by Canadian and American Indians.

PENNYROYAL. A variety of mint, but less pungent than peppermint or spearmint.

PEPPER. A name applied to several pungent spices, i. e. black, white, cayenne or red, Ashanti and Jamaica pepper, but derived from three different orders of plants. White and black pepper are the seeds of the same shrub, but the white has the dark husks removed. See also *Paprika* and *Capsicum.*

PEPPER MIGNONETTE. Ordinary white pepper with husks removed, crushed but not ground. Also a herb belonging to the mint family.

PEPPERMINT. A pungent flavouring. See also *Mint.*

PEPPERMINT CORDIAL. A peppermint-flavoured beverage produced by blending oil of peppermint and proof spirit with sugar and water.

PEPPERMINT CREAMS. See recipe.

PEPPERMINT DROPS. A boiled sweet. (See recipe)

PEPPERMINT OIL. Oil distilled from the flower of the herb — very strong. A concentrated flavouring used medically and also for certain culinary purposes, such as sweet-making, crème de menthe, etc.

PEPPER PICKLE. A sweet pickle made with sweet red and green peppers.
(See recipe)

PEPPER-POT. A West Indian stew of meat, poultry, game or fish, highly spiced and seasoned. Philadelphia pepper-pot is a stew of tripe and dumplings, highly seasoned.

PEPPERS. Name given to capsicums and pimentoes. In their fresh state they are brightly coloured — red, green and yellow. They lend themselves agreeably to pickling, cooking and stuffing, eating raw in salads etc. Strips of red peppers (fresh or tinned) make attractive garnish.
(See recipes)

PERCH. One of the most common — and one of the best — of freshwater fish. They weigh from 1 to 8 or 9 lbs. Their flesh is firm, white, of good flavour and easily digested. They are difficult to scale, the best way being to plunge the fish into boiling water for 1 minute, then scrape. When fresh these fish have a shining appearance, with rosy-red gills, but injury from their spiky dorsal fin can be painful — and dangerous. In season from end of May to beginning of February.

PERIWINKLE (WINKLE). Found in abundance round the coast of England and Scotland and in season all the year round. A small round black shell, inside which is a sea-snail, which is edible. Winkles should be well washed, then boiled for 20 minutes in salted water and cooled quickly. The snails are easily removed from shells with a long pin, first removing the 'cap' or operculum. Usually eaten with bread and butter — the snails sometimes being first sprinkled with vinegar, pepper and salt.

PERLARDON. A fermented French cheese nade in Languedoc.

PETITS POIS. Small peas.

PETTITOES. Pig's trotters.

PHEASANT. A sporting bird with enjoyable flesh. The cock birds are extremely beautiful, with brilliant plumage; the female bird is protectively covered with mottled brown feathers. A brace of pheasants always comprises one male and one female bird. (See recipes)

PICCALILLI. A mixture of chopped vegetables preserved in a mustard and vinegar sauce. (See recipe)

PICKLE, TO. A method of preservation of flesh, fish or vegetables, fruit, etc., in a solution of salt and water or vinegar. To the brine used for preserving meats saltpetre is added to give a better appearance to the meat, which would otherwise be an unappetising grey colour.

PICNIC. An entertainment or excursion in the open air with al fresco meals.

PIE. Food of almost any kind cooked under a covering of dough. The basic idea, very early in origin, was preservation — usually by covering with unleavened dough to exclude air.
(See recipes under their respective headings)

PIECE DE RESISTANCE. The dish by which the chef reveals his culinary skill to the full. The most important course or dish of the meal.

PIG. The name given to swine, both hogs and sows, before they reach mature age. The pig provides more dishes than any other animal — in fact, it has been said that every part of the animal can be utilised except its squeal!   (See recipes)

PIGEON. There are several varieties. Tame pigeons should be cooked as soon as possible after killing, as they soon deteriorate. Wood and rock pigeons, however, should be allowed to hang for a few days after killing and before being dressed. House pigeons are considered best, but wood pigeons are largest. Rock pigeons are inferior to both the others. Choose young birds where possible for cooking. When the legs are large and dark the birds are usually old ones.   (See recipes)

PIG'S FRY. The interior parts of the pig.   (See recipe)

PIG, SUCKING. Baby pig. At its best when no more than three weeks old. It should be cooked as soon after killing as possible, as it quickly deteriorates.   (See recipe)

PIKE. Sometimes referred to as the freshwater shark, because it not only devours other fish, but also its own kind. A large fish, sometimes attaining a length of 3 feet and a weight of 40 lb. A small pike, not more than 3 lb. in weight and not exceeding 2 feet in length, is referred to as a 'jack'. The flesh is coarse and rather dry. It is also very bony, the bones constituting a drawback and a danger as they are sharp and so peculiarly hard that they will not dissolve in the stomach. Before cooking, the fish should be salted for about 12 hours, forcing as much as possible down the throat and hanging the fish by the jaw. Otherwise, cut the fish in slices and rub with salt on both sides.

PIKELETS. North country name for crumpet .   (See recipe)

PILAU (PILAF, PILAW). A preparation of chicken or meat cooked with rice.   (See recipe)

PILCHARDS. A small fish resembling in appearance and flavour the herring, but smaller. Chiefly caught off the shores of Devon and

Cornwall. Except in areas where they are caught, these fish are mostly exported in large quantities to all parts of the Continent, especially during Lent. At their best between July and the end of December.

PILSNER BEER. Best known of all lager beers. From Pilsen in Bohemia.

PIMENTO. Allspice or Jamaica pepper. These berries of a West Indian tree are much used in cookery. The flavour resembles a blend of nutmeg, cinnamon and cloves.

PIMIENTO. Large fruit of the Spanish capsicum, from which the mild red pepper called paprika is obtained. The ripe fruit may be bought tinned. Very popular for its flavouring for special dishes, also as a garnish because of its bright red colour.

PIMM'S CUPS. Name given to four well-known cups. The original — No. 1 — has gin and bitters as its base; No. 2 whisky; No. 3 brandy; No. 4 rum.

PIMPERNEL. A herb. See also *Burnet.* Has a flavour somewhat similar to cucumber and is often used in soups and salads.

PINEAPPLE. A fruit principally grown in South America, Africa and West India, but also elsewhere, including this country. Resembles a pine cone in general appearance, but is topped with broad, spreading and tapering leaves. The pulp is juicy with a strong pleasant flavour, but with a tough core that is usually removed. If required for setting in a jelly, it must be cooked first. Tinned pineapple can be used in any of its many forms — rings, pieces, cubes, spears or crush. The juice is also canned. It is considered that the best pineapples come from Hawaii. As well as being eaten raw, tinned or frozen, pineapples can also be cooked.   (See recipes)

PINT. Standard English measure: one-eighth of a gallon or half a quart.

PINTAIL. A wild waterfowl, so named because of its long tail feathers of a greenish-black. Sometimes called a Sea Pheasant. Can be cooked (roasted), requiring about 30 min. in a moderately hot oven. Must be basted well and should be served with a good gravy. An average bird is sufficient for 3 persons.

PIPE. Standard cask for port in this country; contains about 115 gallons, averaging 56 dozens when bottled.

PIPING. A term given to the decoration of cakes, etc., when the icing or other decorating medium, is forced through tubes or small pipes to form fancy shapes or outlines.

PIPING BAG. A bag made of greaseproof paper, or closely woven material, or waterproofed material — or, nowadays, polythene — used for holding the piping tubes and ingredients for decorating.

PIPPIN. Name given to certain varieties of apples, some of which are Cox's orange pippin; golden pippin; Ribston pippin, etc.

PIPPIN TARTS. Name given to pastry shells containing apples cooked with the rind and juice of a bitter orange and a little butter.

PIQUANT. Pleasantly pungent and appetising. (See recipe for *Sauce piquante*).

PISTACHIO NUTS. Kernels of the reddish brown fruits of the pistachio tree. In the best of these (they vary in quality considerably) the nut when blanched is a pretty green colour. It is used extensively for flavouring and decorating cakes, biscuits, sweets, etc., also some savoury dishes. Sometimes referred to as the green almond. Its shape is oblong and pointed (rather like a small filbert); it is obtained from Syria, Arabia, Persia and other places.

PITCAITHLY BANNOCK. A type of almond shortbread containing finely chopped peel and, sometimes, caraway seeds. ·   (See recipe)

PITHIVIERS. A town in France noted for its dainty pastries.

PITHIVIERS CREAM. A butter cream consisting of equal weights of butter, castor sugar and ground almonds, blended with a little beaten egg and sufficient rum or essence to flavour to taste.

PIZZA. Italian word for a type of open pie made with tomato sauce, with or without the addition of cheese, salami, etc. A word also used for almost any flat dough product.   (See recipe)

PERRIER WATER. One of the best of table waters. A natural mineral water from the South of France. Colourless and odourless.

PERRY. An alcoholic beverage made from pears, bearing a similar relation to the pear as cider does to the apple, but not so alcoholic. (See recipe)

PERSIMMON. A yellow egg-shaped fruit, 1—2 in. in diameter. Has flattened end nearest the stem. Its astringency decreases as it ripens, until it virtually becomes a sugar-plum. In America it is sometimes called a date-plum.

PESTLE. An instrument for pounding food in a mortar.

PETITE MARMITE. A French broth cooked and served in individual earthenware pots — usually with snippets of toast and a sprinkling of grated cheese.

PETIT GRUYERE. A small portion of processed cheese wrapped in tinfoil.

PETIT POUSSIN. A baby chicken. Not to be confused with *poisson*, the french word for fish.

PETITS FOURS. A general term for a variety of tiny iced and decorated cakes, sugared fruits, also bonbons.

PLAICE. A flat fish at its best between June and the end of December, but available at other times of the year, when it is thinner and lacks its otherwise good flavour. It loses half its weight in cleaning and filleting. A favourite fish, but considered second in favour to sole. Plaice can be recognised by yellow to reddish brown spots on the dark side, the other side being white. The age of plaice can be determined by the number of rings in the otolith or 'earstone'.   (See recipes)

PLANKED STEAK OR FISH. This consists of a piece of steak or fish placed on a well-oiled, well-seasoned oak plank, cooked under a hot grill, then tastefully garnished and served on the plank.

PLANTAIN (BANANA). A fruit varying in length from a few inches to a little short of a foot. The small varieties are sweet with a mellow flavour, whilst large varieties are less sweet and rather mealy. Popular for many dishes, both sweet and savoury.   (See recipes)

PLATTER. A flat plate or dish.

PLOVER. There are several kinds of plover known to naturalists, but two only are used for consumption — the golden and the grey. Roast like woodcock without being drawn. They are better for being kept a while before cooking. Baste the bird constantly whilst in oven and serve on toast.

PLOVERS' EGGS. Considered a delicacy. They are usually boiled hard and sent to table either hot or cold. Sometimes they are shelled and masked with a sauce. Time for boiling the eggs — ten minutes.

PLUCK. The lights, liver and heart of an ox, sheep or other animal. The word is sometimes used to describe the removal of feathers from poultry and other birds.

PLUM. A stone fruit extensively cultivated in England and other countries. There are many varieties, some of which are used for cooking, others, more choice (such as the greengage or Victoria) being used for dessert. Dried plums are called prunes.   (See recipes)

PLUM PUDDING. See *Christmas pudding.*

POACH. To cook at simmering heat (just below boiling point) in an open pan.

POISSON. French for fish. Not to be confused with *poussin* — French for young chicken.

POLENTA. An Italian pudding. Originally made from chestnut meal, but now generally made of semolina or maize flour. When cold, it is sliced and served with grated cheese and seasonings.

POLLACK. A species of codfish which is considered inferior to cod. The under jaw projects beyond the upper; by this feature a whole pollack can be identified as such.

POLONAISE. Polish style. Dishes under this title frequently have red cabbage, beetroot, horseradish or sour cream among their constituents.

POLONY. Name given to various kinds of partly cooked sausages.

POMEGRANATE. A fruit mentioned in early religious writings. The fruit is the size of a large orange and has a leathery skin varying in colour from light yellow to a deep red. Its interior consists of a sub-acid pinky red juicy pulp enclosing in mass formation seeds of purplish white.

POPCORN. Grains of maize. When heated in a greased covered pan they expand and burst, releasing the puffy white starchy interior.

POPE'S EYE. A name given to the circle of fat found in the centre of a leg of pork or mutton.

POPE'S NOSE. See *Parson's nose.*

POPOVERS. Very light puddings made from a rich Yorkshire pudding batter, cooked in dariole moulds in high heat to make the batter rise and pop over the top of the mould.

POPPY SEED. Seeds of the large poppy, used for sprinkling over Continental breads and confectionery.

PORK. The flesh of the pig.   (See recipes)

PORPOISE. A mammal, eaten in some countries. It was once a favourite dish at the feasts of King Henry VIII. The flesh of young porpoises has been compared with that of veal. To cook, it is sometimes thinly sliced, egg-and-breadcrumbed, then fried. No longer brought to market.

PORRIDGE. Derived from the biblical word 'pottage'. An every-day Scottish breakfast dish — also popular elsewhere. It consists of cooked oatmeal served with salt, or with sugar and milk. Palatable and nourishing.

PORTER. The original "arf and 'arf" for the porter. Beer of a quality between ale and stout.

PORTERHOUSE STEAK. A steak cut from the thick end of the sirloin. The name originates from the old porterhouse.

PORTUGAISE. Portuguese style. Dishes bearing this title usually have tomato, onion or garlic as some of the constituents.

PORT WINE. A wine from Portugal, made from grapes of varying qualities. It falls into two categories, white and red. A sweet heavy wine usually served at the end of a meal, with dessert or cheese.

POSSET. Milk curdled with wine, sweetened with sugar or molasses.

POTAGE. French for soup.

POT ALE. A residue from a grain distillery.

POTATO. A vegetable, supplies of which originally came from Peru. Much cultivated now as the one vegetable it seems impossible to tire of, for it can be cooked in so many ways. The waxy varieties are best for frying (sautéing) and for salads and the white floury kinds for boiling and making mashed potatoes, etc. See also *Sweet potato.* (See recipes)

POTATO CHIPS. Potatoes peeled and cut into strips about $1/2$ in. wide and thick, washed in cold water, dried well and fried in deep fat until cooked and brown.

POTATO CRISPS. Potatoes peeled and very thinly sliced, washed and soaked in cold water for at least 30 min., then drained and dried before frying in deep fat until crisp and golden brown.

POTATO SALAD. Waxy-type potatoes boiled in their skins, peeled and diced, then tossed in salad cream whilst still warm, and sprinkled with chopped chives.

POTATO STRAWS. Potatoes peeled and cut into match-like strips, washed and soaked well, then drained and dried before frying in deep fat until crisp and brown.

POT-AU-FEU. The national soup of France, but claimed as of Spanish origin. There are many variations, but it is usually a stew of various meats and vegetables, poured over French bread or toast.

POT-POURRI. A stew of various meats and spices, etc.

POT-ROAST. A method of cooking tough meats or poultry. The general procedure is first to fry the meat or joints on all sides in a thick pan with enough fat to cover the bottom. A little stock or water is added — with flavouring vegetables, sometimes — and seasonings. The pan is covered with a tightly fitting lid and cooking continued over low heat, or in the oven, so that the simmering pace is no more than about 300° F. or Regulo 1. Allow about 1 hr. per lb.

POTTAGE. See *Potage.*

POTTED. Meat, poultry game or fish may be pounded to a paste and preserved in *pots* or jars.

POTTLE. A wine measure recognised in England as equivalent to $1/2$ gallon.

POULARDE. Fat fowl.

POULE. Boiling fowl.

POULET. Cock chicken.

POULET. Spring chicken.

POULET DINDE. Young turkey.

POULETTE. Hen chicken.

POULTRY. Domesticated fowls. They are in season as follows:

Chicken	All the year round
Duckling	March to September
Ducks	August to March
Fowls	All the year round
Geese	September to February
Green geese	August to November
Guinea Fowl	February to August
Pigeons	All the year round
Turkeys	September to March

(Poultry keepers are now trying to make small turkeys for the table available all the year round).
Also obtainable frozen at all times of the year.

POUSSIN. See *Petit poussin.*

PRALINE. A rich paste composed of pounded nuts (usually hazel nuts or filberts) and sugar, used for many confectionery purposes, etc.

PRAWNS. Shellfish similar to shrimps, but larger and more delicately flavoured. In season all the year round, but at their best from February to October.
When freshly caught they are semi-transparent, but change colour, when boiled, to a pink or reddish shade. Cooking time 7—8 min. in salted boiling water. Should not be over-cooked.   (See recipes)

PRESERVES. Food maintained in edible condition by various means — canning, bottling, use of chemicals, etc. (See recipes under *Jams, Pickles, Preserves).*

PRESSURE COOKER. A cooking vessel with a tightly fitting lid to prevent loss of steam, controlled by a pressure valve. Very little liquid is used and the steam is generated under high pressure to a temperature much higher than that of boiling water, with the result that foods are cooked in much shorter time. There are several kinds on the market, their prices varying according to size.

PRETZELS. Hard brittle biscuits — originally called Bretzels. The pieces of dough are shaped into a knot-like letter 'B', then dipped in lye (an alkaline solution), sprinkled with salt and baked.

PRICKLY PEAR. Cactus of the genus Opuntia, bearing pear-shaped fruit covered with prickles and in varying colours. The fruits are juicy and refreshing, those with the thinnest skin being considered the best. Weight varies from 1 oz. up to 1 lb.

PRINTANIER. 'Spring style'. A term used to imply that fresh spring vegetables are included in the dish, either as a garnish or in the form of a macedoine.

PROFITEROLE. Tiny shapes made from choux paste — balls or finger shapes — filled with cream or creamy mixtures, or pea-sized pieces sometimes used as garnish for clear soups.   (See *Choux pastry*)

PROMESSI. A soft cream cheese of Italian origin.

PROTEIN. A Greek word meaning 'first'. A complex and unstable organic compound, containing carbon, oxygen, hydrogen and nitrogen, usually with some sulphur — found in all organic bodies and forming an essential constituent of animal foods. Originally applied to a nitrogenous compound supposed to form the basic material of all organisms; the essential principle of food, obtained from albumen, fibrin or casein.

Protein of high food value is contained in meat, fish, milk, cheese and eggs. Ripe peas and beans show a high protein content, but are deficient in quality. Soy beans and peanuts are high in protein content.

PROUENÇALE, A LA. From Provence, a former province of southern France. The terms is applied to certain French dishes containing garlic or onion and olive oil.

PRUNELLE. Sloe — wild plum. A name also given to a pale green liqueur with the flavour of sloes — crème de prunelles.

PRUNES. Dried plums. Principal source of supply of this excellent food is California. The word *prune* is French for plum.

PTARMIGAN (MOUNTAIN GROUSE). A bird which feeds on the wild herbage of the hills of Scotland and other places as far north as Greenland, their feeding giving the flesh a slightly bitter but not unpleasant flavour. The young birds are usually roasted and the older birds braised. They are about the same size as red grouse. These birds are much relished by epicures.

PTOMAINE. A term invented by an Italian chemist for the basic substances produced in putrefaction (decayed or tainted food), which produces food poisoning. The danger lies in germs which have attacked, or are bred in, the food.

PUDDING. As a culinary term pudding usually means a sweet dish. It can also be used in connection with savoury dishes — i. e. meat cooked inside a suet crust.   (See recipes)

PUFF PASTRY. A very light rich paste.   (See recipes)

PUITS D'AMOUR. Small French pastries made with a light puff paste.

PULLED BREAD. The crumb part of a loaf of bread pulled into conveniently small pieces, usually whilst still warm, then baked in a moderately hot oven until crisp and golden.

PULLET. A young hen chicken.

PULQUE. The national drink of Mexico, made from the fermented juice of the maguey plant. It is a yellowish, sweet and pleasing beverage — also known as 'honey-water'.

PULSES. Seeds of leguminous plants — e. g. peas, beans, etc.

PULVERISED SUGAR. Finely powdered sugar.

PUMPERNICKEL. German (Westphalian) wholemeal rye bread. The crust is almost black, but the crumb is only dark brown. Sometimes called 'black bread'.

PUMPKIN. Specimens resemble a very large yellow melon. They have higher fame as a fruit in such dishes as pumpkin pie, etc., than as a vegetable or in soups, etc. May also be eaten raw. Sometimes reach 200 lb. in weight, but are about 90 per cent water.   (See recipes)

PUNCH. A potent beverage sometimes served hot, sometimes cold. From the original 'panch', meaning 'five', made by the Hindus (when it consisted of five ingredients, arrack, spice, lemon juice, sugar and water), the English punch in its simplest form combines the ingredients of rum, lemon juice, sugar and water. It has many variations, however, some of which include brandy, ale, milk, etc.

PUNCH A LA ROMAINE. A kind of soft white lemon-flavoured ice served between courses — usually in a kind of goblet — intended to assist the functions of digestion.

PUREE. A smooth pulp. Cooked food rubbed through a sieve.

PUREE DE LEGUMES. Vegetable purée.

PURL. An old fashioned cold-weather drink made of ale and beer heated, then added to gin and bitters.

PURSLANE (PURSLAIN). A pot herb used in salads and pickles. The young shoots and leaves are succulent and refreshing eaten raw. More frequently seen in Continental markets.

PYROMETER. An instrument for measuring high temperatures.

QUAB. A river fish mostly found in Russia.

QUADRILLE. Indicating thin strips of paste laid net, or chequered, fashion across open jam or fruit tarts and flans. Sometimes styled 'lattice-patterned'.

QUAIL. Tiny birds — best roasted wrapped in vine leaves — of the partridge species. Mostly imported from Egypt and Africa, these delicately flavoured birds were once a feature of the buffet at country and hunt balls, where they were served stuffed, cooked and dressed in aspic. Usually in demand when game is out of season. In best condition from September to January.

QUART. The imperial quart is equivalent to a quarter of a gallon or two pints.

QUARTERN. A quarter or fourth part of various measures — especially of a loaf of bread; a pint, peck or pound. A quartern-loaf weighs about 4 lb.

QUARTIER D'AGNEAU. Quarter of lamb.

QUARTIER DE DERRIERE. Hindquarter.

QUARTIER DE DEVANT. Forequarter.

QUASS. See *Kvass.*

QUASSIA. A tree of the South Americas, the bitter bark and wood of which are used as a tonic — e. g. an infusion of quassia chips makes the basis for quassia cup. This is flavoured with outer rind of orange, borage and spices, sweetened and fortified with alcohol in some form.

QUEEN CAKES. Small cakes containing currants, baked in patty tins.
(See recipe)

QUENELLES. Forcemeat of different kinds — composed of meat, game, poultry, fish, pounded to a paste, then formed into small shapes and used fried or poached for garnishing dishes.   (See recipe)

QUETCH. A colourless French liqueur with the flavour of plums.

QUEUE. Tail. Queue de boeuf — ox-tail, for example.

QUEUX. Name given to cooks during the middle ages.

QUICHE LORRAINE. Egg and bacon open pie, baked in a pie-plate.
(See recipe)

QUICK-FROZEN FOODS. Foods labelled as quick-frozen are frozen in a few minutes or in a number of hours, depending on size and internal temperature. Slow freezing breaks down the tissue of the food, causing it to collapse when defrosted.

QUINCE. A yellowish-green somewhat pear-shaped fruit of a shrub or small tree, *pyrus cydonia,* used in cookery for flavouring and preserving. The flavour is too harsh and sour to be used alone and is often combined with apples in pies, jams and jellies.   (See recipes)

QUINNAL. The king-salmon of the Pacific coast of N. America.

QUOORMA. Name of a very mild Indian curry preparation.

QUTAIF. An Arab dish similar to our pancakes — paper-thin, they are fried in almond oil and served with a rich syrup and sprinkling of rose-water.

RABBIT. A burrowing rodent with edible flesh of a delicate flavour and good food value. Its fur is marketable. Both wild and tame (domesticated) rabbits are edible — the former weigh from 2—3 lb. the latter, when mature, upwards of 7 lb. Owing to their destructive habits in farming areas, rabbits are often destroyed by farmers as a pest.   (See recipe)

RACAHOUT (RACAHOU). An Arabian preparation with pulverised roasted acorns as its base, sweetened and containing other flavouring ingredients.

RACINES. Root vegetables usually used as a garnish.

RACK (ARRACK). A spirit distilled from rice, palm juice or sugar cane — principally in Russia and India.

RADICCHIO. A favourite Italian vegetable not unlike a radish, with edible root and leaves. Eaten both raw and cooked.

RADISH. A salad plant with a bulbous root of somewhat pungent flavour. Some roots are white, some red, some red and white; varying in shape also, some globular, some evenly elongated, some tapering to a point, etc.

RAFFINADE. Best quality refined sugar.

RAFRAICHIR. To cool, to refresh. *Glace à rafraîchir* — ice to put in drinks, etc.

RAGOUT. A rich and highly seasoned stew of meat and vegetables. A kind of goulash, usually browned and thickened.   (See recipe)

RAHAT LAKOUM. Turkish Delight — a sweetmeat of Turkish origin.

RAIE. A large flat sea-fish with a long tail. See *Skate.*

RAIL. A very small bird frequently found in marshy areas. Can be roasted or cooked in a pie.

RAILWAY PUDDING. A plain sponge pudding usually served cold, split and sandwiched together with jam and sprinkled on top with castor sugar.

RAISED CRUST (PIE). A paste used for meat pies which do not require a dish. It is made usually by stirring heated water and melted lard into flour. Also referred to as hot-water pastry.   (See recipe)

RAISIN. The dried fruit of the grape vine. The choicest raisins come from California. Sun raisins are those obtained by leaving clusters of fruit on the vine until they dry on the stalks.

RAISINEE. A syrupy jam made by very slowly cooking pears with a proportion of quince in sweet wine or cider. Another type is made with grapes and quince.

RAKIA. Hungarian liqueur made from fully ripened grapes.

RAKPAPRIKAS. Hungarian dish consisting of crayfish, tomato purée, and spices flavoured prominently with paprika.

RAM. A male sheep.

RAMBOUR. A large, early, sour baking apple.

RAMEKINS. Individual small baking dishes, usually of ovenproof porcelain or earthenware. Savouries or small entrées are usually served in these.

RAMPION. See *Radicchio.*

RANCID. In a state of decomposition, producing a rank taste and/or smell in foods with a high fat content, such as butter, cheese, oils.

RANGPAR. A citrus fruit about the size of a lemon, but with compressed ends. Has a reddish skin and an orange-coloured flesh.

RAPE. A plant allied to the turnip. Cultivated in most European countries for its oil-producing seeds. Rape oil is obtained from the crushed seeds, and a cattle-cake is made from the crushed seeds and husks afterwards. This residue is also used for manure.

RASPBERRY. Small red berries allied to the bramble or blackberry. Two varieties: red and white (yellow when quite ripe), each of delicious flavour. Its soft pulp is easily perishable. Used extensively for cooking and preserves, also for dessert. Raspberry vinegar is an acidulated syrup of raspberries.   (See recipes)

RASPBERRY BUNS. A scone-like mixture formed into small balls and arranged on a baking tin. A hole is pushed in each, into which a little jam is put and the dough pinched up over to enclose it. After brushing with milk and sprinkling with sugar they are baked, when the buns will break on top, showing the jam.

RASPINGS. Very fine crumbs of stale bread.

RATAFIA. Name of a flavouring essence; also a liqueur flavoured with the kernels of peaches, plums, cherries, apricots and bitter almonds. Also the name of a sweet small biscuit, almond-flavoured.

RATION. A fixed amount of food given out for a fixed time.

RATON. A kind of cheesecake.

RATONNET. Small skewers of meat — usually mutton.

RAVIGOTE. A richly flavoured green herb salad dressing containing besides herbs, vinegar and garlic; served cold. Also the name of a hot sauce.

RAVIOLI. Very small squares or shapes of *nouille* (noodle) paste enclosing a savoury mixture of meat or spinach, cheese, etc. Usually highly seasoned. Cooked in boiling water, then served with a savoury sauce and sprinkled with Parmesan cheese.   (See recipe)

RAY. A flat fish of the same genus as the skate or thornback. Should be hung for at least a day before it is dressed. The wings are cut into strips and put into a light brine for 5 or 6 hours before using. May be boiled or fried in the same manner as skate. At its best from September to February.

RECEIPT. A written formula for the preparation of food. (See *Recipe* below.) 'Receipt' is a word nowadays used more generally as an acknowledgement of payment.

RECHAUD. Chafing or warming dish.

RECHAUFFE. Re-heated. Cold food re-warmed or re-dressed.

RECIPE. The terms given to any formula setting out details for the preparation of food. Originally applied to a formula for a medical prescription.

RECREPI. A term applied to crimped (i. e. gashed) fish.

RED CABBAGE. A species of common cabbage with dark red leaves. Used largely for pickling, but is also cooked, especially in Germany, France and Switzerland, where it is shredded and stewed with a rich broth. (See recipes)

REDCURRANTS. Small soft red berries growing in clusters on bushes. Sometimes wall-trained.   (See recipes)

RED HERRING. A cured and smoked fish.

RED MULLET. See *Mullet*.

REDUIRE. To reduce or concentrate liquids by boiling.

REFORME, A LA. This name was given by a French chef to certain dishes which he prepared whilst at the Reform Club, London. The best known dish is the now well-established 'Cutlets Réforme'. The garnish consists of thin strips of cooked carrots, truffle, ham and the white of hard-boiled egg, served in a rich Espagnole sauce.

REFRIGERATOR. A cabinet, insulated and mechanically controlled, to lower the temperature of the enclosed air, so as to preserve food in a fresh condition.

REFROIDI. Chilled but not frozen.

REGAL. A feast or banquet.

REGGIANO. An Italian cheese similar to Parmesan, but rather more strongly flavoured. A cheese that improves with keeping. Not usually marketed until a year or more after maturing.

REGINETTE. Very thin wavy noodles. Cook and use like ordinary noodles.

REGLISSE. Licorice or liquorice. The familiar black sticks are prepared from the condensed juice of the boiled and crushed roots of the licorice plant and mixed with starch. The extract of the root is known as 'Spanish juice' or 'black sugar'.

REGULO. A regulating dial fixed to modern gas-cookers to control the flow of gas to the oven. The temperature will vary somewhat, depending upon the pressure of gas in the particular area. See *Comparative temperatures*.

Mark	$1/2$	1	2	3	4	5	6	7	8	9	10	11	12
Degrees F.	250°	275°	315°	325°	350°	375°	400°	425°	450°	475°	500°	525°	550°

REHOBOAM. A bottle, equal in size to 6 ordinary wine bottles, containing a gallon. Accepted standard of measure for wine bottles is 26⅔ fluid oz.

REINDEER. A species of deer inhabiting the sub-arctic parts of the northern hemisphere. Domesticated for its milk and as a draught animal in its own habitat. Reindeer tongues were imported in the guise of ox tongues before the last war, making excellent eating. Both sexes are antlered. The flesh of the cows and steers is similar to mild venison and that of a three-year-old is considered best. The meat of the buck is considered too strong in taste for most palates.

REISWUERSTCHEN. A type of Austrian rice sausage.

RELEVE. The French term for a substantial course such as a large joint of meat, game and occasionally fish.

RELISH. A highly seasoned or flavoured food used as an accompaniment.

REMOUILLAGE. The French term for a thinner, second stock.

REMOULADE. A rich cold sauce similar to mayonnaise, used as a salad-dressing.

RENDER. To separate fat from connective tissue by heating.

RENNET. Name given to the preparation obtained by an infusion of the inner skin of a calf's stomach, usually, but also obtainable from that of a pig's, hare's or fowl's stomach. Rennet's chief importance is its property of coagulating milk for cheese manufacture and jellying milk for junket. The best quality rennet is obtained from the animals that have received no other form of food than milk.

REPASSE. A French word meaning 'repeatedly strained'. A process usually carried out when preparing fine sauces and aspics.

RESTAURANT. An establishment where substantial meals are served. Originally the name was applied to a highly spiced chicken broth invented by a Frenchman in 1557 and later (1765) a tavern was opened in Paris under the title 'Restaurant' for the purpose of supplying this wonderful soup. Gradually catering establishments as we know them to-day were evolved.

RHUBARB. This is a name applied to both a garden plant and a drug. The garden plant has a leaf stalk which possesses a pleasing acid flavour. It is used stewed or in pies, puddings, etc. Rhubarb is looked upon by most as the first fruit of the season, but it is a mistaken notion to call it a fruit, it being the stalk of the plant.

The drug is an extract of the root of the plant. There are two kinds — the kiln-dried and the sun-dried. This extract has natural purgative qualities.   (See recipes)

RHUM, RUM. A spirit distilled from the fluid residuum of cane sugar. There are two main types — Jamaica and Demerara — Jamaica being considered the better. The Demerara is smoother and of lighter flavour than Jamaica.

RIBOFLAVIN. The water-soluble Vitamin B (known in America as Vitamin G) found chiefly in offal (particularly in liver) and dairy products.

RIBS OF BEEF. There are five joints that come under this heading — wing rib, top ribs, fore ribs, back ribs, and flat ribs. The wing rib is the cut generally most esteemed and commands a higher price than the other ribs.

RICE. A grain largely used throughout Europe — perhaps more extensively for human food than any other. It is the staple food in China, Japan and India. Chiefly marketed with the outer layers removed. Rice when threshed is brown and the husk is removed by milling, which gives us white rice. There are many varieties and qualities — Carolina rice is considered best for puddings and Patna rice for curries. (See recipes)

RICE FLOUR. Ground rice made from defective rice broken in the husking stage.

RICE PAPER. A white, smooth, glossy, edible paper made from the pith of the Formosan — a tree peculiar to Formosa. Macaroons and other similar biscuits are baked on it. Used also by Chinese artists for painting on.

RICE, WILD. A rather long thin grain, chiefly greenish and with a slightly smoky flavour which is not at all unpleasant. Grown extensively in the southern States of America, wild rice has always been relished as a food by Indians, and in recent years has become popular in American restaurants.

Also known as 'zizanie'.

RICHELIEU. Name of a noted French Cardinal, also of two famous French statesmen (all of whom were celebrated gourmets), besides the name of many French dishes.

RIGATONI. Fluted elbow-shaped pieces of macaroni; the largest made.

RILLOTES. Pork meat preparation, in paste form, highly seasoned. Used in France for hors-d'œuvres and savouries. Rillotes and rillons de tours are renowned.

RISENGROD. A Danish dish of rice.

RISOTTO. An Italian dish composed of rice, cheese, tomatoes, usually flavoured with garlic. Sometimes a little saffron is added. (See recipe)

RIS PISI. An Italian soup containing rice and green peas.

RISSOLES. A savoury meat or fish mixture enclosed in rich pastry, formed into half-moon shapes, usually egg-and-breadcrumbed or rolled in finely crushed vermicelli and fried.
In this country they are usually interpreted to mean a savoury meat mixture (or fish) coated with egg and crumbs only and fried.

RIZZARED HADDIE. A Scotch term for sun-dried haddocks.

ROACH. A fresh-water fish of the carp family. Seldom weighs more than $1^1/_2$ lb. White-fleshed, turning reddish when boiled. Bony and not much relished. In season from September to March.

ROASTING. A favourite method of cooking meat, etc. At one time carried out before a fire — the meat being suspended by means of a jack or spit — but nowadays more often in ovens. Roasting means cooking by radiated heat.

ROASTING JACK. A mechanical device for turning the spit upon which food (usually meat) is hung by means of hooks for roasting.

ROBERT. Name of a brown spicy sauce made with onions, chilli vinegar and mustard, served with pork and other meats. Invented by a restaurant keeper of that name.

ROCAMBOLE. Member of the onion family which bears its fruits at the top of its stem. Also called tree-onion.

ROCK SALMON. A name sometimes given to coal-fish. Actually, a long fish with a tough skin which is usually stripped off before sale. Sometimes called dogfish.

ROE. Eggs and milt of fish. There are two types — hard and soft. The hard roe is that of the female and the soft of the male.

ROGNON. Kidney.

ROKELAX. Norwegian smoked salmon.

ROLLMOPS. See *Herring.*

ROOK. A common bird of the countryside, sometimes used as a filler for game pies, giving bulk but not any particular flavour. Once fairly extensively used for pies and puddings, but finds few buyers nowadays. The flesh is dry and somewhat coarse. It is best stewed, or in a pie (as above), but never roasted.

ROOT BEER. An infusion of roots, barks and herbs, fermented with yeast.

ROQUEFORT. A well-known French cheese made from sheep's milk.

ROSE-HIPS. See *Hips.*

ROSEMARY. An evergreen shrub — very fragrant. Occasionally used for seasoning food and in the manufacture of preserves. In medicine it is used as a stimulant.

ROSETBAKKELS (ROSETTES). A kind of German waffle, fried on rosette-shaped irons. Usually served with honey or syrup.

ROUGHAGE. Fibre of cereals, fruits and vegetables, which acts as an aid to intestinal alimination if eaten in reasonable quantities.

ROULADE. Meat roll or galantine.

ROUT CAKES. Small rich almond biscuits. Sometimes handed round at the end of a meal, or served with sweet wines between meals.
(See recipe)

ROUX. A preparation of butter and flour, used for thickening soups and sauces. There are three kinds — white, fawn and brown.

ROYAL. Name applied to an icing made with whites of egg and icing sugar, used for coating cakes and decorative purposes. Also a name given to a savoury egg custard used for garnishing clear soups.

RUDD. Fish of the same family as the roach. Rather bony and not of particularly good flavour. Can be fried, but better for soup-making.

RUM. See *Rhum.*

RUMKIN. A type of drinking vessel.

RUNDERGEHAKT. A Danish dish of minced beef.

RUNDERLAPPEN. A Danish dish of stewed steak.

RUNNER BEANS. A climbing plant bearing green pods larger than French beans. If picked whilst young the beans have a flavour not unlike French beans. If left growing too long they become coarse and stringy, developing large scarlet bean-seeds. Usually sliced thinly before boiling in salted water.

RUSKS. A name given to twice-baked slices of bread, cake or sweet bread. To make: bake dough in an oblong or square tin; when the baked dough is cold, cut into slices or shapes, and rebake in a slow oven until crisp and golden.

RUSSE, A LA. 'In Russian style'.

RUSSET APPLE. A rough-skinned late apple with a delicious flavour. In the dessert class.

RUSSIAN DRESSING. Mayonnaise dressing to which have been added Worcester sauce, chilli sauce, chopped pickles and various seasonings.

RUSSIAN SALAD. A variety of mixed cooked vegetables cut to dice shapes where suitable, masked with a salad-dressing. Sometimes anchovy fillets, hard-boiled eggs and a little diced cooked ham are added.

RUTABAGA. A Swedish turnip with a similar flavour to kohl rabi. Some varieties have white flesh, others yellow.

RYE. Cultivated in England as food for cattle and horses. In parts of Germany and in Russia rye is the principal grain for bread-making. It is similar in appearance to barley. In America and Canada whisky is distilled from it. The Russians also make a drink from it called kvass (q. v.).

RYE BREAD. Made from rye, this bread is very dark in colour, but is nutritious and of pleasing flavour.

SABAYOR (SABAYON) SAUCE. A sweet sauce, thick and frothy.
(See recipe under *Sauces*)

SAO. A pouch or receptacle in an animal or a vegetable.

SACCHARINE. A commercial product estimated to have 400 to 500 times more sweetening-power than sugar. Of no value as food, as it passes through the system unchanged. A derivative of coal tar.

SACCHAROMETER. An instrument used for measuring the volume of sugar in liquids.

SACK. An old name for various white wines, especially those from Spain and the Canaries.

SADDLE OF MUTTON. Two loins not cut asunder, complete with kidneys. Considered the finest part of lamb or young mutton.

SAFFRON. A bright yellow preparation obtained from the stigma of the autumn crocus, used for colouring and flavouring foods.

SAGE. A shrub with narrow greyish-green leaves. This herb is often combined with onions in the preparation of stuffing for pork, duck and goose. (See recipe)

SAGO. Edible starch obtained from the trunk of the sago palm. This starchy substance goes through a process which results in producing seed, pearl and bullet sage. Used for making milk puddings and thickening soups, etc.

SAINT-GERMAIN. A name sometimes given to a special pea soup enriched with cream. As a garnish it takes the form of a purée of green peas.

SAITHE. A Scottish name for coal-fish.

SAKI. A Japanese spirit distilled from rice.

SALAD. A dish usually composed of edible green plants, sometimes including other items such as tomatoes, cooked vegetables, cooked meats, fish, shellfish, poultry, etc. Sometimes served in a salad bowl, or arranged on a flat serving dish, sometimes with hot meats, etc., as a side-plate. (See salad recipes in their alphabetical order — e. g. chicken salad, lobster salad, etc.)

SALAD DRESSING. This takes various forms to suit the dish with which it is served, a light French dressing (usually consisting of oil, vinegar or lemon, and seasonings) being considered ideal for a plain green salad. When served with more substantial salads the dressing is usually of the creamy variety.   (See recipes)

SALADE DE LEGUMES. A vegetable salad.

SALAD HERBS. See *Salad plants.*

SALAD OIL. An ingredient used extensively in salad dressings, also for frying and other cooking purposes. Main source: the olive. Other varieties of oils used for similar purposes include tea-seed and nut oils.

SALAD PLANTS. These include lettuce, watercress, mustard-and-cress, curly endive, radishes, spring onions, cucumber, chives or scallions, young cabbages, etc. Ideally, these should be young and quickly grown.

SALAMANDRE. A thick plate of iron with a handle, once used, when heated, for holding over food to brown the surface. Modern gas and electric grills have taken its place.

SALAMI. A highly spiced Continental sausage of Italian origin, which, if properly dried, will keep a long time. The main ingredients are veal and pork meats, garlic, caraway seeds, black, red and white peppers, spices and food colouring.

SALLY LUNN. A sweetened spongy yeast cake, first made, it is said, by a girl named Sally Lunn.   (See recipe)

SALMAGUNDI. A colourful old English salad-type dish, consisting of a variety of cooked vegetables, pickled fish, cold chicken, hard-boiled eggs, pickles, etc., diced and arranged with regard to flavours and colours on a bed of fresh green salad plants. A definite pattern is given to the ingredients, and with it is served a dressing of oil, vinegar (or lemon juice), pepper and salt.

SALMI (OF GAME). A ragoût or stew made of par-cooked, and sometimes left-over roasted game.   (See recipe)

SALMON. A choice and nourishing fish which leaves the sea and ascends the river to spawn. Popular fish among those who love fishing and good food. Medium-size fish are best for cooking and eating. May be cooked in many ways — baked, boiled, poached, grilled or fried. In season from beginning of February to end of August. Generally cheapest in July and August.   (See recipe)

SALMON TROUT. Resembles salmon in flavour and appearance (though not so red), but is not really of the same species. Justly considered a delicacy, and may be cooked according to recipes for salmon and trout, adjusting cooking times where necessary. Smaller than salmon — seldom exceeding 2—3 lbs. in weight. In season March to August.

SALPICONS. Appetising mixtures, finely minced or diced small, of poultry, game, fish, ham, tongue or foie gras, with forcemeat, truffles, mushrooms, etc. The various ingredients are usually prepared and cooked separately, then heated in a thick sauce of appropriate flavour and nature. Sometimes different ingredients are put into little patty cases (usually puff pastry) or they are put into a dish with the different ingredients divided by sippets of fried or toasted bread sprinkled with breadcrumbs and lightly browned on top before serving.

SALSIFY. A vegetable plant with long white roots which, when boiled, provides a good winter vegetable. Sometimes referred to as the oyster plant, though without any noticeable reason, except, perhaps, its appearance after cooking.

SALT. A preparation used for seasoning and preserving food. Most salt is manufactured from rock salt obtained in the Middlesborough district. There are different grades — superfine, medium or fine crystals — as well as a coarse salt obtained by the natural evaporation of sea water, used for other purposes than cooking. Cooking salt is considered indispensable in the diet.

SALTPETRE. Potassium nitrate. Used for pickling meats, etc., also for preserving the red colouring of meats.

SALTED FISH. Many fish — cod, ling and similar large fish — are frequently salted when newly caught and either dried by air or kept in pickle. When dried, it should be washed well and soaked in cold water for from 24—36 hr. before cooking. When pickled, the fish is also soaked — usually for up to 12 hr.

SALZGURKEN. Small salted cucumbers. A German pickle served with cooked meats.

SAMP. A type of porridge made of boiled coarse-ground maize eaten with milk.

SAMPHIRE. A herb which grows wild mostly among rocks and cliffs round the coast. Used sometimes in salads and can also be cooked and used as a vegetable.

SAMSHU. A Chinese beer brewed from rice.

SAND CAKE. See *Cakes.*

SAND EELS. Small eel-like fish caught at low tide on the sands. Used mainly for bait, but edible if cooked.

SANDWICHES. A term applied to two slices of bread with meat or other filling between — said to have been invented by the 4th Earl of Sandwich as a convenient means of eating a meal during gambling sessions. Nowadays, a popular form of finger-food, especially for informal entertaining.   (See recipes)

SANGAREE. A type of punch popular in the West Indies, made with port or madeira wine, lime juice, water and sugar with added spices.

SAPODILLA. The plum-like fruit of a tree from which chicle is obtained for making chewing-gum. The fruit is edible when ripe.

SARATOGA CHIPS. Name given to a certain type of potato crisp. Another name is game chips.

SARDINES. Small fish mostly preserved in oil and packed in hermetically sealed tins. The name was first given to the young of the pilchards caught off the coast of Sardinia, but has since been applied to the young of herrings, anchovies, etc. The fish caught off the French coasts are considered best and when tinned in best quality oil are usually the most expensive.

SARSAPARILLA. A flavouring made from the bitter-flavoured roots of a certain species of smilax. The flavour is used extensively in some carbonated beverages.

SASATIES. Dutch kebabs — see *Kebabs.*

SASSAFRAS. A North American beverage prepared by infusing the bark, leaves and leaf buds of a laurel tree. In some areas it is drunk as a substitute for tea.

SAUCE. A thickened liquid served with different foods to enhance their flavour. The four chief sauces are Allemande, Béchamel, Espagnole and Velouté.   (See recipes)

SAUERKRAUT. Thinly sliced white cabbage fermented with salt, caraway seed and juniper berries. A familiar accompaniment to many German dishes.   (See recipe)

SAUSAGE. Saucisse (Fr.); *Wurst* (Ger.). A manufactured food consisting of minced pork and/or other minced meat, spices and seasonings, stuffed into a thin skin covering once made only from animal's gut, but also, nowadays, from a synthetic substance which answers the same purpose. It is claimed that the making of sausages originated in Germany. The preparation was originally started as a means of preserving meat from deterioration and has become a highly developed art. There are now many varieties, some richly spiced, some hard and dry, etc. There are well over a hundred varieties to suit all tastes, including the popular American varieties — 'frankfurters' and 'hot dogs'.

SAUTER. A process of frying food in a little fat — usually sliced vegetables or mets when required for adding to stews, braises, etc.

SAUTERNE. A French white wine — one of the best of the naturally sweetened wines. Much esteemed for culinary use.

SAVELOY. A highly seasoned smoked pork sausage with a red colour resulting from the addition of saltpetre in its preparation. This sausage was originally made only of pigs' brains.

SAVORY. A flavouring herb.

SAVOURY. A word with two interpretations. 1. The final course of a meal before serving coffee — usually some small tasty well-seasoned tit-bit of food. 2. Indicating an appetising tasty dish.

SAVOURY BUTTERS. Butter or margarine, seasoned and flavoured with such items as tomato purée, paprika and lemon juice, anchovy paste, horseradish cream, pounded lobster coral, blanched and pounded green vegetable such as spinach, parsley, chives, etc. A little appropriate colouring matter is added where necessary. May be added to sandwiches, used as a garnish to otherwise plain fish or meat dishes, etc.

SAVOY. A hardy curly-leafed variety of cabbage, in season through the winter. Improved by the frost, making it more crisp. Savoy is also the name of a kind of sponge cake or sponge finger originally introduced to this country from Savoy, France.

SAVOY CAKE. A light sponge cake baked in a tall tin or fancy mould which is often used in the making of Tipsy Cake.

SCALD. A name applied to the pouring of boiling water over food, or, in the instance of milk, bringing to boiling point.

SCALLION. A young onion which has developed no bulb.

SCALLOP. A flat shellfish with two shells, the flesh tasting something like crab. Usually in season from October to April or May. Translucent white colour with a bright orange roe. May be cooked on the shell, first removing black or gristly parts. After being cleansed the shells can be used again for other purposes.   (See recipes)

SCAMPI. A giant Italian prawn, similar to the Dublin Bay prawn.

SCARLET RUNNERS. A long thin green vegetable.

SCAROLE (ESCAROLE). A broad-leaved endive or chicory plant with wavy instead of curled leaves.

SCHNAPPS. Gin originally distilled at Schiedam, Holland. Sometimes known as 'square-face'. Sold in black bottles with flat sides.

SCHNITZEL. A term used in Austria and Germany to describe a thin slice of meat (usually veal), coated with egg and crumbs, and fried.
(See recipe for *Wiener Schnitzel*)

SCHWARZBROT. A German brown bread made from rye. See *Rye Bread.*

SCONE. A tea-cake of Scottish origin. There are many varieties. (See recipes)

SCORE. To cut grooves. For example, the rind of pork is usually scored in thin grooves before reasting to facilitate cooking and for easier carving. Sometimes the skin of cucumber is grooved, so that when cut in slices the edges have a pretty serrated effect.

SCORZONERA. Similar to salsify, but with a black root.

SCOTCH BUN. See *Black bun.*

SCOTCH EGGS. Hard-boiled eggs, shelled, dusted with seasoned flour, coated thinly with sausage meat, then coated with egg and crumbs and fried in deep fat.   (See recipe)

SCOTCH MUTTON BROTH. A stew of mutton or lamb with mixed vegetables, containing barley.   (See recipe)

SCOTCH WOODCOCK. A savoury: thin crisp toast, spread with anchovy butter and topped with softly scrambled eggs, usually garnished with rolled anchovy fillets.

SCOTTISH KALE. Name given to a thin broth popular in Scotland. Kale is a component part of this broth.

SCRAPPLE. A savoury mixture of pork trimmings, spices, maize and chopped sage, moulded into cakes and fried. An old-time favourite at pig-killing times.

SCRIPTURE CAKE. See *Bible cake.*

SCROD. A young cod.

SEA BEEF. See *Whale meat.* Best kept frozen up to time of cooking. Its flavour resembles that of beef, if pot-roasted or casseroled. If allowed to thaw out, the fishy flavour is more noticeable.

SEA BREAM. A delicately flavoured fish with head large in proportion to body. Usually reasonably priced. Plentiful round the coasts of Cornwall and the South.   (See recipe)

SEA KALE. A green vegetable — best blanched before cooking.
                                                       (See recipe)

SEAR. To expose food to fierce heat in order to harden or colour the surface.

SEASONING. This usually applies to pepper and salt, but also has reference to forcemeat and stuffings.

SEC. Implies 'dry'. With champagne it means that a little liqueur has been added to make the wine less sweet.

SEKT. A German designation for champagne, indicating 'dry'.

SELTZER. A well-known mineral water.

SEMOLINA. Consists of the small hard particles of wheat left in the bolting machine after the finer flour has passed through. Used in this country for milky puddings and for thickening stews, etc. Semolina also forms the basis of most Italian pastes, from the finest vermicelli to the large type of macaroni called *zitoni.* Another form of semolina is made from maize 'or Indian corn.   (See recipe)

SERVIETTE. A French word meaning table napkin.

SHAD. A salt-water fish with an average market weight of about 4 lbs. In season March to June. It is not, however, highly esteemed in this country. It may be boiled, fried or baked. The best part of the shad is its roe, which is at its best from January to March.

SHADDOCK. Grapefruit was formerly called shaddock because it was originally brought from India to the West Indies by a Captain Shaddock. Later this large coarse fruit was cultivated to the normal sizes with which we are familiar today.

SHALLOT. A small onion differing slightly from the common onion, being a little milder.   (See recipe)

SHANDY GAFF. A drink consisting of equal parts of ginger-beer and ale.

SHARK'S FINS. When sold in this country this commodity has a seaweed-like appearance. It is a delicacy much esteemed in China. For culinary purposes the fins are par-boiled, then stripped of skin, bone, etc., after which the remaining soft yellow cartilage is dried. Cooking makes the fins tender and gelatinous, so that they absorb the flavour of the foods cooked with them.

SHASHLIK. Food — frequently lamb or chicken flesh — cooked on skewers and mostly served with rice. See also *Kebabs.*

SHCHI. The Russian national soup — made with fresh cabbage.

SHEEP'S MILK. A milk containing a higher percentage of fat and sugar than cow's milk. Used in the manufacture of several French cheeses such as roquefort, cachat, etc.

SHEPHERD'S PIE. A meat pie with a potato crust, prepared from par-cooked meat or leftovers from a roast or boiled joint minced and moistened with gravy or stock.

SHERBET. A beverage of the East consisting of scented, spiced fruit drinks. In England it is interpreted as a cooling drink consisting of water, tartaric acid, lemon juice and sugar. In America the term is given to flavoured water ices from whence we get our 'sorbet'.   (See recipes)

SHERRY. A wine made from white grapes grown in the Jerez district in the South of Spain.

SHERRY COBBLER. An American long drink made with sherry, soda-water, a dash of liqueur, sugar and a little ice.

SHIN OF BEEF. Forepart of the leg of beef. Because of its very gelatinous nature it is used extensively in the making of broths, consommés, etc.

SHIRR. To break eggs into a dish which has been greased and sprinkled with crumbs.

SHORTENING. An edible fat used in pastry and cake-making, etc.

SHOT PEPPER. Mignonette peppercorns processed into granules the size of a mignonette seed.

SHRED. To slice very thinly.

SHREWSBURY BISCUITS (CAKES). A crisp biscuit-like flat cake.
(See recipe)

SHRIMP. A small sea crustacean. There are several varieties, the best known being the brown and red shrimps. The brown shrimp is considered the better-flavoured of the two.   (See recipes)

SILLSILLAT. A Swedish dish consisting of pickled herring.

SILVERSIDE. A joint of beef which is usually pickled in brine. The joint is cut from the top of the round of beef. It takes its name from that tissue on part of its side which has a silvery sheen.   (See recipe)

SIMMER. To cook in liquid just under boiling point. The surface should be just 'trembling'. (About 185° F.)

SIMNEL CAKE. An Easter cake. Usually the ingredients include mixed fruits and spices, and the cooked cake is given an almond paste crust round the sides and top edges, with a pool of pale green icing in the middle. The decorations usually include fluffy imitation chicks and imitation speckled eggs. Sometimes this cake is also given a layer of almond paste inside.   (See recipes)

SINGE, TO. The operation of holding poultry (after plucking) over a smokeless flame to shrivel off remaining down and fine hairs.

SIPPETS. Small cut-outs of bread, sometimes fried in hot fat, or toasted. Used as a garnish with savoury dishes, soups, etc.

SIRLOIN. Name given to a loin of beef. French chefs claim that the name was derived from the French *surlonge,* but the term 'Sir Loin' was in vogue in England in the time of Henry VIII, who, it is said, bestowed the title on this his favourite joint.

SIROP. Fruit or flavoured liquids cooked with sugar to a syrup.

SKATE. A large flat fish of which there are three varieties — the long-nosed, flapper, and grey skates, the latter being the best known. Rarely seen whole — usually cut in pieces for sale. At their best in April, but available before and after.   (See recipe)

SKEWERS. Sometimes referred to as brochettes or hatelets, chiefly used for holding meat in shape while cooking. Metal skewers — especially aluminium ones — are heat conductors and said to assist in getting the heat to the centre of the meat. Some skewers are made of wood.

SKILLET. A medium deep frying-pan type of cooking vessel with a lid.

SKILLY. A thin watery porridge or gruel; the term was once given by paupers in workhouses to this type of food.

SKIMMED MILK. Milk left after it has been skimmed of its cream.

SKINK. A Scottish term for a strong beef soup.

SKINKLADA. A Swedish ham omelette.

SLAPJACK. See *Flap jacks.*

SLAW. See *Cole slaw.*

SLING. The name given to a number of alcoholic beverages composed of spirits and sliced orange or lemon, or to rum or gin and sugar to which a little water ice is added.

SLY CAKES, CORNISH. See *Cornish sly cake.*

SLOE. Fruit of the blackthorn, small and dark purple in colour with a very tart flavour, sometimes used for making liqueurs. In this country used quite extensively for sloe gin and sloe wine.   (See recipes)

SMELT. In Scotland known as spurling or sparling. A small fish with a characteristic cucumber smell. At their best from September to March. Coat in egg and crumbs, cook in deep fat, and serve with lemon.
                                                            (See recipe)

SMOKED. Foods pickled and cured in wood chip smoke to give added flavour after the brining process. Foods treated in this way are Findon haddock, salmon, kippers, pork, etc.

SMORGASBORD. A Swedish form of hors-d'œuvres.

SMORREBROD. Danish type sandwiches. An open sandwich consisting of one slice of Vienna bread topped with an assortment of delicacies, meat, fish, vegetables, etc., like a salad.

SNAILS. Edible snails are regarded as a delicacy in France where they are known as *escargots*, the best variety being the Burgundy White. The flavour of snails is somewhat similar to oysters.

SNAPDRAGONS. A Yuletide game of snatching raisins from a dish of blazing spirit — rum or brandy.

SNIPE. A class of small game bird which includes the common snipe, pin-tailed snipe, great snipe, jack snipe, red-breasted snipe, etc. Much esteemed from both the gastronomic and sporting point of view. They should be cooked and eaten whilst young and fresh-killed. Usually cooked without being drawn — roasting time being about 15—20 min.

SNOEK. A fish very common in Australia and New Zealand where it is known as the barracouta. Rarely heard of in this country until the post war period of World War II.

SNOW EGGS. Whites of eggs whipped very stiffly with sugar and poached in milk — to be shaped, if possible, like small birds.   (See recipe)

SODA. From bi-carbonate of soda, a by-product of washing-soda.

SODA WATER. Aerated distilled water to which purified filtered air has been added to improve the flavour.

SOLE. The real sole is called Dover sole — not to be confused with lemon sole, megrims, witches, etc., which are sometimes offered when the real sole is not available.
    Dover sole has a uniformly dark surface with white underside, and is of a flat long oval shape. Available almost all the year round, but not at its best during February and beginning of March. (See recipes)

SOLE BONNE FEMME. One of the best-known methods of cooking sole.
(See recipe)

SOLE VERONIQUE. Sole fillets cooked similarly to Sole Bonne Femme, with grapes for garnish.

SORBET. A deliciously flavoured fluffy white water-ice. See also *Sherbert*. An iced Turkish drink is also called sorbet.

SORREL. A perennial herb with an acidulous flavour sometimes used for flavouring soups and adding to salads. Not in general use in this country.

SOUBISE. Dishes à la Soubise usually have a strong onion flavour. Sauce Soubise is a smooth onion sauce mixed with cream sauce. A noted epicure, Prince Charles Soubise, gave his name to many dishes having onions in their composition.

SOUFFLE. A very light baked or steamed pudding. The term is also sometimes applied to a fluffy sweet cream mixture served in soufflé cases.   (See recipes)

SOULT. A South African dish — pigs' trotters cooked, then steeped in a marinade for some days, and eaten cold.

SOUP. A savoury liquid consisting of water in which meat, poultry, game, fish, vegetables — even fruits sometimes — are stewed to extract their flavour and goodness.   (See recipes)

SOUR. Acid or sharp. The word may also be applied to foods which have fermented or gone bad through long keeping.

SOUSING. A process of pickling food, usually in a brine or pickling vinegar.

SOY. Soy sauce is a dark brown extract of soy beans and pulverised roasted wheat, with other ingredients. Used with caution, this sauce imparts an agreeable flavour and improves the colour of such dishes as soups, stews, gravies and sauces.

SOY (SOYA) BEANS. Next to rice these beans form one of the main foods in China, Japan and other parts of Asia. They are a good source of vitamins A, B and C, and owing to their nutritive value and similar protein composition can take the place of meat. Because of their lack of starch, soya beans are suitable for diabetics.

SPAGHETTI. An Italian paste — finer than macaroni, coarser than vermicelli. The thin lengths are solid, not hollow like macaroni.

SPANISH JUICE. See Liquorice.

SPARE RIB OF PORK. A term applied to the ribs of pork when separated from the side of the back. There is not much meat on the spare rib which probably accounts for the supposed origin of the name in olden times, when 'spare a rib' was the poor man's cry at farmsteads at pig-killing time.

SPARROWGRASS. A corruption of the word 'asparagus'.

SPATCHCOCK. A corruption of 'dispatched cock' — a survival of the days when cock-fighting was fashionable and the cock killed at the fight was often roasted on the spot for the assembled guests. Nowadays, any small poultry or game bird split and flattened in similar fashion for grilling or frying bears the term 'à la Crapaudine'.

SPATULA. A broad-bladed knife, or flat wooden spoon. Generally used for spreading icing or soft substances, or for lifting fragile food from one place to another.

SPEARMINT. A species of mint used mainly for the manufacture of chewing gum, medicines and some culinary purposes.

SPECK. Bacon.

SPELT. A coarse European wheat mainly used for cattle food.

SPICE. Aromatic condiment used whole, ground into paste or used in liquid form. For flavouring dishes.

SPINACH. A leafy green vegetable considered to have certain medicinal qualities and highly regarded in other ways. Needs to be well washed to rid leaves of sand and grit. In cooking it requires no more water than remains on the leaves after washing. Cooks in about 7—10 min.

SPIRIT. An alcoholic liquid obtained by distillation of various fermented liquors.

SPIT. An iron prong (fitted with a device to ensure that it constantly revolves) upon which meat is roasted in front of an open fire.

SPONGE CAKE. Cakes made from well-whisked eggs, sugar and flour. No fats are added, as this would make a closer texture.

SPRAT. A small silvery cheap fish of the same family as the herring. It has a short season — October to March.

SPRING OF PORK. A thin flank or breast and belly.

SPROUTS, BRUSSELS. See *Brussels sprouts.*

SPRUCE BEER. Beer infused with the tips of the spruce fir and various spices.

SQUAB. A word applied to young chickens small enough for individual servings. On the menu the birds are usually termed poussins. In America the term is applied to young pigeons which are at their best when about 4 weeks old.

SQUAB PIE. A Devonshire dish, usually composed of young pigeons with the addition of apples under a crust.

SQUARE FACE. Hollands gin. See also *Schnapps.*

SQUASH. A term given to a variety of gourds of all shapes and sizes, the most common being the vegetable-marrows and pumpkins. The term also applies to juices extracted from citrus fruits.

SQUID (CUTTLEFISH). This sea creature has a bell-shaped body with tentacles. Rarely seen near our shores. It can be cut up (both body and tentacles) and given the same preparation for cooking as skate, i. e. cut in conveniently sized pieces, coated with egg and crumbs and fried — never boiled.

SQUIRREL. As a food the flesh of squirrels is not much in demand in England, though when young it is tender, with a flavour similar to that of wild rabbit.

STABILISER. A substance added to manufactured foods to check crystallisation and to give firmness — e. g. frozen ice-cream often contains gelatine or gum tragacanth.

STARCH. The best known edible forms of starch are those obtained from corn, wheat, barley, rice, potatoes and arrowroot. Pure starch is a glistening white powder with a characteristic texture when rubbed between the fingers.
Starch is used extensively as a thickening agent, as when heated with liquids it swells; it is also used for other domestic purposes — e. g. stiffening flimsy fabrics, etc.

STEAK. A slice or cut of meat or fish. As applied to meat it usually means a slice from a choice part of the animal. Thick fish (such as cod, hake and so on) are cut in slices known as steaks or cutlets.

STEAMING. A slower process than boiling, carried out in a large vessel with two and sometimes three compartments. The lower one contains water and the upper vessels contain food. Steam from the bottom vessel passes up to the other compartments by way of tubes or perforations. Alternatively, if a vessel is large enough, a pudding may be steamed by standing it in a pan containing boiling water rising no more than halfway up the basin lowered into it.

STEEP. To soak in liquid.

STERILISE. A method of destroying micro-organisms by boiling or steaming, as in a pressure-cooker or similar process.

STERLET. A small sturgeon seldom seen in this country. The finest golden caviar comes from its roe.

STEWED. Cooked by simmering in liquid.

STILL. An apparatus for distillation of spirits in which the alcoholic liquid is separated from all or part of its water content by vaporisation.

STILTON. A popular cheese which takes its name from Stilton, a village on the Great North Road. It is said that the first Stilton cheese was made by a Miss Elizabeth Scarbrow at the Angel Inn.

STIRABOUT. An Irish dish similar to porridge.

STOCK. A liquid in which meat, poultry, bones or fish have been boiled, and from which soups and sauces are made.   (See recipes)

STORING FOODS.

>   *Flour.* Not more than 3 months, as it is subject to attack by tiny weevils or mites. Keep in a tin canister. Must be kept very dry, especially self-raising flour.
>
>   *Cereals, such as beans, peas, barley, lentils, rice, sago, etc., macaroni, spaghetti.* About 6 months if kept very dry, otherwise they become rancid and have weevils, especially sago.
>
>   *Oatmeal.* Not more than 3 months.
>
>   *Sugars.* Indefinitely if kept very dry, otherwise they become hard and lumpy.
>
>   *Syrups.* Golden syrup and treacle for at least a year, in a cool place.
>
>   *Honey.* Will keep, but becomes crystallised after about a year.
>
>   *Dried Fruits.* About 3 months in a moderate temperature, otherwise they ferment. Best kept in wood boxes so that they may 'breathe'.
>
>   *Packet goods, custard powders, breakfast cereals, etc.* About 3—6 months in a cool, dry place.
>
>   *Tinned goods.*

Fruits	About 1 year
Honey and jam in tins	About 3 years
Vegetables	About 2 years
Fish and meat	About 3 years
Ham	About 6 months
Unsweetened evaporated milk	About 3 years
Sweetened condensed milk	6—9 months, after which it may turn solid and sugary.

>   *Tea.* Indefinitely, but it gradually loses its flavour.
>
>   *Cocoa.* In tins 12 months, after which it may be lumpy and flavourless.
>
>   *Coffee.* Loses all flavour after a week.
>
>   *Fish and meat pastes in glass containers.* From 1—2 years in a cool place.
>
>   *Tinned soup.* Up to 3 years.

STOVE. A cooking appliance.

STRAWBERRY. A popular soft fleshy red fruit with an exquisite flavour. Esteemed as a dessert and for preserving as a jam.   (See recipe)

STUFFING. A name given to all forms of forcemeat for filling poultry, fish, certain joints of meat after boning, vegetables, etc.   (See recipes)

STURGEON. A large fish of fine flavour, usually found in the Caspian, Black, Baltic and Mediterranean seas. Regarded as a royal fish, and if caught round the shores of this country was once considered the property of the crown. The roe is made into caviar. The flesh is supposed to resemble veal. In season from September to March.

SUCCOTASH. An American dish composed of green corn and lima beans.

SUCCULENT. Juicy.

SUCKING PIG. An unweaned pig.

SUGAR. A substance obtained from various plants, such as sugar beet, sugar cane, the maple, corn, etc. The most common forms produced are loaf (lump), granulated, castor and powdered (icing) sugars. Other kinds include Barbados, Demerara, coffee crystals (sometimes white and sometimes multicoloured), etc.

SUGAR MELON. A variety of cantaloup melon with a grey ribbed skin and very sweet juicy flesh.

SUISSE, A LA. In Swiss style. Often used when describing a variety of iced pudding or shape served with a sponge-cake base.

SUKI YAKI. Name of a Japanese beef stew containing such other items as bamboo sprouts, bean curd and Japanese curry. Usually served with rice.

SULTANAS. Small, seedless sun-dried grapes. Some of the best come from Australia and Turkey. The pale golden ones from California are sulphur-bleached, giving a better appearance than flavour.

SUMMER PUDDING. An uncooked pudding compounded of bread slices and stewed fruit.   (See recipe)

SUNDAES. A variety of fancy ice-cream, usually served with fruits, sweet sauces and syrups, and sometimes sprinkled with chopped nuts.

SUPPE. Soup.

SUPREME SAUCE. A richly flavoured cream sauce made from chicken stock well reduced by boiling, to which cream is added.

SURLOIN. See *Sirloin.*

SWEDE. A large root vegetable with a flavour resembling turnip, but stronger. Its flesh is a yellowish colour.

SWEETBREADS. The thymus and pancreas glands of a calf, lamb or other animal used for food. The glands are divided into 'throat sweetbread' and 'heart sweetbread'. Easily digested and of a delicate flavour. Can be purchased fresh or frozen.   (See recipes)

SWEET HERBS. A term describing culinary herbs such as basil, mint, marjoram, parsley, sage, thyme, etc. Where a recipe recommends a *bouquet garni* this is understood to refer to 2 or 3 sprigs of parsley, 1 or 2 sprigs of thyme and 1 bay leaf, tied together for easy removal during or after cooking.

SWEET PAPRIKA. See *Paprika.*

SWEETMEAT. Usually means confectionery consisting principally of sugar; a bon-bon; a fruit coated with sugar, etc.

SWEET POTATOES (BATATA). A tuber cultivated in South America, New Zealand and the tropics. Recently imported to this country in small quantities. The appearance is that of an old potato; the flesh is tender and sweet. It is served boiled and mashed or sliced, roasted in hot ashes, or sliced and fried. May also be grated and cooked with milk and spices.

SYLLABUB. A dish made by blending wine or cider with cream or milk, producing a light, frothy appearance. There are several versions, but a popular one is made by flavouring sweetened half-whipped cream with rum. Less rich is the one using unseparated fresh milk with sherry or brandy to taste and a dash of grated nutmeg.

TABLE D'HOTE. A general term for a meal consisting of several courses at a fixed inclusive price.

TABLE WATERS. Bottled natural or mineral waters.

TAGLIARINI. An Italian paste that is cut into thin strips of about a third of the width of ordinary noodle strips.

TAGLIATI. A type of noodle paste that is cut into irregular extremely thin pieces.

TALMOUSE. Individual pastry-like soufflés served as a sweet or savoury course.

TAMALE. A Mexican dish consisting of scalded cereal or grain, a little chopped meat, sweet red peppers and garlic. It is wrapped in a securely fastened plantain leaf, and boiled.

TAMARA. A form of Italian curry powder which is composed of crushed cloves, aniseed, cinnamon, coriander seed and fennel.

TAMARIND. The fruit of a tropical plant, a plump brown pod several inches long and about an inch wide, the pulp of which is edible, being acid yet sweet in flavour. Used for sauce-making, condiments, etc.

TAMMY. A cloth used for straining liquids — sauces, soups, etc. — refining them more completely than in putting them through even a fine sieve. Tammy is sometimes made of fine linen, flannel or felt, and should be scalded before use.

TANGELO. A cross between a tangerine and a grapefruit.

TANGERINE. A small citrus fruit with orange-like segments, usually with a lot of pips.

TANSY. A perennial herb with a strong aromatic flavour, used as a flavouring, though not so much nowadays as formerly.

TAPIOCA. A farinaceous food substance obtained by a heating process which extracts starch from the roots of the cassava (manioc plant). During the process the granules burst into irregular pieces, which are then baked to extract the remaining moisture. These pieces are known as flake tapioca, which is used extensively for making milk puddings. This is an easily digested food, suitable for invalids and children.

TARRAGON. An aromatic herb with leaves of a pungent flavour. Much used for flavouring vinegar, sauces, mustard, etc.

TARRAGON SAUCE. Espagnole sauce (see recipe) with chopped tarragon.

TARRAGON VINEGAR. An infusion of tarragon leaves with white wine vinegar, though malt vinegar may also be used.

TARTARE. A sauce made from yolks of eggs, oil, chopped gherkins, capers, mustard, etc. Served with fish, cold meats, and as a salad dressing.

TARTLETS. Small tarts. Small cup-like circles of pastry usually filled with fruit, custard, etc.

TASSE. Cup. Demi-tasse is a term for a half-cup, usually coffee.

TEA. A beverage first introduced into this country about 1660, when it was very costly. The difference between black and green tea lies in the method of drying the leaves, all of which may have been picked from the same plant. Tea is extensively cultivated in Ceylon, India, Assam and China.

TEAL. A water-fowl of the duck family. A full-sized bird is sufficient for only two portions. The flesh has a delicate flavour and is at its best from November to January. Usually roasted.

TENCH. A fresh-water fish similar to carp, but smaller. It seldom weighs more than 4—5 lbs. To scale, put fish into boiling water for about 30 seconds. In season from October to May.

TENDERLOIN. Tender meat found under the loin of pork or mutton — much smaller in younger animals.

TENDON. Gristle; cord of tissue forming a connection in the fleshy part of a muscle.

TERRAPIN. Small American turtle used for soups. The female is the only one used for food. It is distinguished by a diamond-shaped marking on its shell.

TERRINE. A china or earthenware pot or jar used for pâtés and similar savoury mixtures.

TETRAS. French grouse; prairie chicken.

THERMOMETER. Instrument for ascertaining degrees of temperature.

THICKENING. A term used in cookery to indicate the inclusion of a farinaceous substance to thicken liquids. *Liaison* is a French term signifying a similar process.

THYME. A low-growing plant cultivated for its fragrant leaves, which are used for flavouring. Usually found in a *bouquet garni* — a bunch of herbs. There are several varieties. The lemon thyme, having a delicate lemon flavour, is used for veal and poultry stuffings.

TIFFIN. A mid-morning refreshment. The word originated among Anglo-Indians.

TIMBALE. Thimble-shaped moulds of savoury foods.

TOAD-IN-THE-HOLE. Sausages or pieces of meat baked in a batter. It is believed that the dish originated by accident. A cook was preparing a batter pudding and placed it at one end of the table where some cutlets were being chopped. One of the chops fell into the batter unnoticed and was cooked in it. The resulting dish was found to be so appetising that it was repeated intentionally. It is now a popular and typically English dish, and the batter can contain almost any kind of meat.   (See recipe)

TOAST. Slices of bread browned on each side under direct heat. The term also applies to the browning of other food by direct heat.

TOBASCO. The name of a pungent sauce used extensively in hot climates. In recent years the sauce has also become more widely used here for such purposes as 'pepping up' other sauces, tomato-juice cocktails, etc.

TODDY. A type of rum punch.

TOFFEE. A hard-boiled sugar syrup, said to have been first made in Lancashire.   (See recipes)

TOKAY. A sweet Hungarian wine of long keeping. When fully matured, it is said that Tokay still remains unchanged for a hundred years. Made from Hungarian blue grapes.

TOMATOES. Sometimes called Love Apples. Introduced into Europe by the Spaniards, there are now many varieties ranging from the small currant tomato to large specimens weighing up to a pound. Tomatoes have low food value, but are popular because of their piquant flavour and bright colour.   (See recipes)

TONGUE. A popular meat delicacy, classed as 'offal'. Canned tongues are usually those of the sheep or ox.

TONIC WATER. Carbonated table water containing quinine. Popular as an addition to gin to make a long drink.

TONKA BEAN. Seed pod with an aroma similar to the vanilla bean, used extensively for cheaper imitation vanilla essences.

TORBAY SOLE. Another name for lemon sole.

TORTE. An open tart baked in a round shallow tin.

TORTILLAS. Thin Mexican bread-cakes made from manioc flour or yucca. Consumed as a form of bread.

TOT. A small liquid measure.

TOURNEDOS. Small thin pieces of tender steak, usually cut from the tenderloin. The pieces are cut thinner than for filet mignon, for quick cooking.

TREACLE. A thick dark syrup formed during the manufacture of cane or moist sugar. In food value it is similar to sugar. Sometimes called molasses.

TRIFLE. A sweet-course dish composed of sponge cake sandwiched with jam and soaked in wine — usually sherry — and interleaved with ratafias and topped with whipped cream. Sometimes decorated with nuts, glacé cherries and pieces of angelica, etc.   (See recipe)

TRIPE. The inner lining of the cow or ox. The best parts are called 'blanket', 'honeycomb' and 'monkshood', the latter being darker than the others. When cooked, tripe is easily digested, and the dish is regarded as having good nourishing properties.   (See recipe)

TROUT. A much esteemed fresh-water fish — in season from February to September. At its best in August.   (See recipe)

TRUFFLE. A variety of fungus which grows in clusters underground usually under the roots of young trees such as the oak. These fungi of irregular globule form are much sought after for their excellent flavour — their black colouring makes an effective garnish, too.

TRUITE AU BLEU. Trout plainly cooked, the essential point being that the fish must be alive when it reaches the kitchen, for all its natural beauties to be retained.

TRUSS. To secure the wings and legs of birds to the body by means of skewers and string in order to preserve the shape during the process of cooking.

TUNNY FISH. Similar in shape to the mackerel, this fish is of a pale red colour, but smaller than salmon. Found mostly round the Mediterranean coast.

TURBOT. A choice fish in much demand on account of its excellent flavour. Available all the year round, but best during the summer months. Usually grilled or boiled.

TURKEY. A large species of domestic fowl introduced from North America. Norfolk birds are considered the best, but many imported ones are excellent and so are those bred in this country elsewhere than Norfolk. Once regarded as a Christmas-season food, but now available all the year round. Young birds have the best flavour. They can be recognised by the blackness and smoothness of their legs.

TURKEY POULT. A young turkey.

TURKISH DELIGHT. Also called *rahat lakoum*. A jelly-like sweetmeat of Turkish origin. The real Turkish delight often has nuts and preserved fruits in it.   (See recipe)

TURMERIC. An aromatic root stock of a plant grown in India and Southern Asia. Sold in powder form, it is used as a food flavouring and is the principal ingredient of curry powder.

TURNIP. A white round root vegetable with a pronounced flavour. Low in food value, being about 90% water, but mineral content good.

TURNIP TOPS. The young leaves of the turnip. May be cooked as a vegetable, though the flavour is a little pungent and slightly bitter.

TURNSPIT. A revolving spit for cooking meat, poultry or game birds, used in olden times before the introduction of modern gas and electric ovens.

TURTLE, SEA. Edible tortoise. The green turtle is most highly prized as a food delicacy, being used for the famous turtle soup and other dishes.   (See recipe)

TUTTI-FRUTTI. An Italian term applied to fruit and vegetables (mostly fruit) cut into small dice.

TWELFTH CAKE. A large cake made for Twelfth Night celebrations.

UCHA. A Russian fish soup.

ULLAGE. A cask or bottle which has become defective and lost some of its contents.

UMBRE. Grayling. A fresh-water fish resembling trout.

VACUUM-PACKED. A term used to describe the method of packing in cans from which the air is extracted and which are then hermetically sealed.

VAN DER HUM. A South African liqueur which obtains its flavour from tangerines. Similar in flavour to Curaçao.

VANILLA. The fruit, in the form of a bean, of a fragrant plant of the orchid family. The bean can be used whole for flavouring sweet milky dishes, removed after sufficient flavour has been imparted, and saved for another occasion. A flavouring in general use for cakes, icings, etc., the essence being a more convenient form of flavouring for these.

VEAL. Flesh of the calf. It should be pink and firm with the fat (of which there is very little) clear and white. Cooking takes a little longer than for beef, as veal must be well cooked.   (See recipes)

VEGETABLE MARROW. A variety of squash. At its best when quickly grown — 12—14 inches in length and 6—7 inches in diameter. Cut when very small vegetable marrows are known as 'courgettes' and are a delicacy. Avoid over-cooking.

VELOUTE. One of the four 'mother' sauces which form the basis of all others. It has a smooth velvety texture and is made from reduced chicken stock to which cream has been added.   (See recipe)

VENISON. Flesh of all kinds of deer. The best joint for cooking is the haunch, or hind quarter. Leg and loin are also good. Other edible parts are suitable for pies and casseroles, etc.

VERJUICE. The extracted juice of unripe fruit which flows with a green tint.

VERMICELLI. Thin threads of Italian paste, formed by the dough being forced through cylinders or pipes. It is then dried and used for various dishes — puddings, soups, etc.

VERMOUTH. The two principal Vermouths are from Italy and France. French Vermouth is drier than Italian. Italian Vermouth is a white wine with tonic properties and is infused with certain aromatic herbs. French Vermouth, cheaper, is infused with camomile flowers.

VICHY WATER. A mineral water from the springs of Vichy, a French watering-place. Vichy is a name also given to a style of garnish, using sliced carrots cooked in cream.

VINO. Wine.

VIN BLANC. White wine.

VIN ROUGE. Red wine.

VINAIGRETTE. A salad dressing of vinegar, oil, pepper, salt and herbs.

VINEGAR. Made from malt, wine and cider by a process whereby acetic acid is produced extensively in cookery, assisting in softening the fibres of tough meat, in the composition of many sauces and pickles etc. Vinegar is also an antiseptic; in small quantities it helps to promote digestion by stimulating the digestive organs to greater activity. Harmful if taken to excess.

VITAMINS. Food elements necessary to the maintenance of life. Found in animal fats and tissues, liver, kidney, butter and cream, fruits, and in various forms in plant life. Vitamin A is found in animal fats, fish oils and green leafy vegetables, etc.; vitamin B in cereals, fruits, nuts, animal tissues, etc.; vitamin C in most fresh vegetables and citrus fruits; vitamin D in fish liver oils (cod-liver oil, halibut oil, etc.), fat fish, liver, oysters — and sunshine, which causes vitamin D to be formed in the oils of the skin. Vitamin E is found in most types of food, especially in wheat, corn, peanut and soya bean oils, and occurs also in salad plants (watercress, lettuce, mustard-and-cress), carrots, tomatoes, eggs yolks and nuts. In most kinds of food other known vitamins are present in varying degrees and natural foods ensure the reasonable certainty of our getting at least some of these vital elements. (See also under *Foods.)*

VITELLIN. The chief protein in egg yolk.

VODKA. A potent spirit mostly distilled in Russia, where it is the national drink. At one time distilled from wheat and rye, but now mostly from potatoes. The spirit is colourless and practically flavourless; as a drink it is usually swallowed at one gulp.

VOLAILLE. A term covering all kinds of poultry.

VOL-AU-VENT. A rich savoury mixture (poultry, shellfish, mushrooms, etc.), served in a puff pastry case.

WAFERS. Especially thin light biscuits, usually sweetened. They are made in oblong and cone shapes for serving with ice-cream. Further varieties of shape and thickness (for some are sandwiched together with a soft filling like butter-cream) are marketed by various biscuit manufacturers whose recipes are a professional secret. A common variety is a rice mixture baked in wafer-irons.

WAFFLES. A light spongy batter mixture baked between two electrically heated honeycomb-patterned metal plates until puffed up and golden brown. May be served with different types of food — with eggs, ham, sausages, etc., for breakfast or snack meals, or as a dessert with syrup, clear honey or chocolate sauce, etc.   (See recipe)

WALEWSKA. A style of fish garnish consisting of sliced lobster and truffles cooked in white wine. So named after a Polish lady of rank.

WALNUT. A brown-shelled nut which has a green husk when growing. If picked before July, the intact 'fruit' can be pickled. If left to ripen on the tree the shells harden. The shelled nuts can be served with fruit as a dessert, or used for general culinary purposes.   (See recipes)

WASSAIL BOWL. A spiced beverage that at one time was served specially to carol singers on Christmas Eve, as well as used on other festive occasions. It was usually composed of strong ale, roasted apples, nutmeg, ginger and other spices in agreeable proportions.

WATER. A transparent fluid essential to life. It is composed of oxygen and hydrogen.

WATER CHESTNUT. A chestnut-like tuber popular in oriental cookery. Eaten uncooked, or may be cooked in dishes like ordinary chestnuts.

WATERCRESS. A semi-aquatic plant rich in mineral salts and vitamins A, B, C and G. There are three varieties — the green-leafed, the small brown-leafed and the large brown-leafed. Originally found growing wild, it has since been cultivated. It has a slightly pungent flavour and is popular as a salad vegetable.   (See recipe)

WATER MELON. See also *Melon*. A kind of sweet gourd of which there are many sizes and shapes. The rind is rather thick and varies in colour from dark to light green, but is sometimes striped. When ripe it is sweet and juicy. Low nutritive value.

WEDDING CAKE. A rich dark cake with decorations in sugar work. Has its origin in the Roman form of marriage, when a simple cake made of flour, salt and water and the holding by the bride of three wheat ears were symbolical of plenty. Subsequent years brought a change in the cakes, which became richer, until to-day we have cakes both rich and artistically iced and decorated. Most wedding cakes are coated with the traditional white icing, but with second and even subsequent marriages, pastel shades are in some demand.

WELSH RAREBIT (RABBIT). A slice of toast covered with melted cheese sauce composed of grated cheese heated with a little beer, with added seasonings including mustard. Sometimes the coated toast is slipped back under the grill to brown appetisingly. A buck rarebit has a poached egg on top.   (See recipe)

WENSLEYDALE CHEESE. A subtly-flavoured cheese made in the valley of Wensleydale.

WETHER. A castrated ram.

WHALE MEAT. 'Sea beef' is another name. Flesh of the whale — a mammal — usually bought in frozen condition, in which it should be kept until required for cooking. When thawed out, it develops a fishy taste. This can be counteracted to some extent by steeping in a solution of bi-carbonate of soda. If casseroled, the flavour resembles beef.
                                                                (See recipes)

WHEAT. An annual cereal grass cultivated for its grain which is ground into flour for making bread. Next to rice it is the most widely used grain.

WHELK. A rather indigestible shell-fish about the size of a small egg. When caught alive, whelks should be well cleansed in several waters, then boiled in salted water for half an hour or so before removing them from the shells. Frequently they are eaten with a dressing of vinegar and seasonings, but they can also be coated with egg and crumbs and fried in deep fat.

WHEY. The watery part of milk that remains after the casein, etc., have formed curds and been separated. A pale chalky fluid, slightly sweet, which is quite pleasant to drink.

WHIPPED. Beaten or rapidly whisked. Liquid foods such as cream, eggs, partially set jelly, etc., are beaten or whisked rapidly to expand them, their bulk being increased by the injection of air.

WHISK. To agitate quickly — beat (eggs, etc.) — or the term can apply to the implement used for agitating or beating.

WHISKEY (WHISKY). Spelt 'whiskey' in Ireland, 'whisky' in Scotland. A potable spirit obtained by the distillation of the fermented extract of grain — usually barley, but also wheat, rye, etc. 'Bourbon' is an extract of maize.

WHITEBAIT. Smallest known edible fish — fry of the herring or related
families. A silvery fish resembling miniature herring, usually eaten
when about $1^1/_2$—2 in. long. Should be cooked in perfectly fresh
condition. Usually floured and fried crisply, then served with lemon
and brown bread-and-butter. Seasonable from January to September.
(See recipe)

WHITING. A delicately flavoured, easily digested fish, not unlike fresh
haddock in appearance. Seasonable most of the year, but at its best
from October to March.   (See recipes)

WHORTLEBERRY. Bilberry. A small dark edible berry found in various
parts of the country — usually on wooded hillsides — which is in
season towards the end of August and through September. Other names
given to this berry are worts, hurts, whinberries and blaeberries.
(See recipes)

WIDGEON. A small bird of the same family as the wild duck. Usually
roasted, taking about 20 min., basting well with butter or bacon
dripping. In season August to March.

WIENER SCHNITZEL. A favourite Viennese dish of veal cutlets.
(See recipe)

WILD BOAR. The flesh of this animal is considered finer than that
of the pig. In years gone by the head of a wild boar was cooked and
garnished and served as the *pièce de résistance* at the feast given after
each kill. The custom survives at some of the present-day banquets,
except that it is usually the domesticated boar's head that is now used.
It is in districts where the wild boar roams that truffles are found.
The boar roots under trees for them. His fondness for truffles probably
accounts for the esteemed characteristic flavour of his flesh.

WILD DUCK. Known also as the mallard. Requires quick roasting, so
that the outside becomes brown and crisp while the flesh remains
somewhat underdone and so that the juices run when the bird is
carved or divided (for one bird will serve only two persons). At its
best in November and December, but available for a few months both
before and after that time.

WILD RICE. A long thin greenish grain with a slightly smokey flavour
which is quite pleasant. Known in America as 'zizanie'. To cook, allow
a little longer than for polished rice.

WINDBERRY. See *Bilberry.*

WINE. Fermented juice of the grape.

WINKLE. See *Periwinkle.*

WINTERGREEN. A low-growing shrub with evergreen leaves from which
an oil is distilled that is used to relieve muscular pains, etc. It is also
used in confectionery. Its red double berries are said to have a
medicinal value, also, as a tonic.

WITCH SOLE. A flat fish similar to plaice or sole, though inferior in flavour to both. The white skin side has a noticeable roughness, and the other side is a very light brown. Cook as for plaice or sole.
(See recipes)

WOODCOCK. A game bird in high favour for its unusually good flavour. It should be cooked without being drawn, the trail being considered a delicacy. Allow 1 small bird per portion, or a larger bird for 2 portions.
(See recipe)

WOOD PIGEON. Similar for cooking purposes to the common dovecote pigeon, but should first be hung until tender. Year-old birds are usually roasted, older birds casseroled or put in a pie.

WORCESTER SAUCE. A dark pungent sauce with soy as its chief character ingredient. A useful ready-made sauce for many culinary purposes, especially for serving with chops, steaks, etc., as well as with fish.

WORMWOOD. A herb with bitter and tonic properties. Used with other aromatic herbs in the making of absinthe, vermouth, etc., also in certain medicines.

XAVIER. A clear soup named in honour of a Count Xavier of Saxony. Identifiable by its garnish of tiny cheese quenelles.

XERES. A full flavoured richly coloured Spanish sherry.

YAM. Edible tuber of a tropical climbing plant — similar in appearance to the sweet potato, but larger.

YEAST. Also called balm. Used in small quantities with flour to make bread dough. A minute plant or vegetable germ of the fungus family which warmth, moisture and a suitable soil — found in bread dough — will start into growth. In the process of growing carbonic acid is given off, which causes the bread to rise. The compressed yeast is the simplest to use, and when fresh (which it should be for best results) it is like a firm cream cheese, with the same moistness and tendency to crumble. Dried yeast can also be bought, but this requires soaking before use.

YOGHOURT. Cultured milk of custard-like consistency. Made from fresh pasteurized cow's milk, to which cultures are added. Action of the cultures ceases when yoghourt is cooked.

YORKSHIRE PUDDING. A baked batter — made with flour, eggs and milk — which should be light and moist-eating, with a golden brown crispness at the edges. Usually served with roast beef, but also with gravy, before the meat course.

YORKSHIRE RAREBIT. A Welsh rarebit topped with a slice of grilled bacon and a poached egg.

YUCCA. A type of flour from which tortillas (a form of Mexican bread) are made. See *Tortillas.*

YUETTE, CREME. A liqueur based on an extract of violets.

ZABAGLIONE (ZABAIONE). A rich Italian dessert, foamy, made with wine and eggs. Served in glasses and eaten with a spoon.

(See recipe)

ZAKUSKA. A Russian word meaning 'foretaste' — applied to hors-d'œuvres.

ZEST. The thin coloured oily outer skin of citrus fruits, particularly orange and lemon, which are frequently used for flavouring and colouring instead of commercial preparations.

ZITONI. The largest unfluted type of Italian macaroni. Zitoni Rigati is similar, but fluted.

ZIZANIE (ZIZANIA). Another name for wild rice (q. v.).

ZOOLAK. A fermented milk similar to Yoghourt.

ZUPPA. An Italian word meaning soup, e. g. *zuppa al brodo* — a fish soup garnished with sippets of toasted bread and cheese; *zuppa d'erbe* — a fresh greens soup poured into soup plates in which there is a slice of toast, then sprinkled with Parmesan cheese.

ZUURKOOL. Dutch sauerkraut.

ZWIEBACK. The German name for a kind of rusk made from a rich bread dough (ordinary bread dough to which butter and eggs have been added). Sometimes the rusks are sugar-coated.

PART II

RECIPES

COMPARISON OF
ENGLISH AND AMERICAN
WEIGHTS AND MEASURES

English weights and measures have been used throughout this book. In case it is wished to translate these into their American counterparts, the following table gives a comparison:

Liquid Measure

One pint of liquid may be regarded as equal to two American measuring cups for all practical purposes.

3 teaspoonfuls equal 1 tablespoonful.

16 tablespoonfuls equal 1 cup.

Solid Measure

English		American
1 pound	Butter	2 cups
1 pound	Flour	4 cups
1 pound	Granulated Sugar	2 cups
1 pound	Brown (Moist) Sugar	$2\frac{2}{3}$ cups
1 pound	Rice	2 cups
1 pound	Chopped Meat (finely packed)	2 cups
1 pound	Lentils or Split Peas	2 cups
1 pound	Coffee (unground)	$2\frac{1}{3}$ cups
$\frac{1}{2}$ ounce	Flour	1 level tbsp
1 ounce	Flour	1 heaped tbsp
1 ounce	Sugar	1 level tbsp
$\frac{1}{2}$ ounce	Butter	1 tbsp smoothed off

(Tbsp = tablespoonful)

TABLE OF EQUIVALENT OVEN HEATS
(classified according to the manufacturer)

	Slow	Moderate	Mod. Hot	Hot	Very Hot
Exact Temperature	250-325 350	375	400	425	450
Cannon (Autimo) / Parkinson (Adjusto)	3–4 4–5	5	6	7	8
Flavel with Nos. / Main with Nos. / G. L. C. / New Herald	4 5	6	7	8	9
Radiation (Regulo)	2 3	4	5	6	7
Flavel (Letter)	D–E F	G	G–H	H–I	I–J
Main (Letter)	C C–D	D–E	E	E–F	F–G

TABLE OF EQUIVALENT TEMPERATURES

Fahrenheit	Centigrade	Réaumur
212	100.0	80.0
200	93.3	74.6
176	80.0	64.0
167	75.0	60.0
150	65.5	52.4
122	50.0	40.0
100	37.7	30.2
86	30.0	24.0
65	18.3	14.6
32	00.0	00.0

COOKING TEMPERATURES

Simmering (water)	180º F.
Boiling (water)	212º F.
Very slow oven	250º F.
Slow oven	300º F.
Moderately slow oven	325º F.
Moderate oven	350º F.
Moderately hot oven	375º F.
Hot oven	400º F.
Very hot oven	450º–500º F.

ADAM AND EVE PUDDING

1 lb. apples, 6 oz. flour, 4 oz. butter or margarine, 4 oz. granulated sugar, 2 eggs, a little milk, 1 oz. extra sugar, 1 clove.

Peel, core and slice the apples and stew them with the ounce of sugar and clove until tender, but not pulpy.

Put them into a deep pie dish and cool them.

Cream together the 4 oz. sugar and fat, add the eggs and mix to a smooth thick cream. Fold in the sifted flour, add a tablespoonful or so of milk, spread the dough smoothly on top of the apples, sprinkle with a little more sugar and bake at Regulo 6 or 425⁰ F. for about 25—30 min.

Serve with cream or custard.

AILLADE

2 lb. shoulder or leg of veal, ¹/₄ lb. tomato purée or 1 lb. fresh tomatoes cooked and sieved, 2 tablespoonfuls of lard, 2 tablespoonfuls thick gravy, 1¹/₂ oz. garlic cloves, 1 dessertspoonful fine stale crumbs, salt and pepper.

Cut the meat into cubes, fry it in the heated lard until golden brown, add the crumbs, garlic, tomato and gravy. Season with pepper and salt, cover the pan closely and simmer very slowly for about 1¹/₄ hr. Shake the pan frequently. The garlic may be removed before dishing up if preferred. Serve with plain boiled rice.

AILLOLI

8 cloves of garlic, 4 tablespoonfuls olive oil, 2 egg yolks, juice of ¹/₂ lemon, pinch of salt.

Skin and pound the garlic and salt to a fine paste, add the slightly beaten eggs gradually to the paste, then slowly stir in the olive oil and lemon juice as if making mayonnaise. The sauce should be very thick. Serve with any fish, vegetable salad, potatoes in their jackets or potato salad.

ALMOND CAKES

8 oz. self-raising flour, 8 oz. ground almonds, 1 egg, 4 oz. margarine, 4 oz. castor sugar, 1 teaspoonful almond flavouring, a little milk.

Rub the margarine very finely into the flour, stir in the sugar and ground almonds. Beat the egg lightly with the almond flavouring and 4 tablespoonfuls of milk. Stir into the dry ingredients and mix to a creamy dough. Use a very little more milk if required.

Drop spoonfuls of the mixture into small paper cake cases or lightly greased patty pans, and bake at Regulo 6 or 425⁰ F. for about 15 min.

Sprinkle tops with finely chopped almonds.

ALMOND PASTE

See *Marzipan.*

ALMOND PETITS FOURS (ROUT CAKES)

8 oz. ground almonds, 8 oz. castor sugar, 1 egg yolk, 1 tablespoonful orange or rose water (obtainable from chemists), 1 egg white, blanched almonds, glacé cherries, halved walnuts, rice paper.

Mix almonds and sugar together, pour in the rose or orange water and egg yolk, and knead all to a soft dough.

Pat out on a board, to a thickness of about $3/4$ in., scatter with castor sugar, and cut into small rounds and diamonds.

Lift the shapes on to a baking tin upon which sheets of rice paper have been placed. Whisk the egg white until it is just liquid, brush the shapes over to glaze them and decorate with pieces of walnut, cherry, or almond. Put into a pre-heated oven at Regulo 3 or 350° F. and bake for about 15 min. to glaze the biscuits and just make the marzipan firm. When cool, snip round the rice paper tidily.

ALMONDS, SALTED

1 lb. almonds, $1/2$ pint olive oil, 4 tablespoonfuls fine salt; if liked, mix with the salt $1/4$ teaspoonful of cayenne pepper.

Blanch the almonds. Put the oil into a very clean, smooth, frying pan, make it very hot, and fry a handful of nuts at a time, until they are a golden brown colour. Take up the nuts with a slice, drain them well, turn on to greaseproof paper and dredge with the salt and pepper, turning them over and over, until they are evenly coated with salt. When cold, shake free of superfluous salt, and keep in a jar until ready to arrange in small dishes for the buffet or table.

While almonds are considered the best nuts for salting, halved walnuts and whole hazel nuts are also very good.

ALMOND SLICES

Rich short crust, 4 oz. castor sugar, 4 oz. icing sugar, 4 oz. ground almonds, 2 oz. finest semolina, 3 egg whites, 1 teaspoonful almond flavouring, a little raspberry jam.

Cut the short crust into strips $2^1/2$ in. wide, and in length to fit the baking tray. Flute the edges of the strips well to make troughs. Spread the bottoms of the troughs sparingly with raspberry jam.

Mix all the dry ingredients together, and stir to a soft paste with the unbeaten egg whites and the almond flavouring.

Half fill the slices with the mixture, and arrange slivers of blanched almonds on the top.

Bake at Regulo 5 or 400° F. until pastry is a light golden brown and the mixture risen. When cold, cut across into fingers and put away in an airtight tin.

ANGEL CAKE (American Version)

8 egg whites, 6 oz. castor sugar, 6 oz. self-raising flour sifted with 3 oz. cornflour.

Beat the egg whites until quite stiff. Fold in the castor sugar, then fold in the sifted flour and cornflour. If the mixture needs it, add a tablespoonful or so of cold water. The dough should be very light and soft.

Turn into a cake tin lined with greaseproof paper, preferably a real angel cake tin, with a tube running up the centre. Put into an oven which has been pre-heated for 20 min. at Regulo 3 or 350° F., then bake for about 1 hr. at the same temperature.

ANGEL CAKE (English Version)

4 oz. butter, 4 oz. castor sugar, 8 oz. arrowroot, $1/2$ teaspoonful baking powder, 3 well-whisked egg whites. $1/2$ teaspoonful vanilla in 1 tablespoonful warm water.

Beat the butter and sugar together until you have a thick, soft cream. Beat in the vanilla and water until thoroughly blended with the fat and sugar. Fold in the arrowroot, then finally, fold in the egg whites. Bake on the angel cake tin for about 45 min. at Regulo 4 or 375⁰ F.

ANGELS ON HORSEBACK

See *Oyster Savoury.*

APFELSTRUDEL

For the dough: *12 oz. best plain flour, 1 whole egg, 1 tablespoonful melted butter, pinch of salt, ¹/₄ pint lukewarm water or more as required.*

Make a well in the sifted flour, drop in the salt, whole egg and a little of the lukewarm water and work the flour into it with a knife, adding more water until dough is firmly knit and no longer sticky.

Put this dough on a floured board and work it well, then put aside in a warm place for an hour.

Cover the table with a linen cloth and dust it with flour. Put the ball of dough in the centre, then roll gently until it is as large and as thin as possible without stretching it into holes. It should be as thin as paper and almost transparent.

To make the strudel: Butter a large baking sheet, cut the dough into pieces, the width of the sheet, but longer. Make a mixture of apples and small breadcrumbs, sugar, sultanas and cinnamon, and spread it evenly on the strips. Roll up like a swiss roll, put the rolls sealed sides down on the tray. Seal the ends. Brush with melted butter and bake for about 45 min. at Regulo 3 or 350⁰ F. When cold, dust with icing sugar and cut in slices.

APPLE AMBER (APPLE MERINGUE)

1¹/₂ lb. good cooking apples, with 2 oz. butter and just enough water to prevent them from burning, and from 2—4 oz. sugar, according to taste.

Line a pie dish with good rich short crust.

Cook the apples until soft, and rub through a sieve.

If you do not wish to use a sieve, peel, core and slice the apples, then beat them to a foam with a fork until they are soft. Add the grated rind and strained juice of a lemon and the yolks of 2 eggs. Beat all together very well.

Pour the mixture into the lined pie dish and bake in a moderate oven at Regulo 5 or 400⁰ F. for 30 min. The pastry should be lightly browned round the edges and the mixture firm.

Whisk the whites of the two eggs very stiffly, fold in 2 oz. castor sugar, pile on top of the amber and bake in a cool oven for 20 min. to set and lightly brown the meringue. Serve hot or cold.

APPLE CAKE

8 oz. self-raising flour, 3 oz. margarine, 3 oz. sugar, 2 oz. sultanas, 1 teacupful stewed apples, well drained from juice, 1 level teaspoonful powdered cinnamon.

Cream the margarine and sugar together until creamy and light. Stir in the sultanas. Sift together the flour and cinnamon. Add this to the fat, sugar and sultana mixture a little at a time alternately with the apple. Mix gently to a soft dough, and put it into a greased cake tin.

Bake in a moderate oven for about an hour.

This cake is quite good without an egg, but you may add one, and in that case, use an extra 2 oz. flour.

APPLE CHARLOTTE

2 lb. good cooking apples, 4 oz. brown sugar, juice of half a lemon, 1 oz. margarine or butter if possible, thin slices of bread, oiled margarine or butter.

Peel, core and slice the apples, cook them to a pulp with the lemon juice (a clove could be substituted) and half the sugar. Stir in 1 oz. butter or margarine.

Take a plain mould and line it closely with thin slices of crustless bread dipped first in oiled margarine or butter and then sprinkled with brown sugar. Fill with the apple purée, cover the top closely with more bread dipped in oiled butter, sprinkle the top with the remaining brown sugar.

Bake in a moderate oven at Regulo 5 or 400° F. for about 30 min.

Note: Make sure that the pieces of bread overlap closely in the mould. or the apple will get through and spoil the crisp outside.

APPLE CHEESE OR BUTTER

4 lb. apples, sugar, 1—2 cloves, juice of 1 lemon.

Wipe the apples well, cut them up without peeling or coring, but taking away any bruised parts. Simmer the apples in a heavy preserving pan with only enough water to cover the bottom. Continue to cook until the apples are reduced and the juice has evaporated considerably.

Rub all through a sieve, and for every lb. pulp allow ¾ lb. sugar. Stir well together with the lemon juice and cloves. Boil gently until the preserve is very thick. Pot while very hot and cover when quite cold.

APPLE CHUTNEY

4 lb. windfall apples, 1 lb. onions, 1 lb. sultanas, 1 lb. soft brown sugar. 1 pint vinegar, 1 teaspoonful salt, 1 teaspoonful ground ginger, 1/2 teaspoonful black pepper, 1 clove of garlic.

Peel and core the apples, chop them roughly, peel and chop the onions and garlic. Cook the apples, onions, garlic and sultanas in the vinegar, until the apple and onions are tender. Add sugar, ginger, salt and pepper. Bring gently to the boil and boil until the chutney is thick and brown.

Pot while hot and be sure to fill the pots right to the tops.

APPLE DUMPLINGS

1 lb. short crust, 5 medium-sized apples, brown sugar, castor sugar and a little milk, cloves.

Peel and core the apples, roll the pastry to about ¼ in. thickness and cut it into the required number of equal-sized squares. Place an apple on each square, pack the centres closely with brown sugar, fold the pastry up round the apple and seal the edges firmly, so that no seams show, cutting off any superfluous paste. From the cuttings, make two small leaves to each dumpling and a small ball. Push a clove into each little ball and press one on top of each dumpling with two leaves.

Brush all over with milk and scatter with caster sugar. Bake at Regulo 7 or 450° F. for 10 min., then reduce to Regulo 5 or 400° F. for a further 20 min.

APPLE JAM

6 lb. apples, 4 oz. sugar, thinly pared rind of a small lemon or 2 cloves, 4—6 drops cochineal if liked, 1 pint water.

Wipe the apples with a damp cloth, cut them all up, remove any bruised or worm-eaten ones, do not peel or remove the cores.

Put the apple into the preserving pan with the water, and either the cloves or the lemon peel, according to preference.

Cook gently until the apple is reduced to pulp. Rub it all through a sieve, return it to the preserving pan, stir in the sugar, and boil moderately fast until a little of the jam will set when tested on a plate.

If you wish to give a faint pink tinge, add the colouring while the apple is boiling to a set.

APPLE JELLY

Choose apples of good flavour, or crab apples; windfalls may be used, provided that all the bruised or maggoty parts are cut away.

Having washed the apples, cut them into small pieces without peeling or removing the cores. Put them into a preserving pan with water, allowing 2 pints to 4 lb. of prepared fruit.

Simmer gently for 1 hr. Strain the juice through a jelly bag or 2 or 3 thicknesses of fine clean muslin. Measure the juice and for each pint, allow 1 lb. sugar. Put the sugar and juice into the preserving pan, stir well together until the sugar has melted, bring to the boil and boil moderately fast until a little of the jelly will set firmly on a cold plate when tested. Pot while hot, and cover when quite cold.

Note: Sometimes a plain apple jelly is rather flat in flavour. One may add 1 or 2 cloves, a strip of lemon peel, or the strained juice of a lemon if liked. A favourite country flavouring is scented geranium. Add 1 leaf to the fruit and water while it simmers, taste during the cooking time and remove the leaf when the required flavour is obtained. Some cooks also like to colour the jelly with a few drops of carmine colouring.

APPLE PIE

1/2 lb. short crust, 1¹/2 lb. good cooking apples, 1—2 cloves, brown or granulated sugar, milk and caster sugar for glazing.

Peel, core and slice the apples, and cook them in a very little water for 5—10 min. with the cloves. Drain thoroughly and arrange in layers in a pie dish round a pie funnel with sugar to taste, scattered among the fruit. Sugar should never be put on the top layer of fruit as its steam makes the pastry sodden.

Roll the crust a little larger than the top of the pie dish, cut thin strips and arrange them on the damped edge of the pie dish, and damp the strips. Take up the pastry on the rolling pin and roll it loosely over the top of the pie, taking care not to stretch it. Trim away superfluous paste, flute the edges of the pastry with thumb and spoon handle. Make little apples and leaves with the scraps of crust, brush all over with milk and scatter with caster sugar. Bake at Regulo 7 or 450° F. for 20 min., reduce heat to Regulo 5 or 400° F. for a further 10—15 min.

APPLE PUDDING

³/₄ lb. suet crust, 1¹/₂ lb. apples, brown or granulated sugar, 2 cloves, 2—3 tablespoonfuls hot water, lard or margarine.

Grease a 2 lb. pudding basin, line it with thinly rolled suet crust, leaving sufficient crust at the top to lap over to seal the pudding. Fill the basin closely with peeled, cored and sliced apples. Sprinkle generously with sugar between the slices and the 2 cloves hidden in the fruit. Fold the superfluous crust over the top and seal well. Cover with 2 layers of greaseproof paper, tie securely. Steam for 2 hr.

APPLE PUDDING, SWISS

1 lb. apples, ¹/₄ lb. breadcrumbs, 3 oz. sugar, 1 oz. suet, 1 oz. butter, grated rind of ¹/₂ lemon, about 2 tablespoonfuls crisped, browned breadcrumbs.

Cook the apples until tender, having prepared them as for a pie. Add half the sugar and the lemon rind.

Mix together the rest of the sugar with the 4 oz. crumbs and the suet. Grease a cake tin and coat it with the browned crumbs. Put a layer of the dry mixture in the bottom of the tin, fill with alternate layers of apple and crumb mixture, finishing with crumbs. Put the butter, cut into small pieces, on the top, bake at Regulo 7 or 450⁰ F. for 30 min. Turn out and serve with custard sauce.

APPLE SAUCE

1 lb. cooking apples, 1¹/₂ oz. sugar, 1 oz. butter, enough water to cover the bottom of the pan.

Peel and core the apples, cut them into small pieces, put them into the pan with the sugar and butter. Cover with the saucepan lid and simmer until reduced to a pulp. Rub through a sieve and re-heat as required.

APPLE WATER

Boil chopped apples or apple cores and peelings only with water. Strain, add sugar and lemon juice to taste.

A cooling drink in summer. In winter it may be served hot.

APRICOT JAM (FRESH)

4 lb. ripe, firm apricots, 4 lb. sugar, 2 level teaspoonfuls citric acid, ¹/₂ teacupful water, blanched kernels from the stones.

Slice and stone the apricots without skinning them. Put them into the preserving pan with the water, the kernels and the acid, and simmer very slowly until the fruit is tender.

Add the sugar, stir it well in, simmer again until the sugar has dissolved, then boil moderately fast until a little will set when tested on a cold plate.

Pot while hot, cover when cold.

APRICOT JAM USING DRIED APRICOTS

1 lb. dried apricots, 3 lb. sugar, juice of 1 lemon, ¹/₂ teaspoonful almond flavouring, 3 pints water.

Wash the apricots, put them into a bowl, cover with warm water and leave to soak for 24 hr.

The swelled fruit may then be cut into small pieces, or put through the mincer, according to taste.

Simmer the prepared fruit in the water until tender, add the sugar and flavourings, and boil moderately fast until a little of the preserve will set on a cold plate. Pot while hot, and leave until quite cold before covering.

APRICOT MERINGUE

1 pint milk, 2 breakfastcupfuls fine stale breadcrumbs, 2 eggs, 2 oz. granulated sugar and 2 oz. castor sugar, ¹/₂ lb. stewed apricots or 1 tin apricots, 3—4 drops almond flavouring.

Boil the milk, stir in the crumbs and almond flavouring and leave to soak for 15 min.

Add the beaten egg yolks and the sugar. Stir in half of the fruit, cut into small pieces, and put the mixture into a pie dish.

Whisk the egg whites until stiff, fold in the castor sugar and spread over the top of the crumb and fruit mixture.

Bake at Regulo 4 or 375⁰ F. until the meringue is firm and slightly golden. Serve with the rest of the fruit made hot, with the juice thickened with a little cornflour.

APRICOT SAUCE

4 oz. apricot jam or marmalade, ¹/₂ pint water, 2—3 tablespoonfuls sherry (optional), 1 teaspoonful arrowroot.

Put the jam and water into a saucepan. Mix the sherry with the arrowroot, otherwise use water for mixing. Stir smoothly into the jam and water. Heat all together slowly, stirring all the time. Stir until the mixture thickens.

ARRACK LIQUEUR

1 quart arrack, 1 quart water, 1 lb. sugar candy, very finely pared rind of a small lemon.

Boil the sugar candy and lemon rind in the water until it forms a thin syrup. When cold, strain and add to the arrack. Mix well, bottle and cork securely and store in a moderately warm place for three months.

ARROWROOT BISCUITS

4 oz. arrowroot, 4 oz. plain flour, 4 oz. caster sugar, 2 oz. butter, 1 egg.

Sift the flours together. Rub the butter in very thoroughly, stir in the sugar and mix in the egg. Use a dessertspoonful of cold water if necessary to mix to a very stiff dough. Sprinkle a board with arrowroot. Roll the dough out very thinly. Cut into round biscuits, prick the centres with a fork and bake at Regulo 4 or 375⁰ F. for 10—15 min.

The biscuits should only be very lightly coloured.

ARROWROOT PUDDING

1 rounded tablespoonful powdered arrowroot, ¹/₂ pint milk, 2 tablespoonfuls golden syrup, 1 tablespoonful caster sugar, grated rind of half a lemon, 1 egg.

A pudding usually made for invalids or children.

Stir the arrowroot and sugar to a smooth cream with a little of the milk, bring the rest to the boil and pour it into the cream. Put into the top of a double boiler and stir and cook over a gentle heat until it is thick and creamy. Remove from the heat, stir in the beaten egg and lemon rind. Pour the golden syrup into a warmed and greased pie dish, pour the arrowroot mixture in, then bake at Regulo 3 or 350° F. for about 25—30 min.

ARROWROOT SAUCE

1/2 pint cider or equal quantities water and fruit juice, 1 oz. sugar, 1 level dessertspoonful arrowroot, if using fruit juice, a few drops of appropriate flavouring.
Mix the sugar, arrowroot and liquid together, cook slowly, stirring all the time, until the sauce thickens and turns transparent.

ARTICHOKES, GLOBE, TO COOK

Strip off the outer tough leaves, keeping for soup. Cut off the stalk and trim the base and rub it with lemon juice.

Snip off the end of each leaf with scissors. Remove the inner choke which is rough and unpleasant to eat. Tie the leaves with thread to keep the artichokes in good shape, and put them into fast boiling water to which a little vinegar or lemon juice, and a little salt, have been added. Boil for 15—20 min., according to size; when a fork can pierce the bottom of the vegetable, drain and dry them.

Serve hot with Hollandaise sauce or plain melted butter. Serve cold with Vinaigrette sauce.

Artichoke bottoms are used as a garnish for more elaborate dishes, or the artichokes may be stuffed with chicken purée, etc.

ARTICHOKES, JERUSALEM, CREAMED

Well scrub 1 lb. Jerusalem artichokes, and boil in enough slightly salted water to cover them. Cook for 20 min.

Drain, keeping the water, and rub off the skins. Make a sauce with the artichoke pot liquid and hot milk, half and half, butter and flour.

Slice the artichokes, put them into a buttered pie dish, pour the sauce over, top with fine crumbs and curls of butter and heat in the oven long enough to crisp the crumbs.

ARTICHOKES, FRIED

Prepare as before. Cut into thin slices, drop into boiling fat, cook until the slices are golden coloured, drain thoroughly on kitchen paper, sprinkle with finely chopped parsley. Very good with roast veal.

ARTICHOKE SOUP

Boil 2 lb. well-washed artichokes until tender in enough salted water to cover them. Rub off the skins, and then rub the artichokes through a sieve.

Stir 2 oz. butter and 1 oz. flour into the purée. Put back into the saucepan with the water in which they were cooked and 1 pint very hot milk. Cook and stir over a very low heat until thick and smooth. Add a little more milk to thin the soup as required.

ASPIC JELLY

1 pint meat or poultry stock, 1 oz. gelatine, 1 pinch thyme and dried tarragon, juice 1 lemon, 6 peppercorns, parsley sprigs and 1 chopped shallot.

Boil the stock with the seasonings for 15 min., add the gelatine previously dissolved in 2 tablespoonfuls of cold water. Simmer for 5 min., then strain through a clean cloth. If the jelly is not clear, boil up again with a beaten egg white, strain once more.

A tablespoonful of Madeira improves the flavour.

AUBERGINES, BASQUE FASHION

Peel the egg plants and cut them into 1/2 in. thick slices. Sprinkle with salt in a shallow dish and leave for 1 hr. Throw away the liquid and dry the pieces, sprinkle them with flour and fry them gently in a saucepan in olive oil, adding a clove of finely minced garlic, 1 large green and 1 large red pepper finely shredded, and 3—4 large tomatoes skinned, sliced and seeds removed. Season with salt and coarsely ground black pepper. Cover and simmer gently until all the items are tender. Pour over grilled chops or a small roasted chicken cut into joints.

AUBERGINES FARCIES (STUFFED)

Allow 1 large half or two small halves of aubergine for each person.

Remove the stem, cut in halves lengthways and scoop out most of the flesh. Peel and finely chop 2 small onions and one clove of garlic, chop the aubergine pulp and 1/2 lb. spinach, and cook lightly in a little olive oil. Stir in enough fine white breadcrumbs to make a smooth paste, season with salt, pepper and 1 saltspoonful of paprika.

Fill the prepared aubergine halves with the mixture, top with grated cheese and a sprinkling of crumbs. Put the halves on a greased baking tin, cover with greased paper and bake for 25 min. Remove paper and brown the tops for 10 min.

BABA

8 oz. plain flour, 1/2 oz. yeast, 4 oz. butter, 1 dessertspoonful caster sugar, 2 eggs, 1/3 pint tepid milk.

Sieve 4 oz. flour into a warm basin, make a well in middle, and pour in yeast dissolved in a little of the tepid milk. Knead to a smooth dough, cover with a cloth and leave in warm place.

Sieve remaining flour into another warm bowl, drop eggs into centre with sugar, warm butter and rest of milk, and beat together for about 15 min. Cover with a cloth and leave until first dough has risen to twice its original size. Knead the two doughs together very thoroughly. Have ready 1 large mould or about 8 small ones, buttered. Half fill with dough. Stand in a warm place to rise again, then bake at Regulo 4 or 400° F. for 30—35 min. Turn out and while still warm pour over the following syrup:

1/2 pint water, 2 oz. sugar, 2 tablespoonfuls sieved apricot jam, 1 wine-glassful rum.

Put into a saucepan and bring to the boil, and use at once.

Note: In some recipes for baba, 2 oz. currants are added when the two doughs are blended.

BACON, TO BAKE

Prepare as for boiling. Cook for 15 min. per lb. only.

Cook and remove rind. Encase the bacon in a paste made with flour and water well kneaded together and rolled to a thickness of $1/2$ in. Seal the edges well together.

Bake on a greased baking tin at Regulo 5 or 400° F. allowing a further 15 min. and a little extra if the dough case seems to need longer.

Sometimes the crust is discarded, but some people like to eat portions with the bacon because it is savoury with fat and juices from the bacon.

BACON, TO BOIL

Soak the piece of bacon in warm water for 2 hr. or more, according to its saltness. (If pale pink, it should not be over salt; if the flesh is reddish, it will be salt.)

Cut off any brownish parts on the underside, and thoroughly scrape the rind. Put into a saucepan with one small onion stuck with a clove. Bring to the boil, remove all scum, then replace the saucepan lid and simmer gently allowing 25 min. per lb. Allow to cool in the water, then carefully strip off the rind and cover with bread raspings if it is to be eaten cold.

If served hot, take up and remove rind and put into the oven for a few minutes to dry.

BACON, HOME CURING

The pieces of pig to be cured are well rubbed with rough salt, laid in tubs or troughs for 48 hr., then rinsed. They are then rubbed with a mixture of salt, brown sugar and saltpetre. Every 2 days, the pieces are reversed in position. The flitches are taken out of the pickle after 14 days, the hams after 21 days.

All pieces are washed in lukewarm water, rubbed well with pea flour to dry up superfluous moisture and then hung to dry.

A special Derbyshire 'cure' has stout and treacle added.

Many home-curers send their bacon to be smoked by expert smokers.

BAKED ALASKA

1 large oblong sponge cake, 1 ice-cream brick, 4 whites of eggs, 8 tablespoonfuls caster sugar.

Line an ovenproof oblong shallow dish with white paper, or with rice paper, and place cake in middle. The ice-cream brick, when required, should be about $3/4$ in. smaller all round than the cake. (A tinted or two-colour ice-cream brick is much more effective than a plain one.)

Make the meringue, whisking whites with a few grains of salt until solid. Fold in caster sugar 2 tablespoonfuls at a time, whisking well after each quantity.

When the ice-cream is in place on the cake, cover completely, top and sides, with a thick coating of meringue. If liked the shape can be given a decorative finish with an icing bag and large rosette nozzle. Place at once in a hot oven, Regulo 7 or 450° F., for 5 min. or until delicately browned, and serve at once.

BAKEWELL TART

1/2 lb. rich short pastry, 3 tablespoonfuls raspberry jam, 2 oz. ground almonds, 2 oz. caster sugar, 2 oz. butter, 1 egg, 6—8 drops almond flavouring.

Cream butter and sugar together until it looks like Devonshire cream, beat in the egg, stir in the almonds and almond flavouring.

Line a tart tin with the paste, add a layer of jam, then spread the creamed mixture on it.

Bake at Regulo 7 or 450° F. for about 25—30 min. Serve hot or cold.

BAKING POWDER

Mix together 4 oz. ground rice, 4 oz. bicarbonate of soda, 3 oz. tartaric acid. Shake through a sieve. Store in an airtight tin.

BANANA CAKE

12 oz. self-raising flour, 6 oz. caster sugar, 6 oz. butter or margarine, 1/4 teaspoonful salt, 3 bananas, 2 teaspoonfuls lemon juice, 2 eggs, 2 oz. finely chopped walnuts, milk.

Beat the fat and caster sugar together until very soft and creamy. Add the eggs lightly beaten together, then the bananas mashed to a cream with the lemon juice.

Fold the flour in gently until all the ingredients are mixed to a soft smooth dough, with a little milk if necessary, and stir in the nuts.

Put the dough into an 8 in. cake tin lined with greaseproof paper. Smooth evenly and sprinkle with caster sugar. Bake at Regulo 3 or 350° F. for 1 1/2—2 hr.

BANANAS WITH BACON

4 bananas, 8 rashers of streaky bacon, 4 slices of bread cut from a sandwich loaf to fit the length of the bananas, a little lard.

Remove rinds from bacon. Cut the bananas in halves lengthwise. Put them in the grill pan with the pieces of bread and lay the bacon on the grill grid over them, dotted with small pieces of lard.

Grill on both sides under a quick grill. Remove bacon to a hot dish and take away the grid. Grill the bread and the bananas in the fat dripped from the bacon.

Serve 2 banana halves and 2 rashers of bacon on each piece of fat bread.

BANANA PUDDING

A swiss roll, 3 ripe bananas, 1 wineglassful each sherry and water, 2 tablespoonfuls apricot jam, 1 pint boiled custard, whipped cream.

Slice the roll thinly, also the bananas. Arrange in alternate layers in a glass dish, moistening with the jam previously warmed in the water and mixed with the sherry.

Pour the custard over. When ready to serve, cover the top of the custard with whipped cream, flavoured with sherry.

BANBURY CAKES

1/2 lb. rough puff or flaky pastry (see recipe), 1 oz. butter, 1 dessertspoonful finely chopped candied peel, grated rind 1/2 lemon, 2 oz.

brown sugar, 4 oz. cleaned currants, good pinch mixed spice or a little grated nutmeg, a little rum (optional), egg white and castor sugar for glaze.

Make pastry. Prepare filling, melting butter and adding sugar, fruit, peel, etc.

Roll out pastry fairly thinly and cut into saucer-sized circles. Put a portion of filling on each and moisten edges all round. Fold two sides to overlap slightly in middle and pinch up ends, so that filling is quite enclosed. Turn joined side to board with smooth side uppermost, and roll each shape lightly, continuing to accentuate the pointed ends. Make two short slits on each flat surface, brush over with white of egg and dredge with caster sugar. Bake in hot oven, Regulo 7 or 450° F., for 15—20 min.

BANNOCKS

1 oz. butter or margarine, about ¹/₂ pint warm milk, ¹/₂ oz. yeast, 1 teaspoonful sugar, 1 lb. plain flour, 1 teaspoonful salt, 1 yolk of egg.

Melt the fat, add the milk and pour over the creamed yeast and sugar. Leave in a warm place for 20 min. Mix together the warmed and sifted flour, salt, egg yolk and yeast mixture. Cover and leave in a warm place for about 1 hr. or until the dough has doubled in bulk. Turn on to a floured board and knead well, roll to a depth of ¹/₂ in., cut out with a small circular cutter, leave in a warm place for 20 min., then drop the cakes, 2—3 at a time, into deep hot fat and cook until puffed and golden. Drain on soft paper and sprinkle with caster sugar.

BARLEY SUGAR

1 lb. granulated sugar, ¹/₄ pint water, 6 lumps sugar, body and juice of 1 lemon.

Rub the lumps of sugar on the lemon until all the colour and oil has been removed; strain the juice.

Put granulated or lump sugar and water into a strong saucepan and dissolve very slowly over a very low heat, until the syrup is clear: boil to 270° F., add the lemon juice and then boil up to 300° F. very slowly, when the syrup should be straw-coloured. Pour out thinly on an oiled slab or large flat oiled dish. When slightly cool, cut into thin strips and twist them. Leave on greaseproof paper to become very hard, then store at once in an airtight tin or jars to prevent softening again.

BARLEY WATER

1 tablespoonful ground barley, 1 quart boiling water, 2 tablespoonfuls cold water, juice of one lemon, sugar or honey to taste.

Mix the ground barley to a smooth cream with the cold water. Put into a saucepan and stir in the boiling water and boil gently for 10 min. Strain, add the lemon and sugar or honey. Cool and strain before using.

BASIL SHERRY

Fill a wide-necked bottle with small pieces of basil, cover with sherry, cork and leave for about 10 days. The sherry is then strained off and poured over fresh basil and again left for 12 days.

The strained sherry is added, a spoonful at a time, to soup just before it is served. The sherry-impregnated basil may be used for flavouring stews or soups.

BATH BUNS

14 oz. plain flour, 1 oz. yeast, 1/2 oz. sugar, 4 oz. sugar nibs (or crushed sugar loaf), about 1/2 pint milk, 3 oz. butter, 2 oz. citron peel, 1 egg.

Cream yeast and 1/2 oz. sugar well together. Add milk (warm). Rub the butter into the flour and make into a dough with milk, yeast and egg. Allow to rise for 3/4 hr., then work chopped peel and half the sugar nibs into the mixture. Make into round buns, put on greased sheet, brush with beaten egg, dredge with sugar nibs. Leave to rise in a warm place for 15 min. and bake for 10 min. at Regulo 6 or 425° F. A handful of raisins may be added if desired.

BATH CHAP, TO COOK

Put the chap into warm water with a small onion stuck with a clove. Bring to the boil and remove all scum. Simmer gently until the meat feels tender when a fork is driven in. Allow 20 min. per lb. and 20 min. after. Leave to cool in the water, remove skin, roll up in a funnel shape, tie and roll in browned crumbs.

BATTENBERG CAKE

6 oz. margarine, 6 oz. caster sugar, 3 eggs, 8 oz. self-raising flour, 1 teaspoonful raspberry flavouring, several drops cochineal colouring, apricot jam, almond paste.

You will need 2 oblong cake tins, about 6—7 in. long and 4—5 in. wide. Line them with greaseproof paper.

Cream the margarine and sugar together until light and soft and almost white. Beat in the eggs, 1 at a time. When the mixture is like a soft, yellow cream, gently stir in the sifted flour. Use a little milk if necessary, to make a creamy dough that will spread very easily in the tins. Divide the mixture into 2 equal portions, add the raspberry colouring and flavouring to 1 part and put the white and the pink doughs into the 2 tins.

Bake in a fairly moderate oven, Regulo 4 or 375° F., for about 40—45 min. Turn on to cake cooling wires until cold.

Trim the pieces of cake at sides and top until level, then cut each into 2 equal-sized pieces lengthways.

Place a pink piece of cake beside a white piece, and spread apricot jam between them to keep them together. Spread the top of the cakes thus arranged with more jam and place a pink strip on the lower white portion, a white strip on the lower pink portion, with jam between them. Press this square of cake thus made, closely together so that the jam is holding them well together.

Roll the almond paste to an even-sided strip of a length and width to go completely round the square of cake. Brush the inside with a little jam, lay the cake on the jam, then fold the paste firmly round the cake and press the edges closely together. Lay the cake seamed side down, trim off the ends and flute the upper edges at either end. You may make a criss-cross pattern on the top of the cake with a blunt knife if you wish.

BATTER FOR FRUIT FRITTERS

Put 6 oz. flour into a bowl with a pinch of salt and 2 tablespoonfuls of oil or oiled butter. Mix to a smooth cream with 1/8 pint of ale and a little tepid water or mix with milk and water. When ready to use the batter, stir in a well-whisked egg white. This batter must *not* be thin. A tablespoonful of brandy, rum or liqueur may be added, but take out the equivalent quantity of water.

BATTER FOR VEGETABLES

Put 8 oz. flour into a bowl with a pinch of salt and 1 tablespoonful of melted butter or olive oil. Mix together with 1 beaten egg and enough cold water to make a thin batter. Stand for several hours before using.

BATTERS FOR YORKSHIRE PUDDING

4 oz. flour, 1—2 eggs, a small saltspoonful salt, milk.

Sift the flour and salt in a basin, break the egg or eggs into the centre and stir in the flour, gradually adding milk, until a batter the consistency of thick cream is made; this usually makes about 3/4 pint.

Beat this for about 10 min., let stand for 1 hr. Heat 3 tablespoonfuls of dripping in a Yorkshire pudding tin until sizzling, stir 1 tablespoonful of this into the batter, pour in the batter and bake at Regulo 7 or 450° F. for 25—30 min.

Alternatively, brush 8—12 deep patty pans with fat, make them very hot and half fill the pans with batter. Bake at the above temperature for about 25 min.

BEANS, BUTTER, TO COOK

Cover the required quantity of beans with warm water to which 1 level teaspoonful of bicarbonate of soda has been added.

Leave to soak all night.

Rinse in fresh cold water and boil in slightly salted water until the beans are tender. They must not boil too fast or the skins will peel off.

Flavourings may be added to taste, such as an onion, a sage leaf or two, a pinch of herbs or a clove of garlic.

BEANS, SALTING FOR STORE

For every 3 lb. beans, allow 1 lb. kitchen salt. Do not use less than this, as too little salt will result in a failure.

The beans should be young and fresh. Wash and dry, then remove the side strings. Runner beans should be sliced, French beans left whole. Use a glass jar or stoneware jar. Put a thick layer of salt in to the bottom of the jar, then a thin layer of beans, continue to fill the jar in this manner, pressing down each layer very firmly. Cover the jar and leave for a few days. As the beans and salt shrink down, add more beans and salt. Have a thick layer of salt at the top. The salt will absorb juice from the beans and will form a strong brine. Cover the top of the vessel very closely with 2 or 3 thicknesses of brown paper stuck together with melted paraffin wax (melted candle ends). Store in a cool place.

To use the beans, remove from the jar, wash very thoroughly in several waters, then soak for 2 hr. in warm water. Drop into quickly boiling water, cook without salt, for about 25—30 min.

BEEF, CASSEROLE OF

1 1/2 lb. good stewing steak, 1/2 lb. tomatoes, 1/2 lb. carrots, 1/2 lb. onions, 1 bayleaf, 4 oz. par-cooked butter beans, 2 meat cubes, salt, pepper, flour, hot water.

Cut the meat into small strips, slice the tomatoes, carrots and onions. Roll the pieces of meat in flour seasoned with salt and pepper. Arrange in layers with the vegetables, tomatoes and butter beans in an earthenware or ovenglass casserole. Put the bayleaf on top. Dissolve the meat cubes in $3/4$ pint of water, and pour into the dish.

Cover closely and cook at Regulo 2 or 325⁰ F. for about 4—5 hr.

A boiling fowl steamed for 1 hr., then cut into neat joints, may be used instead of the beef. In that case, use only 1 onion and leave out the beans.

1 or 2 pigs' trotters, well blanched, may be added to give richness to the gravy.

BEEF OLIVES

1 lb. rump steak, veal forcemeat, 3/4 pint stock or water, 1 oz. margarine or butter, 1 oz. flour, 1 small sliced onion, a few slices of carrot, salt and pepper.

Remove all the fat from the meat, cut it into very thin slices about 4 in. long and 2 in. wide, and flatten them with a wet cutlet bat or a rolling pin. Spread a little forcemeat on each slice of meat, roll up tightly and tie securely with twine.

Heat the butter in a stew-pan, fry the olives until their entire surface is lightly browned, then remove them from the stew-pan.

Now put in the carrot and onion, fry quickly for a few minutes, then sprinkle in the flour, fry brown, pour in the stock, and stir until boiling.

Replace the olives in the stew-pan, add salt and pepper, cover with a greased paper and the lid of the stew-pan, and simmer slowly for about $1^1/_2$ hr.

Remove the strings, dish the olives on a bed of mashed potato, season the sauce to taste and strain it over them.

BEEF TEA

1 lb. gravy beef or shin of beef, 1 pint cold water, 1/4 teaspoonful salt.

Chop the meat finely, or put it through the mincer, taking care to catch all juice. Put the meat, water and salt into an earthenware jar, cover it, stand it in a pan of water and simmer in the oven for 3—4 hr. Strain, cool, remove all fat from the top. Serve hot or cold with thin fingers of crisp toast.

BEETROOTS, TO BAKE

6 small globe beetroots with leaves, 2 oz. margarine, 1 tablespoonful vinegar, 4 tablespoonfuls water, salt, pepper, flour.

Remove the fresh leaves, wash and boil them in a very little salted water. Drain well. Parboil the washed beetroots, carefully remove the skin. Put them into a casserole with the water, vinegar and margarine. Cover with a lid and bake at Regulo 5 or 400⁰ F. for 35 min.

Put the cooked leaves in the centre of a hot dish, put the cooked beets round. Thicken the liquid with a little flour to make a smooth sauce and pour over the contents of the dish.

BEETROOTS, TO BOIL

Wash the beets thoroughly but gently to remove soil without breaking the skins. Leave a small short tuft of leaves on them to prevent bleeding.

Drop them into boiling water, cover the pan and boil gently until they are tender. Allow 1¹/₂ hr. for medium-sized beets.

To serve hot, rub off the skins, slice and cover with melted butter or with parsley sauce.

BEETROOT, TO PICKLE

To pickle beetroot, boil until tender in salted water. Peel and slice thinly while hot, pack into jars and cover with boiling spiced vinegar.

BEIGNETS SOUFFLES

Choux pastry (see recipe), lard for frying.

Heat the lard. Drop teaspoonfuls of the pastry into boiling fat, a few at a time, and turn the pieces about with a long spoon until they have swelled and turned golden. Lift from the fat with a slice and drain on soft paper. Keep hot until all are ready. Serve on a paper doyley sprinkled with sugar, whipped cream or brandy or rum sauce.

BERCY SAUCE

2 oz. chopped shallots, ¹/₄ pint white wine, ³/₄ pint fish stock, ¹/₄ pint thick cream sauce, 2 oz. butter, juice of ¹/₂ lemon, 1 tablespoonful finely chopped parsley.

Simmer the chopped shallot in the wine and fish stock until soft. Stir in the sauce and simmer again until reduced a little. Stir in the butter, lemon juice and parsley.

Served usually with any poached white fish.

BIBLE CAKE

1¹/₂ cups Judges v. 25 (butter)
2 cups Jeremiah vi. 20 (sugar)
6 Jeremiah xvii. 11 (eggs)
4¹/₂ cups I Kings iw. 22 1st. clause (flour)
2 cups I Samuel xxx. 12 2nd. clause (raisins)
1 cup Nahum iii. 12 (figs)
¹/₂ cup Numbers xvii. 8 (almonds)
2 teaspoonfuls 1 Samuel xiv. 25 (honey)
Season to taste 2 Chronicles ix. 9 (spice)
Pinch Leviticus ii. 13 (salt)
3 teaspoonfuls Amos iv. 5 (baking powder)
¹/₂ cup Judges iv. 19 (milk)

Follow Solomon's prescription for making a good *boy* and you will have a good *cake*. Proverbs xxiii. 14 is best. Mix well.

Note: Use an average tea cup for the above measurements.

BIGARADE

Cook the very finely shredded peel of 1 bitter orange, free from pith, with ¹/₂ pint of red wine, add ¹/₄ teaspoonful of dry mustard mixed to a paste with a tablespoonful of red wine and stir into the hot wine with 4 tablespoonfuls of redcurrant jelly; add strained juice of the orange and ¹/₂ lemon.

Serve cold with cold pheasant, grouse, etc.

BIRD'S NEST SOUP

To prepare, soak about 3 oz. bird's nest material in water for 3 hr., pick out the bird's feathers which may be in it, wash it gently in cold water, then cook it in chicken broth for 2 hr. over a medium heat. Alternatively, to stuff a chicken with it, steam or boil the chicken and serve with its broth and the bird's nest stuffing.

It may also be used as a sweet, simmered in plain water for 2 hr. and then served scattered with fine sugar.

BISHOP

To every bottle of good red wine, allow 1 orange. Seville oranges are preferable, otherwise use thin-skinned fruit, not the thick-skinned type. 1/4 lb. sugar to each orange.

Put washed and dried oranges in a grill pan under low heat. Lightly grill until skins are pale brown and aromatic. Whilst oranges are still hot, puncture them several times with the point of a sharp knife, then put them into a tureen, sprinkle with sugar to cover and pour in the wine. Cover tureen with lid and leave fruit steeping for 24 hr. Strain and serve.

BLACK BUTTER SAUCE

2 oz. butter, 1 packed teaspoonful chopped parsley, 1 dessertspoonful vinegar.

Heat the butter until richly browned, taking care not to burn it. Skim, and stir in chopped parsley and fry lightly. Stir in vinegar and when re-heated, but not boiling, pour into warmed sauceboat.

BLACK CAP PUDDING

6 oz. self-raising flour, 2 oz. caster sugar, 2 oz. well washed and dried currants, 1/2 pint milk, 1 egg, blackcurrant jam.

Grease a pudding basin with margarine and put 2 tablespoonfuls of blackcurrant jam into it.

Put the sifted flour into a basin, break the egg in the middle and gradually stir in half the milk, working the flour into it. Beat well, stir in the sugar, currants and rest of the milk. Beat the batter well, pour into the prepared basin and steam for 1 1/2 hr.

BLACK OR SCOTCH BUN

About 3/4 lb. short crust, 1 1/2 lb. dried fruit, more currants in proportion ot the rest of the fruit, 4 oz. finely chopped peel, 2 oz. finely minced or shredded almonds, 4 oz. sugar, 8 oz. fine stale cake crumbs, 1 level teaspoonful each black pepper, ginger and cinnamon, 1 egg, 3 tablespoonfuls black treacle, a little stout or milk, 1 level teaspoonful bicarbonate of soda.

Mix together all the ingredients, first dissolving the bicarbonate of soda with the slightly warmed treacle and beaten egg. Only enough stout or milk should be used to bring the ingredients to a stiffish dough.

Roll the crust to a circle, put the mixture into the centre of the circle of dough and gather up the edges to make a large dumpling. Be sure to pinch the seams of the dough well together so that none of the rich mixture oozes through. Put the dumpling upside down on a greased baking tin, brush over with egg and milk, then bake for 45—50 min. at Regulo 3 or 350⁰ F.

If you prefer it, roll the crust thinly and line a small cake tin with it, fill with the mixture, put a circle of paste on top and pinch the top and the side edges of the paste very well together, brush with egg and milk and bake at Regulo 4 or 375⁰ F. for about 35—40 min.

BLACK PUDDING

1 quart pig's blood, 1 quart fresh milk, ³/₄ lb. stale bread, 4 oz. cooked rice, 4 oz. coarse oatmeal, 8 oz. finely shredded suet, salt, black pepper, 1 teaspoonful powdered sage or mint.

Dice the bread, put it into a large dish, pour in the milk and put into the oven to warm through. Also, having soaked the rice, put that also in the oven and heat at the same time.

Mix the soaked bread, partly cooked rice, oatmeal and blood with all the seasonings very thoroughly. Put into a large greased baking tin. Bake for about 35—45 min. at Regulo 4 or 375⁰ F.

Serve cut in squares with mashed potatoes and pickled cabbage or cold for breakfast.

BLACKBERRY JAM

6 lb. blackberries, 5 lb. sugar, 3 teaspoonfuls citric or tartaric acid.

Pick the berries over and remove any that are mouldy and all stalks. Put them into the preserving pan with the acid, and cook over a very low heat until juice begins to run. Raise the heat and cook until the fruit is quite tender.

Pour in the sugar, stir to dissolve it, then boil until a little will set when tested on a cold plate. Pot when very hot, cover when quite cold.

BLACKCURRANT JAM

To 1 lb. currants allow 1 lb. loaf or granulated sugar and ¹/₄ pint water.

String the currants, wash them, put them into the preserving pan with the water and simmer very gently until the fruit is very tender. Stir in the sugar and allow to stand for 15 min. while the sugar melts. Bring to the boil, then boil moderately fast, stirring all the time, until a little of the jam tested on a cold plate will set with a wrinkled skin when the plate is tilted.

Note: It is most important to cook the fruit until tender with the water only, for if the sugar is added before the fruit is soft, the currants will remain as tough little pellets, and spoil the consistency and flavour of your jam.

BLACKCURRANT JELLY

4 lb. blackcurrants, 1 pint water, sugar.

Wash currants; there is no need to string them. Put into the preserving pan with the water, and simmer gently until the currants are quite tender.

Strain juice through a jelly bag, measure, and allow 14 oz. sugar for each pint.

Return juice to the preserving pan, stir in the sugar. Bring slowly to the boil, then boil moderately fast until a little of the mixture will jell on a plate when tested.

Pot into small clean dry pots, and cover when quite cold.

BLANCMANGE, ARROWROOT

4 heaped tablespoonfuls arrowroot, $1\frac{1}{2}$ tablespoonfuls sugar, $1\frac{1}{2}$ pints milk, lemon rind, vanilla or almond flavouring.

Mix the arrowroot smoothly with a little cold milk. Bring the rest of the milk to the boil with 2—3 pieces of lemon rind if using. Strain the boiling milk over the arrowroot while stirring, return to the top of a double boiler and sweeten to taste, adding vanilla or almond if using, then cook and stir until the mixture is thick. Pour into a mould rinsed in cold water and put aside to set.

BLANCMANGE, CORNFLOUR

$2\frac{1}{2}$ oz. cornflour, 1 tablespoonful caster sugar, 2 pints milk, flavouring.
Make the pudding in exactly the same way as above.

Alternatively, when the boiling milk is stirred into the cornflour cream, the mixture can be boiled in a single saucepan, stirring all the time, until thickened, then cook a further full minute before transferring the mixture to a rinsed mould to set. Use flavourings as in previous recipe.

BOBOTEE

1 lb. finely minced mutton or beef, 1 breakfastcupful pieces of bread soaked in $\frac{1}{2}$ pint milk, 2 thinly sliced onions, 2 eggs, 2 level table-spoonfuls curry powder, 1 tablespoonful lemon juice, 1 oz. dripping, 8 finely chopped blanched almonds, 1 dessertspoonful sugar, salt.

Squeeze out as much milk as possible from the bread, and beat the bread with a fork until smooth. Fry the onion in the dripping, add the curry powder, lemon juice, sugar, salt, finely chopped almonds, meat, bread and 1 egg. Mix well. Turn into a greased pie dish.

Beat the other egg with the milk taken from the bread and pour over the contents of the dish. Bake until the custard is set, at Regulo 2 or 325° F.

BOILED FROSTING

$\frac{3}{4}$ lb. granulated sugar, $\frac{1}{4}$ pint water, pinch of cream of tartar, 3 egg whites, 1 teaspoonful vanilla, almond or lemon flavouring.

Mix the sugar, water and cream of tartar together in a saucepan and bring to the boil. Boil and stir until the syrup will run off the spoon in threads.

Have the egg whites stiffly whisked in a bowl. Pour the syrup slowly into them, beating all the time. Beat or whisk until the mixture stands up in peaks and then use at once.

BOILED FRUIT CAKE

12 oz. self-raising flour, 4 oz. lard, 4 oz. sugar, 8 oz. dried fruit, or to taste, 1 tablespoonful golden syrup, $\frac{1}{2}$ teaspoonful grated nutmeg, a pinch of cinnamon, 1 level teaspoonful bicarbonate of soda, $\frac{1}{2}$ pint hot water.

Sift the spices with the flour and stir in the sugar.

Put the lard, fruit and syrup into a saucepan with the water and boil for 3—4 min. until the lard and syrup have melted together. Cool the mixture until luke warm, stirring well to keep the ingredients well blended together. Stir in the bicarbonate of soda, pour it into the dry ingredients and mix all together to a soft dough. Do not use more moisture, as an eggless mixture must be stiffer than one with eggs.

Turn the dough into a cake tin lined with greaseproof paper, put into a pre-heated oven at Regulo 6 or 425° F. Turn heat to Regulo 3 or 350° F. and bake for $1^1/_2$—$1^3/_4$ hr.

BONNE FEMME

To make a dish *à la Bonne Femme:*
1/2 lb. fresh mushrooms, washed but not peeled, sliced and minced, 2 chopped shallots, 1 teaspoonful chopped parsley, 1 level teaspoonful salt, 1 wineglassful dry white wine, 1/4 pint stock, 2 tablespoonfuls White Cream sauce, 2 tablespoonfuls butter, 1 tablespoonful whipped cream.

Put the butter, shallots, parsley and mushrooms into a saucepan. Add the wine and stock (preferably fish stock) and cook very slowly for 10 min. Cook until the liquid is reduced. Add the cream sauce, season to taste with salt and pepper. Add a tablespoonful of whipped cream. Pour the sauce over poached soles or other white fish and glaze beneath a hot grill.

BORSHCH

1 lb. raw beetroot, 1 quart stock from a piece of boiled bacon or beef, 1 teaspoonful sugar, salt, pepper, 2 tablespoonfuls vinegar, sour cream or yoghourt.

Peel the beetroot and cut it into strips like match sticks. Cook with the vinegar in sufficient water to cover. When tender, add the stock, sugar and seasonings, and boil all together. Strain and serve a tablespoonful of sour cream or yoghourt on top of each portion.

A second version is a thick soup, with shredded cabbage, diced potato and the beetroot left in the soup.

BOSTON BAKED BEANS (HARICOT BEANS)

1 lb. small haricot beans, 1 large chopped onion, 1/4 lb. belly of pork (salt), 4 tablespoonfuls dark treacle, 1/2 teaspoonful mustard, 1 teaspoonful salt, 2 tablespoonfuls tomato purée.

Soak the beans overnight with 1 level teaspoonful of bicarbonate of soda in water.

Boil for 5 min. in the soaking water, then rinse in cold water.

Lay the piece of pork in the bottom of a casserole with the onion. Pour in the beans. Mix the mustard, treacle, purée and salt with 1 quart of water and add to casserole. Bake gently for about 6 hr. Add more water occasionally as required.

Finally, take the pork from under the beans, cut it into dice and mix with the beans.

Serve with brown bread and butter.

BOUILLABAISSE

About 3 lb. white fish including John Dory, whiting, rock salmon and eel, 1 lb. lobster, Dublin Bay prawns, 2 medium-sized onions, the white parts of 2 leeks, 4 tomatoes skinned and pulp removed, 1 dessertspoonful chopped parsley, 2 cloves of garlic, 1 bayleaf, pinch of saffron, 4 tablespoonfuls olive oil, salt, pepper.

All the fish should be cut into pieces or slices.

Cook the tougher sliced fish and shellfish, onions, leeks, tomatoes and garlic in the oil for about 5 min. Add seasonings, cover with water and boil for 5 min.

Now put in the more tender fish and boil for about 8 min.

Put thick slices of untoasted French bread into soup plates and sprinkle them with the parsley, then ladle in the fish and its rich liquor.

BOURGUIGNONNE

1 tablespoonful chicken or beef dripping, 4 oz. diced salt pork or bacon, 6 small onions, 3 medium carrots sliced, 2 chopped shallots, 1 clove of garlic crushed, 2 tablespoonfuls flour, bouquet garni, 2 stalks of celery, 1/2 pint red wine, 1 pint stock or water, 2 tablespoonfuls butter, salt, pepper.

Put the fat and pork or bacon with the onions and carrots, add shallots, garlic and flour. Mix well. Add the wine, stock, bouquet and celery. Bring to the boil, then simmer slowly for 1/2 hr.

Rub the sauce through a strainer and season to taste with salt and black pepper.

BRAMBLE JELLY

4 lb. blackberries, 1/2 pint water, 1 teaspoonful citric acid.

Pick the berries over and remove all stalks and mouldy ones. Put them into the preserving pan with the water and citric acid.

Simmer over a moderate heat until the fruit is quite soft. Strain off all the liquid through a jelly bag. Measure it and allow 1 lb. sugar for every pint of juice. Return to the preserving pan together and, after the sugar has dissolved, boil moderately fast until a little of the jelly will set firmly when tested in the usual manner.

Pot into small clean dry jars. Store in a cool place.

BRANDADE DE MORUE

2 lb. salt cod, 3/4 lb. warm mashed potato, 1/3 pint warm olive oil, 2 cloves of garlic, 1/4 pint cream or top of the milk, black pepper.

Soak the salt cod for 12 hr., changing the water once or twice. Cut it into small pieces and simmer until it can be removed from skin and bones.

Mix it with the warm mashed potatoes and beat it to a paste, gradually adding the olive oil, crushed garlic and cream.

Season well with pepper, and when it is creamy and very hot, serve with small croûtons of fried bread.

BRANDY SNAPS

3 1/2 oz. butter or margarine, 4 oz. golden syrup, 3 oz. sugar, 4 oz. plain flour, 1/2 teaspoonful lemon juice, 1/2 teaspoonful ground ginger.

Warm together the fat, golden syrup, sugar and ginger. Mix in the sifted flour and lemon juice. Beat well together. Drop teaspoonfuls of the mixture well spaced apart on greased baking tins.

Bake at Regulo 3 or 350° F. for about 8—10 min.

Lift each snap from the tins with a palette knife and roll quickly round the greased handle of a wooden spoon.

Slip off as soon as the rolls set. If the mixture stiffens as it is being used, add a few drops of lemon juice.

BRAN MUFFINS

8 oz. self-raising flour, 6 oz. bran, 1/2 teaspoonful salt, 2 oz. dark treacle, 2 eggs, 1/4—1/2 pint warm milk.

Stir the flour, bran and salt together. Mix the treacle, beaten eggs and warm milk together and stir it into the dry ingredients. Mix to a soft dough and divide into 12—16 small well-greased deep patty pans. Bake at Regulo 5 or 400° F. for about 15 min.

BRAN POSSETT

Boil 1/4 lb. bran in 1 quart water for 15 min. Strain through a fine strainer and add honey or brown sugar to taste. Shreds of lemon peel may also be added. Use hot for a sore throat.

BRAWN

1/2 pig's head, 1 pig's trotter, split, 1 small onion, bouquet garni (sprig of thyme, parsley and a bayleaf, tied together), 1 doz. each allspice and peppercorns, pepper and salt, 1/4 teaspoonful grated nutmeg, pinch mace, 1/4 oz. gelatine.

Wash and blanch head and trotter. Scrape and rinse well. Put these ingredients into a pan with flavouring and add boiling water to cover. Cover pan and boil these ingredients until the meat leaves the bones cleanly, skimming occasionally. Remove head and trotter to a large plate or dish. Remove tongue and skin it. Return all the bones to the pan and continue boiling without the lid until liquor is reduced considerably — it should not be more than a pint. Stir in the gelatine and adjust seasoning to taste. While stock is being reduced, chop the meat into small neat pieces. Strain reduced stock over meat and mix altogether. Transfer to a rinsed mould or basin to set. When shape is firm, turn out.

BREAD, BROWN

1 1/2 lb. wholemeal flour, 1 1/2 teaspoonfuls salt, 1 oz. lard, 1/2 oz. yeast, 1 teaspoonful caster sugar, 1 pint warm water.

Method is the same as for white bread.

BREAD DOUGH DUMPLINGS

Roll 1/2—1 lb. uncooked bread dough into 8 or 16 small balls. Roll them in flour.

Drop into fast boiling salted water, put on the saucepan lid and boil quickly for about 10 min. Skim out of the water and add to a stew or casserole, or serve as a sweet with syrup, jam or fruit.

BREAD, MILK

2 lb. plain flour, 1/2 oz. salt, 1 oz. yeast, 1 pint milk, 1 egg, 1 table-spoonful sugar.

Cream the yeast with the sugar until liquid, then stir it into the lukewarm milk.

Sift the flour with the salt and work it to a soft, smooth dough with the milk and yeast. Turn it into a warm bowl and cover with a cloth. Leave in a warm place for 2 hr. Turn on to a floured board and knead again, very lightly. Cover again and leave for another hour.

Divide the dough into 4 equal portions, mould into flattish round loaves and mark the tops with a crisscross diamond pattern with the back of a large knife, cutting rather deeply to preserve the pattern in the baking. Brush each loaf with beaten egg. Place the loaves on lightly greased baking tins and bake at Regulo 5 or 400° F. for about 45 min.

BREAD PUDDING

1/2 lb. stale bread without crusts, 3 oz. shredded or chopped suet, 2 oz. demerara sugar, 4 oz. dried fruit, 1 or 2 eggs, 1/2 teaspoonful mixed spice, milk.

Cut the bread into small pieces, put into a basin and cover with milk. Leave to soak, then squeeze till dry and beat with a fork. Mix with the suet, sugar, fruit and spice. Stir in the eggs. Press the mixture into a greased sandwich tin and bake for about 35 min. at Regulo 5 or 400° F. or put into a basin and steam for 1 1/2 hr. Serve with custard.

BREAD SAUCE

Simmer a small onion stuck with 2 cloves in 1 pint of milk for 30 min., taking care that it does not boil.

Remove the onion and stir in 3 oz. fine white bread crumbs and leave to soak for 1 hr. or more.

Cook gently without boiling, season with pepper and salt to taste. Stir in 1 oz. butter, whisk the sauce until smooth before serving very hot. If liked, the onion may be left in until the last moment and if the sauce has thickened too much a little extra hot milk may be stirred in.

BREAD, WHITE

2 lb. plain flour, 2 teaspoonfuls salt, 1 oz. yeast, 1 teaspoonful sugar, 2 oz. lard or margarine if liked, 1 pint lukewarm water.

Setting the sponge. Sift the flour and salt into a large bowl and put to warm. Cream the yeast and sugar together until liquid and stir in 1 pint of the lukewarm water. Pour this into a well in the centre of the warmed flour, sprinkle a little of the flour on top, cover and leave in a warm place for about 20 min. and until the surface is covered with bubbles.

Work in all the flour by hand adding more of the lukewarm water as necessary to make an elastic dough. Turn out on to a wooden surface and knead thoroughly for 5—10 min. to distribute the yeast through the mixture.

Rising. Put the dough into a clean bowl sprinkled with a little flour, cover to protect from draughts and stand in a warm place for about 1 1/2 hr. or until the dough has doubled in size.

Turn out and knead again. Cut in two to see if the air holes are evenly distributed and continue kneading until this is so. Shape the loaves and put into greased tins. The dough should half fill the tins.

Proving. Cover with a cloth and stand in a warm place for about 30 min. or until the dough just reaches the tops of the tins.

Bake in a pre-heated oven for 45—60 min. according to size at Regulo 6 or 7 or 425—450° F. When cooked the bread should be well browned and sound hollow when tapped on the bottom with the knuckles.

BRIOCHE

1 lb. plain flour, ¹/₂ oz. yeast, 6 eggs, ¹/₂ lb. butter, 1 teaspoonful salt, 1 tablespoonful sugar, about ¹/₄ pint milk.

Take 8 oz. flour for a raiser and mix in the yeast thinned out in a little warm water to form a paste. Make 4 cuts in the top of this paste and let it rise in a warm place until double in bulk.

Mix together the remaining flour, eggs, butter, salt and sugar. Work or knead this paste well, moistening with the milk, and then stir in the raiser and mix together well. Let it rise until it is light, then punch it down like bread and set in a cool place until needed. Cut the brioche into small or large pieces as desired. Put in moulds or shapes like buns or rings on a baking sheet. Let rise. Make small cuts over the surface. Brush top with beaten egg. Bake in a hot oven at about Regulo 7 or 450° F.

BUTTER, ANCHOVY

Pound 6 fillets of anchovy to a paste, beat smoothly with 4 oz. butter and a teaspoonful of the oil from the tin of anchovies.

BUTTER, CURRY

Put 4 oz. butter into a warm bowl and gradually beat in sufficient good curry powder to give a decided flavour, or according to taste. Add a few drops of lemon juice.

BUTTER, LOBSTER

Pound together ¹/₄ lb. lobster meat, 2 dessertspoonfuls of the coral and ¹/₄ lb. butter. Rub through a sieve.

BUTTER, PAPRIKA

Infuse ¹/₄ teaspoonful paprika in 1 dessertspoonful white wine. Beat into 4 oz. fresh butter.

BUTTER, SALT HERRING

Remove the bones and skin from a salted and smoked herring, beat with 4 oz. butter and rub through a sieve. Add 3—4 drops of tarragon vinegar.

BUTTER, SHRIMP

Pound 4 oz. unpeeled shrimps very finely, add 4 oz. butter and beat well. Rub through a fine sieve twice.

BUTTER SAUCE

4 oz. fresh butter, 1 oz. flour, 1 pint boiling water, 3 egg yolks, 4 tablespoonfuls thin (single) cream, juice of ¹/₂ lemon.

Mix 1 oz. butter smoothly with the flour, stir in slightly salted boiling water until well blended, without boiling.

Whip egg yolks, cream and lemon juice together, and add gradually to the hot liquid. Cook and stir until sauce thickens, without boiling. Rub through sieve and add remaining butter in small pieces. When sauce has absorbed butter, it is ready to serve.

CABBAGE, CREAMED

Melt 1 oz. margarine in a small saucepan, stir in ½ oz. flour, add the boiling cabbage liquid and stir to a smooth, thick sauce.

Thin with a little milk if required, season with pepper and a dash of nutmeg. Stir the cabbage in the sauce until coated. Serve very hot.

CABBAGE, PLAIN BOILED

Remove the outer leaves and bottom stump of the cabbage. Divide into leaves, cut out the thickest middle ribs and slice the whole cabbage coarsely. Wash well. Drop into enough boiling salted water to barely cover the cabbage. Put on the saucepan lid and boil fast for 10—15 min. Drain well.

Cabbage should not be soaked in cold water before cooking, as this results in loss of mineral and vitamin content.

CABBAGE, RED

1 medium firm red cabbage, 1 finely chopped onion, 2 tablespoonfuls butter or margarine, 2 sliced green apples, 1 tablespoonful vinegar, ¼ pint white stock or water, 1 teaspoonful sugar, caraway seeds if liked, nutmeg.

Remove outer leaves and cut the rest into fine strips. Wash and drain. Brown the onion in the fat, add the vinegar, cabbage and stock, season with salt and pepper. Simmer for about 30 min., add the sliced apples unpeeled, but with cores removed, caraway seeds, sugar and nutmeg. Simmer again until the shreds of cabbage are tender. If any liquid is left, thicken it very slightly with flour and pour it over the cabbage.

CABBAGE SALAD (COLE SLAW)

1 small crisp white cabbage, 2 tablespoonfuls salad oil, 2 tablespoonfuls vinegar, 1 teaspoonful dry mustard, salt, pepper, a clove of garlic.

Trim the cabbage, removing outer tough leaves, shred the rest, cutting away centre ribs of leaves. Wash well in cold water. Drain and dry in a cloth.

Crush the garlic in a salad bowl with the mustard, season lightly with salt and pepper, beat in the oil and vinegar, then toss the cabbage in the dressing until it is well coated.

CABINET PUDDING

6 stale sponge cakes, 2 eggs, 8 ratafia biscuits, ½ pint milk, ½ teaspoonful vanilla, 2 oz. castor sugar, a little angelica, 2 oz. glacé cherries, 2 oz. chopped peel.

Grease a mould with margarine, decorate the bottom and sides with pieces of cherry and angelica and thin slices of sponge cake. Crumble the rest of the cake to small pieces, put them with the ratafia biscuits into the mould with the rest of the cherries, angelica and the peel. Beat the eggs with the milk and vanilla and sugar. Pour into the mould. Cover with greaseproof paper and steam for 1 hr.

CALF'S FOOT JELLY

4 prepared calf's feet, 1½ quarts water, 3 lemons, 1 pint white wine, 4 egg whites, sugar.

Simmer the feet in the water until quite tender. Strain and leave the liquid overnight. Remove all the fat. Melt the stock, add the strained juice of the lemon, wine and whisked egg whites, add sugar to taste.

Boil for 10 min., whisking, then strain. It will be ready to serve.

CARROT PUDDING

1/2 lb. deep yellow carrots, 4 oz. margarine, 4 oz. demerara sugar, 1/2 lb. breadcrumbs, 2 oz. self-raising flour, 2 eggs, 2 oz. finely chopped candied peel, 2 oz. currants, 1/2 teaspoonful mixed spice.

Wash and peel the carrots, grate on a fine grater.

Cream margarine and sugar together, beat in the eggs, and grated carrot. Stir in the crumbs, flour, currants, peel and spice.

Turn mixture into a well greased basin. Cover with greaseproof paper and steam for 2 hr. Serve with hot golden syrup.

CARROT SANDWICHES

Grate 2 or 3 medium-young carrots finely. Season with salt, pepper and a dash of tarragon vinegar. Use as a sandwich spread with brown bread and butter and mustard and cress.

The carrot may also be mixed with 2 or 3 finely mashed sardines and seasoned with vinegar, pepper and salt.

CARROT SOUP (SOUP CRECY)

1 lb. carrots, 2 oz. fine semolina, 1 quart white stock, 2—3 tablespoonfuls cream, 1 teaspoonful salt, finely chopped parsley, a pinch of sugar.

Peel and chop the carrots, boil them in the stock with the semolina and salt until quite tender. Rub through a strainer or sieve. Return to the saucepan, stir in the cream and sugar.

Serve with parsley sprinkled on top of each portion.

CARROTS AU GRATIN

1 lb. young carrots, 1 pint creamy white sauce, 1 tablespoonful finely minced parsley, 1/4 teaspoonful sugar, a little grated nutmeg, 2 oz. grated cheese, either Cheddar or Parmesan.

Scrape the carrots and slice them finely. Boil gently with the sugar in enough water to cover them until they are tender. Make the sauce with the liquid from the carrots made up to 1 pint with hot milk.

Stir the parsley into the sauce and season it with nutmeg, pepper and a pinch of salt. Toss the carrots in the sauce, pour all into a pie dish greased with a little butter. Spread the cheese on the top and heat in a brisk oven or beneath the grill to crisp and lightly brown the cheese.

Serve with jacket potatoes as a meatless dish, or with grilled rashers of bacon or grilled gammon.

CARROTS, GLAZED

1 lb. new or small carrots, water, 1 level teaspoonful caster sugar, 2 oz. butter or margarine.

Scrape the carrots, slice very thinly and cook in enough water to cover them until tender and water has practically evaporated. Scatter in the sugar, add the butter or margarine and cook over a very low heat until the carrot slices have absorbed the sugar, rest of the liquid and the fat.

Turn into a hot dish, sprinkle with finely chopped parsley.

CELERY, BRAISED

Remove the outer stems and roots of 2 large heads of celery, also the green leaves. Cut the rest into lengths of about 6 in. Wash very thoroughly and wipe to remove all water. Pack the celery into an earthenware dish, top with about 2 oz. margarine or butter shaved into small pieces. Season with salt and pepper. Put on a lid or cover with a buttered paper or piece of aluminium foil and cook in the oven at Regulo 5 or 400° F. for about 40 min.

The braising may be done in a saucepan closely covered.

Serve with a cream sauce in which a little of the finely chopped green of the celery tops are stirred.

CELERY SALAD

Mix together diced raw celery, apple, carrot and cooked potato and dress with thick mayonnaise. Serve on lettuce leaves or piled into cases made of polished raw red apples with the centres scooped out.

CEPES A LA BORDELAISE

Choose mushrooms of equal size. Remove stalks but do not skin the mushrooms. Sauté on both sides in olive oil. Chop the stalks with a clove of garlic, mix with parsley and cook in the remaining oil. Fill the mushroom cups with the mixture and serve hot.

CHAPPATTIS

1 lb. wholemeal flour, 1/4—1/2 pint cold water, pinch of salt.

Mix flour, water and salt to a stiff dough. Knead it well. Divide into portions the size of walnuts and roll them in wholemeal flour. Roll each ball to the size of a very thin pancake. Cook them in a large ungreased, very hot frying pan. Fry on either side for 2 min. Butter lightly on either side and fry again for a minute or two. Eat while hot, usually with curry.

The chappattis may be bought ready made from oriental grocers.

CHARLOTTE RUSSE

Savoy finger biscuits as required, 1/2 pint lemon jelly, 1/3 pint custard, 1/3 pint double cream, few drops vanilla essence, sugar as required, 1/2 oz. gelatine (powdered), 3 tablespoonfuls water, few glacé cherries and some 'leaves' of angelica.

Trim finger biscuits to depth of mould, cutting at both ends. Dissolve the jelly and make the custard, leaving them to cool.

When jelly is cold and showing signs of thickening pour sufficient into a soufflé mould to make a thin layer at the bottom. Before it sets firmly decorate with glacé cherries and angelica cut into small shapes like leaves. Spoon a very little more jelly over the decorations to secure them in place. Leave remaining jelly to set firmly elsewhere. Now brush one side of the finger biscuits with a little white of egg and press these round the sides of the soufflé mould, arranging them close together without any space between.

Whip cream, but not to piping consistency, and sweeten to taste. Put gelatine with water and stand container over boiling water until clear. Stir into cooled custard. When mixture is quite cold blend with lightly whipped cream, mixing well. Pour into prepared mould and place in a refrigerator or other cold place to set. When firm turn out on to a serving dish and decorate round the base with chopped remaining lemon jelly.

CHEESE CAKES

First make the curd for the filling.

1 pint milk, 1 egg, 1 pint sour milk, 1 teaspoonful lemon juice.

Put the pint of fresh milk into a saucepan, beat the egg with the sour milk, add to the fresh milk which should be brought to the boil first, add the lemon juice and stir the mixture together until curds rise to the top. Pour the mixture into a piece of muslin, gather up the corners and allow the curds to strain in this as the whey runs off. When the curds are firm and free from whey they are ready.

Line small tartlet tins with short crust, rolled thinly; mix the curd with 2 tablespoonfuls of cream, 2 tablespoonfuls of well washed currants, 1 beaten egg and a good pinch of nutmeg.

Fill the little pastry cases with spoonfuls of the mixture and bake at Regulo 5 or 400° F. for 15—20 min.

Note: Puff pastry may be used instead of short crust.

CHELSEA BUNS

12 oz. flour, 3 oz. butter or margarine, 4 oz. caster sugar, 3/4 oz. yeast, 2—3 tablespoonfuls milk, 2 large eggs, 2 oz. currants, 1/2 oz. chopped peel, good pinch mixed spice.

Warm flour and sift into a warm bowl. Rub in half the fat and add half the sugar. Crumble yeast and mix with a teaspoonful sugar until liquid. Warm the milk and mix with beaten egg. Stir mixture into the yeast, then add to flour, etc. Mix to a soft dough (if required, adding a little extra warmed milk) and beat well. Cover and leave in warm place until doubled in bulk. Turn out on to a well-floured board and knead lightly. Then roll out to a square and spread with remaining butter. Sprinkle with sugar. Fold ends to middle, turn dough sideways, and roll out again thinly. Sprinkle with remainder of sugar, currants, peel and spice. Roll up as for swiss roll, then cut in thick slices (about 1—1 1/2 in. thickness) and arrange these touching on a greased warmed baking tin, cut sides downwards. Leave again in a warm place to prove for about 20 min. Brush over with milk and sprinkle with sugar. Bake in a hot oven for about 20 min.

Pull buns apart whilst still warm, when they should be in the traditional squarish shape.

CHERRY CAKE

8 oz. self-raising flour, 6 oz. margarine, 6 oz. caster sugar, 3 eggs, 4 oz. glacé cherries, about 1—2 tablespoonfuls cold water and, if liked, a few drops cherry flavouring and 1/2 teaspoonful carmine colouring. (The last two ingredients may be omitted, if extra flavour and a pink tinted cake are not required.)

Prepare a 7 in. cake tin by lining it with greaseproof paper, letting the collar of paper come up 1 in. beyond the rim of the tin to prevent over-cooking.

Wash the glacé cherries and dry them well, cut them into rings, small pieces or halves, according to taste. Whisk the eggs thoroughly.

Cream the fat and sugar together until they are smooth, light and like Devonshire cream. Stir in the fruit well. Add a little egg, then a little sifted flour alternately, folding in the flour and not beating the mixture any more, until all the ingredients have been mixed to a smooth, creamy dough.

If using the flavouring and colouring, add to the fat, sugar and fruit. The dough should be soft enough to drop easily from the shaken mixing spoon, and if more moisture is needed to obtain this consistency, use cold water and not milk.

Bake at Regulo 3 or 350° F. for 1¼—1½ hr.

CHESTNUT STUFFING

2 lb. chestnuts, ½ pint stock or water, 1 oz. butter, a good pinch of sugar, salt and pepper.

Cut off the tops of the chestnuts, and bake or roast them for about 20 min. Remove both the outer and inner skins, put the chestnuts into a stewpan, add the stock (no more than will barely cover them) and simmer until they become tender and dry. Rub through a fine sieve, add the butter, salt and pepper, and use as required.

CHICKEN A LA KING

4 tablespoonfuls chicken fat or butter, 4 oz. flour, ½ teaspoonful salt, pepper, 1½ pints chicken stock (can be made with chicken broth), 2 tablespoonfuls sherry, 1 small cooked chicken cut into joints and portions, ½ lb. sliced cooked mushrooms, ½ lb. green and red peppers very finely shredded and freed from white seeds.

Cook flour and fat together until thoroughly blended, then stir in the broth and make a smooth, creamy sauce. Season. Add the chicken, mushrooms and peppers. Heat through thoroughly, add sherry and serve. Some cooks add a little diced ham to the dish.

CHICKEN, FRICASSEE OF

A medium-sized boiling fowl, 1 onion, 6 peppercorns, 6 cardamom seeds, ½ pint chicken broth, ½ pint boiling milk, 1 oz. butter or margarine, 1½ oz. flour, salt, a little extra pepper.

Put the fowl, onion, peppercorns and cardamom seeds into a large saucepan with ½ teaspoonful salt, cover with warm water.

Bring to the boil and remove the scum. Put on the saucepan lid and simmer gently for 2 hr.

Remove the meat from the bones in large pieces.

Boil the carcase and skin with the broth for 20 min., strain and measure about ½ pint.

Melt the butter or margarine in a saucepan, stir in the flour and cook and stir together; do not allow it to brown.

Gradually stir in the chicken broth, then the boiling milk, and continue to cook and stir until the sauce is smooth and creamy. Put in the pieces of chicken, heat through.

Transfer to a large hot dish, garnish with mushrooms stewed in milk, and serve with plain boiled rice, or if preferred, very tiny dumplings.

CHICKEN, FRIED

2 small chickens, beaten egg, fine crumbs, a deep pan of hot fat.

Steam the chickens until tender, cut up into joints and portions. Dry, dip into the beaten egg, then coat with crumbs. Drop the pieces into the very hot, but not boiling fat and cook until golden brown. Drain on kitchen paper and serve on a paper doyley on a very hot dish. Garnish with parsley.

CHITTERLINGS, TO COOK

About 1 lb. chitterlings from calf or pig (or sheep's pluck; and, in fact, the heart, liver and lungs or lights of any animal used for food), 1/2 teaspoonful salt.

Wash the chitterlings well. Put into a pan with salt, and cover well with water. Cover with lid and bring to the boil. Simmer for about 20 min. May be sliced (after draining) and coated with seasoned flour to which a pinch of powdered sage has been added. Fry in a little dripping until nicely browned and serve with apple rings also fried in dripping.

CHITTERLING TURNOVER
(Old English recipe)

After cooking chitterlings, drain and chop finely. Mix with chopped apples, currants, a little mixed spice and sugar to taste. Enclose in a pastry crust and bake in a fairly hot oven for about 25—30 min.

In some country districts cooked chitterlings are esteemed as a tea-time delicacy, when they are eaten with vinegar and seasonings.

CHOCOLATE CAKE

4 oz. margarine, 4 oz. caster sugar, 5 oz. self-raising flour, 1 oz. good cocoa or chocolate powder, 1/2 teaspoonful vanilla flavouring, 1 level tablespoonful golden syrup, 2 eggs.

Sieve the flour and cocoa together. Whisk the egg whites and egg yolks separately until very thick and foamy, then stir them lightly together.

Beat the margarine, sugar and syrup together until you have a thick, smooth cream. Measure the syrup with a spoon dipped in boiling water, then you will not take up too much.

Stir in the foamy egg mixture and the vanilla flavouring, then the flour and cocoa. Mix all to a soft creamy dough and if you need more moisture than the eggs, use a few teaspoonfuls of cold water.

Put the mixture into a cake tin lined with greaseproof paper. Smooth evenly on the top, put into an oven which has been pre-heated to Regulo 4 or 375° F. Lower the heat to Regulo 3 or 350° F. and bake for about 1 1/2 hr.

When the cake is cold, you may either dust it with sugar and serve it plain, or slit it into 2 or 3 layers and sandwich it with chocolate butter cream and ice it with chocolate glacé icing.

Note: On no account use more than the given quantity of golden syrup or make the cake too wet, or it will sink in the middle.

CHOCOLATE GLACE ICING

8 oz. sieved icing sugar, 1 dessertspoonful cocoa, a walnut-sized knob of margarine or butter, a little hot water.

Add hot water, a teaspoonful at a time, to the icing sugar, beating well until you have a thick, smooth cream. Beat in the chocolate powder and the melted fat and beat again until the icing is like thick but smoothly running cream. Pour it over the cake and smooth with a knife dipped in hot water.

CHRISTMAS CAKE

1.

8 oz. butter or margarine, 8 oz. brown sugar, grated rind of 1 small lemon, 5 eggs, 10 oz. plain flour, 1/2 teaspoonful baking powder, 1/2 teaspoonful each mixed spice and cinnamon, 1/4 teaspoonful salt, 1 tablespoonful treacle, 2 oz. chopped glacé cherries, 1 oz. chopped angelica, 12 oz. cleaned currants, 2 oz. chopped mixed candied peel, 12 oz. seedless raisins (or raisins and sultanas mixed), 1/2 teaspoonful vanilla essence, about 2 tablespoonfuls sherry.

Soften butter and beat well. Add sugar and beat together until soft and creamy. Add grated lemon rind, and beat in eggs, one at a time, sifting in a little flour after each. Stir in treacle, then stir in remaining sifted powdered ingredients in three stages, mixing in about a third of the cleaned fruit, etc. after each addition of flour, etc. Stir in sherry at the last, making a good consistency that requires a shake to leave the mixing spoon.

Put mixture into a 8 1/2—9 in. cake tin, previously lined with triple thickness of greaseproof paper. Spread mixture level to sides of tin. Bake in a very moderate oven for about 3—3 1/2 hr. Pre-heat oven to 350° F. and reduce to 300° F. after 15 min. Do not remove cake from oven until richly browned and very slightly shrunk from sides of tin, or test with warmed skewer.

When cake is sufficiently browned, cover top with greaseproof paper until end of cooking time.

2.

6 oz. margarine, 6 oz. granulated sugar, 1 tablespoonful black treacle, 12 oz. self-raising flour, 1/2 lb. raisins, stoned or seedless, 1/2 lb. sultanas, 4 oz. currants, 2 tablespoonfuls marmalade or 4 oz. finely chopped candied peel, 4 eggs, juice of 1 fresh lemon, 1 teaspoonful mixed spice, 1/2 teaspoonful grated nutmeg, 1 teaspoonful almond flavouring, 1 level teaspoonful bicarbonate of soda, 1/2 teacupful hot milk, 2 tablespoonfuls rum or brandy.

Cream the fat and sugar together as thoroughly as if making a feathery sponge cake, because this is as important in a heavy rich cake as in any other kind. Beat in the treacle next, then stir in all the fruit and the marmalade or peel.

Now prepare the liquid, lightly beat the eggs, stir into them the lemon juice and the bicarbonate of soda; this should froth up. Stir into it the spice, nutmeg, almond flavouring, hot milk and spirit.

Add a little of this egg nogg to the fat, sugar and fruit, etc., then add a little of the sifted flour. Continue like this until all the liquid and all the flour have been well blended into the rest of the ingredients. The mixture should be a soft, creamy consistency that will fall easily from the mixing spoon. If it seems at all stiff, use a very little more warm milk.

Have ready a cake tin lined with two layers of greaseproof paper. Put the cake mixture in it and smooth it down evenly, making a hollow in the centre of the mixture so that it will rise beautifully smooth and even and will not rise up in a central peak. Put the cake into a hot oven, then shut the oven door immediately, turn it down to low and bake for 3½—4 hr. at Regulo 2 or 325° F.

Note: On no account open the oven door until the cake has been cooking for 1½ hr.

For such a cake it is always best to use a larger cake tin than usual; first, because it gives it opportunity to cook evenly all through and, secondly, it is easier to cut even-sized slices with a shallow cake than with a narrow, high cake. Finally, if the cake is to be iced and decorated, the wide, smooth top gives scope for an uncrowded and graceful decoration scheme.

When the cake is quite cold, and it should be left to cool for 12 hr., wrap it in a fine, clean cloth, then in greaseproof paper, until ready to ice.

CINDER (OR HONEYCOMB) TOFFEE

½ lb. granulated sugar, ½ lb. golden syrup, 2 level teaspoonfuls bicarbonate of soda.

Put the sugar and syrup into a strong saucepan over a low heat until the sugar and syrup have melted together.

Bring to a moderate boil and boil until a little of the syrup dropped into a cup of cold water forms a small hard pellet.

Remove the pan from the heat, stir in the bicarbonate of soda and as the toffee bubbles and fizzes, pour it into a flat tin lightly oiled with olive or almond oil. When cold break into pieces.

Note: Be sure to use a large saucepan, as the toffee bubbles up a great deal when the bicarbonate of soda is added.

COCKTAIL SNACKS, SAVOURY

Devilled Almonds: Fry blanched split almonds in oil (see recipe), but add ¼ teaspoonful cayenne pepper and ½ teaspoonful paprika to salt.

Stuffed Olives: Soak these in dry sherry for about 20 min., drain and impale on cocktail sticks.

Stuffed Dates: 4 dozen dates, 4 oz. cream cheese, 1 heaped tablespoonful chopped walnuts, 2 oz. minced preserving ginger, 1 piece of tinned pimento, finely chopped, celery salt, pepper, cayenne pepper.

Slit dates and remove stones. Mash cheese and work in remaining ingredients, using seasonings to taste. Fill cavities in dates, pressing the halves together. Impale on cocktail sticks for serving.

Ham and Egg Snippets: Mince 4 oz. lean ham and mix with 2 finely chopped hard-boiled eggs. Bind with a little well flavoured white sauce. Spread on small cracker biscuits and sprinkle with chopped parsley.

Stuffed Celery: Cut white sticks of celery into short lengths. Cream soft cheese and add chopped olives and walnuts. Press firmly into hollows of celery pieces.

COCONUT CAKE

4 oz. margarine, 4 oz. sugar, 6 oz. self-raising flour, 3 oz. desiccated coconut, 1 teaspoonful vanilla, 2 eggs, milk.

Cream the margarine and sugar together until they are very soft and almost white. Beat in the eggs to make a smooth, yellow cream. Mix in the coconut and vanilla flavouring, then slowly stir in the sifted flour, with enough milk to make a soft, creamy dough.

Put the dough into a cake tin lined with greaseproof paper, smooth evenly on the top, then bake at Regulo 3 or 350° F for about 1¼ hr.

This should make a nice moist cake, but the addition of 1 tablespoonful of golden syrup, beaten into the egg and fat and sugar, would make it more so.

COCONUT ICE

1 lb. lump sugar, ½ lb. desiccated coconut, ½ oz. butter, ¼ pint milk, ½ teaspoonful lemon juice.

Melt the sugar in the milk, then bring to a gentle boil and cook until a drop of the white syrup will form a soft ball when dropped in cold water. When this point is reached, stir in the butter, remove the pan from the heat and beat the mixture until it is very thick and creamy. Stir in the coconut and lemon. Beat well again and pour the mixture into a tin sparingly rubbed with almond oil.

When firm, mark into bars or squares and, when cold, cut up and wrap in waxed paper.

If pink ice is required, colour with a few drops of cochineal and add 4—6 drops of raspberry flavouring.

COCONUT PYRAMIDS

6 oz. desiccated coconut, 12 oz. castor sugar, 3 egg whites, ½ teaspoonful raspberry flavouring, 6 drops carmine colouring, ½ teaspoonful vanilla flavouring.

Mix the sugar and coconut together and mix to a soft consistency with the very slightly beaten egg whites.

Divide into 2 parts. Flavour and colour one with the raspberry and carmine, and the other with the vanilla.

Form into small pyramids, put them on rice paper, and bake at Regulo 2 or 325° F. until faintly tinged with golden brown.

COCONUT TOFFEE

1¼ lb. granulated sugar, ¼ lb. desiccated coconut, ¼ lb. glucose, 1 gill water, 1 teaspoonful vanilla flavouring.

Dissolve the sugar in the water over a very low heat. Stir in the glucose and boil to 290° F. with a sugar thermometer, or until a little will form a soft ball when dropped in water. Take the pan from the fire, stir in the coconut and flavouring, return to the heat and boil to 312° F. or until a drop will form a hard ball in cold water. Pour into oiled tins and mark into bars or squares as it hardens. Break up when quite cold.

COD'S ROE, FRESH

1 cod's roe, 1 tablespoonful vinegar, salt, pepper.

Poach the roe in sufficient water to cover, with the vinegar, salt and pepper for 15 min.

Cool it in water.

Cut into slices about $1/2$ in. thick, put into a fireproof dish and dot with margarine or butter. Bake for 15 min. at Regulo 5 or 400° F. Serve with egg or tartare sauce.

CORNISH HEAVY CAKE

$1/2$ lb. self-raising flour, 2 oz. butter, 2 oz. lard, 4 oz. stoned raisins, 4 oz. currants, 2 oz. chopped peel, 3 oz. granulated sugar, $1/4$ teaspoonful mixed spice, 1 saltspoonful grated nutmeg, 1 egg, milk.

Rub the butter into the flour; stir in the fruit, sugar and spices. Mix to a stiff dough with the 2 beaten eggs and a little milk. Roll out to about $1^1/2$ in. thick, press into a flat greased tin, brush with milk and bake at Regulo 4 or 375° F. for about 35—45 min.

Cut into squares and serve while warm.

CORNISH (OR DEVON) SPLITS

$1^1/2$ lb. plain flour, 4 oz. butter, 2 oz. lard, 1 oz. yeast, $1/2$ pint warm water, 1 tablespoonful sugar, pinch of salt, $1/4$ pint milk.

Put the sugar, yeast and warm water into a bowl, add 1 teaspoonful of flour and leave to work in a warm place.

Dissolve the fats in the milk. Put the flour in a bowl, add all the liquid ingredients, mix to a soft dough and leave for $1^1/2$ hr. Knead well, roll out to $1/2$ in. thickness, cut into pieces and roll into balls.

Flatten the tops a little and bake for 15—20 min. When cold, split almost through, open and fill with thick cream and jam.

CORNISH SLY CAKES

See *Sly cake, Cornish.*

COURT BOUILLON

1 large sliced onion, 1 large chopped carrot, 2 stalks chopped celery, 2 sprigs parsley, 1 bay leaf, $1/2$ teaspoonful thyme, 1 level teaspoonful peppercorns, $1^1/2$ pints water, $1/4$ pint white vinegar, 2 level teaspoonfuls salt.

Simmer all these ingredients together for 1 hr. Strain off the liquid and use as required.

For use with fish dishes, a cod's head or trimmings and bones of any fish may be cooked with the other ingredients.

COW-HEEL, BOILED

1 prepared cow-heel, 1 oz. margarine, 1 oz. flour, 1 tablespoonful finely chopped parsley, $1/2$ teaspoonful dry mustard, salt and pepper, 1 onion.

Wash the cow-heel, put it into a large saucepan with the onion and a teaspoonful of salt and cover with water. Bring to the boil, remove the scum, then boil gently for 3 hr.

Remove the jellied meat from the bones. Mix the flour and margarine together in a small saucepan until blended, stir in about $3/4$ pint of the liquid, cook until thickened, stir in the parsley and mustard, season with pepper.

Pour the sauce over the cow-heel and serve with boiled potatoes.

CREAM CHANTILLY

1 pint double cream, 3 oz. icing sugar, 1/2 teaspoonful vanilla flavouring.

Whisk the cream until it is stiff enough to cling thickly to the whisk.
Fold in the sugar and stir in the vanilla. Use to fill meringues or
éclairs, or to decorate trifles and puddings.

Other methods of flavouring are: (1) with a tablespoonful of liqueur
such as Maraschino. Curaçao or Kümmel; (2) with a few drops of
violet essence; (3) with a teaspoonful of rose water.

CREAM HORNS

1/2 lb. puff or flaky pastry, jam, whipped cream.

Roll out pastry fairly thinly and cut into 3/4 in. wide strips. Moisten
down 1 side of each and wind pastry strips overlapping on dampened
side over cornucopia moulds. (If small shapes are required, wind only
half way from pointed ends.) Glaze with white of egg or water, and
dredge with castor sugar. Bake at Regulo 6 or 425° F. for 15—20 min.
Slip shapes off moulds and leave to cool.

To fill, put a spoonful of jam into each shape and top up with
whipped, slightly sweetened cream. Pipe a line of sieved red jam or
jelly round pastry edges.

CREAM, MOCK (USING CREAM MAKER)

2 oz. unsalted butter, 4 oz. milk (about 1 small teacupful).

Put butter and milk into a saucepan and heat until butter is melted;
do not allow to boil. Stir mixture and put through cream maker
immediately, first making sure that nozzle nut of machine is screwed up
tightly. Stir cream as soon as made, to assist cooling. When cooled,
cream will be found to have thickened considerably.

To make an even thicker cream — i. e. for whipping — use 3 oz.
unsalted butter with the same quantity of milk as given above.

CROISSANTS

*2 lb. plain flour, 1 teaspoonful salt, 1 1/2 oz. yeast, 1 pint tepid milk,
6 oz. butter or margarine, 2 oz. sugar, 1 egg yolk, 2 tablespoonfuls cold
milk.*

Cream the yeast with the sugar and add to the tepid milk.
Put the flour and salt into a warm bowl, gently pour the warm
yeast liquid into the flour and work to a soft moist dough. Knead it
until smooth, then leave it in the bowl under a warm cloth for 60 min.

Roll out the dough on a floured board to 1/8 in. thickness.
Cut the butter into small pieces and space over the surface.

Fold sides to middle and seal the ends. Turn the dough over and
roll it again into a square. Fold, turn and roll 4 times more. Rest it for
15 min.

Roll to a long rectangle 1/8 in. thick, cut into 4 in. squares and cut
them across in triangles. Roll each triangle towards the point with the
palm of the hand. Put the rolls point side down on greased baking
sheets and turn into crescent shapes. Leave for 30 min. in a warm place.

Brush with egg yolk and milk, and bake at Regulo 5 or 400° F. for
about 15 min.

CRUMPETS

1 pint water, 2 oz. potato, well cooked and sieved, 1 oz. yeast, a pinch of salt, plain flour.

Add the water, just warm enough for the fingers to bear easily, to the potato; dissolve the yeast in this, add the salt, and stir in enough flour to make a thick batter, of a consistency a little thicker than that of a Yorkshire pudding. Cover the basin with a warm cloth and leave in a warm place to rise. At the end of the rising time, beat up the mixture with a wooden spoon, leave for another 30 min., beat up again.

Stand the greased crumpet rings on a hot baking sheet, pour into each enough batter to-half fill the rings and bake at Regulo 6 or 425° F. until the crumpets are risen and a pale brown, then turn them all with a broad knife, rings and all, and cook to set on the other side.

CUMBERLAND RUM BUTTER

¹/₂ lb. soft brown sugar, 4 oz. butter, 6—8 tablespoonfuls rum, a good pinch of grated nutmeg, cinnamon and mixed spices, according to taste.

Beat the butter and sugar to a very soft creamy consistency, add the spices, taking great care not to add too much or the delicate flavour of the butter will be spoiled.

Now beat in the rum a little at a time, until the mixture is soft and creamy. Press the mixture into a shallow dish and put it away in a cold place. To serve with Christmas pudding, it should be firm enough to cut into small cubes, but it may be softer to spread on cake or biscuits.

CURRANT TEA LOAF

Take 1 lb. milk bread dough. Work into it 4 oz. well washed and dried currants and 2 oz. finely minced peel.

Put into a tin-loaf-shaped bread tin, brush the top with a syrup made by melting 1 oz. demerara sugar in 2 tablespoonfuls of water 10 min. before the loaf is finished.

CURRY OF RAW MEAT

1 lb. raw beef (cut into dice), 1 tablespoonful desiccated coconut, 2 oz. butter or dripping, 1 medium-sized onion, 1 rounded dessertspoonful curry powder, 1 oz. plain flour, 1 medium-sized apple (chopped), 1 pint stock, 1 teaspoonful lemon juice, 1 dessertspoonful chutney, salt.

Prepare meat. Put coconut into a small basin and cover with ¹/₄ pint boiling water. Leave to infuse.

Melt fat and fry peeled and chopped onion and meat. When onion is soft and golden, add curry powder and flour. Stir for a few moments over low heat, then add chopped apple. Mix well, then add stock and strained liquor from infused coconut. Bring contents of pan to the boil and add lemon juice, chutney and salt to taste. Transfer mixture to casserole, cover and cook for about 1¹/₂—2 hr. (depending on quality of meat) in slow oven at 265° F. or Regulo mark ¹/₂.

CURRY OF FISH

1 lb. filleted fish (cut into neat pieces), 1 small clove garlic, 1 medium-sized onion, 1 dessertspoonful curry powder, 1 oz. butter or margarine, 1 medium-sized tomato, salt, water.

Prepare fish, peel and chop onion and garlic. Fry onion and garlic in melted fat until soft. Stir in curry powder, skinned and quartered tomato, and about 2 tablespoonfuls water. Mix well and simmer for several minutes. Add pieces of fish, salt to taste and about 1/4 pint hot water. Simmer gently until fish is tender — about 10 min.

CURRY OF VEGETABLES

1 oz. butter or margarine, 1 large onion, 1 dessertspoonful each curry powder and flour, about 1 lb. mixed cooked vegetables (carrots, potatoes and sprigs of cauliflower), 1 tablespoonful chutney, salt, 1/2 pint stock or water.

Fry chopped onion in melted fat until golden and soft. Stir in curry powder and flour, mixing well. Add stock and chutney and simmer 15 min. Stir in vegetables, salt to taste and make piping hot.

DAHL

1/2 pint Egyptian lentils, 1 small onion finely chopped, 1 oz. butter or margarine, 1 pint stock, 1 teaspoonful curry powder, pinch of salt, pepper.

Wash the lentils, put them into the stock and leave to soak all night. Put stock and lentils into a saucepan with the onion and bring to the boil, taking care that they do not boil over.

Simmer until the lentils are reduced to a purée, add salt, pepper and butter or margarine and serve, either with boiled rice or with fingers of toast.

The lentil mixture may be cooled, stirred into enough cooked rice to make a firm mixture, formed into little croquettes, egg-and-bread-crumbed, and fried and served with chutney.

DAMSON CHEESE

6 lb. damsons, 2 pints water, sugar, kernels from some of the crushed stones.

Boil the damsons with the water until quite soft. Rub through a sieve. For each lb. of the fruit purée allow 1 lb. of granulated or preserving sugar. Stir well together in the preserving pan and boil gently, stirring all the time until a little of the preserve will set on a cold plate. Add the kernels. Pot while very hot, cover when quite cold.

A little brandy or port wine may be added to the preserve just before it is potted. This is optional.

DAMSON GIN

Choose ripe damsons, prick them well with a large darning needle. Put them into 1/2 gallon jars, cover with unsweetened gin and add preserving sugar. Allow 1/4 lb. damsons and 2 oz. sugar to each pint of gin.

Cork securely and shake the jar well every day. At the end of three months strain off the gin. The damsons may have a second soaking, but use only half the quantity of gin this time.

DAMSON JAM

4 lb. damsons, 1/2 pint water, 3 lb. sugar.

Wipe all the damsons, simmer them gently with the water until they are soft, and have made plenty of juice. Stand by with a wooden spoon and catch up all the stones as they loosen and come to the top. It is always better to remove as many stones as possible before adding the sugar, because this prevents wastage.

Pour in the sugar, stir to dissolve it, then bring to the boil. Boil moderately fast until a little will set when tested, stirring constantly.

Pot while very hot and cover when quite cold.

DATE CAKE

12 oz. self-raising flour, 6 oz. demerara sugar, 2 oz. black treacle, 6 oz. margarine, 2 eggs, 3/4 lb. dates, 1/4 pint milk, 1 level teaspoonful bicarbonate of soda.

Cream the fat and demerara sugar together until very soft and light. Beat in 1 egg at a time, to make a smooth, thick, fawn-coloured cream. Stir in the well washed and chopped dates.

Melt the treacle in a small saucepan with the milk; when hot but not near boiling, remove from the heat and stir in the bicarbonate of soda. Add the sifted flour and the warm liquid alternately, a little at a time, to the fruity mixture, then blend all to a smooth, moderately soft dough. A cake dough containing syrup or treacle should always be slightly stiffer than one without.

Turn the dough into an 8 in. cake tin lined with greaseproof paper, put into a pre-heated oven for 15 min., then bake at Regulo 3 or 350° F. for about 2—2 1/4 hr.

DATE PUDDING

1/2 lb. dates, stoned and chopped, 6 oz. finely shredded suet, 4 oz. soft brown sugar, 12 oz. self-raising flour, 1 level teaspoonful bicarbonate of soda, milk.

Mix together the dates, suet, flour and 3 oz. sugar, dissolve the bicarbonate of soda in 1/2 teacupful warm water and with it mix all to a soft dough. Grease a 2 lb. pudding basin with margarine and scatter sides and bottom with the last oz. sugar. Put in the dough, cover with 2 layers of greaseproof paper. Steam for 2 hr.

DATES, STUFFED

Use smooth large dates from boxes. Slit them without halving and remove the stones.

Fill the cavities with rolls of marzipan of various flavour, stuck with blanched almonds, pieces of cherry, quarters of walnut, etc.

Fondant icing may be used instead of marzipan.

DATES, STUFFED FROSTED

1 box dates, 1 egg white, 4 tablespoonfuls caster sugar, marzipan paste.

Slit the dates at one side and remove stones. Slip a small roll of marzipan paste into each date and close firmly.

Whisk egg white — but not so stiffly as for meringues — and stir in castor sugar. Coat each stuffed date and place on a tin lined with waxed paper or oiled greaseproof paper. Set the tin in a slow oven (250° F. or Regulo 1/2) until coating on dates has candied. Cool and place each bonbon in a paper sweet cup. (Use middle shelf of oven.)

DAUBE A LA PROVENÇALE

2 lb. stewing beef, 1 glassful red wine, 2 tablespoonfuls vinegar, 12 tiny onions, 2 sticks celery cut into 1 in. lengths, 1 lb. carrots cut into thin rings, 2 cloves of garlic, 4 oz. fat bacon, strips of bacon for larding, salt, pepper, small bayleaf.

Cut the beef into cubes and lard each with a small strip of bacon. Put into a deep dish with the wine, vinegar and seasonings. Leave to marinade for 3—4 hr.

Heat the 4 oz. fat bacon, finely chopped, and brown the onions, carrots and garlic and celery with it.

Add the meat, fry together for about 5 min. Add the marinade and 2 more glasses of red wine, 1/2 lb. bacon rind, well blanched and cut into small pieces, and a bouquet garni.

Cover the pan tightly, then allow to simmer on the hot plate for about 4 hr. or in the oven for about 7 hr.

DEVILLED CHICKEN (OR TURKEY) LEGS

Simmer cooked chicken or turkey legs in chicken stock with a sliced onion, carrot and a pinch of marjoram until tender. Remove all skin and score the flesh to the bone in several places. Season with salt and pepper, rub with a thin paste of mustard and Worcester sauce. Leave for 12 hr., then grill quickly until golden brown.

Put on a very hot dish and brush over with melted butter.

Serve with toast and a watercress salad.

DEVIL'S FOOD CAKE

12 oz. self-raising flour, 6 oz. soft brown sugar, 6 oz. margarine, 1 level teaspoonful bicarbonate of soda, 4 oz. cocoa, 1/4 pint cold water, 1 teaspoonful vanilla, 1 whole egg and 3 egg yolks.

Sift together the flour, cocoa and bicarbonate soda.

Cream the fat and sugar very thoroughly. Beat the egg and yolks lightly with the water and vanilla. Stir in a little liquid and a little flour alternately until all the ingredients have been well blended to a soft creamy dough, using a little more water if necessary.

Put the dough into an 8 in. cake tin lined with greaseproof paper, smooth the top evenly and bake at Regulo 3 or 350° F. for 1 1/4—1 1/2 hr.

When cool, slice into 3 layers and sandwich together with chocolate butter cream. Ice with white or chocolate icing.

DEVIZES PIE

Lay in a pie dish slices of cold calf's head, cold lamb, cold cooked calf's brains, calf's tongue and cooked streaky bacon in alternate layers with sliced hard-boiled eggs, seasoned with salt, pepper and a very little allspice. Fill the dish with gravy made from the calf's head. Cover with rich short crust and bake at Regulo 7 or 450° F. for 35—40 min. When quite cold, turn from the dish with crust under the jellied meats and serve cut in wedges.

DIGESTIVE BISCUITS

1 lb. wheatmeal or wholemeal flour, 4 oz. butter, 2 oz. sugar, 1 egg, 1/2 level teaspoonful bicarbonate of soda, warm water.

Rub the butter well into the flour, add the sugar and bicarbonate of soda, drop the lightly beaten egg into the centre, then gradually work the dry ingredients into the egg with enough warm water to make a smooth but dry dough.

Roll the dough to the thickness of 1/4 in. on a cloth well scattered with wholemeal flour. Cut into round biscuits, prick the centres. Place them on a lightly greased baking tray and bake in a brisk oven at Regulo 6 or 425° F. for about 15 min.

DOUGH CAKE

1³/4 lb. plain flour, 1 teaspoonful salt, ³/4 oz. yeast, 6 oz. sugar, ³/4 pint tepid milk, 6 oz. lard, 1/2 lb. margarine, 1/2 lb. currants, 1/4 lb. finely chopped mixed peel, 1/2 teaspoonful mixed spice, if liked.

Sift together 12 oz. flour and the salt into a warm bowl.

Cream the yeast with a teaspoonful of the sugar and add 1/2 pint of tepid milk. Mix with the warm liquid 12 oz. flour. Beat well together, cover and leave in a warm place until the dough has doubled in bulk. Sift the remaining flour into another bowl, add the rest of the sugar, rub in the fats. Turn on to a board, and work in the risen dough with the remaining 1/4 pint of tepid milk, spice, fruit and peel. Knead well and divide into 7 in. cake tins. Prick well with a skewer, cover and leave to prove in a warm place for 1 hr.

Bake for 1¼—1½ hr. at Regulo 4 or 375° F. As soon as the cakes are removed from the tins, brush over with syrup, or with 6 knobs of sugar dissolved in 2 tablespoonfuls of hot water.

DOUGHNUTS

12 oz. plain flour, ³/4 teaspoonful salt, 1 oz. butter or margarine, 1/2 oz. yeast, 1¹/2 oz. sugar, 1 egg, warm milk, raspberry jam, sugar.

Sieve the flour and salt together, rub in the fat and put to warm. Cream the yeast and sugar together until liquid. Beat the egg, make up to 1/2 pint with warm milk and mix with the creamed yeast. Add to the warmed flour and beat well. Cover and put in a warm place until the dough has doubled in bulk (1¹/2 hr.). Turn on to a floured board, knead and divide into 18 pieces. Re-knead each piece, put a teaspoonful of jam in the centres and form into balls. Cover and prove in a warm place for about 15 min. Fry in faintly smoking hot fat for 8—10 min., turning when necessary. Drain, and toss in sugar.

DOUGHNUTS (WITH YEAST)

8 oz. plain flour, pinch of salt, 1¹/2 oz. butter or margarine, 1/2 oz. yeast, 3 tablespoonfuls milk, 1 egg, raspberry jam, deep fat or oil for cooking.

Sift flour and salt into a bowl. Sprinkle in all but 1 teaspoonful of sugar. Rub in butter.

Cream yeast with the teaspoonful of sugar. Warm the milk and beat the egg. Mix and stir into the liquid yeast. Mix lightly with the flour, etc. Cover bowl and put to rise in a warm place.

When dough has doubled its bulk, divide into about a dozen pieces and mould these into balls. Place on a floured tin and set aside in a warm place for a few minutes to prove. Then make a hole in each ball of dough and put in a small teaspoonful of raspberry jam. Damp edges and seal in neatly. Place again on floured tin, join side down, and leave in warm place for 10 min. Heat fat or oil to faintly smoking point. Drop in small balls, one or two at a time, and cook in a hot oven for about 7—8 min. Skim out with draining spoon and place on crumpled kitchen paper. Then roll in caster sugar, or in a mixture of sugar and powdered cinnamon.

DOUGHNUTS (WITHOUT YEAST)

1 lb. plain flour, 2 teaspoonfuls baking powder, 4 oz. granulated sugar, caster sugar for coating, 1/2 teaspoonful salt, 2 tablespoonfuls melted lard, 1 egg. milk, 1/2 teaspoonful vanilla flavouring, raspberry jam.

Sift flour and baking powder together, add the sugar. Beat the egg into a teacupful of milk, stir in the melted lard and vanilla, and pour into the dry ingredients. Mix to a soft dough. Divide into about 12—16 pieces, put a teaspoonful of jam on each piece, then roll into balls to cover the jam. Drop into hot lard and cook for about 4—5 minutes until brown all over. Drain well and roll on a sheet of paper covered with castor sugar.

DOVER SOLES
See *Soles.*

DOVER SPLITS

1 lb. plain flour, 1/2 pint of milk, 2 oz. lard, 1 oz. butter, 2 teaspoonfuls of baking powder, 1/2 teaspoonful salt.

Sift baking powder and salt together. Rub in the lard and butter. Mix to a stiff dough with the milk. Roll out on a floured board to 1 in. thickness, cut into small round shapes, brush tops with milk and bake for about 15 min. at Regulo 6 or 425⁰ F.

DRIPPING CAKE

1 lb. self-raising flour, 1/4 lb. demerara sugar, 1 tablespoonful of golden syrup, 6 oz. dripping, 1 tablespoonful lemon juice, 1/2 lb. well-washed and dried currants, 1 oz. finely chopped candied peel, 2 eggs, milk.

Cream together the sugar, dripping, syrup and lemon juice. Beat in the eggs one at a time until thoroughly blended. Stir in the fruit and peel, gradually fold in the sifted flour, adding milk a tablespoonful at a time, to make a soft dough that will drop easily from the mixing spoon. Turn the mixture into an 8 in. cake tin lined with greaseproof paper. Smooth evenly on top with a milky spoon. Make a deep depression in the centre. Put in an oven pre-heated for 20 min. at Regulo 3 or 350 ⁰ F. and bake at that temperature for 1¹/₂—1³/₄ hr.

DUCK, WILD, BRAISED

Season a prepared wild duck with black pepper and a little salt. Put it into a saucepan upon several rashers of streaky bacon with a bouquet garni and a walnut of butter. Put on lid and allow to simmer gently for 15 min., turning the duck once during the process.

Take the bacon and duck from the pot and cut the bird into joints. Chop the carcass and return it to the saucepan and fry it in the fat left there. Add 1 pint of stock made with giblets and 1/2 pint of brown sauce to the pan and stir and simmer for 10 min. Strain the liquid. Return all the duck and bacon to the pan and simmer together for about 30 min. Add a glass of red wine and cook for 5 min.

Serve with mashed potatoes and mashed turnips.

DUMPLINGS, SUSSEX HARD

1/2 lb. self-raising flour, 1/4 pint water, pinch of salt.

Mix to a stiff dough, make into small balls, roll them in flour and drop them into boiling water. Boil for about 30 min. or put into the baking tin when roasting meat.

DUTCH CRACKLINGS

4 oz. butter or margarine, 4 oz. soft brown sugar, 1/4 lb. plain flour, 1 dessertspoonful of ground ginger, 1/2 level teaspoonful of cinnamon, halved walnuts, 1 egg.

Cream together the fat and sugar, beat in the egg, add the sifted flour, ginger and cinnamon. Knead to a smooth dough, then roll into small balls. Put these on greased baking trays, press half a walnut on top of each and bake for 15 min. at Regulo 4 or 375° F.

EASTER CAKES

8 oz. flour, 4 oz. margarine, 1 egg, 4 oz. caster sugar, 1 oz. ground almonds, 4 oz. currants, pinch of salt, milk.

Rub the butter into the flour, add salt, stir in the sugar, almonds and currants. Beat the egg with a tablespoonful of milk, stir into the dry ingredients. Mix to a firm stiff dough. Roll out thinly on a floured board, stamp with a round cutter about 3 in. in diameter.

Bake on lightly greased tins for about 20 min. at Regulo 5 or 400° F. While still hot, dust with castor sugar.

EASTER EGGS, TO MAKE

The origin of decorating hard-boiled eggs and presenting them to friends and children on Easter Sunday morning is of great antiquity, and is observed in many countries; it used to be a great ceremony in Russia, as well as in our own country villages.

The eggs are decorated in many ways, but the simplest, and the one most followed in England, is to dye them by boiling in various liquids.

To make green eggs, boil with chopped spinach; bright pink ones, with plenty of cochineal in the water; and yellow-brown, tied in onion skins.

The custom of tying the eggs in pieces of coloured material is no longer a hundred per cent effective as so many materials to-day are colour fast.

Designs may be drawn, or a child's name written, with a candle sharpened to a point. The colour will not take on the candle grease, and the design or name stands out well.

Amusing faces may be painted on the eggs after they have been hard-boiled with poster colours or oil paints.

Little hats of coloured paper may be stuck on with glue.

ECCLES CAKES

1/2 lb. flaky rough-puff pastry, 4 oz. currants, 1 oz. butter, 1 oz. chopped (minced) candied peel, little mixed spice or grated nutmeg, little grated lemon rind, 1 1/2 oz. brown sugar.

Roll out pastry fairly thinly and cut into 4 in. diameter circles. Put a spoonful of filling ingredients in the middle of each and moisten edges of pastry with water. Pinch up edges, drawing them together to make a ball. Turn them over, smooth sides uppermost, and roll with rolling pin until fruit is just visible through paste. Make two or three slits on top — or mark a lattice pattern with back of knife over surface — and brush with white of egg, milk or water, sprinkling quickly with caster sugar. Bake in a hot oven for 15—20 min. at 450° F. or Regulo 7.

EDINBURGH ROCK

1 lb. loaf sugar, ¹/₄ teaspoonful cream of tartar, ¹/₂ pint water, lemon, raspberry, orange, ginger flavouring.

Dissolve the sugar in the water and bring to the boil, add the cream of tartar, and continue boiling without stirring until a little will form a hard ball in cold water. Put the chosen flavouring into the syrup, or divide it into 2—3 portions and flavour them differently. Pour the mixture on a marble slab or a very large china dish and with a broad buttered knife, push the edges back as they spread. When nearly firm, dust with icing sugar and pull the portions out until the sugar looks dull. Twist and cut into short lengths and stand them in a warm place for a day. The rock should then be powdery and soft.

EEL PIE

1¹/₂ lb. eels, 1 tablespoonful flour, 1 level teaspoonful salt, a good dash of pepper, 1 onion, 1 clove, a blade of mace, ¹/₄ pint water, ³/₄ pint milk, rough puff pastry.

Skin, clean and cut the eels into 2 in. lengths. Dip each piece into the flour seasoned with the salt and pepper. Put into a casserole with the onion stuck with the cloves and the mace. Cover with the milk and water. Put the lid on the casserole and cook in the oven for 1¹/₂ hr. at Regulo 4 or 375° F.

When cool pack the pieces of eel into a pie dish round a pie funnel, just cover with some of the liquid, and then with puff pastry. Brush with egg and bake at Regulo 7 or 450° F. for about 30—35 min. Serve hot with creamed mashed potatoes, or cold, with slices of lemon.

EELS, JELLIED

2—3 medium sized eels, 2 onions, 1 small piece of bayleaf, 1 teaspoonful of whole pickling spice, a dozen peppercorns, ¹/₂ pint of water, ¹/₄ pint of vinegar, salt and pepper.

Skin the eels, and cut into small pieces. Put into a pie dish with all the seasonings. Mix vinegar and water. Pour over the eels, and bake in a very slow oven for 2¹/₂ hr.

Leave until cold, when the pieces of eel should be very tender and surrounded with a spiced jelly.

EELS, PLAIN JELLIED

Eels, 1 onion, parsley, salt and pepper, water.

Skin and cut the eels into small pieces. Put into saucepan with onion, salt and pepper and several sprigs of parsley. Cover with water and bring to boil; remove any scum. Simmer gently for 1¹/₂ hr.

Take up the pieces of eel carefully and put into a basin. Strain the liquid in, and leave until cold.

EGGS

SOFT-BOILED: Lower gently into boiling water. Lower heat and simmer 3—4 min., depending on size and condition. New-laid eggs take a little longer to set. If put into cold water, bring gently to the boil and cook 1 min. or thereabouts.

HARD-BOILED: If put into cold water, bring slowly to the boil and simmer about 15 min. If put into boiling water, cook at simmering pace for about 15 min.

Eggs lowered into boiling water are more likely to have their yolks centred than those put in cold water. To avoid a dark ring round the yolk, do not over-boil, and plunge the eggs after cooking into cold water.

A small teaspoonful of salt in the cooking water will help to prevent the shells cracking.

Eggs taken from the refrigerator usually require an extra $1/2$ min. cooking and the cold water method is best.

CODDLED: Place eggs in their shells in a pan of boiling water. Cover and remove pan from heat. Leave for 10 min., then serve.

POACHED: Have ready a shallow pan containing lightly salted water. Break eggs, one at a time, into a cup or saucer, and slip gently into the simmering water. Cover and draw pan from heat, and leave in warm place until whites have set and a thin film has formed over the yolks. Skim out with perforated spoon, and serve on buttered toast.

If muffin rings, or plain tart cutters are used to confine the eggs whilst poaching, butter these inside before placing in the cooking water and adding the eggs. If egg poacher is used butter shells before breaking an egg into each. Cover and steam until set.

SCRAMBLED: *3—4 eggs, pepper and salt, 2 tablespoonfuls milk, 1 oz. butter.*
Beat eggs with seasonings and milk. Melt butter in small saucepan, pour in egg mixture and stir over moderate heat until mixture is set creamily, but still moist. Serve on hot buttered toast.

FRIED: Heat a little fat (butter, bacon fat or lard) in a frying pan. Break each egg into a cup before slipping it into the hot fat. Cook over low heat, spooning a little fat over the eggs whilst cooking. When set they are cooked.

SCOTCH: *4 hard-boiled eggs, flour, $1/2$ lb. sausagemeat, pepper and salt, breadcrumbs for coating, little beaten egg, fat or oil for frying.*
Shell the eggs and dust with seasoned flour. Divide the sausage meat into four equal portions and enclose an egg in each, moulding the sausagemeat evenly. Brush with a little beaten egg and coat each shape closely with baked crumbs. Lower into smoking hot fat or oil and cook until richly browned. Drain well and eat hot or cold.

SHIRRED: Melt $1/2$ oz. butter in each individual shallow dish before adding eggs. Dust with pepper and salt and bake in moderate oven (350° F. or Regulo 4) until set. Shirred eggs are always served in the dish in which they are cooked.

EGGS, PICKLED

12 hard-boiled eggs, 1 quart of good malt vinegar, $1/2$ oz. black peppercorns, $1/2$ oz. allspice, 1 teaspoonful of salt.

Shell the eggs, and arrange them in large wide-necked glass jars. Boil the peppercorns and allspice in the vinegar for 15 min. Strain while hot over the eggs, to cover them completely.

When cold, cover with an air-tight cover and store in a cool dry place.

EGGS, TO STORE

1. Immerse eggs not more than 24—48 hours old in a solution of water-glass. This is obtainable in tins from most chemists. Follow instructions on the tin in making the solution. The eggs must be covered completely at all times, and a lid or covering placed on the container. A zinc-lined bucket or small bath is best.

2. A commercial liquid into which each egg is dipped separately for a few seconds and placed on a rack to dry. The dipped eggs can then be put into baskets or boxes, separated by thin layers of straw or shavings. It is not necessary to keep them air-tight.

3. Grease the eggs thoroughly with lard, lay them in a box of bran and cover each layer with bran to keep them air-tight.

Experts say that it is not advisable to preserve duck's eggs.

ELDERBERRY CHUTNEY

8 lb. elderberries, weighed after removing from stalks, 3 lb. green cooking apples, 2 lb. onions, 1 bulb of garlic, 1½ lb. brown sugar, 4 oz. cooking salt, 2 oz. ground ginger, 2 oz. dry mustard, 1 teaspoonful ground mace, ¼ teaspoonful ground cloves, 20 peppercorns, 1 quart of malt vinegar, 1 lb. sultanas.

Peel, core, and chop the apples, peel and chop the onions and garlic.

Simmer these three ingredients very slowly until a little juice runs, raise the heat and cook until the apple is soft. Stir in the elderberries, salt, sugar, sultanas and peppercorns. Mix the ginger, mustard, mace and cloves with the vinegar. Stir into the other ingredients, then boil gently until the chutney is thick and jammy. Pot into clean, dry pots, filling them to the tops; when cold, cover securely.

ELDERBERRY JELLY

6 lb. ripe elderberries, sugar, strained juice of a lemon if liked.

Wash the berries and strip them from the stalks into a preserving pan. Put over a very low heat, and cook very slowly until a little juice begins to run. Crush the softened berries, and simmer until pulpy.

Strain through a jelly bag, taking care not to let any pulp through. Measure the juice, add the lemon, and for each pint of liquid, allow 1 lb. sugar.

Stir juice and sugar in the pan until the sugar is quite dissolved, then bring to the boil and boil moderately fast until a little will set when tested on a plate.

ELDERBERRY WINE

4 lb. ripe elderberries, 3 quarts water, 2½ lb. sugar, 2 cloves and a small piece of root ginger if liked, ½ oz. yeast.

Wash the berries if they have been picked near a highway. Put them into a large crock. There is no need to string them.

Mash well with a wooden spoon or vegetable press. Bring the water almost to the boil, pour it over the mashed fruit, add the cloves and ginger if you like the flavour. Stir in the sugar, making quite sure that it dissolves completely and does not lie in a cake at the bottom of the crock. When the liquid is luke-warm, take off a teacupful, dissolve the yeast in it, stir thoroughly into the rest of the liquid, then cover the top of the crock with a folded cloth or blanket to keep out dust and tiny wine flies. Leave for 7 days, strain off through three thicknesses of clean muslin, or clean blotting paper, or specially prepared filter papers, into clean, perfectly dry bottles. Press the corks in quite lightly and leave thus for 14 days. When the working has ceased, fill each bottle to cork level from the contents of one of them, press the corks right home and leave the wine to mature for at least 6 months — 12 is better.

ELDERFLOWER WINE

Pick a dozen fine clusters of elderflowers, full-blown ones so that the pollen is rich on them, on a dry day and away from the road so that they are not dusty. Put the flowers carefully in a basket as you pick in order not to shake off the pollen.

Snip the flowers from the stalks, put them into a crock, pour a gallon of luke-warm water over (on no account let it be hot, merely blood heat). Add the rind of two lemons, and the fruit very thinly sliced and free from pith.

Leave for 3 days, stirring occasionally, and covered with a cloth. Put in 4 lb. white sugar, stir well to dissolve it and leave for 7 days.

Put a piece of cotton wool into the mouth of a filter, or on a piece of muslin, and filter the wine through it. Bottle the clean liquid, filling the bottles up right to the cork; cork, but not very tightly.

Leave for 14 days, then cork securely, and lay the bottles on their sides until you want to use the wine. Try not to use any of it for at least 4 months, but better still 6 months. No yeast is used.

ENGLISH FRONTIGNAC (ELDERFLOWER WINE)

24 heads of elderflowers, 3 lb. granulated or preserving sugar, 1 gallon of water, 4 tablespoonfuls of best white wine vinegar, or lemon juice, 1 egg white, 1 teaspoonful of yeast, 1 lb. good plump raisins.

Wash the raisins, put them with the flower heads, and vinegar or lemon juice into a large dry crock.

Bring the water and sugar, with the egg white well whipped into it, to the boil; boil for 10 min., cool a little, remove the scum and pour the liquid into the crock over the flowers, etc. When the liquid is luke-warm, take off a teacupful and dissolve the yeast in it. Stir it back into the rest of the liquid in the crock.

Cover the top of the crock with a board or thick cloth. Stir every day for 6 days, keeping it well covered between stirrings. Leave to rest for 24 hr., then strain carefully into very clean, dry bottles. Fill the bottle necks with thick tufts of twisted cotton wool and leave for 14 days, then replace the wool with well-cleaned, or new corks. Store in a cool place for at least 9 months.

EVE'S PUDDING

1 lb. cooking apples, 4 oz. sugar, 1 clove; dough made from: 2 oz. butter, 2 oz. caster sugar, 4 oz. self-raising flour, 1 egg, grated rind of 1/2 lemon, milk.

Cook the peeled, cored and sliced apples with the clove and sugar and only enough water to moisten the saucepan.

Turn them into a pie dish. When cold, cover them with dough made as follows:

Cream butter and sugar, add beaten egg, the flour, lemon rind and enough milk to make a soft dough. Bake at Regulo 6 or 425° F. for about 20 min.

FADGE (IRISH POTATO BREAD)

Peel and boil 3 lb. of old potatoes until tender. Drain well and dry over a low heat. Mash very smoothly. When cool enough to allow a finger to remain in it, add salt and work in enough self-raising flour to make a pliable dough. Knead it well on a floured board. Form into large rounds about 1/2 in. thick. Cut into wedge-shaped pieces. Cook the pieces on a griddle very lightly brushed with lard until brown on one side, then turn and brown on the other. Split and butter while hot, or fry with bacon or sausages.

FAGGOTS

1/2 lb. raw liver, 2 medium-sized onions, 2 rashers bacon, 2 or 3 slices bread, 2 eggs, 2 tablespoons flour, milk, seasoning to taste, a few herbs if liked.

Beat up the eggs and make into a batter with the flour and milk, adding the seasoning and herbs. Mince the liver, onions and bacon, soak the bread in milk, mix all the ingredients together and blend very thoroughly with the batter. Put into greased tins with covers and stand them in a pan of water in the oven for about 3/4 hr. or more. Delicious when served, cold or hot, in slices.

FARLS

See *Oatmeal Biscuits.*

FAT RASCALS

8 oz. butter, 1 lb. plain flour, 4 oz. currants, 1 oz. brown sugar, a little caster sugar, a pinch of salt, milk, water.

Rub the butter into the flour, add the currants, sugar and salt, and sufficient milk and water to make a slack dough. Turn on to a floured board and roll out to 1/2 in. thick, cut into rounds, dust with a little caster sugar, place on a baking sheet and bake for 20 min. in a quick oven.

FAVE DEI MORTI

1 lb. plain flour, 8 oz. castor sugar, 8 oz. butter or margarine, 4 eggs, 2 tablespoonfuls orange water or 1 teaspoonful powdered cinnamon, 2 tablespoonfuls brandy.

Rub the fat well into the flour, stir in the sugar and cinnamon, if used. Beat the eggs and put a little aside for brushing.

Add brandy and orange-flower water to the eggs if using them. Mix the dry ingredients to a stiff dough with the egg mixture. Roll out, cut to broad bean shapes, brush with egg, sprinkle with sugar and bake at Regulo 5 or 400° F. for about 20 min.

FIG JAM, GREEN

4 lb. green figs, 3¹/₂ lb. granulated sugar, strained juice of 2 lemons, ¹/₂ pint warm water.

Use the figs when they are quite ripe, then the skins should be thin and the pulp juicy.

Cut off stalk ends and calyx ends, slice the figs thinly or cut them into small pieces. Put the fruit and water into the preserving pan, and simmer gently until soft and pulpy.

Stir in the lemon juice, then the sugar. Bring slowly to the boil, and boil moderately fast until a little of the preserve will set when dropped on a cold plate.

While the jam is boiling, stir frequently, to prevent it from burning.

Pot the jam while it is still very hot, and cover when quite cold.

FIG JAM USING DRIED FIGS

2 lb. dried figs, 3 lb. granulated sugar, strained juice of 2 lemons, 1¹/₂ pints water.

Soak the figs in a bowl of water for 12 hr., rinse in fresh water, cut into small pieces, removing any hard little pieces of stem.

Put into a preserving pan with a pint and a half of fresh hot water and simmer until tender. Stir in the lemon juice and sugar and continue to cook until the preserve is thick.

Pot while hot, cover when quite cold.

FISH PIE

1¹/₂ lb. fresh haddock, hakes or codling, 2 tablespoonfuls crumbs, 3 tablespoonfuls finely grated cheese, 2 teaspoonfuls finely chopped parsley, 1 tablespoonful minced onion, salt, pepper, 1 pint milk, 2 eggs, 2 oz. margarine.

Poach the fish in a little salted water until it can be removed easily from skin and bones, then divide into flakes.

Put the flakes into a pie dish greased with a little of the margarine, sprinkling the parsley and onion between the layers.

Beat the eggs into the milk, season with salt and pepper, pour over the fish. Bake in a slow oven, Regulo 3 or 375⁰ F., until the top feels firm to the touch. Run the remaining margarine over the top, cover with the minced onions and cheese, then put under a hot grill to brown the cheese, for 3—4 min.

The crisp cheesey top contrasts beautifully with the creamy custard and well-seasoned fish inside the pie.

FISH POT

A selection of fish, whiting, herrings, plaice, codling, fresh haddock or any kind of fish obtainable, 1 or 2 sliced onions, 2 oz. butter or margarine, salt, pepper, small piece of bayleaf.

Clean and scale the fish, removing heads. Put all into a large casserole. Cover with the lid, and cook in a slow oven until all the bones and skin can be removed easily.

Flake the fish, put it into a pie dish with the liquid slightly thickened with flour. Cover with a thick layer of well-mashed potato and brown it in the oven.

FISH STOCK

Fish trimmings, bones and fish, salt, 1/2 teaspoonful peppercorns, 1 small bayleaf, 1 strip of celery, 1 small onion, cold water to cover well.

Rinse trimmings of fish, etc., and put into pan with flavourings and water. Cover and bring slowly to the boil. Simmer gently for about 40 min., then strain.

A second method is to cook the flavourings and water for 20 min. steadily. Then add fish etc. and bring again to simmering point. Continue simmering for 20 min., then strain.

FLAMRI

4 oz. small semolina, 1/2 pint sweet white wine, 1/2 pint water, 2 oz. castor sugar, 2 eggs, purée of strawberries or raspberries or red currants.

Bring the wine and water to the boil, sprinkle in the semolina and cook over a very slow heat for 25 min. Stir in the sugar, the beaten egg yolks and the whites separately, whisked to a stiff froth. Put into small buttered moulds and cook gently in a large pan of water for 15 min. Cool in the water, then turn out the moulds and mask with fruit purée sweetened and if liked, flavoured with a tablespoonful of port wine.

FLAP JACKS

6 oz. butter or margarine, 6 oz. Demerara sugar, 8 oz. rolled oats, pinch of salt.

Cream the fat until soft. Mix together the sugar, oats and salt and stir into the fat. Transfer the mixture to a greased tin 9 in. by 12 in. and spread evenly, smoothing the surface. Bake for 30 min. at Regulo 5. When cooked leave to stand for a few minutes in the tin and then cut into 16 squares or fingers.

FLORENTINES

1 oz. butter, 3 oz. sugar, 1/2 teacupful cream, 1 teaspoonful honey, 2 oz. sifted flour, 4 oz. blanched and chopped almonds, 4 oz. candied orange and lemon peels, finely shredded or minced coarsely, 1 oz. chopped glacé cherries, about 4 oz. plain chocolate.

Put butter, cream, honey and sugar into a pan and make very hot. Allow to bubble for a moment or so, then draw pan from heat and stir in sifted flour, nuts and candied peels with glacé cherries. Mix well. Place dessertspoonfuls spaced well apart on well-greased baking tins. Flatten with floured fingers. Place in moderate oven (350° F. or Regulo 3) for about 25 min., or until richly browned. Loosen cakes from tin with broad-bladed knife, but leave on tin to cool.

Melt grated or chopped chocolate in a pan standing in a vessel containing very hot water. When melted, spread chocolate over flat sides of cakes. When partially set, these can, if liked, be turned, chocolate side down, on lightly oiled wire trays for the pattern to be imprinted on the chocolate. Lift off when set.

FONDANT

(Basic recipe for cream used in making sweets)
2 lb. granulated sugar, 2/3 pint of water, 1 dessertspoonful glucose.

Put sugar and water into a strong saucepan and leave to soak for 1 hr.
Heat slowly, stirring until the sugar has completely dissolved, then add
the glucose, and cover with the saucepan lid until boiling point is
reached. Test with the thermometer until 235° F. is reached. Leave to
stand until the bubbles have subsided. Pour gently into a wide bowl
rinsed in cold water. Allow to cool, then stir with a wooden spoon until
quite thick and smooth. If the mixture is stirred too soon, the sugar will
grain and become coarse.

FONDUE

*4 eggs, 3 oz. grated Gruyère cheese, pepper and salt, 1 oz. butter,
1 saltspoonful made mustard, fingers of crisp toast, or cheese crackers.*

Separate eggs, whisking whites first and adding yolks one by one. Beat
eggs together and put with grated cheese, etc., in a pan over low heat.
Stir until mixture is soft and creamy. Serve very hot with toast or
biscuits.

For large quantities, use ingredients in these proportions: one-third
of the weight of the eggs in grated Gruyère cheese, and one-sixth in
fresh butter, using salt to taste and plenty of freshly ground pepper.
Add a pinch of cayenne, if desired.

FORCEMEAT

*1/2 lb. veal finely chopped, 1/4 lb. bacon finely chopped, 2 tablespoonfuls
breadcrumbs, 1 dessertspoonful finely chopped parsley, 1/2 teaspoonful
powdered mixed herbs, 1/4 teaspoonful finely grated lemon rind, 1 egg,
nutmeg, salt and pepper.*

Mix the veal, bacon, breadcrumbs, parsley, herbs and lemon rind well
together and season to taste. Add the egg, which should thoroughly
moisten the dry ingredients; if too small to do this, use a little milk
or water in addition. Mix well, and use as required.

FRANGIPANE FILLING FOR FLANS OR TARTS

*3 oz. plain flour, 3 egg yolks and 1 whole egg, 2 oz. castor sugar, 1 oz.
butter, 3 oz. ground almonds, 3—4 drops of almond flavouring, cold
milk, 1 pint hot milk.*

Mix the flour to a smooth paste with cold milk, then add the egg yolks
and whole egg and sugar, stir for 5 min. to mix thoroughly. Gradually
add the hot milk and the butter cut into small pieces, stir well again,
then turn into the top of a double saucepan and cook and stir until the
mixture is like thick cream, but do not allow it to come to the boil.
Remove from the heat, beat in the almond flavouring and ground
almonds. Use in a plain tart or flan pastry, or poured over a flan filled
with fruit of any kind.

FRIAR'S OMELETTE

12 apples, 1/4 lb. butter, 1/4 lb. white sugar, 4 eggs, breadcrumbs.

Boil the apples, as for sauce; stir in the butter and the sugar. When
cold, add the eggs well beaten. Put into a greased baking dish thickly
strewn with breadcrumbs, so as to stick to the bottom and sides, then put
in the apple mixture; strew crumbs over the top. When baked, turn it
out and grate loaf sugar over it.

FRITTER BATTER
See *Batters.*

FROMAGE DE PORC (PORK CHEESE)

About 1 lb. cooked pork, which could be taken from a leg, or hand and spring, cut into small dice, 1/4 level teaspoonful powdered sage, a good pinch grated nutmeg, 1 dessertspoonful chopped parsley, 1 tablespoonful minced onion, 1/2 pint jelly stock made with pig's trotters.

Mix all the ingredients together, pour into a mould and bake for 1 1/2 hr. at Regulo 5 or 400° F.

When cold, turn out and serve sliced with mustard sauce.

FRUIT BOTTLING

Fruit for preserving should be fresh, firm and ripe—even slightly under-ripe, especially in the case of soft fruits. Gooseberries should be green and hard.

Grade fruit according to size and ripeness. Wash well and drain. Fruits that require peeling, such as apples or pears, should not be left exposed to the air. See directions below.

Fruit may be bottled in water or syrup, using a thin syrup (2 oz. sugar to 1 pint water) for small, soft fruits, a medium syrup (4 oz. sugar to 1 pint water) for peaches, gages and other stone fruit, and a heavy syrup (6 oz. sugar to 1 pint water) for large sour fruits.

To make the syrup, put sugar and water into a pan, bring to the boil, stirring until sugar is dissolved, and simmer for 5 min. Use hot or cold as directed.

If golden syrup is substituted for some of the sugar, remember that 1 tablespoonful equals 1 oz. sugar.

Apples and pears may be par-boiled for 5 min. in plain water before being put into the jars, as this softens them a little and they mature in the jars well. With the very hard winter pears, cook them for several hours in a casserole in a slow oven, or they will remain hard even when bottled and cooked later. (Save this cooking liquor and use when making syrup or botling in water.)

These fruits should be prepared very quickly, and each piece, as it is peeled and cored, and sliced or halved, dropped at once into a bowl containing a solution of 1 tablespoonful salt to 1/2 gallon water. This prevents the fruit from browning, as it does very easily.

Rinse the fruit in clean water, par-cook as directed, then pack the pieces into the jars which should be ready rinsed out with very hot water and drained. Use two spoon handles or two slim pieces of wood to help you arrange the pieces of fruit, or any whole fruits, in the jars in a neat and regular manner. Fruit heaped into the jars anyhow not only takes up too much room, so that too little is put into each jar, but allows large pockets of air to form between the pieces, apart from the fact that the jars look untidy and unprofessional when finished.

Plums of moderate size may be bottled whole, but very large ones are more successful if halved. In halving the fruit leave stones on one half of the fruit because they impart an almond flavour richer than when stones are removed.

Oven Method: Having packed fruit into jars — almost to the brim to allow for shrinkage whilst heating — cover tops with the glass lids of Kilner-type jars, or with patty-tins, to prevent fruit browning. Place jars in the oven — not touching each other — at low temperature for $3/4$—1 hr., when fruit will have changed colour slightly. Remove one jar at a time from the oven and place on a wooden or paper-covered surface. Fill to the brim with boiling water or syrup. Adjust seals without delay, tightening screw band as far as possible. Repeat the process with each jar and bringing water or syrup to boiling point before pouring over fruit. Leave until cold before testing the seals by removing metal band and lifting the jar by the lid.

Water-Bath Method: Having packed the fruit into the jars, prepare the syrup, using any liquor in which hard fruit may have been par-boiled. Fill jars to overflowing with cold syrup or water. Adjust covers according to their type. Place in a large deep pan holding sufficient cold water to keep jars submerged. The bottoms of the jars should rest on a false bottom, and if a proper sterilising pan is not used, see that there is a folded cloth or newspaper to protect the jars from direct contact with bottom of pan. If screw bands (Kilner-type jars) are used, give these a half-turn back after screwing as tightly as possible. Clip top closures require no attention. Cover pan and heat slowly to simmering point (about 185° F) taking about $1^1/2$ hr. Maintain this temperature for 15 min. for most fruits, and 30 min. for pears and whole tomatoes.

Remove jars one at a time. Tighten screw tops at once. Spring clips require no further attention.

Test seals when cold, as for Oven Method.

Note: If jars are to be sealed with a synthetic skin or with paraffin wax, the jars should be submerged in water up to their shoulders only, and the skin covering fitted, or hot wax poured in immediately after removal from the water-bath.

A further Method: If desired, the fruit and syrup may be put into the jars and these contents preserved as follows, preferably in Kilner-type jars.

Having packed the prepared fruit in the jars, prepare the syrup or water. If doing apples and pears, use the water in which the fruit was par-boiled. For syrup, add the required quantity of sugar, bring to the boil and remove any scum that rises. Then allow to go off the boil, and pour very slowly and gently into the jars (which can have been well heated before filling with the fruit), filling until the fruit is well covered. If jars are filled slowly, it will prevent as far as possible any formation of air bubbles which form if the liquid is poured in quickly. Let the liquid settle down, then add more if necessary, until top layer of fruit is covered completely. Tap jars gently on every side, to expel any air bubbles low in the jars, and as they come to the top, prick them to explode them.

Put rings, lids and metal bands in place, first making sure they are all in perfect condition. It is advisable to soak rubber rings in hot water for about 15 min. before using, and dry well. Tops of jars should also be dried, as if wet and slippery they may not engage the glass, and a good seal will not be possible. Having put on the rings, etc., screw bands tightly, then give a half turn back to allow for expansion of the glass in the heat.

Heat the oven to 250⁰ F. — Regulo ¹/₂ — and stand the jars, not touching one another, on the lowest grid shelf. Leave for 90 min. for solid fruits, and for 75 min. for soft fruits.

Turn off heat, open oven door, but do not touch jars until they are quite cool. Test for seal, then store away.

The reason for the rising of fruit in the jars is almost always because the jars have been left in the heat too long — even ten minutes over the stated times may bring about this result. Other causes could be too high a temperature, or a too heavy syrup in the case of light fruits.

FRUIT. PULPED

See *Pulped fruit*.

FUDGE

1 lb. loaf or granulated sugar, just over ¹/₄ pint milk, 3 oz. margarine.

This is a basic fudge recipe and to it may be added any flavouring required.

Put the milk and sugar into a stout saucepan and leave for about 20 min., then bring slowly to the boil without stirring. Boil for 5 min., this time stirring and adding the margarine cut into little pieces. Stir and cook to 240⁰ F. if you have a sugar thermometer, or until the mixture thickens and forms a soft ball when a little is dropped into a cup of cold water. Remove the saucepan from the heat, allow to stand for about 2 min., then beat thoroughly with a wooden spoon, scraping down the mixture from the sides of the pan in order not to waste any. When the mixture is smooth and creamy, pour it into a well-oiled tin and, as soon as it stiffens, mark into squares with the tip of a sharp knife. When cold, break up and wrap the pieces in waxed paper.

Variations

1 teaspoonful vanilla flavouring.
1 tablespoonful coffee essence and 2 oz. finely chopped walnuts.
2 tablespoonfuls orange juice and grated rind of ¹/₂ orange.
2 oz. minced glacé cherries; 1 oz. chopped nuts and 1 oz. chopped candied peel.

GAME PIE

Rich short crust, flaky pastry, the meat from a roast pheasant, 2—3 grilled rashers bacon, 3—4 thinly sliced mushrooms. 1 carrot, 1 egg, 1 shallot minced and browned in butter, gravy thickening, salt, pepper.

Line a pie dish or casserole with rich, short crust; arrange the pheasant meat on it with the shallot, salt, pepper, bacon and mushrooms in layers.

Cover with gravy made by boiling the carcase with the carrot, salt and gravy thickening. Add a lid of flaky pastry, brush with egg and bake at Regulo 7 or 450⁰ F. for 35 min.

Short crust may be used for the lid if it is not possible to have two kinds of pastry ready.

Serve hot or cold, cut into small wedges. The same recipe does for grouse, partridge or other game.

GARLIC BREAD

1 long French loaf, butter, a clove of garlic.

Crush the skinned garlic to a pulp, mix with 3 oz. butter. Cut the loaf through in slices down to the bottom crust, but not right through. Spread one side of each cut slice with garlic butter. Press the slices together and put the loaf into a hot oven for a few minutes until the crust is very crisp.

To serve, cut right through into separated slices.

GENOA CAKE

12 oz. self-raising flour, 8 oz. caster sugar, 8 oz. butter, 8 oz. each sultanas and currants, 4 oz. finely chopped candied peel, 2 oz. finely chopped blanched almonds, 1/2 oz. split almonds, grated rind and strained juice of one small lemon, milk as required.

Cream the butter and sugar together until soft and almost white. Add the eggs one at a time, beating in each very thoroughly. Stir in the fruit, peel and chopped almonds, fold in the sifted flour, adding a little milk as required to make a soft creamy dough.

Put into a cake tin lined with greaseproof paper, smooth the top evenly with a milky spoon, drop the split almonds gently on the surface.

Bake at Regulo 3 or 350° F. for about 2 hr.

GENOESE CAKE (OR PASTE)

6 oz. butter, 8 oz. caster sugar, 4 eggs, 6 oz. plain flour well sifted, 1/2 teaspoonful vanilla flavouring.

Melt the butter over hot water, then put aside to cool. Beat the eggs and sugar into the melted butter until it is so thick and fluffy it appears to have doubled.

Add the flour very gently by sifting it in little by little, by means of a wire strainer. Fold in the flavouring. Pour the mixture into a greased square tin. Bake at Regulo 4 or 375° F. for about 30—35 min.

GENOESE SAUCE

1 oz. each of pistachio and pine kernel nuts pounded to a paste, 3 egg yolks, 1 pint olive oil, juice of 1 lemon, 1 tablespoonful Béchamel sauce, salt, pepper.

Add seasonings, sauce, egg yolks and oil to the nut paste as for making mayonnaise.

GHERKINS, PICKLED

Put the required quantity of gherkins, picked when they are mature, into a large china bowl and cover them with a brine of 4 oz. kitchen salt to 1/2 gallon of water and a walnut-sized piece of alum. Leave for 7 days. Soak in fresh water for 24 hr., then drain and dry them and pack them into small jars.

Cover with cold spiced vinegar, that is, good malt vinegar, boiled with 1 oz. allspice and 24 peppercorns to 1 quart vinegar.

GIBLET PIE

1 set of giblets if goose or turkey, 2 if fowl giblets, 1 lb. good stewing steak, 1 onion, a bouquet garni (parsley, thyme, bayleaf and rosemary), salt, pepper, rough puff paste, 1 egg yolk beaten with a tablespoonful of milk, flour.

Wash the giblets, put them into a saucepan with the steak cut into small dice and rolled in flour, seasoned with salt and pepper, the sliced onion (only remove top layer of skin and root), the herbs and sufficient water to cover.

Bring to the boil, remove all scum, then simmer gently for 2 hr. Cut the giblets into pieces and arrange them with the steak in a pie dish. Pour in enough stock to cover the meat.

Put on a cover of puff pastry, decorate with roses and leaves of cuttings of paste, brush all over twice with egg and milk. Bake at Regulo 7 or 450° F. for about 35—40 min.

GINGER BEER

5 quarts boiling water, 1¹/₄ lb. sugar, 1 oz. whole ginger, well bruised, 2 lemons, ¹/₂ oz. cream of tartar, 1 oz. yeast.

Remove the rinds of the lemons as thinly as possible, cut into small strips and put them into a large earthenware crock or large china bowl. Strip off every particle of the white pith from the peeled lemons, cut the fruit into very thin slices, removing all the pips, add the sliced lemon to the peel, then add the sugar.

Boil the water with the ginger for 10 min., pour it over the contents of the bowl and leave until just lukewarm. Take off a teacupful of the lukewarm liquid, dissolve the yeast in it and stir it back thoroughly into the rest. Cover the top of the crock and leave for two days. Strain into clean dry bottles and cork. The beer is ready to drink the next day. As this very good ginger beer is apt to turn flattish after about 10 days, it is best to make up half the quantities, unless you need a lot at a time.

GINGERBREAD, DARK

8 oz. butter or margarine, 4 oz. granulated sugar, 4 oz. soft brown sugar, 4 oz. dark treacle, 2 eggs, 12 oz. self-raising flour, 1¹/₂ teaspoonfuls ground ginger, 1 level teaspoonful ground cinnamon, 2 oz. split blanched almonds, a little milk.

Beat the butter or margarine, the sugar and treacle to a soft cream. Add the flour sifted with the spices alternately with the eggs (beaten), using a little tepid milk if necessary to make a soft dough.

Line a baking tin with greaseproof paper. Scatter the almonds over it, then spoon the cake mixture into the tin. Smooth the top and brush with milk. Bake at Regulo 2 or 325° F. for about 1—1¹/₄ hr.

GINGERBREAD, WHITE

1 lb. self-raising flour, 6 oz. butter or margarine, 4 oz. granulated sugar, 2 oz. golden syrup, 1¹/₂ teaspoonfuls ground ginger, 2 eggs, tepid milk as required.

Sift together the flour and ginger, stir in the sugar. Warm the fat and syrup together, beat in the eggs and pour all into the dry ingredients.

Mix to a soft dough, using a little tepid milk as required.

Smooth the dough evenly into a greaseproof paper lined baking tin, brush with milk, bake at Regulo 3 or 350° F. for about 1 hr.

GINGER NUTS

¹/₂ lb. plain flour, 2 teaspoonfuls ground ginger, ¹/₂ teaspoonful ground cinnamon, 4 oz. brown sugar, 2 oz. dark treacle, ¹/₂ teaspoonful bicarbonate of soda.

Sift together the flour and spices, stir in the sugar. Melt together the treacle and fat, stir in the bicarbonate of soda, and pour the mixture into the dry ingredients. Mix to a stiff dough without using any other liquid. Roll the dough into balls the size of walnuts. Space out on greased tins. Flatten a little with a milky spoon. Bake at Regulo 3 or 325⁰ F. for about 14 min.

GINGER PUDDING

4 oz. margarine, 4 oz. granulated sugar, 4 oz. golden syrup, 8 oz. self-raising flour, 1 egg, ¹/₂ teaspoonful bicarbonate of soda, 1¹/₂ teaspoonfuls ground ginger, ¹/₂ small teacupful warm milk.

Cream together the fat and sugar, beat in the egg. Sift the flour with the ginger. Mix the golden syrup, warm milk and bicarbonate of soda together. Add flour and liquid to the fat and sugar. Blend to a smooth dough.

Grease a 1¹/₂ lb. pudding basin with margarine, pour the rest of the syrup into it, then put in the dough.

Cover with two thicknesses of greaseproof paper and steam for 2 hr.

GINGER WINE

1. *3 lbs. sugar, 1 gallon water, 1¹/₂ oz. bruised root ginger, the thinly pared rind of 2 lemons and the strained juice of the fruit, 1 oz. yeast.*
Boil the lemon rind, ginger, sugar and water together for 1 hr. Pour the hot liquid, with rind and ginger, into a large crock or tub, then stir in the lemon juice. When the liquid has cooled to a lukewarm temperature, take off a teacupful and dissolve the yeast in it.

Cover the top of the vessel with a thick cloth or folded blanket, and leave until the working ceases, which should be about 6 days. If using bottles, strain into clean dry bottles and cork loosely for about 10 days, then fill all the bottles to cork level from the contents of one of them, and cork securely.

If using a cask, bung tightly after the working has ceased, and do not bottle for 3 months. Mature the wine for 6 months.

2. This is a good drink, but is unfermented. Buy from the chemist 3 drachms each of tincture of capsicum, essence of lemon and essence of ginger, 2 drachms each of tartaric acid and of cream of tartar and 1 pennyworth of burnt sugar. Boil 2 lb. loaf sugar with 3 quarts of water, then stir in the ginger mixture. Bottle when cold, cork securely, and allow to mature for 2 months.

GIRDLE SCONES

1 lb. plain flour, 2 teaspoonfuls baking powder, 1 teaspoonful salt, ¹/₂ pint milk.

Sift flour, baking powder and salt together. Mix quickly with the tepid milk. Knead lightly, roll to a thickness of about ¹/₄ in. Cut into round scones. Lightly grease the girdle and bake the scones on either side.

GNOCCHI ALLA PIEMONTESE (POTATO GNOCCHI)

1 lb. potatoes, 3 oz. flour, 1 whole egg and 1 egg yolk, 3 oz. butter or margarine, 6 oz. grated Parmesan cheese, salt, pepper.

Boil or steam the peeled potatoes and rub them through a sieve while hot. Mix with the flour, egg and egg yolk, season with pepper and salt.

Roll into small sausage-shaped pieces. Drop into boiling salted water, cook for 15—20 min. Drain and serve with tomato sauce and grated cheese, or Espagnole sauce and cheese.

GNOCCHI ALLA ROMANA (SEMOLINA GNOCCHI)

4 oz. semolina, 1 oz. butter, 2 oz. grated cheese, 2 eggs, milk, salt.

Cook the semolina in $3/4$ pint boiling milk. When thick and smooth, add 1 oz. butter and 1 oz. cheese. Take from the heat and beat in the eggs. Pour the mixture, $1/2$ in. thick, on to a large dish. Leave until cold.

Cut the mixture into small squares, circles or diamonds. Arrange these overlapping one another in a buttered dish, cover with 2 oz. melted butter and about 3 oz. grated Parmesan or Gruyère cheese and brown in the oven.

GNOCCHI, SEMOLINA

1 pint milk, 4 oz. semolina, 2 oz. grated Cheddar cheese, pepper, salt, pinch nutmeg, 1 oz. butter, 1 egg, little Parmesan cheese, chopped chives and marjoram.

Heat milk with flavourings (pepper, salt, nutmeg and herbs). Just before milk boils sprinkle in semolina, stirring all the time with a wooden spoon. When quite thick, draw pan from heat and stir in butter, beaten egg and Cheddar cheese. Mix well and pour into a fairly shallow buttered tin, spreading it out level about $1/3$ in. thick. When cool and set, stamp out rounds with an egg cup or cutter of similar diameter. Arrange overlapping in a buttered shallow baking dish. Sprinkle with Parmesan cheese and dot with tiny pieces of butter. Brown under grill, or on top shelf of fairly hot oven, and heat through.

GOLDEN SAUCE

4 oz. butter, 4 oz. soft brown sugar, 1 egg, 1 wineglassful brandy, a small dusting of grated nutmeg.

Beat sugar and butter together to a soft cream, beat in the egg, then over a very low heat, gradually stir in the brandy until all the ingredients are perfectly blended. Flavour with nutmeg.

GOOSEBERRY CHUTNEY

3 lb. green gooseberries, $1/2$ lb. brown sugar, $1/2$ lb. sultanas or seedless raisins, 1 lb. onions, 1 level tablespoonful mustard seed, 1 piece root ginger, weighing about 1 oz., $1/2$ oz. mixed spice, $1/2$ level teaspoonful celery seeds, 1 teaspoonful peppercorns, $1^1/2$ pints vinegar, preferably white vinegar.

Top, tail and wash the gooseberries, skin and chop the onions, chop the sultanas. Tie the mustard and celery seeds, ginger, spices and peppercorns in a small piece of muslin. Put all into the preserving pan with 1 pint of the vinegar and simmer gently until the chutney is thick. If desired, the celery seeds may be put into the ingredients loose and cooked and left in the chutney.

Taste the chutney from time to time to test for hotness, and remove the bag with the mustard seeds and the ginger if the flavour is too pronounced.

GOOSEBERRY FOOL

1 lb. ripe gooseberries, 4 oz. sugar, ¹/₄ pint thick cream.

Top and tail the gooseberries, stew them with the sugar with 2—3 tablespoonfuls of water, until they are quite tender.

Rub through a sieve. When cold, stir in the stiffly whipped cream, until well blended with the fruit. Divide into individual glasses and serve with extra cream if possible and small sponge cake fingers.

GOOSEBERRY JAM

4 lb. small green gooseberries, ¹/₂ pint water, 4 lb. sugar.

Top, tail and wash the gooseberries and put them into the preserving pan with the water. Cook gently until the gooseberries are quite tender, then stir in the sugar. Leave for 15 min. off the heat to help dissolve the sugar. Bring gently to the boil, stirring well, then boil moderately fast until a little of the preserve will set when tested on a plate or until it will coat the wooden stirring spoon thickly and only slide from the spoon (held high over pan) in thick flakes.

Pot while the jam is quite hot, leave until quite cold before covering.

A walnut of butter stirred into the jam while it is cooking gives a rich flavour; while in season, a head of elderflowers gives a very unusual and delicate flavour. Remove the flowers before potting the jam.

GOOSEBERRY JELLY

Wash the desired quantity of fruit and put it into the preserving pan with water just to cover. Simmer until tender, and mash the soft fruit well.

Put it into a jelly bag and leave until all the juice has dripped through. Now put the pulp from which the juice has been extracted back into the pan with just enough cold water to make a thin soupy mixture. Simmer this slowly for about 40 min., then strain as before.

Mix the two extracted liquids together and measure them. Allow 1 lb. of sugar to every pint of juice and dissolve it all together in the pan, then bring to the boil and boil rapidly until a set is obtained.

GOULASH, BEEF OR VEAL

Veal is the meat most generally used in making goulash, although good stewing steak may be used.

2¹/₂—3 lb. of breast or fillet of veal cut into cubes or pieces about 1¹/₂ in., 3 tablespoonfuls lard, 4 medium-sized onions, thinly sliced, 1 clove garlic skinned and crushed, 1 tablespoonful paprika, ¹/₂ teaspoonful caraway seeds, 6 medium-sized potatoes, peeled and cubed raw, stock which can be made from a veal bone stewed, salt and pepper.

Melt the fat in a good-sized saucepan, add the onions and garlic and fry lightly, taking care not to let the onions brown. Put in the cubed meat and toss in the fat and onions until seared all over. Mix enough stock to cover the meat with the paprika, seasoning to taste, add the caraway seeds. Cover the pan closely and simmer gently for 40 min.

Put in the cubed potatoes and continue to cook until the potatoes are soft but not mashy.

Serve with plain boiled rice or plain boiled broken macaroni, lightly moistened with butter.

GRAPES, FROSTED

Divide small sweet white grapes into clusters of about 6—8.

Whisk the white of an egg fairly stiffly, coat the clusters with the egg white, roll thickly in caster sugar and lay the clusters on sheets of greaseproof paper spread on flat baking tins.

Put the tins into a very cool oven, not more than Regulo ¼ or 200⁰ F,. with the oven door ajar, and leave until the egg white and sugar have crusted.

Bunches of red or white currants, dates, sections of orange or tangerines may be treated in the same manner.

GREENGAGE JAM

4 lb. greengages, 3¹/₂ lb. sugar, ¹/₄ pint water.

Wash the fruit, cut it in halves and take out the stones, or as many as possible. Crack a few stones, and remove the kernels and bleach them.

Put the water, fruit and kernels into the preserving pan and cook gently until the fruit is very soft. Remove any stones that did not come out before. Pour in the sugar, stir to dissolve it, then bring to the boil and boil moderately fast until a little of the jam will set when tested on a cold plate.

GREEN PEPPERS, STUFFED

For two people allow 1 large pepper, 2 uncooked sausages, ¹/₂ teacupful fine crumbs, ¹/₄ teaspoonful marjoram, ¹/₄ teaspoonful thyme, 1 teaspoonful chopped parsley, 2 tablespoonfuls tomato sauce, 1 tablespoonful melted dripping or margarine, salt and pepper.

Mix the meat, crumbs and herbs together, mix the sauce and dripping and moisten the dry ingredients with it, season with salt and pepper. Cut off the stalk, halve and remove the inside and small seeds from the pepper, drop the pieces into boiling salted water for 5 min. Remove the outer skin if you wish, but the pepper retains its shape better if you do not. Drain the halves, fill them with stuffing, bake in a tin with a little dripping until the peppers are tender enough to pierce with a fork. Serve hot with tomato sauce.

GROSERT FOOL

See *Gooseberry Fool.*

GUARDS PUDDING

4 oz. butter, 4 oz. caster sugar, 2 eggs, 3 oz. self-raising flour, 2 oz. fine breadcrumbs, 3 tablespoonfuls raspberry jam.

Cream the butter and sugar together until as thick and white as Devonshire cream, add well-beaten eggs, then lightly stir in the flour and jam (the jam may be sieved if preferred).

Butter a pudding basin and also line the bottom with a buttered paper. Pour the mixture into the dish, cover with another buttered paper and steam for 1¹/₂ hr. Turn out on to a hot dish and pour over it a sauce of sieved raspberry jam boiled with a little water and thickened with cornflour.

HADDOCK, DRIED

1. Cut off 'ears and tails' of a dried haddock and cut it into portions. A haddock for 2 people should be cut across the middle, a larger fish just down the centre, then into two or more portions according to size.

Put into a flat earthenware or oven glass dish and cover with milk. Season with pepper and add a few thin curls of butter. Bake at Regulo 5 or 400° F. for about 25 min. Drain and put on a hot dish. Boil up the liquor with a large piece of butter and pour over the fish as it is served.
2. Put the portions of fish into a large pan with hot water. Bring to the boil and boil for 5—7 min. Drain and serve with a pat of butter on each portion.

HAKE

One of the best known ways of cooking hake is to poach steaks of the fish in water, drain well, cover one side of each generously with grated cheese and breadcrumbs, place in a buttered dish and pour in enough lobster sauce to leave the breadcrumbed surface above the liquid. Bake until the surface of the fish has a light golden crust.

HALIBUT

A typical rich dish is made by seasoning each side of a halibut steak cut from a moderately sized fish, putting it into a oven-proof dish, dusting it with flour and covering it with small dabs of butter. Place round the fish soft herring-roes first poached in slightly salted water until they are firm but not broken, then scalloped, well buttered and crumbed. Cook for 20 min. in a moderate oven, turn and cook for 10 min. more.

HARE, JUGGED

1 hare, 1¹/₂ pints good stock, the strained juice of 1 small lemon. 2 oz. dripping, 1 oz. butter, 1 oz. flour, 1 onion, 2 cloves, 12 peppercorns, a small bayleaf, 3—4 good sprigs of parsley, a small piece of thyme, a small piece of mace, salt and pepper.

Cut the hare into joints, then if possible cut them again with a small saw, fry the pieces in the dripping until they are brown, and put them into a deep casserole. Add the onion stuck with cloves, the peppercorns, parsley, thyme, bayleaf, mace, lemon juice, salt, pepper and stock.

Cover the casserole closely and put into a moderate oven. Regulo 3 or 375° F. for 3 hr.

Mix the flour and butter together, stir it into the stock and return the casserole to the oven. Pile the pieces on a very hot dish, strain the gravy over. Put the forcemeat balls round, and serve the dish with red-currant jelly.

HARICOT BEANS

See *Beans, Boston baked.*

HERRINGS, BISMARCK (ROLLMOPS)

Fillet the herrings; on each fillet sprinkle some peppercorns and a little salt. Roll up, secure with piece of matchstick, put into jars with a ring of onion and a small chilli, cover with white wine vinegar. Leave for 3—5 days.

HERRINGS, FRESH BOILED

Herrings, as required, little vinegar or lemon juice, pepper and salt, few peppercorns.

Behead fish and clean, leaving roes intact. Put into a saucepan with water to cover. Add 1 dessertspoonful vinegar or lemon juice and seasonings, etc. Heat slowly until contents of pan are bubbling. Cook for 5—10 min. at simmering pace.

HERRINGS, FRIED

Split, remove backbone, coat with seasoned oatmeal, and fry in shallow fat, or fry in pairs, coating outsides only with seasoned flour.

HERRINGS, GRILLED

Sprinkle the cleaned, beheaded and scaled fish with pepper and salt. Cook on either side under a quick grill. Serve with mustard sauce.

HERRINGS IN WINE

6 herrings with soft roes, 1 tablespoonful finely chopped parsley, 1 finely minced shallot, 3 oz. butter, 1/4 pint medium dry red wine.

Behead and clean the fish, remove all scales and make 3 cuts on each side of the fish. Put them into a deep pie dish, laying them heads to tails to fit them in.

Sprinkle with parsley, put the butter in thin curls over the fish and heat in the oven until the butter has melted, then pour in the wine and cook at Regulo 5 or 400° F., for 20—25 min. Serve with slices of crisped French bread.

HERRINGS, SOMERSET

Split the fish down the backs; remove the soft roes and beat with thick cream and chopped onion, season with pepper and salt and replace in the fish and poach the fish in cider.

When cold, remove from the sauce, beat this with cottage cheese or sour cream and garnish with thin slices of cucumber, or with stewed cucumber.

HODGE-PODGE

See *Hot-pot.*

HOLLANDAISE SAUCE

See *Sauces.*

HONEY CAKE

12 oz. self-raising flour, 1 level teaspoonful mixed spice, 4 tablespoonfuls honey, 4 oz. sugar, 4 oz. margarine, 2 eggs, split almonds, milk.

Mix together the flour, spice and sugar. Warm the margarine, honey and 6 tablespoonfuls of milk, add the beaten eggs, and pour into the dry ingredients.

Mix to a soft dough. Put into a shallow square tin lined with grease-proof paper. Brush with milk and scatter the top with split almonds.

Bake at Regulo 3 or 350° F. for about 1 hr. Cut into small squares.

HOP BEER

3 oz. hops, 3 gallons water, 1¹/₄ lb. brown sugar, 3 level tablespoonfuls yeast.

Boil hops and water for 45 min., stir in the sugar until dissolved, strain into a small tub or big bowl. When luke warm, mix 1 teacupful of the liquid with the yeast and stir it back into the rest. Cover the top of the vessel with a thick cloth and leave for 48 hr.

Skim off froth, strain into clean bottles or a small cask, cork or bung securely and leave for six days before using.

HORSERADISH CREAM

(To serve hot with fish)
¹/₂ pint thick cream sauce, 2 tablespoonfuls freshly grated horseradish, 1 level teaspoonful French mustard, salt, 1 tablespoonful tarragon vinegar.

Stir the horseradish, mustard and salt into the cream sauce and heat together. Remove from the stove and stir in the vinegar.

HORSERADISH SAUCE

(Everyday method of making sauce to serve with roast beef)
2 tablespoonfuls finely grated fresh horseradish, 1 level teaspoonful made mustard, 1 tablespoonful vinegar, preferably white, 1 teaspoonful sugar, ¹/₄ pint thin cream or top of the milk, salt.

Leave the horseradish to soak in the milk or cream for 1—2 hr. Stir in the sugar, mustard and a little salt, and beat well, then add the vinegar.

HOT CROSS BUNS

1 lb. plain flour, 4 oz. butter or margarine, 3 oz. sugar, ³/₄ pint warm milk, 2 eggs, 1 oz. yeast, 4 oz. currants, ¹/₂ teaspoonful mixed spice, glazing syrup of 2 oz. brown sugar boiled in ¹/₄ pint water.

Sift the flour and spice into a large bowl. Melt the fat in the warm milk. Cream the yeast with a little of the sugar and mix well with the warm milk and fat. Make a well in the centre of the flour and pour in the warm liquid. Mix lightly to a soft dough. Cover the bowl with a warm cloth, and leave for 1¹/₂ hr. in a warm place.

Now blend in the beaten eggs and currants very thoroughly. Leave to rise again for 30 min.

Turn out on to a floured board, knead lightly, then form into sixteen buns. Space out on lightly greased baking trays. Leave once more to prove and when risen, mark a cross with the back of a knife and bake at Regulo 7 or 450° F. for 10—15 min. As soon as they come from the oven, brush quickly with the glaze.

HOT-POT OR HODGE-PODGE

1 lb. scrag end of mutton, 1 lb. small loin chops, 1 lb. onions, 2 lb. potatoes, pepper and salt, dripping.

Cut off excess fat, put meat and onions into cold water with a little salt, bring to the boil, take off the scum, then simmer for 30 min. Put a thick layer of potatoes in a buttered casserole, fill it up with layers of meat, onions, and potato seasoned with pepper and salt. Finish with potatoes. Pour in enough of the broth to cover. Spread a little dripping on the top potatoes. Bake in a moderate oven for 1 hr., when the potatoes should have absorbed the liquid.

Kidneys halved may be cooked with the meat and onions

HOT WATER PASTRY

1 lb. self-raising flour, 1/2 teaspoonful salt, 1/4 teaspoonful pepper, 6 oz. lard, about 1/4 pint water.

Sift the flour, salt and pepper together into a warm bowl. Melt the lard and water in a little saucepan and bring to the boil. Pour this into the flour and mix well with a wooden spoon. Turn out on a lightly floured board and knead until smooth. Quickly shape with the hands before the dough becomes cool or it will be difficult to handle.

ICE CREAM (FOUNDATION RECIPES)

1. *2 whites of egg, 1/4 pint cream (or prepared evaporated milk), 4 level tablespoons sieved icing sugar (1 1/2 oz).*

Whip the whites until stiff. Whip the cream until thick but not stiff, adding sugar and flavouring as required. Gradually whip the egg whites into the cream. Pour into ice drawers and freeze for approximately 2 hr.

2. *Half tin evaporated milk, 1/4 teaspoon gelatine, 1 egg white, 1 table-spoon caster sugar.*

Whip the egg white until stiff. Whip the milk, adding sugar and the dissolved gelatine a little at a time. Add flavouring to taste, then gradually whip the egg white into the mixture. Pour into ice drawers and freeze.

3. *1/2 pint evaporated milk, 1/4 pint cream, 1 saltspoon gelatine, 2 level tablespoons sieved icing or caster sugar.*

Whisk the milk and dissolved gelatine. Whisk the sugar into the milk, gelatine and cream with a rotary beater. Add flavouring to taste and when the mixture is light and creamy, pour into ice drawers and freeze.

ICE CREAM, RASPBERRY

1 lb. fresh raspberries, 4 oz. caster sugar, 1/4 pint thin cornflour (unsweetened), 1/4 pint double cream, 1 tablespoonful lemon juice, few drops carmine.

Rub raspberries through sieve into a bowl. Add sugar and lemon juice and mix well. Make cornflour cream and cover with piece of greaseproof paper whilst cooling to prevent a thick skin forming or stir until cool. Whip cream stiffly. Fold into cooled cornflour, then stir lightly into raspberry purée (in which sugar should now be quite dissolved) and add a few drops colouring to give a pretty shade. Put into freezing tray for an hour, then turn out and mix well with wooden spoon. Return mixture to freezing tray, and freeze in the usual way.

ICE CREAM, VANILLA

1/2 pint milk, 3 egg yolks, 3 oz. sugar, 1/2 pint cream, 1 small teaspoonful vanilla essence.

Mix egg yolks with milk and heat, stirring all the time until custard mixture thickens. Have ready a sugar syrup made by boiling together the sugar and 1 tablespoonful water, and stir into custard. Add vanilla

and mix well. Cool, add half the whipped cream and pour into freezing
tray of refrigerator to partially firm up. Then turn out of freezing tray
and whisk well. Fold in remaining cream and mix well. Return mixture
to freezing tray, and freeze.

ICE CREAM, VANILLA (ECONOMICAL)

*1 pint milk, 1 tablespoonful cornflour, 1 egg yolk, 2¹/₂ oz. sugar,
1 teaspoonful vanilla essence, ¹/₄ pint whipped cream, or whipped chilled
evaporated milk.*

Heat milk in a saucepan to boiling point. Have ready cornflour, egg
yolk and sugar, moistened to a thin cream with a little extra milk, and
stir in boiling milk. Mix well and return to saucepan. Stir and cook
for 3 or 4 min., then add vanilla essence and mix well. Strain and cool.
When cool, pour into refrigerator trays and leave for about 1 hr. Turn
out into a bowl, whip well and fold in whipped cream. When blended,
return mixture to freezing tray and freeze.

ICE CREAM (VARIATIONS)

To vary the ice cream, add to the mixture before it is frozen, ¹/₄ pint
crushed strawberries, raspberries, gooseberries, peaches, apricots, or sieved
blackberries, with 2—3 drops of appropriate colouring; or add 4 oz.
grated and melted chocolate, or add strong undiluted coffee to the
evaporated milk, allowing 3 tablespoonfuls of the coffee to any of the
mixtures given here.

A tablespoonful of rum may be added to the chocolate or coffee
creams, other liqueurs to those containing fruit.

Sorbets come under the heading of ice cream. These are made without
cream or milk, example:

Peach and Lemon Sorbet

*6 halves of fresh or tinned peaches, strained juice of 1 lemon, 2 egg
whites, 1 teaspoonful gelatine, 1 pint water, 8 oz. loaf sugar.*

Boil the sugar and water for 5 min., removing scum, stir in the gelatine
thoroughly dissolved in a little tepid water.

When cool, add the well-crushed peaches and the lemon juice. Beat
well and put into the freezing trays. When partially frozen, turn the
mixture into a bowl and fold in the stiffly whisked egg whites. Freeze
again, until firm but not solid.

ICING, BUTTER

*4 oz. salt-free butter (or margarine), 8 oz. icing sugar, flavouring and
colouring as required.*

Soften the fat in a warmed bowl, then gradually stir in the icing sugar.
When all has been added, beat until the icing is quite white and the
consistency of Devonshire cream. Flavour and colour as required. Use
for decorating outsides of cakes and for cream fillings.

ICING, CHOCOLATE

1. *10 oz. icing sugar, 2 oz. good cocoa or chocolate powder, 1 teaspoonful
vanilla, 2—4 tablespoonfuls warm water.*

Mix together 2 oz. cocoa and 2 oz. icing sugar, rub through a sieve or
wire strainer. Sieve the remaining 8 oz. icing sugar into a basin. Stir

in warm water, adding only 1 tablespoonful at a time, until you have a thick, smooth cream. Add the vanilla. Put the bowl containing this cream over a saucepan of hot water, stir in the cocoa and sugar, adding just a little at a time, and beating it thoroughly to blend all well. Use warm water, just a few drops at a time, until the consistency of the mixture is that of very thick cream. Remove from the heat and beat well for several minutes before pouring it over the cake or small cakes.

2. *4 oz. plain chocolate, 8 oz. icing sugar, 2 oz. butter, 2—3 tablespoonfuls milk.*

Put the milk into a bowl over a saucepan of boiling water, at once grate the chocolate into the warm milk and stir until it has quite melted. Now beat in the butter and when that has also melted and is well blended with the chocolate, stir in the icing sugar, already sieved. Beat well again, and if the mixture seems too thick to run, add a teaspoonful or so of warm milk. When the mixture is like very thick cream, beat until cool, then pour it over the cake or cakes.

ICING, GLACE

1/2 lb. icing sugar, 1 teaspoonful flavouring, warm water.

Sieve the icing sugar, pour in a tablespoonful of warm water and the flavouring and stir well. Continue to add warm water, just a teaspoonful at a time, beating the icing all the time to get a smooth consistency, which will coat the mixing spoon thickly. Use quickly. This is the soft icing which is used for coating small cakes and biscuits.

ICING, ROYAL

1 lb. icing sugar, 1 teaspoonful lemon juice, 2 egg whites, 1 dessertspoonful glycerine, 1 or 2 drops of washing blue (optional).

Sift the icing sugar, mix the lemon juice and egg whites lightly together and gradually add the icing sugar. Beat for about 10 min. with a wooden spoon. Add the glycerine, which prevents the icing from becoming brittle, and the blue, which keeps the icing pure white.

When the icing is 'peaky' and stiff enough to hold up the spoon, spread it very quickly and smoothly with a broad knife dipped in hot water.

ILES FLOTTANTES (FLOATING ISLANDS)

1 pint sweet boiled custard, 3—4 egg whites, raspberry or apricot jam, 1/4 pint boiling milk.

Pour the boiled custard into a flat dish.

Whisk the egg whites very stiffly, then shape into spoon-shaped pieces and drop gently into the boiling milk, one or two at a time. Leave for about 2 min. to firm them, drain carefully and drop them on to the surface of the custard. Leave until very cold and spread a little jam on the custard between the 'islands'.

A richer dish is made with cream instead of custard.

IMPERIAL POP

2 oz. cream of tartar, 1 oz. bruised ginger, 1 lb. granulated sugar, strained juice of a lemon, 1 1/2 oz. yeast, 1 gallon boiling water.

Mix all the ingredients with the boiling water. When luke warm stir in the yeast.

Cover with a cloth, leave for 24 hr., then strain, bottle and cork.

INDIAN CHUTNEY

2 lb. sour green apples, peeled, cored and sliced, 1/2 lb. onions, peeled and chopped, 1 lb. soft brown sugar, 1/2 lb. seedless raisins, 4 finely chopped cloves of garlic, 2 oz. salt, 2 oz. ground ginger, 1 oz. dry mustard, 1/4 oz. cayenne pepper, 1 quart malt vinegar.

Cook the apples, onions and garlic with the vinegar until soft, then rub through a sieve.

Return the purée to the pan with raisins, sugar, ginger, cayenne and salt. Simmer gently for 2 hr., then pot into small jars, filling them right to the top.

When quite cold, cover with air-tight covers.

IRISH MOSS JELLY

1/2 oz. Irish Moss or agar-agar, 1 pint water, 1/4 tablespoonful sherry, sugar to taste, strained juice of 1/2 lemon.

Wash the moss thoroughly, then soak it in cold water for 12 hr. Drain it well, put it into a saucepan with 1 pint fresh water and the lemon juice, and allow to simmer for 2 hr. Stir in the sugar and sherry.

Strain into a mould and leave to set in a cool place.

IRISH STEW

About 2 1/2 lb. scrag end of neck of mutton, 2 lb. medium-sized potatoes. 1/2 lb. onions, salt, pepper, 3/4 pint boiling water.

Have the meat chopped into neat pieces, wash to remove scraps of bone. Peel and slice the potatoes, skin and finely slice the onions.

Place alternate layers of meat, potatoes and onions in a stout saucepan, seasoning the layers lightly with pepper and salt, and making the top layer of potatoes.

Pour in the water, put on the lid securely, and bring to the boil, then lower the heat and simmer gently for 3 hr.

The gravy of Irish stew is never thickened.

JAMBALAYAH

1 breakfastcupful Patna rice, 1/2 lb. ham or salt pork, 1 large onion, 1/2 red pepper, 1 pint dried peas, 1 clove garlic, salt, cayenne pepper, butter.

Soak the peas overnight. Bring them to the boil in fresh water, then add the pork or ham, cut into dice, and the finely chopped onion and garlic. Simmer until the peas are tender and the water evaporated.

Having cooked and dried the rice, add it to the peas with shredded pepper. Season with salt and cayenne pepper. Cook together for 5 min., add 2 oz. butter and serve very hot.

Prawns or crab meat may be substituted for the ham or pork.

JAM ROLY POLY

This is a favourite pudding with children and adults alike, and is very characteristic of English desserts.

The rolls may be made with pastry and baked, or with suet crust and steamed. The steamed puddings may be wrapped in two thicknesses of greaseproof paper or cooked in a special cylindrical tin which opens lengthways, called a 'sleeve'. To make the roly poly, use about 1/2—3/4 lb. of good short crust or suet dough.

Roll to an oblong and trim the edges in straight, even lines. Spread the jam generously all over the paste to within 1 in. of the edge all round, then roll up moderately tightly and seal firmly all round to prevent the jam from seeping out.

If the roll is in short crust to be baked, place it on a greased tin sealed side down, brush over with milk, scatter very lightly with sugar, and bake at Regulo 7 or 450° F. for 15 min., to set the pastry, then reduce to Regulo 5 or 400° F. for approximately 25—30 min. to cook the roll through to the centre.

If the roly poly is made with suet dough, make as above, roll in two thicknesses of greaseproof paper, the first lightly brushed with melted margarine or lard. Tie ends and steam for 2 hr. If using a 'sleeve' grease both top and bottom halves, lay the roll in and close it securely. Steam for 2 hr.

JAP CAKES

2 oz. ground almonds, 8 oz. caster sugar, 4 egg whites, coffee-flavoured butter cream, little tinted glacé icing.

Beat whites of eggs until cloudy but not solid. Add 4 oz. of the sugar, two tablespoonfuls at a time, mixing well after each. Blend remaining sugar with ground almonds and fold into first mixture. Brush two average-size Swiss roll tins with oil and line with oiled or buttered kitchen paper, or rice paper. Spread almond mixture over surface of each, making smooth with wetted knife blade. Place tins in moderate oven until just set and lightly coloured on the surface. Take tins from oven, and use a small plain-edged tart cutter to mark out circles without removing the circles from the tins. Continue baking until mixture is pale brown. Remove the circles of almond mixture to a wire tray. Return tins, with remaining trimmings of mixture, to oven and bake a richer brown colour. Leave until cool, then crush finely.

Sandwich two circles of mixture together with coffee butter cream and spread extra cream round sides and tops evenly. Roll sides in crushed almond crumbs, coating firmly. Mark a close lattice design on tops with the back of a knife and centre tops of each with a half-teaspoonful glacé icing dropped from the tip of a spoon to spread in a small even circle, or centre with a chocolate drop.

JELLY MARMALADE

3 lb. Seville, or other bitter marmalade oranges, 6 pints water, 5¹/₂ lb. loaf sugar, 1 level teaspoonful citric acid.

Scald all the fruit, then remove the peel. Cut half a pound of the peel into shreds as fine as you can get them. Put them into a small basin and cover with a little of the water. Now slice the fruit coarsely and cut up the rest of the peel roughly. Put all with the water, pips and acid into a large bowl and leave all ingredients to soak for 24 hr.

Cook the fruit, coarse peel and pips in the water in which they were soaked, for 2 hr. over a gentle heat. Meanwhile simmer the fine shreds and their soaking water in a small pan, until the shreds are tender. Strain off their water into the pan in which the rest of the orange is cooking and gently dry the shreds on a cloth.

Pour the cooked fruit and rough peel, etc., into a jelly bag and allow the liquid to drip until all has been extracted from the pulp. Put the

juice and sugar into the preserving pan. bring to the boil moderately
fast until a little of the liquid will jell when tested. Stir in the dry
shreds. Allow the marmalade to cool a little, stirring frequently, then
pot while still very hot. Stir well between the filling of each pot. When
quite cold, cover securely and store in a cool place.

JELLY, TO MAKE

To make jelly, the fruit is simmered with a little water to barely cover,
until quite tender, poured into a ready-made jelly bag, or a large square
of flannel or double butter muslin, and left to drip for 12—24 hr.
according to the type of fruit.

The juice so obtained is measured, and for every pint, allow $3/4$—1 lb.
of sugar, depending upon the setting properties of the fruit used.

Fruits which make good firm jellies are apples, crab apples, black,
red and white currants, gooseberries, loganberries and quinces, as they
contain a large percentage of pectin and acid. Cherries, pears, strawberries or vegetable marrow are not suitable for making jellies as they
contain so little pectin and acid they will not set by themselves and
need so much extra pectin that all the real flavour of the fruit is lost.

Soft fruits such as blackberries and elderberries are better used with
apples, apple or red currant juice or a commercial pectin bought by
the bottle, and made from apples.

When making the jelly, the strained juice is returned to the pan and
heated, the sugar is added gradually and stirred until dissolved, and
the syrup brought to the boil and boiled until a little of the liquid will
set firmly when tested on a cold plate.

Fill the jars while the liquid is very hot. Leave until quite cold and
cover with discs of waxed paper. Cover with good airtight covers and
store in a cool, dry place.

It is best to put up jelly in jars of not more than 1 lb. It is most
important to cook the fruit very slowly and very thoroughly before
straining it to obtain the juice, in order to break it down so that the
acid and pectin are completely extracted.

JOHN COLLINS

*1 sherry glassful of gin, 1 small bottle soda water. 1 tablespoonful lemon
juice, crushed ice, a thin slice of lemon, 1 teaspoonful caster sugar.*

Put a tablespoonful of crushed ice into a tumbler, pour the gin over it.
Add lemon juice and sugar. Shake well. Fill up with soda water, put
in the slice of lemon.

JOHN DORY, FRIED

Fillet the fish, cut the fillets in halves, coat with frying batter and fry
until golden. Serve with Tartare or tomato sauce.

JOHN DORY SALAD

*1 medium-sized fish, 2 large tomatoes, $1/4$ red pepper, $1/2$ green pepper,
$1/4$ pint thick mayonnaise, lettuce.*

Clean the fish and remove head.

Poach in slightly salted water with 1 tablespoonful of tarragon
vinegar, for 25 min.

When almost cold, lift off all the skin, take fish from the bones and break into small pieces.

Skin the tomatoes, remove the pulp and cut the flesh into strips. Remove the pulp and seeds from the peppers and cut them into very thin strips.

Mix the fish, tomato and peppers lightly. Arrange on a bed of lettuce and mask with the mayonnaise.

JUMBLES

12 oz. self-raising flour, 4 oz. sugar, 4 oz. butter or margarine, 1 egg, the grated rind and strained juice of a lemon, 3—4 tablespoonfuls milk if required.

Cream fat and sugar thoroughly, add egg, lemon rind and juice, fold in the flour. mix to a firm dough, adding milk as required.

Roll the paste thinly and cut into narrow strips, about 6 in. long, and wind these round and round to make small flat cakes. Put on a greased baking tin, brush with milk, scatter with sugar. Bake at Regulo 7 or 450° F. for about 10—15 min.

KEBOBS (KEBABS)

1/2 in. thick slices of lamb, 1 large grated onion, 2 tablespoonfuls olive oil, 2 tablespoonfuls red wine, 1 teaspoonful paprika, pepper, salt, black pepper. 1 level teaspoonful dry mustard, button mushrooms, green peppers. fat bacon.

Cut the lamb into small squares. Put into a bowl with the wine, oil and seasonings. Toss well and leave all night.

Next day. when ready, put a piece of lamb, a mushroom, piece of bacon and piece of pepper alternately on skewers, until the skewers are full.

Grill or bake in the oven.

Arrange on a large oven-proof plate, pour over some heated brandy and set alight. Serve with rice.

KEDGEREE

4 oz. unpolished rice. 1 lb. flaked fish, comprising two-thirds smoked haddock or fillet and one-third white fish. 3—4 hard-boiled eggs, 4 tablespoonfuls margarine or butter, pepper and a little chopped chives or spring onion green.

Boil the rice in a quart of salted water for 20 min., strain, rinse with cold water and put into the oven to dry.

Then mix with the butter and onion green or chives, stir in the flaked fish. season with pepper and arrange in layers with the sliced hard-boiled eggs. Serve very hot.

KENTISH HUFFKINS

1 lb. plain flour, 1 oz. yeast, 2 oz. lard, 2 teaspoonfuls sugar, 1/2 teaspoonful salt. 3/4 pint tepid milk.

Sift flour and salt together into a warm bowl. Cream the yeast with the sugar and stir it into the tepid milk, then pour it into the flour and knead to a soft dough. Cover the bowl with a warmed cloth, and leave in a warm place for an hour. Knead again. Divide the dough into four

round flat cakes. Make a hole in the centre of each with a thick wooden
spoon handle. Flour the tops well, and leave on lightly greased warm
tins in a warm place for 30 min.

Bake at Regulo 7 or 450° F. for 15—20 min., then wrap in a thick
warm cloth at once to keep the crusts soft.

KIDNEYS, GRILLED PIGS'

Pigs' kidneys have a less delicate flavour than sheep's, but are very
good grilled.

Skin one per person, split and skewer to keep open. Brush over with
melted butter. Grill on either side.

Serve with fried onion rings sparingly sprinkled with sage, and
chipped potatoes.

KIDNEYS SAUTE

*4 sheep's kidneys, 1/4 lb. small mushrooms, 1 teaspoonful lemon juice,
1 sherry glassful sherry, 1 shallot, 2 tablespoonfuls butter, 1 dessertspoonful flour, salt and pepper.*

Skin the kidneys, cut in halves, then in thick slices. Stem and wipe the
mushrooms, slice them, mince the skinned shallot.

Heat the butter in a shallow pan, put in the kidney, shallot and
mushrooms and cook quickly, stirring all the time, until the mushrooms
no longer exude moisture. Sprinkle with the flour, pepper and salt,
moisten with the sherry, adding it gradually, until the kidneys and
mushrooms are surrounded with a thick sauce, then sprinkle with chopped
parsley and serve quickly on toast.

KIPPERS, TO COOK

1. Fold the kippers in halves and stand them upright in a large jug.
Fill the jug with boiling water and stand in a warm place for 10 min.
Drain the kippers. Put them on a large dish and put into a hot oven
for 2—3 min.

2. Cut off 'ears and tails'. Put them into a deep pan, cover with water
and simmer moderately for 7—10 min.

Drain, put on a dish beneath the grill for 1—2 min. Serve with small
pieces of butter.

3. Grill first on one side (skin side up) for 3 min. Then turn and grill
the other side 5—6 min. Serve with pat of butter.

KRINGLES

4 eggs, 4 oz. caster sugar, 4 oz. butter, 8 oz. plain flour.

Hard boil 2 eggs, sieve the yolks and mix them with the raw beaten
yolks of the remaining 2 eggs, and 3 oz. of the caster sugar.

Rub the fat very firmly into the flour, then mix with the egg and
sugar and knead to a smooth, crackless dough.

Using small portions of the dough at a time, roll to 1/4 in. thickness
and cut into rings with two cutters, one a little smaller than the other.
Brush with white of egg and scatter with the rest of the caster sugar.
Bake at Regulo 5 or 400° F. until golden brown.

LAMBS' TONGUES, BRAISED

4 lambs' or sheep's tongues, 1 oz. butter or margarine, 1 onion, 2 carrots, 2—3 sticks celery, $^1/_2$ pint stock, small piece of bayleaf, 2—3 sprigs parsley, salt, pepper, 2 rashers bacon cut in halves (optional).

Soak the tongues in water with a little salt for 2 hr.

Slice the vegetables thinly, put them into a saucepan with the butter or margarine, parsley and bayleaf, and fry gently until the vegetables are lightly browned. Lay the tongues on the vegetables, the bacon cut into 4 pieces on the tongues, pour in the stock, put the lid on the saucepan and simmer slowly for 2 hr.

Take up the tongues, skin them and cut each in half lengthways. Dish them on a bed of mashed potatoes with the bacon. Strain the vegetables and arrange them round the mashed potato. Serve the gravy separately. The gravy may be slightly thickened with flour if preferred.

LARDY CAKE

1 lb. bread dough, 3 oz. pure lard, 2 oz. sugar, $^1/_2$ teaspoonful mixed spice.

Roll out bread dough to an oblong shape on a floured pastry board. Spread two-thirds of surface with half the dough and half the sugar (which has been sprinkled with the mixed spice), then dredge lightly with flour. Fold up the plain area of paste halfway over the buttered area and bring top third of paste down, making three folds as for flaky pastry. Give dough a half-turn and repeat with remainder of fat and sugar. Repeat once more, giving dough a dredging of flour only. Roll out once more to about $^1/_2$ in. thick, to a shape that will fit into a tin as used for gingerbread, which has been greased and floured. Score top with a knife. When in tin, set in a warm place to prove for about 15 min. Brush over with a little warmed milk and bake in a hot oven (450° F., reducing to 400° F. — Regulo 8, reducing to 6) until nicely coloured.

LEEK AND BACON PIE

About 6 large leeks, 4 rashers of streaky bacon, $^1/_2$ lb. medium-sized potatoes, 2 oz. butter or margarine, fine bread crumbs, $^1/_2$ pint thin white sauce.

Remove green leaves and outer skins of the leeks, slit them lengthways and wash thoroughly. Peel and thinly slice the potatoes, par-boil them for 15 min.

Butter a flat ovenware dish and put in a layer of sliced potatoes. Arrange the leeks on the potatoes and spoon a layer of sauce over them. Cover with the rest of the potatoes, and sprinkle with crumbs and curls of butter.

Bake at Regulo 6 or 425° F. for 40 min. Cut the rashers of bacon in halves, lay them on top of the pie and return to the oven long enough to crisp the bacon.

LEEK AND POTATO SOUP

6 leeks, 4 medium potatoes, 1 pint water, $1^1/_2$ pints milk, 2 sage leaves, salt, pepper, 1 oz. butter, $^1/_2$ oz. flour.

Cut up the leeks using all the best part of the green, peel the potatoes and cut them into small pieces. Cook in the water with the sage until quite tender. Rub through a sieve. Cook the butter and flour until blended, add the boiling milk, stir in the leek and potato purée and cook and stir until thick and smooth.

LEEK PUDDING

³/₄ lb. suet crust, 6 leeks, ¹/₂ lb. cooked bacon (collar or knuckle is good), 1 oz. butter, pepper, salt, small pinch of powdered sage.

Remove the coarse leaves and roots from the leeks, and cut them into 1 in. lengths, washing them thoroughly. Dice the bacon very small. Line a greased basin with the suet crust, leaving aside enough to make a lid. Fill the basin with the leaks and bacon, with seasoning and tiny pieces of butter scattered among them. Cover closely with crust, then with greaseproof paper, steam for 2 hr. Serve with gravy or parsley sauce.

LEMON CURD

4 large lemons, 1 lb. caster sugar, 6 oz. salt-free butter or margarine, 5 new-laid eggs.

Lightly beat the eggs and strain them.

Put the caster sugar in the top of a double boiler, grate the rind of the washed lemons into it, add their strained juice and the butter or margarine. Dissolve the sugar in the juice and fat over a very low heat, stirring frequently. When the fat, sugar and lemon are well blended, slowly pour in the eggs, and cook and stir until the mixture is thick and creamy. On no account must it boil.

Pot into small dry pots and when cold cover. Store in a cool, dry place.

LEMON MERINGUE PIE

A short pastry shell, 4 oz. caster sugar, 3 egg yolks, strained juice of 2 lemons, 3 level tablespoonfuls cornflour, ³/₄ pint water, 1 oz. butter or margarine, unsalted.

Mix together the sugar, cornflour and water, and cook in the top of a double boiler until thick and smooth.

Remove from the heat, thoroughly mix in the eggs beaten with the lemon juice. Pour the mixture into the pie shell and bake for 5 min. only, at Regulo 5 or 400° F.

Remove from the oven, spread the meringue lightly on the top and return to the oven and bake at Regulo 2 or 325° F., for about 10 min., when the meringue should just feel firm to the touch.

To make the meringue, whisk the 3 egg whites until stiff, fold 6 level tablespoonfuls of caster sugar lightly over and over into the whites. When the meringue is light and well mixed spread it quickly.

LEMON PUDDING

12 oz. self-raising flour, 6 oz. suet, 6 oz. demerara sugar, 4 large lemons, cold water, 1 dessertspoonful granulated sugar, margarine.

Mix the flour, suet and granulated sugar to a soft dough with cold water. Roll out to a thickness of ¹/₂ in. Grease a 2 lb. pudding basin with margarine and scatter it with a little of the demerara sugar. Line with the crust.

Wipe the lemons with a cloth wrung out of hot water, cut each into six sections, remove pips and pack into the pudding basin with the rest of the brown sugar between the pieces. Add 2 tablespoonfuls of cold water. Fold over the superfluous crust at the top of the basin to form a good seal. Cover with 2 layers of greaseproof paper and steam for 3 hr.

LINZER TORTE

6 oz. soft butter, 8 oz. self-raising flour, 6 oz. fine white sugar, 6 oz. ground almonds, 4 beaten egg yolks, 1/2 teaspoon cinnamon, pinch of grated lemon rind, red jam.

Work all the ingredients except the jam into a stiff dough. Divide the dough into three parts. Take two of the parts and roll each out to the shape of the bottom round of a torte tin. Cover two of these tins. Roll out the third part thinly and cut into strips about 1/4 in. wide. With these strips make a 'gate' or trellis to fit a third tin the same size. Finish this with a strip right round the edge. Bake all three tins at 350° F. for 45 min.

When the pastry rounds and the trellis are quite cool brush one of the rounds, still on the tin, with warm jam and put the second round on this. Spread the top with jam, place the trellis carefully on this and pipe the spaces full with red jam. Brush the trellis with a little melted fondant icing.

LOBSTER THERMIDOR

2 small lobsters, 1/2 pint creamy white sauce, 1 tablespoonful tomato purée, 1/2 lb. mushrooms, 2 tablespoonfuls butter, 1/2 small shallot finely minced, 1/2 glass dry white wine, pepper, grated Parmesan cheese.

Cut the lobsters in halves, lengthways, and pick out all the meat from the shells, claws and tails. Dice the meat. Put it with the shallot and chopped mushrooms into a saucepan with the butter and simmer gently for 5 min.

Add the tomato purée and wine and season with pepper. Cook again for 5—7 min., stirring frequently.

Divide the mixture into the four half shells. Cover with a thick layer of cream sauce, then of cheese.

Heat in the oven, then brown beneath a hot grill.

LOBSTER VOL AU VENT

1 large or several individual vol au vent cases, 1 hen lobster, 1/4 lb. mushrooms, 1/2 pint Béchamel sauce, 1 egg yolk, 1 tablespoonful butter, 1 small wineglassful sherry, a little paprika pepper, finely chopped parsley.

Remove all the meat from the lobster and dice it, break up the coral. Wipe but do not peel the mushrooms, slice them thinly and cook them in the butter.

Heat the lobster and sauce in a double boiler, beat in the egg yolk, and stir until the mixture is thick, add the butter and mushrooms, a saltspoonful of paprika and the coral. Finally stir in the sherry.

Pour the mixture into the heated vol au vent case or cases and sprinkle with parsley. Put on the tops of the cases and serve at once.

MACARONI AND MARMALADE PUDDING

4 level tablespoonfuls of orange marmalade, 3 oz. short quick-cook macaroni, 1 pint milk, 2 oz. sugar, 1 oz. butter, nutmeg.

Cook the macaroni in the milk with the sugar until it is tender, stir in half the butter.

Grease a pie dish with the rest. Pour in a little macaroni, cover with marmalade, add more macaroni and another layer of marmalade, finish with macaroni, grate a little nutmeg over the top. Bake at Regulo 2 or 325⁰ F. for 30 min.

Serve hot or cold with cream or custard.

MACARONI CHEESE

There are two versions of macaroni cheese, one with and one without sauce.

1. *1/2 lb. macaroni, 11/2 pints milk, 2 oz. margarine, 2 oz. plain flour, 4 oz. grated cheese, 1/2 teaspoonful mustard, salt, pepper, 1 tablespoonful stale crumbs, grated nutmeg.*

Boil the macaroni in slightly salted water until it is tender between the fingers, but on no account mashy. Drain and rinse in cold water.

Make a creamy sauce with the fat, flour, mustard and boiling milk. A few tablespoonfuls of the strained liquid from the macaroni may be used if the sauce is too thick. Stir in 1 oz. of the cheese. When well mixed, toss the macaroni in the sauce, pour it into a greased ovenproof dish. Spread the rest of the cheese mixed with the crumbs on the top and bake at Regulo 5 or 400⁰ F. near the top of the oven until the cheese is lightly brown and crusty.

2. *Macaroni cooked as before, 4 oz. cheese, 2 oz. butter.*

Make the macaroni hot again after having rinsed it. Stir the butter and half the cheese into it until they have melted. Scatter the rest of the cheese on top and lightly brown it in the oven, or if preferred, hand the uncooked cheese separately.

MACAROONS

4 egg whites, 1 lb. caster sugar, 8 oz. ground almonds, 2—3 drops almond essence, split almonds, rice paper.

Slightly oil baking trays and spread rice paper on them.

Stir the sugar and almonds well together. Drop the unwhisked egg whites and flavouring into the centre and beat until all the ingredients are blended to a smooth paste. Drop small spoonfuls of the mixture on the rice paper at regular intervals. Pat the mixture with a wet spoon, place a split almond on the centre of each. Bake at Regulo 3 or 350⁰ F. for about 20—25 mins. Slide a broad knife beneath the paper and raise the macaroons from the tin, cut away superfluous paper.

MACKEREL, SOUSED

4 medium-sized and very fresh mackerel, cleaned and scaled, 1 bayleaf, 1/2 small onion thinly sliced, 6 peppercorns, liquid to cover made with 2 parts vinegar and 1 part water.

Put the fish into a deep pie dish or casserole, break up the bayleaf and scatter it, with the peppercorns among them. Cover with the vinegar and water.

Bake in a slow oven at Regulo 4 or 375⁰ F. for 35—40 min.

Leave in the vinegar until quite cold. Lift out. Mix the spiced vinegar with a little mustard or grated horseradish to serve with the fish.

MADEIRA CAKE

8 oz. self-raising flour, 5 oz. caster sugar, 5 oz. butter, 3 eggs, 1 slice citron peel, few drops lemon essence.

Beat the butter and sugar together to a soft, light cream. Add the eggs one by one, beating each one in very thoroughly before breaking in the next, add essence.

Lightly stir in the flour, turning it over and over into the wet ingredients with the mixing spoon. Use a tablespoonful or so of milk if required. This depends upon the size of the eggs.

Put the mixture into the prepared tin, then bake at Regulo 3 or 350⁰ F. for 1—1¼ hr. About ¼ hr. before the cake is done, lightly and quickly lay the piece of citron peel over the top. If added before, it will sink through the cake and spoil the appearance of it.

MADELEINES

½ lb. self-raising flour, ½ lb. caster sugar, ½ lb. butter melted but not hot, 3 eggs, ½ teaspoonful lemon flavouring, sieved apricot jam, desiccated coconut, glacé cherries.

Beat the eggs and sugar over hot water until very thick and creamy. Remove from over the hot water and beat until cooled. Gradually add the flour, the warm butter and lemon. When all are thoroughly blended, fill the buttered madeleine moulds two-thirds full and bake at Regulo 7 or 450⁰ F. Remove from moulds, cool a little, then roll first in warm sieved apricot jam, then in coconut. Put half a cherry on top of each.

MAIDS OF HONOUR

Puff pastry, 4 oz. caster sugar, 4 oz. ground almonds, 1 egg, 1 tablespoonful lemon juice.

Line about 10 patty pans with thinly rolled puff paste. Stir the sugar and almonds well together, stir in the egg lightly beaten with the lemon juice. Put a little of the mixture into each lined pan, bake at Regulo 7 or 450⁰ F. for 10 min., then for a further 5—8 min. at Regulo 5 or 400⁰ F.

MAITRE D'HOTEL BUTTER

1 oz. butter, 1 teaspoonful chopped parsley, 1 teaspoonful lemon juice.

Put ingredients on to a plate and work them together with a knife until an evenly green pat of butter is obtained. Drain off any surplus lemon juice and set in a cool place, or on ice, until required.

MALT LOAF

1 lb. self-raising flour, 2 tablespoonfuls sugar, 1 tablespoonful malt extract, 2 tablespoonfuls treacle, ¼ lb. sultanas or seedless raisins, 1 level teaspoonful bicarbonate of soda, ½ pint warm milk, or milk and water.

Put the flour, fruit and sugar into a bowl and mix together. Heat the malt, syrup and milk together until blended, but do not allow to boil. Mix the bicarbonate of soda with a tablespoonful of warm water, stir into the hot ingredients, then pour it into the dry ingredients and knead all to a soft dough. Put into a greased 2 lb. or into two 1 lb. oblong tins and bake at Regulo 3 or 350° F. allowing about 1 hr. for the larger tin and about 45 min. for the smaller ones.

Do not cut this bread for about 24 hr.

MARBLE CAKE

6 oz. margarine, 6 oz. sugar, 3 eggs, 9 oz. self-raising flour, 1 tablespoonful cocoa, ¹/₂ teaspoonful vanilla, ¹/₂ teaspoonful raspberry flavouring, a few drops cochineal, ¹/₂ teaspoonful almond flavouring, a few drops green vegetable colouring, a little milk.

Cream the margarine and sugar together very thoroughly, beat in the eggs one by one until you have a smooth pale yellow cream.

Fold in the sifted flour and make a soft, creamy dough, using a little milk if necessary. Divide the dough into three portions using 2 other bowls for the purpose. Add the cocoa and vanilla to one portion, the raspberry flavouring and colouring to the second, and the almond flavouring and green colouring to the third.

Line a cake tin with greaseproof paper, choosing an 8 in. tin. Spread the chocolate dough in the bottom, drop the pink dough in next, then finish with the pale green dough. Smooth evenly on top, brush with milk. Put into a moderately hot oven, and bake at Regulo 3 or 350° F. for about 1¹/₂ hr.

Ice with pale pink or pale green icing and decorate with candles or other pretty decorations appropriate to the occasion.

MARMALADE, GRAPEFRUIT

2 medium-sized grapefruit, 1 level teaspoonful citric acid, 3 pints water, 3 lb. sugar.

Wash the fruit, remove the peel and cut it all into fine, rather long shreds. Put into a bowl with 1¹/₂ pints of the water. Slice the fruit thinly, removing the pips, put the fruit into a bowl and cover with the rest of the water, and stir in the acid. Also put into this bowl all the pips loosely tied in a piece of well boiled muslin. Leave everything to soak for 24 hr.

Next day, gently boil the pulp in the soaking water for 1¹/₂—2 hr. with the bag of pips. Cook the shredded peel in its own water until tender.

Either rub the grapefruit pulp through a sieve, or mash with a fork and remove as much of the coarse skin as possible. Now put all the water in which pulp and shreds were cooked, the pulp, shreds and the sugar into the preserving pan, bring slowly to the boil and boil moderately fast until a little of the marmalade will set when tested on a plate. Pot while hot, cover when quite cold and store in a cool place.

MARMALADE, LEMON

1. *6 medium-sized lemons, 4¹/₂ pints of water, sugar.*

Wash and dry the lemons, pare off the peel as thinly as you can, not taking off any white pith. Now shred the peel thinly or coarsely, according to taste. Remove every scrap of white pith from the lemons and cut it into little pieces. Put with the lemon pips loosely into a piece of muslin and tie securely. Slice the fruit. Simmer the shredded peel with the water until it is tender.

Add the sliced fruit pulp and the bag of pith and pips. Boil gently all together until the contents of the pan are tender and thick, taking about 1 hr. Remove the bag of pith, etc. Weigh the contents of the pan and for each pound, allow 14 oz. sugar. Stir the sugar into the lemon mixture, bring all slowly to the boil and boil for about 10—15 min., when a set should be obtained. Pot while hot, stirring between each pot filling, cover when cold. If you do not get a set in the time given, boil until it comes, but with this recipe the setting is very quick.

2. *1 lb. lemons, 1 lb. sugar, 2 pints water.*
Wash the lemons and dry them. Cut in halves without peeling, lengthways. Lay the halves cut side down on a board and, with a very sharp knife, slice right across into very thin slices. Remove the pips as you go, and put them in a little bowl with enough water to cover them. Put the sliced fruit into a bowl with the rest of the water and leave all to soak for 24 hr. Put all into the preserving pan, with the water or the thin jelly which may have formed from the pips. Simmer gently until a piece of the lemon peel feels quite tender between the fingers, then stir in the sugar, bring to the boil and boil moderately fast until a set is reached, which should be in about 15—20 min. Pot while hot and cover when quite cold.

MARMALADE, LEMON JELLY

3 lb. lemons, 6 pints water, 5 lb. sugar.

Pour boiling water over the lemons, and leave for 5 min. Now remove the skins and cut half a pound of them into very fine shreds. Put the shreds into a bowl and cover with some of the water. Cut up the lemons into small pieces, and put with the rest of the water, and the remaining peel, also cut up roughly, into another bowl.

Next day, simmer the fine shreds in their soaking water until tender, then drain and dry them. Add the water to the fruit pulp, peel and soaking water, then turn into the preserving pan and simmer moderately fast about 1¼ to 2 hr.

Strain off all the juice through a jelly bag, squeezing the bag gently towards the end to expel as much juice as possible without getting any of the pulp through, which would spoil the clearness of the jelly. Return all the strained juice to the preserving pan, stir in the sugar, and bring to the boil. Boil moderately fast until a little of the jelly will set when tested, stir in the dried lemon peel shreds very quickly. At once pot into clean dry jars, stirring well between the filling of each pot. When quite cold, cover securely, and store in a cool place.

MARMALADE, ORANGE CHUNKY

4 lb. marmalade oranges, 2 lemons, 2 sweet oranges, 6 pints water, 6 lb. loaf sugar.

Wash the fruit well, put it into a preserving pan with the water and simmer it moderately fast until it is soft enough to be pierced with a fork. This usually takes about 1 hr.

Take the fruit from the pan, leaving the water behind. When the fruit is cool enough to handle, cut it all into about eight pieces, then shred each across in fine strips, but not too fine, or the marmalade will not be chunky. Discard all the pips as you go, as they have done their work while being cooked. Return the cut-up fruit and all the juice which may have run while cutting, to the pan with the water in which the oranges were cooked, stir in the sugar, bring all to the boil, and boil moderately fast until a little of the preserve will set when tested. Pot while hot, cover when quite cold and store in a cool place.

MARMALADE, PINEAPPLE

2 lb. pineapple, 1¹/₂ lb. sugar, 1 teaspoonful citric or tartaric acid, or juice of 2 lemons.

Strain off the juice or syrup, cut the pineapple into small pieces, put it into a bowl or on a large dish and sprinkle the acid or the lemon juice over and leave for 2 hr.

Put all into the preserving pan with ¹/₂ teacupful of the syrup, simmer for 1 hr., then add the sugar. Stir to dissolve it, then bring to the boil and boil moderately fast until a little will set on a plate when tested.

Although the pineapple may be very sweet, it must have this quantity of sugar to give bulk and make it set.

The acid or lemon juice is also essential, as pineapple has very little pectin or setting matter in it.

MARMALADE, TANGERINE

2 lb. tangerines, 2 lb. sugar, 1¹/₂ pints water, 2 level teaspoonfuls citric acid.

Wash the fruit, cut it in halves, lay the halves cut side down on a board and slice peel and pulp very thinly with a sharp knife, removing pips as you go. Tie the pips loosely in a piece of well boiled muslin. Put the sliced fruit, pips, juice and acid, also any juice that has run out while cutting, into a bowl with the water and leave for 12 hr.

Turn into the preserving pan and simmer gently until the fruit is tender, which usually takes about 45—60 min. Remove the bag of pips, stir in the sugar, bring to the boil and boil moderately fast until a little will set when tested on a cold plate. Pot while the marmalade is hot, stirring well between the filling of each pot.

When quite cold, tie down, and store in a cool place.

MARRONS GLACES (CHESTNUTS)

2 lb. chestnuts, 3 lb. loaf sugar, glucose, cream of tartar, vanilla essence, water.

Slit the nuts, put them into luke warm water and bring to the boil. Peel, put into another pan of luke warm water, simmer gently until tender, being careful they do not break. Remove and allow the nuts to dry.

Make a syrup with 1 lb. loaf sugar, ¹/₂ pint of water, 1 teaspoonful glucose and boil to 220⁰ F. Bring nuts to boil in this syrup. Remove from heat. Leave in pan for 36 hr. in a warm place. Lift out and drain.

Make second coating with 1 lb. sugar, ¹/₂ pint water, pinch of cream of tartar; boil to 250⁰ F. and add a little vanilla. Put the nuts in carefully and again bring to boiling point. Stir very carefully with confectioner's spoon to be sure syrup is all over the nuts. Take out nuts and drain.

When quite cold and dry, give a third coating. Bring 1 lb. sugar and 1/2 pint water to boil, add 1 teaspoonful of glucose and boil to 235⁰ F. and add a few drops of vanilla essence. Remove mixture from heat and drop in the nuts. Allow syrup to boil for 3—4 min.

Remove nuts singly and place on a greased tray. When set, place in fancy confectionery case.

MARROW AND GINGER JAM

4 lb. vegetable marrow weighed when it has been peeled and seeded, 3 lb. sugar, 2 level dessertspoonfuls tartaric or citric acid, 1 oz. ground ginger, or less if you do not like the preserve too gingery.

This should not be made until the marrows are ripe and yellow. If made when they are soft and new, the jam or preserve will be watery and not set or keep well.

Cut the marrow into small chunks, and leave in a bowl for 12 hr., then drain off any water there may be, and dry the pieces in a clean cloth. Pour the sugar over the marrow and leave for 24 hr.

Put it into the preserving pan with the acid and simmer for half an hour, bring to the boil and boil gently for another hour, when the syrup should be thick and the marrow transparent.

MARROW GINGER

6 lb. marrow weighed after being prepared, 4 lb. sugar, 2 teaspoonfuls citric or tartaric acid, 1—2 oz. ground ginger, according to taste.

Peel the marrow thickly, if it is a hard one, to avoid using the fibrous outside parts; cut out any pulp and seeds and cut the marrow into neat cubes about 1 in. thick.

Put the prepared marrow on a large dish and leave for 12 hr., in order that any excess moisture may dry out. This helps to make clear cubes. If there is any moisture, wipe the marrow dry, then put it back on a dry dish and cover it with the sugar. Leave it for 12 hr. again.

Put the marrow and juice into the preserving pan with the acid, mix the ginger to a smooth paste with a little of the liquid, then stir all the ingredients together and bring to the boil. Simmer gently until the syrup is thick and the cubes clear. Do not over-cook or the preserve will turn dark and treacly.

MARSH-MALLOWS

1/2 lb. icing sugar, 1/4 lb. gum arabic, 3 egg whites, 1/2 pint water, caramel essence.

Soak the gum arabic in the water until soft, then heat gently until dissolved, and strain it through fine muslin. Return to the stewpan, add the sugar and when dissolved, stir in the egg whites, and whisk until the mixture is quite stiff. Flavour to taste, sugar, and let it remain for about 10 hr. When ready, cut into small squares, and dredge them liberally with icing sugar.

MARZIPAN (ALMOND PASTE)

1 lb. ground almonds, 3/4 lb. sifted icing sugar, 1/4 lb. caster sugar, 2 egg yolks or 2 egg whites, depending upon whether a yellow or a white paste is required (as a rule, the yellow paste is used for petits fours, the white paste for cakes), 1 teaspoonful orange flower water, 2—3 drops almond essence.

Mix together the almonds and the sugars.

Work in the yolks or whites of eggs and the flavourings and knead until a smooth well-blended paste is made. If not using at once, wrap the marzipan in waxed paper, put it into a polythene food bag and store in a moderately warm place.

MARZIPAN, BOILED

1¹/₄ lb. sugar, 1 teacupful (¹/₄ pint) water, ¹/₄ teaspoonful cream of tartar, 1 lb. ground almonds, about 1 small teaspoonful each almond essence and orange flower water, 2 eggs.

Put sugar and water into a pan and leave for about 1 hr. to soak. Place pan over low heat and stir until sugar is quite dissolved. Add cream of tartar and boil to about 238⁰ F. or 'soft-ball' stage. Remove pan from heat and stir in ground almonds and flavourings. Mix well and when somewhat cooled, add sufficient of the well-beaten eggs to make a firm paste. Turn on to a sugared board and knead lightly for a few moments. Use as required. (Sufficient for a large Christmas cake.)

MARZIPAN FOR SIMNEL CAKES

8 oz. icing sugar, 4 oz. caster sugar, 12 oz. ground almonds, 1 egg, 1 egg yolk, 1 teaspoonful almond flavouring.

Mix sugars and almonds together. Add 1 egg and the almond flavouring, knead together and if necessary use the second yolk to make a smooth soft paste. Make a flat cake for the middle and the rest of the paste into a roll that will fit round the outside edge of the cake, and when the cake is cold, press it into place and flute it prettily. Brush over twice with egg, and return the cake to a warm oven until the marzipan is golden and glistening.

Fill the centre of the top of the cake with white or pale green icing, and arrange crystallised violets in the shape of a bunch with stalks made of thin shreds of angelica, pressed into the icing close together by the posy, but free-standing otherwise to make them look real.

MAYONNAISE SALAD DRESSING

1 egg yolk, a pinch of salt and of pepper, 1 saltspoonful dry mustard. 1 tablespoonful tarragon vinegar, 1 tablespoonful malt vinegar, ¹/₂ pint salad or olive oil.

Stir the egg yolk, salt, pepper and mustard lightly together in a bowl which has been slightly warmed. Stir in ¹/₂ teaspoonful oil and blend thoroughly with the egg. Add a further ¹/₂ teaspoonful oil and blend thoroughly again. Continue until half the oil has been added, and the sauce is very thick and smooth.

Stir in the malt vinegar, continue with the oil, although you may add it more quickly at this stage. When all the oil has been used, stir in the tarragon vinegar. If the sauce is too thick for your taste, add more vinegar, but too much vinegar spoils this rich sauce. Should the sauce begin to curdle (this happens when too much oil is added at once) stir in a tablespoonful of boiling water and beat thoroughly. This will 'bring it back', as they say.

MEAD

2¹/₂ lb. honey, 1 gallon water, 1 egg white, ¹/₂ oz. yeast.

Use English honey when possible as this gives the better flavour, but thick Empire honey does very well.

Beat the egg white a little, put into a large saucepan with the honey and water. Bring slowly to the boil, whisking frequently until the liquid boils. Lower the heat and simmer gently for 1 hr. Remove scum if necessary.

Allow the liquid to cool, strain it through muslin into a wooden cask, large china jug or earthenware crock. Take off 1 teacupful of the luke warm liquid, dissolve the yeast in it, then stir back into the rest of the liquid. Cover the top of the crock or jug with a thick cloth or folded blanket, and leave undisturbed for 7 days. Listen to see if the working has finished, if not, cover again for a day or so.

Now bottle into very clean, bone-dry bottles, plug necks with thick twists of clean cotton wool. Leave for 14 days, remove twists of wool, then cork tightly with new corks that have been well washed and dried, or old corks that have been sterilised by boiling for 15 min. Store in a moderately warm place for at least 9 months.

If a cask is used, cover the bung hole lightly for 3 days with a cloth, after adding the yeast, then bung tightly for 9 months, before bottling in the usual manner.

In some parts of the country, a very small knob of root ginger and a blade of mace is boiled with the honey and water, but this is a matter of tradition and taste.

MEAT, HOW TO ROAST

Weigh the joint and calculate the time required as follows.

	Low-temperature roasting (Reg. 3 or 350° F.)	High-temperature roasting (Reg. 6-7 or 450° F.)
Beef	20 min. per lb.	15 min. per lb.
Beef (without bone)	27 „ „ „	20 „ „ „
Mutton and Lamb	27 „ „ „	20 „ „ „
Veal	33 „ „ „	25 „ „ „
Pork	33 „ „ „	25 „ „ „
Stuffed meat	33 „ „ „	25 „ „ „
In all cases: for joints up to 6 lb. allow in addition	20 min. extra on total cooking time.	15 min. extra
For joints over 10 lb. deduct from cooking time	20 min. of total cooking time.	15 min.

The times given above can only be a guide for the average joint as the shape and the proportion of bone must also be taken into consideration. If the joint is very thin a shorter cooking time will be required.

Low-temperature roasting

This method of cooking gives very good results, especially with tough or very lean meat, poultry and game and with small joints. When meat, etc., is cooked by this method it is juicy and tender; there is little loss of weight during cooking; the outside of the meat and fat is not dry; smell of cooking is not so noticeable; and there is very little oven splashing.

MEAT, METHODS OF PRESERVING

The following methods are employed for preserving meat.

Refrigeration

This means storing meat in a cold place. 34° to 39° F. is the general temperature for refrigerated meat.

Drying or Dehydration

Dried meat is produced by removing the water and treating with warm air. The meat is first treated with brine to draw out the water; the pieces are then hung in roomy, airy lofts. Streams of warmed air are often directed to the rooms, instead of leaving the natural air to do the work. The very close and hard types of Continental sausages, like salami, are treated in this way. Cod is salted and dried in this way, as well as other fish.

Salting or pickling

Cooking salt is an age-old method of preserving. When large quantities of salt are added, or brine is used, surplus water and certain substances essential to the growth of bacteria, are removed. There is no complete destruction of the germs, but the presence of the large quantities of salt halt the decay.

There are two methods of salting, brining and dry salting. The first is by immersing the whole piece of meat in a solution of salt and water, the second, by rubbing into the meat over several days a mixture of cooking salt, sugar and saltpetre. The saltpetre is used to preserve the red colour of meat, to help arrest the process of decay, and to prevent the odour of hydrogen sulphide.

Smoking

Smoking is as ancient a process as salting, and the two have always gone together in the preservation of meat. The flavour of various smoked meats can be varied by means of the different wood smokes used. Oak sawdust smoke is considered best by many people, while others think that apple wood gives a flavour that cannot be beaten. The wood smoke gives out wood vinegar, formic acid and creosote, minute drops of all of which penetrate the meat and kill the bacteria more effectively than plain salting.

Smoking causes a considerable loss of weight.

Marinating

This means preserving meat by laying it in a mixture of vinegar, herbs and sometimes a small proportion of wine. Two weeks is the longest time meat should be marinated, otherwise it becomes too acid. Large joints of slightly fat beef such as brisket and top side or top ribs are often marinated.

MERINGUE CASES

2 egg whites, 4½ oz. caster sugar.

Prepare the baking trays by covering with two thicknesses of grease-proof paper, the top one lightly brushed with sweet oil.

Whisk the egg whites very stiffly, until they will not fall out when the bowl is inverted. Add 4 teaspoonfuls of caster sugar and whisk until the whites are stiff again. Fold in all but 1/2 oz. of the remaining sugar with a tablespoon or palette knife, no longer whisking, but just turning the sugar over and over into the egg whites.

The mixture may then be put in dessertspoonfuls or tablespoonfuls on the oiled paper, or piped on with a forcing bag and plain tube.

Sprinkle the extra sugar over the meringues and bake on a low oven shelf for approximately 2 hr. at Regulo 1/4 or 200° F. in an electric oven.

If any difficulty is experienced in removing the cases from the paper with a palette or other broad knife, wet the paper on the underside, then the cases will peel off quite easily. Carefully make hollows in the bottoms of the meringues and put them back into the oven, after the gas or electricity has been turned off, to dry. Fill with whipped cream lightly flavoured with vanilla and sugar.

MILK

Milk is almost the perfect food, containing all the constituents essential to health.

There are recent examples of two doctors carrying out normal rounds of heavy professional commitments on milk for a month.

Every child gets free milk at school. Toddlers are entitled to 1 pint of milk a day at 1 1/2d. up to the age of 5 years.

Milk provides 375 calories to the pint, 3% protein, 4% fat, 4.5% carbohydrates, vitamins A and the B Group, D and E, calcium and phosphorus, and 87% water.

The average life of a milk bottle is 30—50 deliveries. About 250 million bottles, or 5 for every person in the United Kingdom are lost or broken every year. Each bottle costs 3 1/2d.

There are 3 million cows in the United Kingdom, one to every 16 people, producing 17 hundred million gallons a year or 5 times the average daily flow of the Thames at Teddington Weir.

There are one hundred and sixty thousand dairy farms in Great Britain. It takes 18 pints of milk to make 1 lb. of butter and 2 3/4 pints to make 4 oz. cream.

Thirty million pints of milk are sold in Great Britain daily.

Milk after it comes from the cow is now subjected to various different processes to make it safe and easy to keep fresh. It is actually one of the natural foods most likely to gather germs and odours from other foods, and to cause summer sickness in babies if it is not perfectly clean.

T. T. Milk

This means that it is from cows kept in the best of hygienic conditions, and that it has been tested to make sure it is tuberculin-free.

Pasteurised

This means that the disease germs, if any, are destroyed and the healthy bacteria left alive. To pasteurise, milk is kept at a temperature of 145° F. for 30 min. Pasteurising of milk is carried out by very efficient heating plant which most dairies now have installed.

Humanised

Milk prepared for babies by pouring off the creamy top after the milk has stood in a cold place overnight, made up to a pint with cold water and with an ounce of cane sugar stirred into it.

Homogenised

Treated by a process which blends the fat globules into the milk so that they remain evenly distributed. No cream rises on this kind of milk, it is all in the milk itself.

Sterilised

Heated slowly to over boiling point and maintained at high temperature for 5 min. then as slowly cooled.

Scalding

Bring milk to a temperature of 145⁰ F. quickly, then pour into a jug immediately and put into the coldest place possible. This is the home method of keeping milk from turning sour, and should be carried out immediately the milk is left by the milkman.

Yoghourt

Fresh milk artificially transformed into a thick creamy consistency by the introduction of a special culture of a harmless bacterium known as *bacillus Bulgaris.*

Yoghourt has been made and eaten for many centuries in Balkan countries, and Bulgars and Turks who make and eat it daily consider it essential to health and long life. The making and eating of Yoghourt has grown enormously in popularity in this country during the last years, and is always found on the menus of vegetarian and many other restaurants specialising in health foods.

Some dairies sell it as freely as milk.

It may be made at home by a simple process; the necessary culture with which to start the making is obtainable from several sources, and from this beginning, fresh supplies may be made daily.

MILK SHAKES

These are made by adding flavouring and colouring matter to fresh milk in order to make it more interesting and attractive, and are an excellent way to induce children to drink more milk.

In milk bars the drinks are made frothy by means of high-speed electric mixers, but home-made ones are easily made by using a good whisk.

Flavours generally used are raspberry, strawberry, pineapple, lemon, chocolate or coffee.

Fruit syrups are also used, but care must be taken to prevent the milk from curdling.

MINCE PIES

Mincement, rough puff or short pastry.

Roll out pastry thinly and cut into circles with a tart cutter. Put a teaspoonful of mincemeat on half the circles, moisten the edges, and place the remainder of the circles on top of the mincemeat, pressing the edges firmly together.

Pierce the top with a fork or skewer, brush with a little water and sprinkle with caster sugar. Bake in a fairly hot oven (Regulo 8 or 425⁰ F.) for 15 to 20 min.

MINCE, TO COOK

1 lb. fresh minced beef, 1 onion, 1 dessertspoonful flour, 1 or 2 savoury meat cubes, 1/2 pint stock, salt and pepper, 1 tablespoonful dripping or butter.

Mince the onion finely, lightly brown it in the fat, add the meat and stir together over a low heat for 5 min., sprinkle with flour, salt and pepper and the meat cubes, gradually add the stock, stir well to prevent the mince cooking in lumps. Bring to the boil to thicken the gravy, then simmer for 10 min.

Serve with sippets of toast or surrounded with grilled mushrooms. Sliced tomatoes may be added to the cooking mince. Also ready-cooked cold meat of any kind may be minced and served in this way.

MINCEMEAT

1 lb. finely chopped or shredded suet, 1 lb. currants, 1 lb. sultanas, 1 1/2 lb. raisins, 1 lb. firm cooking apples, 1 lb. caster sugar, 1/4—1/2 lb. finely minced candied peel, 4 oz. finely minced blanched almonds, 1/4 level teaspoonful mixed spice, 1/2 level teaspoonful grated nutmeg, 1/2 lemon, 1 large wineglassful brandy or rum.

Having well washed and dried the fruit, cut the raisins into quarters, roughly chop the sultanas, and leave the currants whole. Peel, core and chop the apples. Mix all the ingredients together with the brandy, and the strained juice and grated rind of the half lemon. Put into a large, wide-mouthed jar, place a piece of grease-proof paper, cut to fit over the mincemeat, and dipped in brandy, over the top. Seal the jar with two or three thicknesses of greaseproof paper and store the jar in a very cool, dry place.

This mincemeat should remain quite good for at least 4 months. Examine it from time to time, and if it seems at all likely to ferment, spread it on a dish and bake in the oven for 25—30 min. Return to the jar with a little extra brandy or sherry.

MINESTRONE

2 quarts meat or chicken stock, 1 small head celery, 1/4 lb. spinach, 1 onion, 1/2 lb. green peas, 2 carrots, 1 small cabbage heart, 1/2 lb. tomatoes, 2 sage leaves, 2 cloves garlic, salt, pepper, 1/4 lb. lean gammon, 4 tablespoonfuls grated Parmesan cheese, 2 oz. spaghetti broken very small.

Dice all the vegetables and the gammon. Put the carrots, gammon, spaghetti and celery into the stock and oil gently for 30 min. Add the rest of the vegetables and simmer until all are tender. Season to taste, stir in the cheese and serve with more Parmesan cheese.

Another version has diced vegetable marrow and small pieces of aubergine, leeks, sprigs of cauliflower, chopped parsley and basil added.

MINT CAKES

1/2 lb. flaky or rough puff pastry, 4 oz. currants, 2 oz. finely chopped candied peel, a pinch mixed spice. 1 1/2 oz. brown sugar, 1 tablespoonful finely chopped fresh mint leaves, a little butter.

Roll out pastry and cut into 3 1/2 in. circles. Soften some butter and spread a little over one half of these. Mix remaining ingredients and put a spoonful on each of the buttered circles of pastry. Moisten edges and lay a circle of pastry on each, sealing firmly. Press each lightly with rolling pin. Brush with a little egg and make two short slits on each. Alternatively, these cakes may be prepared as for Eccles cakes (see recipe) and given the same finishing touches. Bake for 15—20 min. at Regulo 8 or 450° F.

MINT JELLY

2 lb. cooking apples, about 12 good stalks of fresh mint, 3—4 table-spoonfuls water, sugar.

When in season, green gooseberries may be used instead of apples.

Cut the apples into small pieces without peeling or removing cores, or removing tops and tails of the gooseberries.

Put with the small quantity of water into the preserving pan and simmer over a low heat until the fruit is soft.

Strain carefully through a jelly bag, squeezing a little to help the juice to flow, but taking care that no pulp is squeezed through. Measure the juice and for each pint allow ¾ lb. sugar. Put juice and sugar back into the preserving pan, then add the mint, tied in a bunch. Bring slowly to the boil, then boil until the syrup is thick, and a little will set when tested on a plate. Remove the bunch of mint, pot the jelly into small pots, and when it is quite cold seal with a good seal such as is used for jam. It is a good plan to use well washed fish paste jars, as this gives the quantity required for a meal. If mint is liked in the jelly allow 1—3 tablespoonfuls of mint, very finely chopped and spread on a sheet of clean blotting paper for about 5 min. Stir into the jelly just before potting.

Two or three drops of green vegetable colouring may also be stirred in to give a better green colour.

MINT LEAVES, CRYSTALLISED

Choose fine freshly picked mint leaves, prepare them by washing, then cutting off all but ⅛ in. of the stalk. Dry the leaves thoroughly.

Whisk an egg white until it is thick and frothy, but not too stiff. Dip each leaf in the egg white, allowing it to become completely covered on both sides. Dip into caster sugar, then place on a sheet of greaseproof paper laid on a cake cooling wire.

Put the wire into an oven which is turned as low as it will go, with the oven door open a crack, and let the leaves stay in the warmth until the sugar has hardened and each leaf is encased in sugar.

Take from the oven, stand in a cool draught of air, and when the leaves are quite cold and hard, store between sheets of waxed paper, in a wooden or cardboard box. The leaves do not stay stiff for very long, so only make up enough for a day or two.

MINT SAUCE

4 tablespoonfuls finely chopped fresh garden mint, 1 teaspoonful caster sugar, pinch salt, 6—8 tablespoonfuls malt vinegar.

Mix the mint, sugar and salt together, stir in the vinegar. The mint chops more easily if it is lightly sprinkled with sugar. Lemon juice is sometimes used instead of vinegar.

MOCK TURTLE SOUP, CLEAR

1/2 calf's head, 1/4 lb. lean veal, 2 quarts thin white stock or water, 1 onion, 1 carrot, 1 stick celery, bouquet garni, 12 peppercorns, 6 cardamom seeds, 1 glass of sherry, white and shell of 1 egg, salt.

Soak the head for 24 hr., after having removed the brains and tongue. Put it into a large saucepan with the chopped vegetables, seasonings and herbs and a little salt.

Bring to the boil, remove all the scum, then boil very gently until the meat is ready to slip off the bones. Strain the liquid and leave to get cold. Skim off the fat. (Remove the meat from the bones, cut up with the vegetables and press into a basin as a brawn.)

Return the liquid, bones, chopped veal, crushed egg shell and whisked egg white to the saucepan. Boil for 30 min. Cool, strain carefully and add the sherry.

MONT BLANC, CHESTNUT

1 lb. chestnuts, 1/4 pint cream, 2 oz. icing sugar, 1 teaspoonful vanilla flavouring, chocolate grains, 2 egg whites, 2—3 tablespoonfuls Marsala or sherry if liked.

Split skins of the chestnuts round the centres and boil for 20 min. Strip off the shells and skins and rub through a sieve or mash very smoothly.

Stir in the icing sugar, vanilla and 2 egg whites stiffly whisked.

Pile the mixture in a mound in a glass dish, pour the whipped cream over, in which the wine has been mixed, scatter with chocolate grains.

MOTHERING SUNDAY CAKE

See *Simnel cake.*

MOUSSE, COLD RASPBERRY

1/2 pint cornflour cream, 3 oz. caster sugar, 1/4 pint raspberry purée (from fresh fruit), 1/2 oz. gelatine, 3 tablespoonfuls water, 1/4 pint double cream, few drops carmine colouring.

Make cornflour cream and sweeten with sugar. Set aside with covering of greaseproof paper to prevent a thick skin forming on top. Add water to gelatine and place over hot water until dissolved. Whip cream. Fold raspberry purée into cooled cornflour cream, adding a few drops colouring. Fold in whipped cream, then stir in dissolved gelatine. Pour into a mould, or several small ones, and leave until set.

MOUSSE, HOT RASPBERRY

2 oz. butter, 2 oz. caster sugar, 2 tablespoonfuls raspberry juice, purée from 1/2 teacupful fresh raspberries, sieved, 4 eggs, 1 oz. flour.

Cream butter and sugar well together, then add gradually the egg yolks and raspberry juice and purée. Whisk in bowl resting on the rim of a pan containing boiling water, until thick and creamy. Fold in sifted flour and stiffly beaten whites of eggs. Put mixture into a well-buttered and floured soufflé mould (it should be about half full), then place mould in a tin with water reaching half-way up sides of mould. Cover with greased paper and bake in a moderate oven at 350° F. or Regulo 5 for about 30 min.

MOUSSES, VARIOUS

The luxurious and genuine basic mousse mixtures are made as follows:

1. *3 egg yolks and 3 egg whites, 1/2 pint cream, 2 oz. caster sugar, 1 teaspoonful powdered gelatine, dissolved in a tablespoonful of tepid water.*

Beat sugar and egg yolks together until creamy, then beat in the gelatine. Fold in the lightly whipped cream, then the whisked egg whites. On no account beat the cream and egg whites into the egg and sugar. The whole secret is to keep the whole mixture very light. Add fruit purée or flavourings as required.

2. *1/4 pint thick sugar syrup made by boiling 1/2 lb. sugar with 1/4 pint water, 1/2 pint thick cream, 3 egg yolks, 1/4 pint fruit purée.*

Whip the egg yolks, pouring on the cold sugar syrup. Beat until thick. Fold in the lightly whipped cream and the fruit purée.

Put into the refrigerator.

3. This is a useful and economical recipe.

14 oz. tin evaporated milk, 1 fruit jelly of desired flavour, 1/4 pint water, 2—3 tablespoonfuls cream if possible, 1/4 pint fruit purée if desired.

Dissolve the jelly in the water. Whisk the evaporated milk until it is frothy, stir in the jelly and continue to whisk until the mixture begins to sponge. Beat in the fruit purée if using, until the mixture is again frothy and light, then pour into one large or several individual dishes, and put away to set.

Apricot, strawberry, raspberry and gooseberry purée are excellent for making mousse.

If a savoury mousse is required, make with a purée of chicken or fish. Use the last recipe, omit the jelly and use instead 3 teaspoonfuls powdered gelatine dissolved in 1/4 pint meat or fish stock, 1/4—1/2 lb. chicken or fish purée, and seasonings to taste, with 2—3 tablespoonfuls cream.

MUFFINS

1 lb. plain flour, 1/2 teaspoonful salt, 1/2 oz. yeast, 1 egg, a little tepid milk and water, 2 tablespoonfuls caster sugar.

Sift the flour and salt together. Cream the yeast with the caster sugar and stir it into a third of a pint of tepid milk and water, add the beaten egg and pour into the flour.

Knead lightly to a soft dough, cover the top of the bowl and leave it in a warm place for 1 1/2 hr.

Turn out on to a well-floured board, roll out to a thickness of about 1 in., cut into rounds about 3 in. in diameter.

Lift the muffins on to a floured baking tray, and bake in a hot oven for 7 min. With a broad knife blade, turn the muffins over and cook for a further 7—10 min.

When cold, toast and butter.

MULBERRY JAM

4 lb. mulberries, 4 lb. sugar, 1 teaspoonful citric or tartaric acid, a tiny piece of butter.

As a rule, mulberries do not require washing; go over them carefully, however, to remove cores.

Put into a preserving pan which has been lightly greased on the bottom and sides with the little piece of butter. Do not add any moisture because the mulberries will make all the necessary juice. Simmer very slowly until plenty of juice has run, stir in the citric or tartaric acid and simmer again for 5 min.

Pour in the sugar, bring all to the boil and boil moderately fast until a little jam will set when tested on a plate.

Pot into clean dry jars while the jam is very hot. Cover with a reliable jam seal when quite cold.

MULLED WINE

1 quart claret, or other light red wine, ¹/₂ pint water, 2 oz. sugar, the thinly-pared rind of 1 orange, ¹/₂ nutmeg in one piece.

Put the wine, water, nutmeg and sugar into an aluminium saucepan and bring it all almost to the boil. Serve very hot with a small piece of orange peel in each glass.

MULLIGATAWNY SOUP, CLEAR

2 quarts thin bone stock, 2 large sliced onions, 1 large sliced apple, 1 tablespoonful curry powder, juice of 1 lemon, shells and whites of 2 eggs, 2 teaspoonfuls salt, 1 teaspoonful sugar.

Simmer the stock, onions, apple, salt, sugar and the curry powder smoothly mixed with a little of the cold stock, for 1¹/₂ hr., closely covered. Strain and when cold, return to the saucepan with the egg shells crushed and the whites lightly whisked. Boil up again and leave to settle for an hour, remove scum, strain, add lemon juice and reheat. Serve with a little boiled rice added to each portion.

MULLIGATAWNY SOUP, THICK

2 quarts water, 2 lb. leg of mutton, 2 onions, 2 carrots, 2 apples, a bouquet garni, 2 tablespoonfuls flour, 1 tablespoonful curry powder, juice of 1 lemon, salt, 1 dessertspoonful sugar, 2 tablespoonfuls rice.

Cut the meat into small pieces, remove as much fat as possible and fry the fat until melted. Add the sliced vegetables and apple and cook for 15 min., removing the pieces of fat. Sprinkle in the flour and curry powder, fry for a few minutes, then add the meat cut into very small pieces, the salt, sugar, herbs and hot water.

Bring to the boil, remove all scum, then cook gently, closely covered for 3 hr. Rub all through a strainer, meat as well, return to the saucepan, season to taste, add lemon juice and serve. The rice boiled separately may be added or more rice may be cooked and handed separately.

MUSHROOM KETCHUP

4 lb. large fresh mushrooms, ¹/₄ lb. salt, ¹/₂ oz. pickling spices, ¹/₂ oz. ground ginger, ¹/₄ teaspoonful black pepper, 1 blade mace.

Examine the mushrooms to make sure that they are very sound and not wormy. Put them into a large casserole, sprinkling the salt between them. Leave for three days, each day stirring them well, over and over.

Drain off the brine, put the mushrooms into a preserving pan and cook them very gently over a low heat until they have made a lot of juice. Strain through muslin. Pour the juice off into a jar or bowl that can stand in a saucepan of water. Add the spices, ginger, pepper and mace, bring the water in the saucepan to the boil, then cook slowly for 3 hr.

Strain and bottle the ketchup and put it away for 2 weeks, then boil it up again for 5 min., then return to bottles and cork securely. This second boiling ensures that the ketchup will keep well.

Some people like the flavour of a shallot in the ketchup. The shallot should be cooked in the preserving pan with the mushrooms in the first place.

MUSHROOM SOUP, CLEAR

1 lb. mushroom stems, or stems and whole mushrooms, 2 wings of chicken or a chicken carcase, broken into pieces, 2 tablespoonfuls chopped parsley, 1 medium chopped onion, salt, 2 pints boiling water.

Put all the ingredients into a saucepan and simmer gently for 1 hr. Now remove any meat from the chicken bones, put this, the mushrooms and onions through the fine cutters of the mincer 3 times. Return to the stock and boil for 15 min. Strain and serve.

MUSHROOM SOUP, CREAM OF

1 oz. butter, 1 small onion, very finely minced, 1 level tablespoonful flour, 2 pints scalded milk, 1/2 lb. minced mushrooms, 4 tablespoonfuls cream, salt, pepper, 1 saltspoonful ground mace.

Melt the butter in a saucepan, add the onion and flour, mace, salt and gradually add the scalded milk, stirring to keep it all smooth. Put the mixture into the top of the double boiler and add the mushrooms. Cook gently for 20 min., then pour in the cream. Stir until very hot and creamy.

Serve with croûtons of French bread. If preferred, chicken stock may be used instead of milk.

MUTTON, BOILED

The rule is to put the meat into hot water; this seals the albumen on the outside of the meat, and prevents the juices from going out into the water. If you are stewing meat solely for the purpose of making soup or stock, and wish to extract all flavour from the meat, start it in cold water.

Put the mutton into enough hot water to cover it completely, with an onion, a carrot, a small piece of celery and 1—2 teaspoonfuls of salt.

Begin to cook fairly quickly, until the water comes to the boil, and the scum rises to the top. Remove every particle of this scum with a large spoon, for if left, it spoils the flavour and appearance of the meat.

Having made sure that no more scum will rise, lower the heat to a very slow simmer, put on the saucepan lid, and cook the meat 25 min. for every lb. in weight of the joint.

Dish it up, thicken some of the liquid smoothly with flour, and, if liked, add chopped capers.

Mashed turnips, beaten with butter or margarine, usually accompany boiled mutton.

MUTTON CHOPS

Grill beneath a sharp grill for about 3—4 min. on either side, according to taste.

Serve with grilled tomatoes and mushrooms.

MUTTON CUTLETS

Brush with butter or dripping and grill, or egg-and-breadcrumb them and deep fry. Serve with tomato sauce.

MUTTON, LEG OF, A LA BOULANGERE

So called because cottage people used to take their Sunday dinners to be cooked in the local baker's oven.

A small whole or half a large leg of mutton, 3—4 onions, 8—10 large potatoes, cut into 1/2 in. thick slices, peeled or not, dripping.

Skin and slice the onions; make a bed of the onions and some of the potatoes in a deep meat tin. Lay the joint on the vegetables. Put the rest of the potatoes round it, cover with dripping and roast at Regulo 7 or 450° F. for 20 min., then reduce to Regulo 5 or 400° F. for rest of the cooking time, according to weight of joint.

This is a good method to use for stuffed rolled loin or breast of mutton.

NAPOLEON BISCUITS

1/2 lb. plain flour, 5 oz. margarine or butter, 5 oz. caster sugar, 1 egg, 2 oz. ground almonds, jam.

Cream the fat and sugar together thoroughly, stir in the flour and ground almonds, moisten with the egg beaten lightly with a dessert-spoonful of cold water. Mix to a smooth stiff dough. Leave for an hour.

Roll very thinly, cut out with a round cutter. Bake on lightly greased baking tins for 10 min. at Regulo 5 or 400° F. When cool, sandwich together in pairs with raspberry jam.

NASTURTIUM SEEDS, PICKLED

Nasturtium seeds, salt, 1 oz. pickling spices, 1 quart good malt vinegar.

Put the spices and vinegar into a saucepan and boil rapidly for 15 min. Put on the lid and leave to infuse, off the heat, for 2 hr. or more. When ready, strain through muslin. The spices may be used a second time.

Pick the seeds on a dry day, and discard very large coarse ones. They are best used soon after the flowers have fallen from them. Put into a bowl and scatter kitchen salt thickly over them. Put a saucer or plate over them to keep them down, and leave for 24 hr. Rinse in fresh cold water, and dry well.

Put into small, wide-mouthed bottles. Those used for salad cream are good for the purpose. Fill the bottles with the cold spiced vinegar, so that all the seeds are completely covered with the vinegar, and cover closely. Store for 3—4 weeks before using.

NESSELRODE ICE PUDDING

1/4 lb. chestnut purée, 1 pint rich egg custard, 2 oz. chopped raisins and currants, 1 oz. chopped candied peel, 1 oz. chopped cherries, 1 pint whipped cream, a little Maraschino syrup.

Blend purée with custard and mix in the dried fruit and peel. Fold in the whipped cream, adding a few drops Maraschino syrup. Put in a mould and freeze lightly.

NORFOLK SPOON DUMPLINGS

2 eggs, ¹/₄ pint milk, pinch of salt, self-raising flour.

Break the 2 eggs into a bowl, stir in the milk and salt, then add flour until a thick batter is made.

Drop this into boiling salted water in small spoonfuls. Cook until firm in the centres. Drain in a colander, put on a hot dish and serve with a stew, a thick soup, or melted butter and brown sugar.

NOUGAT

1. *4 oz. icing sugar, 4 oz. honey, 8 oz. almonds, 2 whites of eggs, wafer paper.*

Blanch and dry the almonds thoroughly. Line a box of suitable size first with white paper and then with wafer paper, both of which must be cut to fit exactly. Put the sugar, honey and whites of eggs into a copper sugar boiler or pan, and stir by the side of the fire until the mixture becomes thick and white. Drop a little into cold water; if it at once hardens, remove the pan from the fire and stir in the almonds. Dredge the slab with icing sugar, turn on to it the nougat and form into a ball. Press into the prepared box, cover with paper, let it remain under pressure until cold, then cut up into squares.

2. *2 tablespoonfuls honey or golden syrup, 3 whites of eggs, 12 oz. lump sugar, ¹/₄ pint water, 2 oz. glucose, 4 oz. blanched almonds, roughly chopped, 6 glacé cherries, chopped, a little vanilla essence, rice paper.*

Put honey into top compartment of double saucepan, over boiling water. When heated, add stiffly whisked egg whites. Continue whisking together until thick and white. In a separate saucepan, put sugar and water. Stir over heat until sugar is dissolved, then add glucose. Boil until syrup spins a long thread from spoon — about 260^0 F. — then add to egg mixture, whisking briskly. Stir in chopped nuts and cherries. Have ready a tin lined with rice paper and pour in mixture. Cover with a second piece of rice paper, pressing lightly in place. Leave until set, then cut into bars and wrap separately in waxed paper.

OATMEAL BISCUITS (FARLS)

1 lb. medium oatmeal, ¹/₂ lb. self-raising flour, ¹/₂ lb. butter, margarine or dripping, warm milk and water, pinch of salt.

Mix the oatmeal and flour together with the salt, rub in the fat, then stir in enough warm milk and water to make a dry stiff dough. Roll out thinly on a board scattered with oatmeal. Cut into rounds about 3—4 in. in diameter, then cut each into quarters. Lay on baking sheets scattered with flour, and bake at Regulo 5 or 500^0 F. for 5—7 min. These cakes are dry and crisp, and should be served with butter.

OATMEAL BROSE

Put a cupful of medium oatmeal in a bowl, add a knob of butter and some salt. Pour enough boiling water over it to make a thin porridge. Serve hot with milk. Sometimes whisky is added.

OBLETJES OR OUBLIES (WAFFLES)

1 lb. plain flour, 8 oz. caster sugar, 6 oz. butter, 2 eggs, 1 level tea-spoonful powdered cinnamon, ¹/₄ pint white wine, pinch of salt.

Cream butter and sugar very well together, add the stiffly whisked egg whites.

Stir in the flour, cinnamon and salt sifted together, then add the egg yolks and wine. Beat to a smooth batter. If necessary, thin with a little more wine or cold water.

Pour tablespoonfuls of the batter into the lightly greased waffle iron. Cook quickly over a sharp heat, and roll while hot.

OMELETTE, CHINESE

4 eggs, 4 tablespoonfuls water, pepper and salt, 2 tablespoonfuls oil or melted butter (margarine), 4 small white onions, 1 teacupful bean sprouts, 2 teacupfuls diced cooked lean pork or chicken.

Beat eggs briefly. Add water and seasonings, and whisk together. Prepare ingredients, thinly slicing or chopping onions, and heating with the other ingredients in a little melted butter or in oil, until piping hot.

Heat a small frying or omelette pan and drop in a piece of butter or a spoonful of oil. When hot add about 3 tablespoonfuls of egg mixture. When bottom surface of mixture has set, add a layer of meat mixture. Cover with more egg mixture. Cook like an omelette, shaking pan occasionally, until mixture has almost set. Turn over and brown the other side. Repeat until all the mixtures have been used up. Serve with hot dry rice or with soya sauce.

OMELETTE, SPANISH

5 eggs, pepper and salt, 2 oz. butter, 1 teacupful diced cooked potatoes, 2 oz. chopped or sliced mushrooms, 6 chopped pitted green olives, 1 tablespoonful chopped tinned pimento, 1 onion, par-cooked and finely chopped, 1 clove garlic crushed (optional), chopped chives.

Beat eggs briefly and season to taste. Prepare ingredients and make piping hot with a little melted butter in small pan. Keep hot.

Melt butter in heated omelette pan and pour in half the egg mixture. Add filling ingredients, spreading over surface of pan. Pour in remaining egg mixture. Lift corners of omelette at intervals for any liquid mixture to run over surface of pan and set. Shake pan occasionally to keep contents from sticking. When almost set, slip pan under hot grill for a few moments, sprinkle with chopped chives and serve right away.

ONION FLAN

Line a deep flan tin or cake tin with good short pastry, then fill to the brim with the following mixture:

1¹/₂ lb. onions finely chopped, 8 oz. thick slice of gammon rasher, 1 dessertspoonful flour, 3 eggs, ¹/₂ pint milk or thin cream, salt and pepper, 2 oz. butter.

Fry the onions in the lard with almost all the gammon, cut into small dice. Do not allow the onion to brown. Sprinkle with flour and a pinch of salt, then add the eggs lightly beaten with the milk or cream. Pour this into the pastry case, drop the remaining bacon cubes on top and bake for 30—45 min. at Regulo 6 or 425° F. Serve at once.

ONIONS

To boil: Remove skins, cut off roots and tops. Put into salted water, bring to the boil and throw away the water.

Put into fresh salted water and cook until they can be pierced easily with a fork. Serve with butter, pepper, and salt.

To fry: Peel and slice the onions, drop them into a little milk, leave for about 30 min., drain and dry.

Have ready some hot fat in a frying pan or saucepan, drop in the onions, and cover the pan. Cook slowly for about 10 min., turning them occasionally. To make them crisper, dip in flour, and fry in hot fat until crisp. Serve with steak or pork chops.

ORANGE SAUCE

See *Sauces.*

ORANGE SAUCE, SWEET

2 tablespoonfuls orange marmalade, 1 orange, 1 oz. caster sugar, 1/2 pint water, 2 teaspoonfuls arrowroot, 1 small glassful curaçao.

Boil the marmalade in the water with the grated rind of half the orange and the sugar. Strain. Return to the saucepan with the arrowroot mixed to a paste with the strained juice of the orange. Cook and stir until the sauce thickens and becomes smooth. Add the liqueur. Serve hot with steamed pudding.

OX-CHEEK, STUFFED

1 ox-cheek, 2 oz. butter, 2 oz. flour, 2 onions, 2 medium carrots, 1 bouquet garni, 1 teaspoonful peppercorns, salt, pepper, 1 egg, bread-crumbs, veal stuffing.

Wash the cheek well in warm slightly salted water and leave to soak in more salted water for 12 hr.

Put into a saucepan with the seasonings and diced vegetables. Bring to the boil, remove scum. Simmer until the bones can be taken from the meat. Flatten the cheek with a cutlet bat, spread the forcemeat on it and roll it up. Tie with string. Roll in beaten egg and then in the crumbs. Then bake it in a hot oven, basting frequently with dripping, for 1 hr. at Regulo 6 or 425° F.

Garnish with rolls of bacon and slices of lemon.

OX-HEART STEW

Clean the heart, cut into thick slices. Marinate them with diced vegetables, a small bayleaf, a small wineglassful of dry red wine and 4 tablespoonfuls of vinegar for a whole day.

Put the pieces of heart with 2—3 slices of fat pork into a saucepan with the vegetables and liquid, a clove of garlic, salt and pepper, and enough water to cover.

Simmer until the meat is tender.

Dish up and serve with the liquid strained and slightly thickened.

OX-PALATE

Bone and wash the cheek, roll up and tie.

Put it into a saucepan with a little salt, bring to the boil, remove the scum, then put into the saucepan small whole onions, small carrots split lengthways in halves, a head of celery cut into short lengths, a bouquet garni, salt, peppercorns and a piece of mace.

Simmer together for 3—4 hr. Dish up, put the vegetables round and strain the broth over. Parsley sauce may be served, sharpened with a little vinegar and dry mustard.

OXTAIL SOUP

As stew (see below), but use more water.

Thicken with a gravy thickening, and add a little of the meat from the smaller pieces of the tail. Before serving, stir in a glassful of dry sherry.

OXTAIL STEW

1 large meaty oxtail cut into pieces, 2—3 onions, 3 carrots, small piece of bayleaf, flour, pepper and salt, 1/2 pint of haricot or butter beans, 1 tablespoonful of dripping.

Roll the pieces of oxtail in flour seasoned with pepper and salt. Heat the dripping in the saucepan and turn the onions and oxtail in it until seared all over. Add the beans, sliced carrot and bayleaf. Cover completely with hot water. Bring to the boil and remove scum. Put on the lid of the saucepan and simmer moderately for 3—4 hr. Leave until quite cold. Remove all the fat and re-heat as required. Never serve oxtail without removing the fat; it is far too greasy to be pleasant.

OX-TONGUE, FRESH

Wash a fresh ox-tongue, soak it for 5 hr., then boil it gently for 3 hr. with an onion, carrot, leek, clove of garlic, bayleaf, and peppercorns. Remove the skin and the root. Serve hot with tomato sauce, or with peeled grapes and some of the liquor mixed with a glass of red wine.

OX-TONGUE, SMOKED

1 smoked ox-tongue, peppercorns, 2—3 cubes aspic jelly or 2 teaspoonfuls powdered gelatine, peppercorns.

Soak the ox-tongue for 5—6 hr. Put into a large saucepan with 1 doz. peppercorns, bring to the boil and skim. Boil gently for 2 1/2 hr. Cool in the saucepan, then take out and remove the skin and cut off the root and fat at the root. Press the tongue into a round mould with the tip folded neatly in.

Boil the cuttings for 1/2 hr. Strain and add the gelatine or jelly cubes to about 1/2 pint of the liquor. Pour a little of this into the mould.

When cold, remove and mash with the remains of the jelly.

OYSTER LOAF

A favourite American dish.

Cut the top from a large or small loaf. Scrape all the crumbs from inside it, leaving a shell, and butter the inside.

Simmer 3 doz. small oysters in their liquor for 3—4 min., drain. Add to this liquor 2 tablespoonfuls of flour mixed to a cream with 1/4 pint milk and 1 oz. butter. Season with a pinch of cayenne pepper and a dash of nutmeg. Cook until smooth and creamy. Add the oysters, pour all into the loaf shell, put back the top, brush over with melted fresh butter or margarine and bake at Regulo 7 or 450° F. for 10 min.

OYSTER FRICASSEE

Make a rich sauce with 4 oz. butter, 1 pint cream or thin Béchamel sauce. Season it with salt, 3—4 drops lemon juice and a pinch of cayenne pepper.

Open the oysters and simmer in their liquid for 2 min., stir oysters and liquid into the sauce and serve at once with buttered toast. Allow 2 doz. oysters to the above quantity of sauce.

OYSTER SAVOURY (ANGELS ON HORSEBACK)

Simmer large oysters in their own liquor until the edges curl, wrap each in half a thin rasher of bacon, push on to a skewer and grill until the bacon is crisp. Unskewer, and serve on croûtons of bread fried in butter.

PAELLA

1 lb. rice, 1 large joint of uncooked chicken, which can be bought in many food shops, frozen or fresh, 1/4 pint prawns, 1 pint mussels (in season), 2—3 scallops, 2 crayfish tails, a thick slice ham, 2 onions, 2 large tomatoes, 1 red pepper, 12 green olives, mushrooms, fresh or frozen green peas, saffron, oil, butter, salt, pepper and 1 1/2 pints of chicken stock.

Cut the chicken and ham into small pieces, skin and remove pulp from the tomatoes, wipe the mushrooms and slice them. Open the mussels over a quick heat, take them from the shells and keep the liquid.

Fry the chicken and ham in about 2 oz. butter. Cook the rice in boiling salted water for 10 min., dry thoroughly and put into the pan with the chicken and ham.

Fry the onions and tomatoes and mushrooms lightly. Stir the rice well with the chicken, using a little more butter if required. Add the onions, tomatoes and mushrooms, saffron and stock. Simmer until the stock is almost absorbed, then stir in the peas, mussels, crayfish and scallops, cut in pieces, season with salt and pepper to taste. Be gentle with the stirring in order not to break up the ingredients. Turn into a large flat hot dish and decorate with strips of red pepper cooked in a little butter until soft but not broken.

PANCAKES, IRISH

4 eggs, 1/8 pint thin cream, 1 1/2 oz. butter, 3 oz. plain flour, grated nutmeg, caster sugar.

Beat 2 egg whites and 4 yolks and mix with the cream. Stir in the melted butter, flour and a little nutmeg. Beat gently to a smooth batter.

Fry the pancakes in a pan with a very small piece of butter made very hot. Be sure the pancakes are thin. Sprinkle with sugar and roll up to serve.

PANCAKES, PLAIN

8 oz. plain flour, 2 eggs, pinch of salt, 1/2 pint milk.

Sift the flour and salt together, break in both eggs and begin to stir, gently adding the milk in a trickle as you go and stirring until the flour and eggs are completely blended and you have a smooth creamy batter that will coat the back of the spoon thickly.

Stop adding the milk at this point; you may not need all of the half-pint. Beat the batter until it is covered with bubbles, then leave in a cold place for at least an hour.

Spread a sheet of greaseproof paper and sprinkle generously with caster sugar. Give the batter a last beating up and put it into a jug.

Melt a good knob of lard or cooking fat (never butter or margarine) in a small pan. Use enough fat to film the bottom of the pan lightly, then pour in enough batter to cover the pan thinly.

Stand by with a broad palette knife to lift the batter as it gets firm at the edges, tilting the pan about to let the loose uncooked batter get to the heat. Once the pancake is firm on the bottom pass the knife right under it, and with a quick flip turn it over, unless you like to take a chance and toss it.

Cook on the other side, then at once tilt it on to the sugared paper and roll gently. Stock pile on a hot dish covered with a paper doyley and start at once on the next one. The ideal is to serve each pancake as you make it.

You must never roll a pancake inside out, but always with the first cooked side showing its lacy pattern.

PANDOWDY

Put into a deep dish several layers of sliced apples, with brown sugar generously sprinkled between the layers. Top with slices of new bread from which the crusts have been cut. Sprinkle with fine shavings of margarine or butter and more brown sugar. Bake at Regulo 4 or 375⁰ F. for about 45 min., when the apple will be very soft, and the bread soaked with juice, but crisp on top.

PANDOWDY, NEW ENGLAND

2 lb. juicy cooking apples, 1/4 teaspoonful each powdered cinnamon and nutmeg, 1 teacupful brown sugar, grated rind and juice 1/2 lemon, 2 tablespoonfuls hot water, 1/2 lb. scone dough.

Peel, core and slice apples into a buttered casserole. Cover and cook in hot oven about 15—20 min., or until apples are par-cooked. Remove cover.

Make scone dough and press out lightly to fit over apples. Mark into wedges. Return dish to oven and bake at 450⁰ F. or Regulo 8 until scone topping is golden brown, i. e. for about 35—40 min.

PANOCHA

1 1/2 lb. brown sugar, 1/2 pint milk, 2 oz. butter, 1 teaspoonful vanilla essence, 6 oz. chopped walnuts.

Put sugar and milk into a pan and stir until sugar is dissolved over low heat. Cook until a teaspoonful dropped into cold water forms a soft ball between the fingers. Then draw pan from heat and stir in vanilla. Add butter and leave without further stirring until cool. When luke warm beat mixture until creamy, and stir in chopped walnuts. Pour at once into oiled or buttered shallow tin. When set cut into squares.

PARKIN

8 oz. plain flour, 8 oz. fine oatmeal, 8 oz. cane syrup (the very black kind gives too bitter a flavour), 6 oz. margarine, 4 oz. sugar, 1 teaspoonful each ground ginger, spice and bicarbonate of soda, 1 teacupful hot milk.

Rub the margarine thoroughly into the flour, stir in the sugar and spices. Mix the treacle, bicarbonate of soda and warm milk together and pour it into the dry ingredients, and mix all together to a soft dough.

Put this into a well-greased, oblong-shaped cake tin or square baking tin, brush top with milk and bake for about 1 hr. at Regulo 4 or 375° F.

Turn out to cool on a cake cooling wire, and do not cut the cake for at least 24 hr. after it is cool. Cut into slices and butter.

PARSNIPS, MASHED

Cook as below. Mash thoroughly, add a tablespoonful of dripping or butter. Put into a pie dish, scatter the top with breadcrumbs and brown in the oven. Serve with a roast joint. The mashed parsnips may be mixed with crumbs and an egg, formed into cakes and put into the tin with the roasting meat.

PARSNIPS, TO COOK

Wash and thoroughly scrape the parsnips; if small, slit into 4, if large, cut the thick base into rounds and the thinner portion into quarters.

Boil in salted water until sufficiently tender to pierce with a fork, usually from 1/2—3/4 hr.

Usually served with salt fish or with pickled pork.

Cooked parsnips may be coated with batter and deep fried.

PASTRY

Choux Pastry

1/2 pint water, 4 oz. plain flour, 2 oz. butter, 3 eggs, pinch of salt.

Heat the butter and water in a saucepan, not too large, as it is difficult to beat the mixture in too large an area. Stir in the flour and salt, and continue to stir until a thick paste is formed, which leaves the saucepan sides cleanly.

Take the pan from the heat, allow the paste to cool a little, then add the eggs, one by one, beating in each egg very thoroughly before adding the next. The last egg should be added a little at a time, since if the eggs are very large you may not need the whole of the third, because the mixture should be stiff enough to pipe.

Flaky Pastry

1 lb. plain flour, 10 oz. margarine and lard mixed (real flaky pastry is made with butter), 1 tablespoonful lemon juice, very cold water.

Put the fats or one variety of fat into a large piece of clean muslin and knead it until it is quite soft, then pat it to a large flat piece. Put it into a cold place to become firm again. Sieve the flour into a bowl, cut off about one-third of the fat, put it into the flour and cut it into small pieces, then rub in the pieces lightly, but not as thoroughly as for short crust.

Pour in the lemon juice and about 1/2 small teacupful of very cold water. Work the mixture to a smooth elastic dough, using a little more water if necessary. The dough must not be slack. Now roll it on a floured board to a long, narrow strip. Divide the remaining portion of fat into three equal parts. Take one part and cut it into a number of small nuts, place them all over the strip of paste, sprinkle with a very little sifted flour; if you have no flour dredger, use a small wire gravy strainer. Fold the paste into three, and press the edges closely together to prevent air escaping. Turn with the sealed edges to the right and left hands, roll the pastry away from you into a long strip again. Repeat the process with the remaining two pieces of fat, then cover the pastry and leave in a cold place for 1 hr.

Make up as required, and when baking, use Regulo 8 or 475° F.

Puff Pastry

1 lb. plain flour, 1 lb. butter and margarine mixed, ¹/₄ teaspoonful salt, the strained juice of 1 small lemon, a little very cold water.

First put all your fat, be it butter, margarine and butter or all margarine, into a piece of muslin, and knead it well until it is soft, and all moisture has been squeezed out of it. Put it aside to get firm and cold again.

Put the flour and salt into a large bowl or on a large pastry board, make a well in the centre, pour in the lemon juice and ¹/₄ teacupful of very cold water, iced if possible.

Stir all together, then work to a stiff, firm dough, that leaves the bowl or board cleanly.

Roll the ball of dough, on a floured board, to a strip about 12 in. long and of even width.

Place the prepared fat in the centre of the strip of dough, then fold the ends over the butter, so that you have one thickness of the paste on the bottom and two thicknesses over the fat. Seal the sides by pressing the dough firmly together with finger and thumb.

Now roll the sealed packet of dough and butter or fat away from you, to a 12 in. strip again, keeping the sides of the strip as even as possible. Fold in three again, with a very light sprinkling of flour between each fold of dough. Seal the edges again, give a half turn, so that the folded edges are towards you. Leave in a cool place for 30 min. Roll and fold again twice in succession, then put the dough away in a cool place for 15 min. Roll and fold again twice in succession. Put away in a cool place until ready to make up.

Raised Pastry

1 lb. plain flour, 6 oz. lard, ¹/₄ pint water, ¹/₂ teaspoonful salt, ¹/₄ teaspoonful black pepper.

Sift the flour with the salt and pepper. Boil the lard and water for 5 min., then pour it into the flour. Stir with a spoon until cool enough to touch, then knead to a soft, smooth dough without cracks. The paste must be kept warm during the making or it will crack and be difficult to shape.

Let the paste stand in a warm place for 1 hr., then make up at once.

Short Pastry

8 oz. self-raising flour, 4 oz. lard or 2 oz. lard and 2 oz. margarine, pinch of salt, 1 tablespoonful sugar, water.

Sift the flour and salt, add the sugar. Put the fat into the flour and cut it into the flour with a sharp knife until it is reduced to tiny pieces. Rub these into the flour between fingers and thumbs until fine as crumbs. Use enough cold water to make a firm smooth dough. If a dough is too moist, it will make a tough, dry crust.

For a savoury pie, omit sugar and season with pepper.

Suet Crust

8 oz. self-raising flour, 4 oz. finely-shredded fresh or packet suet (when using packet suet, allow an extra dessertspoonful), 1 tablespoonful sugar, or salt and pepper to taste.

Mix flour and suet, sugar or seasoning, to a soft dough with cold water. Roll out and use as required.

Good beef dripping may be substituted for the suet.

PASTY, CORNISH

Pasties can be made of various kinds of meat and poultry, but the most famous is the Cornish pasty, which differs from others because the ingredients are not previously cooked.

Pastry

1 lb. plain flour, 8 oz. dripping, pinch of salt.

Mix to a stiff dough with cold water. Roll out and cut into rounds about 4 in. in diameter.

Filling

1/2 lb. steak, 1/4 lb. liver or kidneys, 2 raw potatoes, 1 large onion, 1/2 small turnip, 1 large carrot, salt, pepper, 1 beaten egg.

Chop the meat and liver fairly small. Dice the peeled vegetables. Put a layer of vegetables on one half of the pasties, cover with meat and season with salt and pepper. Brush the lower inside edge with egg, then fold the plain half of the pastry over the ingredients. Press very firmly together, and flute round to prevent the pasties opening. The steam must be kept in to cook the ingredients.

Put on greased tins, brush with egg and put into the oven at Regulo 7 or 450° F. Cook thus for 15 min., then reduce to Regulo 4 or 375° F. and cook for a further 35—40 min.

When making chicken or game pasties, use margarine or lard or half and half for the pastry.

PATE OF CHICKEN LIVER

1 lb. chicken livers, 1/4 lb. fresh butter, 1/2 teaspoonful grated nutmeg, 1 teaspoonful dry mustard, 1 small clove well-crushed garlic, a good dash black pepper.

Simmer for 20 min. in slightly salted water with the garlic. Drain thoroughly and put through the finest cutters of the mincer three times, then rub smooth with the back of a wooden spoon. Beat in the butter and all the seasonings. Press into a small earthenware dish and pour clarified butter on the top. Put into the refrigerator or other cool place to become firm.

Serve with sliced French bread and butter.

The pâté may be made with calf's liver, beef, rabbit or chicken.

PEACH MELBA

5 or 6 ripe peaches, 1/4 pint raspberry purée, 1 large vanilla ice cream brick, 4 oz. caster sugar, vanilla flavouring.

Halve and stone the peaches, poach them in a syrup made with the sugar and a few drops of vanilla until the fruit is just tender but not broken. Drain the fruit on a sieve.

When quite cold, arrange them round the block of ice cream. Pour the chilled raspberry purée over and stand the dish on another filled with shaved ice and serve at once.

PEA SOUP

2 quarts stock, preferably that in which ham or bacon bones have been cooked, 1 pint split dried peas, preferably green split peas, 2 onions, 2 carrots, 2 large sticks celery, 1 teaspoonful dried mint, salt, pepper, 1 oz. pea flour, freshly chopped mint.

Soak the peas in water for 12 hr. Put them into a large saucepan with the stock and the vegetables diced small, the salt and dried mint. Simmer gently for 3 hr., then rub through a sieve. Return to the saucepan, add the flour mixed smoothly with a little water, bring to the boil and cook for 5 min.

Serve with a scattering of freshly chopped mint on each portion. If preferred, the soup may be served without the vegetables being put through the sieve.

PEANUT BRITTLE

1 lb. granulated sugar, $^1/_4$ pint water, 1 generous tablespoonful golden syrup, 1 oz. butter, 1 dessertspoonful vinegar, 1 teaspoonful lemon juice, 3—4 oz. roasted peanuts.

Put sugar, water and syrup into a thick saucepan over low heat. Stir until sugar is melted. Add butter and vinegar and bring to the boil. Boil without stirring, until a teaspoonful of the syrup dropped into a cup of cold water become brittle almost at once and snaps when bent. Draw pan from heat and gently stir in lemon juice or lemon essence. Pour into an oiled or greased tin and sprinkle nuts over the surface at once. When toffee is half set mark into squares with a greased knife. Break up when cold.

PEARS, HOW TO BOTTLE

The method of sterilising pears is the same as that for peaches and apricots, etc. Their preparation, however, differs a little. Pears quickly lose colour and to prevent this as much as possible, have ready a bowl containing a solution of 1 oz. salt to 2 quarts of cold water.

Prepare each pear by peeling and halving or quartering and removing the core, and immediately drop the pieces into the solution before starting on another pear. When all the fruit is ready, drain and rinse in clean cold water.

If the pears are ripe and juicy, such as William or Comice pears, they may be packed at once into the jars, the syrup poured over and the jars sealed as usual.

If the pears are inclined to be hard, bring to the boil in plain water and then simmer gently for 5 min. Drain and pack into jars as usual. Use the water in which they were half cooked for making the syrup with which to cover them.

PEAR JAM

For every lb. of pears, weighed when they are peeled and cores removed, allow $^3/_4$ lb. sugar. Since pears do not always cook a good colour, a few drops of cochineal added towards the end of the cooking is an improvement. A small piece of cinnamon, or a little powdered cinnamon is liked by many people, or the juice of a lemon for every 4 lb. fruit.

Peel, core and slice the fruit, and as each pear is dealt with, drop the slices into a bowl containing a solution of salt and cold water, 1 level tablespoonful kitchen salt to $^1/_2$ gallon water. This helps to prevent the pears turning brown.

When all the fruit has been prepared, rinse it in clear water, put it into the preserving pan with enough water to cover the bottom of the pan to prevent sticking. Should the pears, however, be of the very hard winter variety, more liquid will be needed. Simmer the fruit over a low heat until it has become quite soft, stirring now and then, and now add the sugar, cinnamon flavouring or lemon juice. When the sugar has dissolved, bring slowly to a gentle boil and boil and stir until a little of the jam will set when tested on a plate. Add the colouring a little before finishing. Pot into warm, dry jars, cover closely when the jam is quite cold, and store in a cool light place.

PEAR MARMALADE

6 lb. of any kind of pears, 4 lb. sugar, 1 lb. honey, 6 drops cochineal, $^1/_2$ pint water.

Remove the stalks and bruises from pears, cut the fruit into small pieces without peeling or taking out the cores. Simmer with the water until the pear is reduced to a pulp.

Rub through a strainer, return the pulp to the preserving pan with the sugar and honey, stir until the sugar has dissolved, then boil moderately fast until a little of the preserve will set on a cold plate. Stir in the cochineal colouring very thoroughly, pot the marmalade while it is very hot, cover when quite cold.

PEASE PUDDING

1 lb. split peas (yellow), 1 onion, 2 sage leaves (optional), 1 tablespoonful flour, walnut-sized piece of margarine, salt and pepper, 1 egg.

Soak the peas for 12 hr. put them into the saucepan with the onion thinly sliced, sage, salt and pepper. Cover with warm water and bring to the boil, cook slowly until the peas are tender, stirring frequently as the peas burn easily. It may be necessary to add a tablespoonful or so of water.

When the peas are soft, rub them, with the onion, through a sieve or wire strainer. Mix the flour to a paste with the beaten egg, stir into the purée of peas. Season again if required.

Grease a basin with the margarine, press the purée into it, cover with a margarine paper or a piece of greaseproof paper and steam the pudding for an hour.

PEPPERMINT CREAMS

1 lb. icing sugar, milk, few drops of peppermint essence or oil of peppermint.

If using oil of peppermint, less will be required because it is much stronger.

Sift the icing sugar well, mix the required quantity of peppermint flavouring with a tablespoonful of milk and mix with the icing sugar.

Knead well, adding a few more drops of milk at a time, until a thick paste is made.

Turn this out on to a dish or marble slab and knead until soft and smooth, then roll out with a bottle dusted with icing sugar to a thickness of 1/2 in. Cut into small rounds with a small sharp cutter, and place the round shapes in rows on a sheet of grease-proof or waxed paper. Leave to dry, then pack into boxes between grease-proof or waxed paper sheets.

PEPPERMINT DROPS

1 lb. lump sugar, 1/4 lb. brown sugar, 1³/4 gills water, 1 teaspoonful glucose, good pinch cream of tartar, 1¹/2 oz. butter, oil of peppermint (few drops) or about 2 teaspoonfuls peppermint essence.

Put both sugars into a strong saucepan. Add water and stir over low heat until sugars are dissolved. Add glucose and cream of tartar and boil to 240⁰ F. Add oiled butter and boil to 300⁰ F. without stirring. Add peppermint essence or oil and drop in small teaspoonfuls, from the tip, on to waxed or oiled paper.

PEPPERMINT TAFFY

1 lb. granulated sugar, 8 tablespoonfuls water, 2 tablespoonfuls vinegar, 6—8 drops peppermint flavouring, or a little more if you like strong sweets, enough green colouring to give the mixture a pretty green tint.

Put sugar, water and vinegar into a thick saucepan over a very low heat and leave, shaking the pan frequently, until the sugar has dissolved. Now boil it moderately fast, stirring all the time, until a little of the syrup dropped into cold water will make a hard little ball. Take the saucepan from the heat, stir in peppermint and colouring. Pour the toffee on to a lightly oiled dish, keep turning back the edges towards the centre of the mass with the knife, as soon as it is cool enough to handle, lift the mass of toffee from the dish and pull it out as far as it will go without breaking. Fold up and stretch it into one or more long, thin ropes, twist them round and round, like barley sugar, then cut them into short cushions with scissors. When quite cold, wrap the pieces in squares of waxed paper, twisting the ends together.

PEPPER PICKLE, SWEET

1 teacupful finely chopped (or coarsely minced) sweet red peppers, 1 teacupful finely chopped (or coarsely minced) green peppers, 3 teacupfuls coarsely minced onions, 1 heaped teacupful sugar, 2 teaspoonfuls salt, 2 teacupfuls white vinegar.

Combine peppers and onions in basin. Cover with water off the boil. Stand 5 min., then drain well. Put into pan with sugar, salt and vinegar. Mix well and simmer (only) for 25 min. Pack into hot sterilised jam jars. Seal at once. Excellent in sandwiches, or with cold meats, etc.

PEPPERS, STUFFED

10 green peppers, 1 lb. pork, 1 cup of sour cream, small piece of bacon, 1/4 lb. rice, 3 tomatoes.

Boil the green peppers for a few min., then cut off the stalks, remove the seeds and fill them with the following mixture: for each 8 or 10 peppers take 1 lb. pork run through a mincer, a cupful uncooked rice, and a little bacon cut in cubes. Mix and salt to taste and fill the peppers therewith. Meanwhile prepare a thin tomato sauce, sweeten, put the stuffed peppers in it and let them boil for $1/2$ hr. Take care to put the peppers upright in the sauce, lest the filling fall out.

PERRY

Perry is made by maturing a large quantity of pears in a warm place for 15 days, then crushing them through metal or very heavy wooden rollers. The pulp is then crushed again with heavy weights and put into large casks for a week or two, until the sediment falls to the bottom. The clear liquid is then taken off without disturbing the sediment and bottled from the casks as required.

The pulp must be kept at a temperature of not lower than 60º F. while it is setting.

PHEASANT WITH WINE

1 good plump pheasant, $1/2$ lb. small carrots, 1 shallot, $1/2$ lb. pork sausage meat, $1/4$ lb. calf's liver, salt, pepper, $1/4$ pint port wine; an inexpensive wine will do quite well.

Slice the calf's liver thinly.

Put the liver and pheasant into a deep dish and pour the wine over them. Leave for 24 hr., turning several times.

Take up the liver and cook it with $1/2$ oz. butter until tender, then put it through the mincer twice. Mix it with the sausage meat, together with the butter in which it was cooked, and stuff the bird with it.

Slice the carrots very thinly, lay them in the bottom of the casserole, lay the bird on them, cover the breast of the pheasant with slices of streaky bacon.

Pour in the port wine used for the marinade, season lightly with salt and pepper, cover closely and cook in a gentle oven, Regulo 4 or 375º F. for 45 min. Remove the casserole lid and cook for 15 min. more.

Take up the bird, bacon and carrots. Keep very hot. Strain the liquid in the casserole and mix it thoroughly with a little thick brown gravy.

PICCALILLI OR MUSTARD PICKLE

1 lb. cauliflower, 1 lb. cucumber cut into small chunks, 1 lb. small runner or French beans, 1 lb. small onions or shallots, 2 lb. vegetable marrow cut into small cubes, (all these vegetables should be weighed after they have been cut into the required size in order to get the correct proportions), 2 quarts of malt vinegar boiled with 1 oz. allspice and left to infuse for 2 hr. before being strained for use, $1/4$ lb. brown sugar, 1 oz. dry mustard, $1/2$ oz. ground ginger, 1 oz. cornflour, $1/2$ oz. turmeric, kitchen salt.

Put the prepared vegetables into a large china bowl and sprinkle them with salt. Put a large plate on top of the vegetables to keep them from floating out of the salt and leave for 24 hr. Wash quickly with fresh water and drain thoroughly.

Mix the cornflour, dry mustard, ginger and turmeric to a smooth paste with a little of the vinegar. Put the rest of the vinegar into the preserving pan with the sugar and boil all the vegetables in this for just 15 min. Now stir in the thickening paste and boil for 5 min. to make a thick, smooth sauce. It is very important to let this sauce boil for the full 5 min., or later on it will 'run back' or go thin. Pot into clean, wide-mouthed jars, and when the pickle is quite cold, cover well with a good air-tight type of jam pot cover.

PICKLES, CLEAR MIXED

Spiced Vinegar
1 quart best malt vinegar or white vinegar, 1 oz. allspice, 2—3 red chillis.

Put all the spices and the vinegar into a saucepan, bring to the boil, boil gently for 15 min. with the lid on the pan, put the pan aside for 2 hr., then strain off the vinegar, and it is ready for use. The spices may be used a second time with half the amount of vinegar.

Pickle
6 lb. mixed vegetables, such as very small shallots, small cubes of marrow, tiny green tomatoes, tiny runner beans, cauliflower cut into small sprigs with much of the stump and stem removed, gherkins or cucumber, cut into small pieces with pulp and seeds removed.

All vegetables to be pickled must be brined, to remove the superfluous moisture, and in the case of strong-flavoured vegetables to remove a little of the strength and make them more mellow.

Put all the prepared vegetables into a bowl, cover with a solution of 4 oz. salt to 1 quart vinegar and leave for 24 hr. Rinse in clear water, drain very thoroughly, pack into clean wide-mouthed jars and cover completely with cold spiced vinegar (see above).

Cover with good air-tight jam pot seals, closely gummed down to exclude all air. Store the pickles in a cool place. A small chilli may be included in each jar if liked.

PIGEON CASSEROLE

2 plump pigeons, 2 onions, 3—4 medium carrots, 1 doz. unstuffed olives, 1 glass port wine, small piece bayleaf, salt and pepper, 1 pint stock, 1 oz. butter.

Cut the pigeons in halves down the centres. Slice carrots and onions. Brown the pieces of bird and vegetables in the butter, then arrange the pigeons on the vegetables in a deep casserole. Put in the bayleaf and olives, the stock and any juices left in the pan after browning the ingredients. Cover closely and cook in a slow oven (Regulo 4 or 375° F.) for 2 hr. Strain off the stock, thicken it slightly with cornflour, add the wine, pour back into the casserole and cook again for 1/2 hr.

PIGEON PIE

3 plump pigeons, 1/2 lb. rump steak (optional), 1/4 lb. lean gammon, 2 hard-boiled eggs, 3/4 pint good stock, small piece of bayleaf, 6 peppercorns, salt, 2—3 carrots, 1 tablespoonful dripping.

This pie is one of England's oldest dishes, because almost every household had a pigeon cote which kept the family in fresh meat during the days when other meat was not available.

Cut each pigeon in half along along the breast bone. Cut the steak and gammon into dice, slice the carrots. Turn them lightly in the dripping for 15 min., drain from the fat and arrange in a large pie dish with the shelled eggs, and peppercorns.

Stir the stock into the juices left in the pan and boil up with the bayleaf. Pour enough of the stock into the dish to moisten the ingredients. Cover with puff pastry, brush with beaten egg and bake at Regulo 8 or 475⁰ F. for 15 min. Reduce to Regulo 5 or 400⁰ F. and continue for a further 45—40 min. Heat the rest of the stock and pour into the pie through a hole in the crust.

If the pie is to be eaten cold, jell the stock with 1 level teaspoonful of powdered gelatine before using it.

PIG, SUCKING, TO ROAST

Having thoroughly cleaned the pig, which should not be more than 1 month old, and scraped the entire surface, stuff it with sage and onion stuffing to which the liver, sautéed in butter, then finely chopped, has been added; truss and skewer. Make several deep gashes on either side of the back bone.

Put the pig on a rack in a large baking tin, brush whole surface with melted butter or olive oil. Sprinkle with pepper and salt, put a pint of hot water into the pan, cover the pig with buttered paper or aluminium foil. Bake at Regulo 5 or 400⁰ F. allowing 25—30 min. to the lb.

Remove paper or foil 15 min. before end of cooking time.

Dish up whole and serve with sharp apple sauce.

PIG'S FRY

1 fry, consisting of heart, lights, liver and sweetbread with some of the surrounding fat, 1 large sliced onion, flour, salt, pepper, 1 level teaspoonful powdered sage, dripping.

Wash the fry and par-boil in salted water for about 30 min. Drain and dry well, cut into thin pieces, coat with flour seasoned with salt, pepper and sage.

Fry the sliced onion in some dripping until tender, take up and keep hot. Add the fry and cook in the hot dripping until lightly browned.

Put with the onion. Pour a little boiling vegetable stock into the pan, stir well and boil until slightly thickened. Pour round the onion and pig's fry. Garnish with parsley.

PILAU OF FOWL WITH MUTTON

1 medium sized boiling fowl, 1 lb. lean mutton, ¹/₂ lb. rice, 6 onions, ¹/₄ lb. butter or margarine, 12 peppercorns, 12 cardamom seeds, 12 coriander seeds, ³/₄ oz. green or ¹/₂ oz. ground ginger, 1 teaspoonful salt, 3—4 hard-boiled eggs.

Slice the mutton and put it into a large saucepan with 4 onions halved, salt and 4 quarts of water and spices. Bring to the boil, remove scum, then put in the fowl and simmer gently until tender. Remove from the pan and put aside to keep hot, leaving the liquor to boil gently to reduce it.

Slice the remaining 2 onions thinly and fry them in the butter or margarine. Put in the fowl and brown it lightly all over, then take out again. Fry the rice in the hot fat with the onions, gradually adding the liquor.

Put in the bird and pile the rice over it, and leave until the rice has absorbed all the liquid. Serve garnished with hard-boiled eggs quartered.

Mutton only may be used to make a mutton pilau; in that case, 2½ lb. of meat should be used, and 1 oz. of stoned raisins added.

PINEAPPLE, TO SERVE

1. Remove top-knot of leaves and a thin slice from the bottom. Cut away the rind, taking care to remove the 'eyes' on the fruit. Cut into slices ¼ in. thick, remove hard centres of the rings, then build them up into the shape of the fruit. Pour into the centre hole 2—3 tablespoonfuls of caster sugar and replace the top.

2. Prepare slices as before, lay them on a large dish and sprinkle with caster sugar and a little Kirsch. Leave for 2—3 hr. Serve portions with a little of the syrup.

3. Cut the pineapple into small dice, put into a saucepan with enough water to cover and 2—3 tablespoonfuls of sugar. Bring to the boil and simmer for 5 min. Drain well and fill small tartlet cases with pineapple cubes, add 1 teaspoonful of arrowroot to each ¼ pint of syrup, boil until clear and thick and spoon over the fruit. Put aside to become cold.

PITCAITHLY BANNOCKS

12 oz. plain flour, 2 oz. finely chopped orange peel, pinch salt, 2 oz. chopped blanched almonds, 8 oz. butter, 4 oz. caster sugar, 2 oz. rice flour.

Soften butter at room temperature. Cream well and work in caster sugar. Add remaining ingredients with sifted flour and rice flour, and work together with the hands to make a dough. No liquid must be added. Form into one or two large round or square cakes, about 1¼ in. thick. Pinch edges with finger and thumb and prick centre all over. Place in tins of suitable shape and bake in a moderate oven (350° F. or Regulo 4) for about 1 hr., or until cakes are firm and of a light brown colour.

Wrap cakes, when cool, in greaseproof paper and store in an airtight tin.

PIZZA

¼ lb. plain flour, a little under ¼ oz. yeast, a little tepid water, salt, 4 or 5 fresh tomatoes, 6 anchovy fillets, basil, 3 oz. Mozzarella or Parmesan cheese, olive oil.

Pour the flour on to a pastry board, make a well in the centre, and put in the yeast dissolved in a little water. Add 1 small teaspoonful of salt. Fold in the flour over the yeast and blend well. Add sufficient water (about ⅛ pint, but the exact amount depends upon the quality of the flour) to make a stiff dough. Knead with the hands, pressing the dough out and away from you with the palm of one hand while you hold it with the other. When it feels light and elastic, roll it into a ball and put it on a floured plate. Cover with a clean cloth and put in a warm place to rise. In 2—2½ hr. the dough should have doubled in volume. Roll it out on a floured board into a large disc about ¼ in. thick (or divide it in half and make two smaller pizze).

Have ready the peeled and coarsely chopped tomatoes, the cheese and the anchovies. Spread the tomatoes on top of the pizza, season with salt and pepper, put halves of the anchovy fillets here and there, and then the cheese cut in thin small slices. Sprinkle a liberal amount of basil over the top, moisten with olive oil, pour more oil in a shallow round baking dish which should be large enough to allow the pizza to expand during the cooking.

Bake in a hot oven for 20—30 min. When no fresh tomatoes are available use peeled tomatoes from a tin, but not concentrated tomato purée. A few stoned black olives are sometimes added to the pizza. Other ingredients are added according to the provinces from which they originated, such as mussels, anchovies, mushrooms or ham.

PLAICE

To Steam. Put fillets of fish on a heat-proof glass plate, scatter with small pieces of butter, pour 2—3 tablespoonfuls of milk over the fish and season to taste with salt and pepper. Cover with another plate, put the two plates over a saucepan of gently boiling water and cook for 15—20 min.

This is an excellent method of cooking plaice for invalids.

To Bake. Well grease a flat oven-proof dish with butter or margarine, lay fillets of plaice in the dish with a little butter, pepper and salt. Cover with the lid or a piece of buttered paper and bake for 15 min. at Regulo 5 or 400° F. The fish may be lightly coated with fine crumbs before it is baked. In that case it should not be covered.

Tomatoes, mushrooms and white wine may be added.

To Fry in Egg and Breadcrumbs. Dry the fillets well, dip in beaten egg, then coat with crumbs. Deep fry in fat. Drain thoroughly on crumpled kitchen paper. Garnish with parsley and small segments of lemon.

To Fry in Batter. Dry the fillets of plaice, dip in batter and leave for about 30 min. Re-dip, then deep fry, and serve with lemon or tomato sauce. The fish, when small, may be cooked whole, or if large and plump cut across into 3 pieces, the centre piece of course being the prime cut.

Small fillets may be rolled, stuffed with shrimps, stood upright in a shallow dish, moistened with milk and baked at Regulo 5 or 400° F. The milk should be thickened with butter and a very little flour and served as a sauce. White wine may be used instead of milk.

PLANTAIN

See *Banana.*

PLUM CAKE (RAISIN CAKE)

1 lb. self-raising flour, 1/2 lb. butter or margarine, 1/4 lb. caster sugar, 1/4 lb. soft brown sugar, 1 tablespoonful dark treacle, 6—8 oz. stoneless or stoned raisins (the latter make the richer cake), 3 eggs, 1/2 teaspoonful vanilla flavouring, 1/2 teacupful or more warm milk.

Cream together the fat, sugar and treacle until very soft and light. Beat in the eggs one by one until thoroughly blended. Stir in the raisins, then gradually fold in the flour, alternating with a little of the milk mixed with the vanilla.

Make a soft creamy dough, put into an 8 in. cake tin lined with greaseproof paper. Smooth the top evenly with a spoon dipped in milk. Bake at Regulo 2 or 325° F. for about 2—2½ hr.

PLUM CHUTNEY

Pick out the larger plums for this, for the chutney is particularly good if the fruit can be kept in big pieces.

6 lb. large plums, 2 lb. onions, 1 lb. stoned dates, ½ lb. brown sugar, 1 quart vinegar, 1 clove, 1 oz. mustard seed, 1 oz. peppercorns, ½ oz. coriander seeds, 1 oz. ground ginger, ¼ oz. ground mace, 3 small red chillis.

Halve and stone the plums. Skin and chop the onions very finely. Put the sugar, the dates (washed and finely chopped) and the onions into the preserving pan and boil gently together until the onions and dates are very tender and pulpy.

Tie peppercorns, coriander seeds, mustard seeds, clove and chillis in a muslin bag. Stir the ginger and mace with a little of the liquid and add the liquid and spices to the rest of the ingredients. Now put in the halved and stoned plums and cook all together at a gentle simmer, until the plums are tender and almost transparent. Try not to break them while stirring the chutney. Taste frequently in order that you may remove the bag of spices if the flavour begins to get too hot for your palate.

Pot into hot pots, taking care to fill them. Cover when cold.

PLUM JAM

1. *6 lb. plums, 4 lb. sugar, 2 level teaspoonfuls citric acid.*

Halve the plums, take out as many stones as possible, crack a number, skin the kernels.

Spread the fruit on a large dish, sprinkle with half the sugar and the acid. Leave for 24 hr.

Turn fruit and syrupy juice into the preserving pan, and cook gently until the fruit is soft. Add the remaining sugar, and the desired number of kernels, bring to the boil and boil moderately fast until a little of the jam will set when tested on a plate.

2. *6 lb. plums, 4 lb. sugar.*

Wash the plums, halve and stone as many as you are able, crack about 20 of the stones and skin the kernels.

Arrange the fruit cut side up on large dishes and sprinkle with 2 lb. sugar. Cover with muslin or light cloths and leave for 24 hr., at the end of which time the fruit should be swimming in juice. Pour off the juice into the preserving pan, bring it to the boil then add the fruit. Cook it until it is soft, removing as many stones as possible. Stir in the rest of the sugar, bring to the boil and boil and stir until a little of the jam will set when tested. Pot while very hot and cover when cold.

If you make two boilings of jam, one with less sugar than the other, use the lower sugar content one first. Also, if you like a different flavour to your jam, add a clove, or a small head of fresh lavender to the boiling, and remove it before potting.

PLUM PIE

Any plums may be used for making plum pie, but avoid using over- or under-ripe fruit. When possible halve the fruit and remove the stones.

Arrange the fruit in a pie dish round a pie funnel, with sugar between the layers, but be sure that the sugar is completely covered with a top layer of fruit, as sugar produces steam that makes doughy crust.

Cover the fruit with short or rough puff pastry. Brush over with milk and scatter very lightly with caster sugar.

Bake at Regulo 7 or 450° F. for 15 min., then reduce to Regulo 5 or 400° F. for a further 20 min.

PLUM OR CHRISTMAS PUDDING

1 lb. each of sultanas, currants and raisins, 6 oz. finely chopped candied peel, 2 oz. finely minced blanched almonds, 6 oz. self-raising flour, 12 oz. fine bread crumbs, 12 oz. finely shredded suet, 1 lb. demerara sugar, 1 lemon, 1 nutmeg, 1 teaspoonful mixed spice, 1 teaspoonful bicarbonate of soda, 1 teaspoonful almond flavouring, 4 eggs, 1 wineglassful rum or brandy, 1/4 pint warm milk.

Mix together the flour, crumbs, suet, fruit, peel, almonds and sugar. Grate the lemon rind and the nutmeg into these ingredients. Stir the strained lemon juice, spice, almond flavouring, brandy or rum and well-whisked eggs into the milk. Pour the liquid into the dry ingredients and stir thoroughly until all are blended. Cover the bowl and leave until next day, so that crumbs and fruit may swell. If the mixture should seem too dry, add a little more milk.

Put the mixture into well-greased basins, filling them to within 1 1/2 in. of the tops, cover with three thicknesses of greaseproof paper, tie securely, then steam the puddings for 5 hr. and before serving steam again for 2 hr.

PLUM PUDDING (DUFF)

8 oz. self-raising flour, 4 oz. finely shredded suet (packet suet is excellent), 1/4 lb. stoned or stoneless raisins, 1 tablespoonful golden syrup, 3 oz. demerara sugar, 1/4 teaspoonful mixed spice, cold water, margarine.

Sift together flour and spice, mix with the suet, sugar and raisins. Mix to a soft dough with cold water.

Grease a 1 1/2 pint pudding basin with a very little margarine. Put the syrup at the bottom of the basin and drop in the dough. Cover with a double layer of greaseproof paper and steam for 2 hr.

PORK

To Boil. Put a fresh leg of pork into a large saucepan with one split pig's trotter, an onion, a leek, 2 sage leaves, salt and 6 peppercorns. Cover with warm water. Bring to the boil and remove scum. Reduce heat and simmer gently for 4 hr. for an average-sized leg of about 5 lb.

Strain trotter first and remove the meat from it. Chop up and put into a basin with a little of the liquid to which has been added a pinch of mace, to make a small breakfast brawn.

Serve the hot leg of pork with a little of the unthickened gravy, pease pudding and plain boiled potatoes.

To Roast. Score the skin of the piece of pork to be roasted in narrow strips and brush with salad oil. Put into the roasting tin with dripping sufficient to come up the sides of the meat, but not to cover the top. Do not baste, as this makes the skin soft and leathery, instead of crisp and crackling.

Allow 20 min. per lb., roasting at Regulo 7 or 450° F. or 25 min. roasting at Regulo 5 or 400° F.

A leg or a loin of pork may be stuffed with sage and onions, but it is more practical to bake that in a separate dish, well moistened with dripping from the roast, in order not to flavour the whole of the dripping.

PORK CHEESE

See *Fromage de porc.*

PORK PIE

Hot water crust (see recipe), 1½ lb. lean pork, ½ lb. fat pork, 2 sage leaves, pinch dried sage, salt, black pepper, 1 onion, pork bones, pork rinds or 2 trotters.

Mould ball of pastry dough up round a 2 lb. size glass jar or a cake tin, after having cut off a piece with which to make the lid. When the pie mould is ready, fill with the meat, which has been prepared as follows.

Cut lean and fat pork into small dice, put into a saucepan with the onion, seasonings and the bones, rind or trotters and boil gently for 2 hr. Remove meat and cool. Press into the mould and moisten with a little of the strained gravy.

Roll the remaining crust to a circle and fit the top of the pie. Seal edges closely. Decorate the top with leaves cut from remains of the crust. Brush over twice with beaten egg and make two or three holes in it. Tie two thicknesses of greaseproof paper round the pie, then bake at Regulo 4 or 375° F. for about 1½ hr.

Meanwhile boil up the stock and bones, etc., until reduced by half, and when the pie begins to cool, pour some of the strained stock into the pie by means of a little funnel, through holes in the crust.

PORT WINE JELLY

¼ pint port wine, ½ pint water, 2 oz. sugar, 1 oz. gelatine, 2 rounded tablespoonfuls redcurrant jelly, a few drops of cochineal to colour.

Put the water, sugar, jelly and gelatine into a saucepan over a very low heat, and stir until dissolved. Strain through a fine strainer, add half the wine and the colouring. When beginning to cool, add the rest of the wine and put into a wetted mould to set.

POTATOES

Potatoes may be started in cold or in hot water.

Boiled Potatoes

Select potatoes of uniform size. Wash, peel very thinly and drop into cold water. Put the potatoes into a saucepan, cover with boiling water and cook with the water just below the boiling point until the potatoes are tender. Just before cooking is completed add the salt — about

1 teaspoonful to 1 quart water. When done, drain and shake the pan over the fire to dry the potatoes. Serve immediately in a hot dish.

Mashed Potatoes

Milk or cream, 2 teaspoonfuls butter, salt and pepper.
Prepare potatoes as for boiled potatoes. Mash thoroughly with a heavy wooden masher, fork or ricer. Add the butter, seasonings and a small amount of hot milk at a time and beat with a fork until potatoes are very light. Pile lightly in a hot serving dish.

Roast Potatoes

Select medium-sized potatoes, peel and place them in the roasting pan with the roast about $1^1/4$ hr. before the meal is to be served. Turn and baste once or twice when cooking. A fairly hot oven is best. Serve round the joint or in a hot dish.

Potatoes may be roasted without the meat. Place them in a roasting pan in which there is dripping. Turn and baste potatoes once or twice. If potatoes are par-boiled for 10—15 min., they will roast in about $^3/4$ hr.

Baked Potatoes

Choose large even-sized floury potatoes. Scrub, wash and dry. If a thin shiny skin is desired, the potatoes may be brushed over with fat. Place potatoes on a baking tin and bake in a hot oven at 450^0 F. for $^3/4$—1 hr. When soft, make a deep cross-cut on the top of each potato and, holding potato in both hands with a cloth, squeeze it gently until the potato comes up through the opening. Season with salt, pepper and paprika, if liked, to taste. Place a pat of butter in the centre of each and sprinkle with finely chopped parsley.

Potato Chips

1. Wash and peel potatoes. For chips many people prefer a waxy potato. Cut potato into chips and soak in cold water for about one hour. Heat fat in a deep fat pan to a temperature of about 370^0 F to 380^0 F. or until it gives the bread cube test (see Part I). There should be at least three inches of fat in the fryer. Dry the chips thoroughly in a towel. Put into a frying basket, a few chips at a time. and fry until potatoes are just beginning to brown at the edges. It is important to fry just a few chips at a time since a large number would cool the fat too much. Lift the potatoes out and allow the fat to reheat to about 390^0 F. Return the chips to the pan and cook till golden brown. Drain on soft paper. Sprinkle with salt and serve.

2. This is a quicker and much simpler method resembling sautéing which produces very good chips. It requires less time and less fat.

Wash and peel the potatoes; cut them into chips and dry each with a cloth as you place it in the frying pan. Only shallow fat is required, but be sure to turn the chips carefully after they have been cooking on one side for a few minutes. This seals them and ensures that the outside is browned and the inside cooked through. It is advisable to have only as many chips as will lie on the floor of the pan cooking at a time.

Turn all the chips as soon as they begin to brown. When they are a rich golden colour on all sides, they are done.

Many people prefer chips done this way, as they are not greasy, and the interior is softer than that of chips done by a method which crisps them.

Sautéed Potatoes

These may be made with raw (1) or cooked (2) potatoes.
1. Cut the potatoes, after peeling, into neat round slices about ¼ in. in thickness. Melt some fat in a frying pan and fry the potatoes slowly in it. Turn once or twice only, cook until soft and evenly browned. Sprinkle with chopped parsley and serve in a hot dish.
2. Use left-over cold boiled potatoes. Cut into neat rounds, about ¼ in. in thickness. Fry in a frying pan in fat, turning once or twice only. Cook until golden brown. Serve in a hot dish and sprinkle with parsley. Large cold boiled potatoes may be cut into slices ¼ in. thick, dipped into beaten egg and breadcrumbs, and then fried.

Potatoes, Anna (Pommes de Terre Anna)

1½ lb. potatoes, 3 oz. butter, pepper and salt.
Melt half the butter and brush round inside a round shallow cake tin, coating it generously. Leave to set.

Peel potatoes and cut into very thin slices. Stamp rounds from these (doing several at one time) about the size of a penny. Use the rounds to line tin inside, commencing from the centre of bottom surface and working round in overlapping slices to the sides, then continuing up the sides a row at a time in neat formation. Take the potato trimmings; sauté these in butter until lightly coloured, and use to fill up middle of potato-lined tin. Fry remaining butter a golden brown colour and pour over potatoes. (Pepper and salt should be sprinkled between the layers of potato slices as the tin is filled.)

Bake in a fairly hot oven (375° F. or Regulo 5) for about 30 min., then place a warmed plate or dish over tin and turn out potato cake which should be an appetising brown colour. Use top shelf of oven.

Potatoes, Paris

Potatoes, dripping, pepper and salt.
Wash and peel potatoes and drop into boiling salted water for 4—5 min., depending on size of balls. Drain well, sprinkle with pepper and salt and place in tin with hot melted dripping. Roast, basting occasionally, until potatoes are golden all over.

Potato Balls

About 8 oz. cooked potatoes, 1 oz. butter, pepper and salt, flour, yolk of 1 egg, egg and crumbs for coating, deep fat for frying.
Cream potatoes well or rub through sieve. Work in melted hot butter, pepper and salt and egg yolk, mixing smoothly. Leave until cool, then divide into small portions and mould into balls with floured hands. Coat with egg and crumbs and fry in smoking hot fat until golden brown, frying only a few at a time. Drain well, sprinkle with salt and garnish with parsley.

Potatoes à la Duchesse

¾ lb. cooked potatoes, 1½ lb. butter, 1 yolk of egg (if small, part of another yolk), pepper and salt, 2 tablespoonfuls top of milk or cream, little grated nutmeg, flour, dripping or oil, beaten egg.

Beat potatoes well with butter, yolk of egg and seasoning of pepper and salt. Mix in top of milk or cream, again beating well, regulating the amount required as the mixture should not be too moist. Turn on to a board dusted with seasoned flour, sprinkle with extra seasoned flour and lightly press out. Mark out into squares or small rounds, and make a lattice pattern with back of knife. Arrange on a well greased or oiled baking tin, and brush a little beaten egg over each shape. Bake in a fairly hot oven (400⁰ F. or Regulo 6) until golden brown, i. e. about 20—25 min. Serve garnished with parsley.

Potato Rings, Nests, Roses, etc.

Make the same potato mixture as for Potatoes à la Duchesse, making just a little more moist for pressing through a large rose piping nozzle attached to a forcing bag. Shape as required. Arrange on oiled or greased baking sheet, brush lightly with beaten egg and bake in hot oven (400⁰ F. or Regulo 6) until nicely tinged with brown, using top shelf.

Potatoes for borders etc.

Make the same potato mixture as for Potatoes à la Duchesse, but take care not to have the mixture too moist. Turn mixture out on to a board dusted with seasoned flour and shape as required into a ring, straight roll etc. Use tines of fork for making decorative. If using the border for mounting cutlets, etc., use handle of knife to make the sections. Brush over with beaten egg and brown in a moderately hot oven (375⁰ F. or Regulo 5) on the top shelf.

Potato Rösti.

A celebrated potato dish.

Slice raw potatoes very thinly and simmer them in butter until tender, with a little finely chopped onion and a crushed clove of garlic. Use enough butter to cook the potato easily, but not to make it greasy. Add salt, pepper and a few caraway seeds, and sprinkle with a few drops of lemon juice and at the end, a tablespoonful of sherry. The potatoes should be carefully tossed and well mixed with the seasonings and flavourings and should not form a solid cake.

POULTRY AND GAME, TO ROAST

A completely accurate time for roasting cannot be given, as it depends upon the size and age of the bird, and in the case of game and hares, the period of hanging. The following table will, however, give a reliable guide.

Poultry	Low temperature roasting (Regulo 3 or 350⁰ F.)	High temperature roasting Regulo 6—7 or 450⁰ F.)
Chicken	1 hr.—1 hr. 20 min.	3/4—1 hr.
Turkey	See below	See below
Goose	See below	See below
Gosling	1 hr. 20 min.—2 hr.	1—1 1/2 hr.
Duck	1 hr. 40 min.—2 hr. 40 min.	1 1/4—2 hr.
Duckling	1 hr. 20 min.—1 hr. 40 min.	1—1 1/4 hr.
Pigeon	25—40 min.	20—30 min.
Guinea Fowl	1 hr. 20 min.—1 hr. 40 min.	1—1 1/4 hr.

Game	Low temperature roasting (Regulo 3 or 350° F.)	High temperature roasting Regulo 6—7 or 450° F.)
Grouse	40—60 min.	30—45 min.
Partridge	45—65 min.	35—50 min.
Pheasant	1 hr.—1 hr. 20 min.	45—60 min.
Wild Duck	40—55 min.	30—40 min.
Blackcock & Teal	45 min.	35 min.
Rabbits	1 hr. 20 min. or longer	1 hr. or longer
Hares	2 hr.—2 hr. 40 min.	1½—2 hr.
English Turkeys & Geese		
6 lb. bird	1 hr. 40 min.	1 hr. 15 min.
12 lb. bird	2 hr. 20 min.	1 hr. 45 min.
18 lb. bird	3 hr. 10 min.	2 hr. 30 min.
24 lb. bird	4 hr.	3 hr.

Frosting.
Ten minutes before the roast is served remove any paper covering, baste the breast and sprinkle lightly with flour. This will give a good brown appearance.

PRAWN COCKTAIL

For the Sauce
½ pint tomato juice, or sauce, 2 tablespoonfuls chilli vinegar, 1 teaspoonful Worcester sauce, 2 teaspoonfuls horseradish cream, a good pinch celery salt. Mix all very thoroughly.

Line cocktail glasses with finely shredded crisp lettuce leaves, and into the centre of each put 4—6 prawns, cut into 4 pieces each.

The cocktail glasses may be stood on a tray in a ring round the bowl of sauce, which should be surrounded with cracked ice, or a little added to each glass before serving.

If the above sauce is too elaborate, use a good mayonnaise, and sharpen it with lemon juice or chilli vinegar. The cocktails must be very cold.

PRAWN CURRY

For the Sauce
2 onions, 2 tablespoonfuls dripping, margarine or butter, 2—3 tablespoonfuls curry powder, 1 chopped apple, 1 clove garlic, 1 dessertspoonful sugar, 1 tablespoonful sultanas or seedless raisins, 1 pint water or stock.

Chop the skinned onions, peeled and cored apple and skinned garlic finely, simmer gently in the fat until soft, stir in the curry powder, sugar, raisins or sultanas. Stir until thoroughly blended. Add stock or water gradually to make a smooth paste.

Having cooked sufficient rice until tender, turn it on to a clean cloth laid on a hot dish to dry out all moisture. Stir it with a fork to separate the grains. Lay the prepared prawns on the rice and pour the hot curry sauce over them. To prepare the prawns, shell them and keep them in a bowl of hot water for about 5 min. Frozen or tinned prawns are excellent for making curry.

The raisins or sultanas may be omitted if preferred. Some people like sliced banana with a prawn curry.

PULPED FRUIT

Fruit prepared as if for cooking in the usual way.

Melt a knob of butter in preserving pan and put in fruit with a minimum of water. Cook over low heat at first until juices are flowing freely. Then cook steadily until fruit is quite pulped (about 30 min. depending on nature of fruit). Have ready sterilised heated jars and fill one at a time with pulp at boiling point. Adjust each seal at once, fixing securely. Test when cold, before storing away.

PUMPKIN JAM

6 lb. pumpkin, cut into small slices, 4 lb. sugar, 1 oz. citric acid, 2 oz. ground ginger.

Cut the pumpkin into small pieces, put into a bowl and sprinkle with the sugar and acid. Leave for 12 hr. Pour off the syrupy liquid into the preserving pan, bring to the boil, stir in the ginger, then the pumpkin; boil moderately fast until the syrup is very thick and the pumpkin quite soft.

The ginger may be omitted if the delicate flavour of the pumpkin is preferred.

PUMPKIN PIE, DEEP DISH

2 lb. pumpkin cut into small pieces, 2 large apples, 2 tablespoonfuls seedless raisins or sultanas, 3 oz. brown sugar or golden syrup, 1/2 teaspoonful mixed spice, 1/4 teaspoonful ground cinnamon, grated rind of 1 lemon and its strained juice, short crust.

Cook the pumpkin and the apple separately, until both are soft. Drain the pumpkin thoroughly. Beat the apple to a pulp, but cut the pumpkin into small dice. Mix them together with the sugar, spices, lemon and lemon juice. Line a pie dish with short crust, fill with the pumpkin mixture, bake at Regulo 7 or 450⁰ F. for 25—30 min. If you like a thicker filling, add a beaten egg, or a dessertspoonful of cornflour mixed to a smooth paste with a tablespoonful or so of apple juice.

PUMPKIN PIE, SIMPLE

Short crust, 1 1/2 lb. of pumpkin cut small, grated rind and strained juice of 1 lemon, 1 dessertspoonful cornflour, 2 oz. brown sugar, pinch of cinnamon.

Line a pie dish with the crust. Cook the pumpkin until tender. Mash it, add the cornflour mixed to a paste with a little of the water in which it was cooked, the sugar, lemon rind and juice, and the cinnamon. Pour the mixture into the pie shell, bake at Regulo 7 or 450⁰ F. for about 30 min.

PUMPKIN SOUP

2 lb. pumpkin, 2 oz. butter, 1 1/2 pints milk, 1/2 pint hot water, 1 small French roll, salt, pepper and 1/2 teaspoonful sugar.

Cut the pumpkin into little pieces, and boil in the water for about 10 min. Drain and rub through a sieve. Stir the purée into the butter heated in a saucepan, stir in the milk and seasonings.

Toast the sliced French roll until crisp and put the pieces into a large soup tureen and pour in the soup and serve very hot.

QUEEN CAKES

4 oz. butter (or butter and margarine mixed), 4 oz. caster sugar, 3 eggs, 6 oz. self-raising flour (or plain flour and 1 teaspoonful baking powder), pinch of salt, 1 oz. thinly sliced candied peel, grated outer rind of 1/2 lemon, 4 oz. sultanas.

Grease small patty tins. Prepare fruit and peel etc. Cream fat well, add sugar and beat together until soft and light. Add the eggs one at a time, beating well after each. Sift powdered ingredients and add alternately with prepared fruit etc., mixing without beating. Half-fill patty tins and put a small piece of peel on each. Bake in moderate oven (350° F. or Regulo 4) for 15—20 min.

QUEEN OF PUDDINGS

2 oz. breadcrumbs, 1/2 pint milk, 3/4 oz. butter, 2 oz. caster sugar, 1 egg, jam.

Heat milk and butter in a saucepan almost to boiling point and pour over crumbs, adding half the sugar. Stir and leave for 20 min. or so. Separate egg, beat yolk with a teaspoonful cold water and add to crumb mixture. Put into a greased pie-dish and bake in moderate oven for about 20 min.

Whisk white of egg stiffly, then fold in remaining sugar. Spread a little jam over top of baked crumbs etc. and pile meringue mixture on top, spreading roughly. Return dish to oven, lowering heat a little, and leave until lightly browned on top.

QUENELLES, POACHED

1 lb. raw meat — veal, lamb, mutton, game or chicken, 1 1/2 oz. butter, 1 1/2 oz. flour, 1/4 pint white stock or milk, 1 whole egg and 1 extra yolk, pepper and salt, little grated lemon rind, pinch of powdered nutmeg.

Trim meat free from fat and skin. Cut into pieces, then put through mincer twice. Make the panada with butter, flour and stock, or milk, and cook until very thick, forming a ball. Blend minced meat into the panada gradually, alternately adding some of the beaten eggs, seasonings and flavourings. Pound well and rub through a sieve. Divide mixture into portions, shaping each in the form of eggs, using two dessertspoons dipped in hot water. Arrange these in a buttered sauté-pan or deep frying pan and pour in sufficient boiling water to almost submerge them. Poach gently until firm — about 10—15 min. — drain, and arrange them round a mound of creamy potatoes. Pour a little Béchamel or velouté sauce over and garnish with green peas, or with sprigs of parsley.

QUENELLES DE VEAU A LA FLORENTINE
(QUENELLES, FRIED)

Veal quenelles, egg and breadcrumbs for coating, oil or fat for frying, little Parmesan cheese, 2 lb. cooked spinach, tomato sauce as required, heated, fleurons of pastry.

Prepare veal quenelles as in previous recipe, cooking for 10 min. Drain well and leave to cool. Blend a little Parmesan cheese with the breadcrumbs for coating. Brush shapes with egg and coat closely with the crumb and cheese mixture. Fry in smoking hot fat until golden brown. Serve against a mound of cooked spinach leaves, with fleurons of pastry between each. Serve with heated tomato sauce.

QUICHE LORRAINE (EGG AND BACON OPEN PIE)

6 oz. rich short pastry, 6 rashers bacon, 2 eggs, 1/4 pint cream, 1/4 pint milk, pepper and salt, nutmeg.

Roll out pastry lightly and use to line a pie-plate about 9 in. in diameter.

Cut bacon into squares, rejoining them to line pastry-lined plate. Whisk eggs with milk and add pepper and salt to taste. Beat cream lightly to thicken a little and fold into egg mixture. Pour into bacon-lined plate and grate a little nutmeg on top.

Bake at once in a hot oven (450° F. or Regulo 8) for about 30 min., lowering heat a little to 350° F. or Regulo 5 when egg mixture is nicely coloured.

QUINCE JAM OR MARMALADE

1. *4 lb. quinces, 4 lb. sugar, 2 pints water, juice of 2 lemons if liked, but the flavour is very good without.*

Wash the quinces to remove the grey fluff, peel and core them, and boil the cores and peel in the water until these are tender, then strain off the liquid. Meanwhile, cut the prepared fruit into small cubes, put into the strained liquid and boil gently until the cubes are quite tender. Stir in the sugar, add the lemon juice if using, then bring slowly to the boil and boil moderately fast until the jam is rich pink in colour and a little will set when tested on a cold plate.

Pot into clean, warm pots while it is very hot, then cover when quite cold with good air-tight jam pot covers, and store the jam in a cool place.

If you happen to have a solid fuel range, the quince may be put into an earthenware pipkin with the juice from the peel, etc., and left to simmer very slowly all night at a very low heat. This gives it a wonderful colour.

2. *Quinces, water, preserving sugar as required.*

Wash, wipe and peel quinces, then slice them. Put peel, with cores, into a pan and cover well with water. Cook them until soft, then strain through a hair sieve or jelly bag. Weigh the sliced fruit and set aside 3/4—1 lb. sugar to each pound. Put sliced quinces into preserving pan, add strained quince liquor and cook together until the quinces are pulped, mashing occasionally with wooden spoon. Add sugar, stir until dissolved, then boil until marmalade sets when tested. Put into heated jars and seal.

QUINCE JELLY

Quinces, 1/2 pint water to each 1 lb. fruit parings, etc., sugar as required.

Wash, wipe and peel quinces. Weigh parings etc. and put into a pan with water as directed. Boil until parings are soft. Put sliced fruit into another pan and strain liquor over, making up with cold water to cover fruit. Simmer gently until fruit is soft. Put through jelly bag, leaving to drip overnight. Next day, measure juice and allow 1 lb. sugar to 1 pint juice. Stir together until sugar is dissolved, then boil rapidly until jelly sets when tested — about 15 min. Put into heated small jars, and seal.

QUINCE WINE

4 lb. ripe quinces, 4 lb. sugar, 6 quarts cold water, 2 lemons, a little yeast.

Wash the quinces and cut in slices like apple rings, but without removing cores. Cover with the freshly boiled water and leave for 1 week covered with a piece of muslin. When time is up, strain liquid into another bowl and add sugar and lemon juice. Stir until sugar is dissolved, then cover bowl and leave for a further 3 days, stirring daily. Make a slice of toast and whilst still warm spread with a little yeast. Add this. Cover pan and leave until the next day. Remove toast and strain wine into a cask or other large suitable container with a cork or bung, but at this stage leave uncorked. When wine has been left a full week to ferment, cork (or bung) tightly. Leave to mature for several months — not less than nine — as quince wine is slow in maturing.

RABBIT

To paunch and skin

Paunch as soon after killing as possible, first making a slit in the skin underneath, sufficiently long to insert the fingers and draw out intestines, discarding them. Cut away a small piece near the tail so as completely to remove the intestines and gland, also all discoloured parts round this area. To remove skin entirely, separate skin from flesh near middle of body, insert fingers and slip out back legs first. Then pull skin over the body, slipping out forelegs next and head last. Remove eyes with a pointed knife.

When jointing the rabbit, remove kidneys and any fat round them. Use a sharp knife to cut body into joints. Wash these in warm salted water, if possible leaving them to soak for about half an hour or so before cooking.

When jointing the body, cut away flaps of skin of stomach and bony part of breast. These can be used for making stock or gravy. Chop breast into two portions and back into 3 or 4, depending on size of rabit. The legs and back pieces are the choicest joints.

RABBIT, BOILED

1 rabbit, 4 oz. bacon, 1 breakfastcupful sliced mixed vegetables, onion, carrot, small piece turnip, celery when in season, 1 pint water, pepper and salt, 1 oz. flour, 1/4 pint milk, chopped parsley.

Wash and joint rabbit. Trim fat from bacon and render down in pan. Remove pieces and fry onion in fat until soft. Then add remaining vegetables, cover and shake over heat until they are no longer crisp. Add pieces of rabbit and diced bacon, with seasoning to taste. Cover pan and simmer gently for about 1 1/2 hr. Mix flour and milk smoothly and stir into pan. Cook for 6 or 7 min., then add chopped parsley and serve.

RABBIT GALANTINE

1 rabbit, 4 oz. bacon, ¹/₂ lb. sausage meat, grated outer rind ¹/₂ lemon, 1 dessertspoonful chopped parsley, 1 shallot, pepper and salt, breadcrumbs.

Cut away meat from bones of rabbit and put through mincer with trimmed bacon. Mix with sausage meat, lemon rind, parsley and grated shallot. Season well and form into a roll. Wrap in scalded cloth, tying at each end securely. Steam for about 3¹/₂ hr. Unwrap and re-roll firmly in cloth. Fit into a tin of suitable size and shape and place a weighted plate on top. When cold, remove from tin and unwrap. Coat with baked breadcrumbs. Trim ends before serving, with a garnish of watercress or parsley.

RABBIT, ROAST

1 rabbit, ¹/₂ lb. forcemeat or ¹/₂ lb. sausage meat, 2 tablespoonfuls breadcrumbs, few strips fat bacon, bacon rolls.

Prepare rabbit, leaving head on or removing it as preferred. If head is left on, pass a skewer through the mouth to secure it in place. The skewer should be long enough to run through the shoulders, setting the head up. Stuff rabbit with forcemeat, or with sausage meat to which an extra 2 tablespoonfuls breadcrumbs have been added, mixing well. Arrange strips of fat over rabbit and place in greased tin. Roast for about 1 hr. at 350° F. or Regulo 5, basting frequently. Serve with bacon rolls.

RAGOUT

1¹/₂ lb. lean beef or veal, or 2 lb. breast or neck of lamb, 1¹/₂ oz. butter or cooking fat, 1 or 2 onions, 1 tablespoonful flour, 1 pint stock or water, pepper and salt, 1 carrot, small piece turnip, small bouquet garni.

Cut meat into neat pieces. If breast or neck of lamb is used, trim away surplus fat. Coat pieces of meat in seasoned flour (flour mixed with pepper and salt) and fry in hot fat until nicely browned. Lift out meat on to a plate. Sprinkle in remaining seasoned flour and stir over heat until lightly browned. Add stock gradually, stirring all the time until blended, then bring to the boil. Add vegetables cut in strips or diced, and add stock or water. Cover and simmer slowly until meat is tender — about 1¹/₄ hr. To serve, lift meat on to heated serving dish. Reduce liquor by boiling and add a little ketchup, if liked. Adjust seasoning to taste and strain liquor over meat.

RAISIN CAKE

See *Plum cake.*

RAISIN ROLL

4 oz. each plain flour, freshly rubbed breadcrumbs and chopped or shredded suet, 2 oz. sugar, ³/₄ lb. stoned and chopped raisins or raisins cut in halves, ³/₄ teaspoonful bicarbonate of soda, pinch salt, 1 egg and milk to bind.

Sift flour, salt and soda and mix with crumbs, suet and fruit. Stir in sufficient beaten egg and milk to bind to a soft dough. Form into a roll and wrap in a scalded and floured clean cloth, tying at both ends. Steam steadily for about 2¹/₂ hr.

RASPBERRY JAM

6 lb. raspberries, 6 lb. sugar.

Put the prepared fruit into the preserving pan and cook very slowly over a low heat until some juice runs. Raise the heat a little and simmer until the fruit is tender. This does not take long.

Having warmed the sugar on a large dish in the oven for about 10 min. at a low temperature, stir in the warm sugar, and when it has completely dissolved, boil moderately fast until a little of the jam will set when tested on a plate.

RASPBERRY JELLY

8 lb. raspberries, 1 lb. sugar per pint of juice.

Hull the fruit, remove any berries that have mould, wash lightly and gently if necessary.

Place the fruit in the preserving pan. Heat gently until a little juice begins to run, then mash well, turn into a scalded jelly bag and leave to drain. Measure the extracted juice, bring to the boil and add 1 lb. sugar to each pint. Dissolve the sugar in the juice, stirring constantly. Bring to boiling point and then boil without stirring until the jelly will set when tested.

A stronger jelly can be made if 2 lb. of red currants are added to the raspberries as they cook in the first place. The currants will not spoil the flavour of the raspberries.

RAVIOLI FILLINGS

Veal Filling

4 oz. veal, 1 oz. butter, little stock, 1 tablespoonful red wine, 2 tablespoonfuls cooked spinach, 1 oz. grated Parmesan cheese, pepper and salt, 1 shallot or piece of onion, 1 egg, 1 tablespoonful breadcrumbs.

Fry veal and sliced onion in butter until browned, then add sufficient stock to moisten bottom of pan well, and simmer over low heat for about 20 min. Put through mincer and blend with cooked spinach, cheese and breadcrumbs, moistening with egg and adding seasonings to taste. Use on prepared ravioli pastry.

Cheese Filling

4 oz. soft cream cheese, 1 heaped teaspoonful chopped parsley, 2 oz. grated Parmesan cheese, 1/2 oz. butter, pepper and salt, egg yolk to bind.

Blend above ingredients and use in spoonfuls on prepared ravioli pastry.

Spinach Filling

4 tablespoonfuls cooked spinach, pepper and salt, 2 oz. grated Parmesan cheese, 3/4 oz. butter, nutmeg, egg to bind.

Drain spinach well after cooking and chop. Whilst still hot, add butter, cheese, seasonings and nutmeg to taste. Bind with beaten egg and place in spoonfuls on prepared pastry.

RAVIOLI PASTRY

1. *With Eggs*
8 oz. plain flour, 1 egg, salt.

Sift flour and salt. Work in the egg, adding a little water, sufficient to make a pliable dough. Knead until smooth, then leave for ½ hr. Divide dough and roll out each piece to paper thinness. Leave to dry for 1 hr. Put a teaspoonful of filling (see above) on one layer of dough about 2 in. apart. Brush very sparingly between the small mounds, then cover with the other layer of dough, pressing down firmly between the mounds to seal closely. Cut squares apart with sharp knife, making sure each square is sealed all round. Drop into briskly boiling salted water and cook for about 8 min. Skim out carefully with draining spoon and serve with tomato sauce, sprinkling grated Parmesan cheese on top.

2. With water

8 oz. plain flour, good pinch salt, water.

Make a firm dough with sifted flour, salt and cold water. Knead well until dough is pliable. Divide in two and wrap each piece in greaseproof paper brushed over with oil. Keep warm. After two hours, unwrap, and roll out each piece of dough to paper thinness, and use like egg ravioli pastry.

REDCURRANT JELLY

6 lb. redcurrants, 1 pint water, sugar.

Wash the currants, do not string them.

Put them into the preserving pan with 1 pint water, and simmer gently until the fruit is quite soft. Strain off all the juice through a jelly bag. Return the pulp to the preserving pan, stir in the remaining ½ pint water, boil fast for about 20 min., strain off the liquid and add it to the fruit extract. Mix well together, put into the preserving pan, add sugar, stir to dissolve, then boil moderately fast until a little of it will set firmly when tested on a plate.

Pot into small, dry, warm jars, while the jelly is very hot. Cover when quite cold.

RHUBARB JAM

4 lb. rhubarb, juice of 2 lemons, or 1 teaspoonful of citric acid, 4½ lb. sugar.

Wash the rhubarb, cut it into short pieces about 1 in. long, taking care not to remove the skin. Put it into a large china bowl, scatter it with the citric acid, or pour the squeezed lemon juice over it. Stir in the sugar thoroughly, cover the bowl with a cloth and leave for 12 hr.

Turn all into the preserving pan, bring slowly to the boil, boil moderately fast until a little of the jam will set when tested on a plate.

Pot and cover.

Rhubard jam does not, as a rule, set as firmly as some jams made with other fruits, but this method of using no water does help to give a firmer, thicker consistency. Some people like to add ½ teaspoonful of ground ginger, some like about 4 oz. finely minced crystallized ginger added at the beginning of the cooking.

RHUBARB WINE

6 lb. rhubarb, 6 lb. sugar, 1½ gallons water, 1 lemon, 1 orange, ½ oz. yeast.

Wipe rhubarb with a damp cloth and cut into short lengths. Put them into a large bowl and cover with boiling water. Cover and leave for 4 days, then strain into another bowl. Add finely pared outer rind of lemon and orange and add with juice of lemon to rhubarb juice. Add sugar and yeast creamed with a little water and stir well all together until sugar is dissolved. Cover and leave for 3 days, stirring well daily. Strain into a cask or bottles with corks or bung fitting loosely. Leave until all signs of fermentation have subsided before closing cask or bottles tightly. Ready in six months, but even better if kept longer.

RICE

To boil for curries

Use Patna rice. Wash and put into plenty of boiling salted water (1 dessertspoonful to the quart) and boil quickly with lid off pan until grains are soft when tested between finger and thumb — about 15—20 min. Stir occasionally to prevent sticking whilst boiling. Drain well. To separate grains, pour boiling water over the rice in a colander, or run cold water from tap over rice. To re-heat, drain well and place colander over boiling water.

To dry, place rice on a large dish in a moderate oven, and stir lightly with a fork at intervals, to keep grains separate. Keep oven door slightly ajar.

Devilled rice (to eat with meat and vegetables, or alone)

4 oz. Patna rice, 1 small onion, 1 oz. butter, 1 dessertspoonful curry powder, salt, pepper, pinch cayenne, lemon juice.

Cook rice until tender in the usual way (see above), then drain well. Heat butter in a saucepan and fry grated or minced onion until lightly coloured. Stir in rice, curry powder and seasoning, using wooden spoon to stir well until butter is absorbed. Adjust seasoning to taste and add a good sprinkling of lemon juice.

RICE CAKE

4 oz. butter (or margarine and lard or vegetable shortening), 4 oz. caster sugar, 2 eggs, 4 oz. plain flour, 1 level teaspoonful baking powder, 3 oz. ground rice, grated rind 1/2 lemon.

Grease and line a 6 1/2—7 in. cake tin. Cream fats well with sugar and beat in whisked eggs gradually, alternately with sifted powdered ingredients and lemon rind. Mix without beating. Bake mixture in prepared tin in moderate oven at 350° F. or Regulo 4 for about 1 hr.

RICE CAKES, ORIENTAL

1 1/2 teacupfuls rice, 1 pint milk, 2 eggs, 1/2 teaspoonful each cinnamon and nutmeg (ground), 3 oz. caster sugar, 1 oz. butter, glacé cherries and preserved ginger for decoration.

Wash rice and cook in milk until soft — 30 min. or so. Mash and cool, then mix with beaten eggs, spices and sugar. Divide into portions, flatten and fry golden in melted butter, or bake on a well-greased griddle, thick frying pan or cleaned hot-plate of electric cooker. When browned on both sides, which takes about 6 min. per cake, arrange on hot dish and decorate with sliced cherries and pieces of ginger.

RICE CREAM

1 pint milk, 2 oz. ground rice, 2 tablespoonfuls caster sugar, ¹/₄ pint cream, ¹/₄ oz. powdered gelatine, few drops vanilla essence.

Heat milk and before it boils sprinkle in the rice, stirring over heat until rice is cooked, about 10 min., then add sugar. Cool and blend with half-whipped cream and gelatine (softened previously in 2 tablespoonfuls cold water), adding vanilla. Mix well and when commencing to look thick, pour into a mould. When firm, turn out and serve with fruit, or a sweet sauce.

RICE A L'IMPERATRICE

2 oz. rice, 1 pint milk, 2 oz. sugar, vanilla essence, ¹/₂ oz. gelatine, ¹/₂ pint cream.

Wash rice and cook in milk until soft. Stir in sugar and a few drops vanilla essence. Soften gelatine in 3 tablespoonfuls hot water, stirring until clear. Stir into rice mixture and when cool fold in whipped cream. Divide between individual moulds, or put into 1 large mould. When set turn out. If border moulds are used, fruit can be put in the centre and topped with extra whipped cream, or a little cream set aside when mixing.

RICE PUDDING, TO BAKE

1¹/₂ oz. rice, 1 pint milk, ¹/₄ teaspoonful grated outer rind of lemon, 1 rounded tablespoonful sugar, little grated nutmeg.

Put all ingredients into a pie dish, adding grated nutmeg last. Put dish into a slow oven (250° F. or Regulo ¹/₂) and cook gently for about 2 hr. During first ¹/₂ hr., stir mixture two or three times, to distribute flavourings.

   If the oven heat must be raised for cooking other foods, place dish in a pan containing a little water, using low shelf.

RICE SOUP

4 oz. rice, 1 quart good stock, pepper, salt.

Dilute ¹/₂ pint stock with 1 pint water. Heat to boiling point and add washed rice. Cook briskly until grains are tender. Strain through colander. Divide rice between soup cups. Have ready remaining stock heated to boiling point and well seasoned. Pour over rice and serve.

RICE SOUP A LA LYONNAISE

¹/₂ lb. onions, 1 oz. butter, 1¹/₂ pints second stock or water, pepper and salt, 4 oz. rice, chopped chervil.

Peel and slice onions. Fry in melted butter until lightly browned. Add heated stock or water with seasonings and cook for 20 min. Then add washed rice and continue cooking for a further 30 min. Divide between soup plates and sprinkle each with chopped chervil.

RICE WINE

3 lb. rice, 3 lb. sugar, 1 lb. plump raisins, chopped, juice of 1 lemon, 4 quarts water, 1 oz. yeast.

Put washed rice, sugar and lemon juice into a large bowl. Boil water and when cool, but still warm, pour over contents of bowl. Cream yeast with a little extra warm water and stir into ingredients. Cover bowl with piece of muslin and leave in warm place for 12 days. Stir daily for 1 week, then leave without disturbing for the remaining 5 days. Then remove scum and strain wine into bottles. Cork loosely until all fermentation ceases. Test this by dropping a piece of sugar candy into a bottle every few weeks. When the wine does not make a fizzing noise, cork closely and keep for about 6 months or even longer. If any loss occurs through fermentation before corking down at the last, keep one bottle for filling up the others.

RISOTTO

6 oz. Patna rice, 1 small onion, 2 oz. butter, pinch of saffron, 1 pint stock (or chicken bouillon cube dissolved in 1 pint boiling water), pepper and salt, little grated nutmeg, 2 oz. grated cheese.

Melt 1 oz. butter in a pan and fry the chopped onion until soft but uncoloured. Wash and dry rice and add to pan. Stir with wooden spoon until slightly yellow. Sprinkle in saffron, then add stock. Cover and simmer until rice is soft, stirring at intervals, and liquid almost completely absorbed. Add seasonings and a little grated nutmeg to taste. Stir in remaining ounce of butter and the grated cheese. Mix well and serve.

RISSOLES, COLD MEAT

8 oz. cold cooked meat, 2 tablespoonfuls fresh breadcrumbs, 1 oz. butter or margarine, 1 oz. flour, ¼ pint stock, pepper and salt, 1 shallot or small onion, 1 teaspoonful chopped parsley or pinch crushed mixed herbs, good pinch grated nutmeg, little flour, egg and crumbs for coating, fat for frying.

Trim meat, removing skin and gristle. Finely chop or mince remaining meat, then mix with breadcrumbs. Melt butter and fry finely chopped shallot or onion until soft. Add flour and stir with wooden spoon over heat until mixture is lightly browned. Add stock gradually, cooking and stirring until thick. Add to meat and crumbs, sprinkling in seasoning and flavourings and mixing well. Divide into portions and pat into rounds with floured hands. Brush over with beaten egg and coat closely with crumbs. Fry in deep or shallow fat until golden brown on both sides. For deep frying, fat should be smoking hot.

ROSE HIP SYRUP

2 lb. ripe rose hips, 1 lb. sugar, 4½ pints water.
The following method is recommended if a syrup with a high Vitamin C content is required.

Extracting the juice

Have ready 3 pints boiling water, preferably in an aluminium or unchipped enamel pan. Mince the rose hips in a coarse mincer, place them immediately in boiling water and bring this again to the boil. As soon as the mixture reboils, remove the pan from the heat and leave it for 15 min., then pour the contents into a scalded jelly bag and allow the bulk of the juice to drip through. Return the pulp to the saucepan, add 1½ pints boiling water, reboil and allow it to stand without further heating for another 10 min., then drain as before.

Addition of Sugar

Pour the mixed juice into a clean saucepan, and boil it down until the juice measures about 1½ pints, then add 1 lb. sugar and boil for a further 5 min.

Bottling and sterilising the Syrup

Pour the syrup while it is hot into clean, hot bottles and seal at once. If corks are used these should have been boiled for ¼ hr. just previously, as for other fruit syrups, and tied or wired on. Sterilise the syrup by putting the bottles in a deep pan of hot water, standing them on a false bottom and boiling for 5 min. The bottles are then removed, cooled and the corks dipped in melted paraffin wax as for other syrup.

It is advisable to use small bottles, as the syrup will not keep for more than a week or two once it is opened. A dessertspoonful of this syrup each day is recommended if the diet is lacking in Vitamin C.

ROUT CAKES

8 oz. ground almonds, 8 oz. caster sugar, 1 teaspoonful orange flower water, few drops almond essence, about 3 yolks of eggs.

Mix ground almonds and sugar together with finger tips. Then add flavourings and well-beaten egg yolks to make a pliable paste, leaving sides of bowl clean.

Dust pastry board with fine sugar and press out paste about ¼ in. thick. Leave to dry out a little.

Cut into fancy shapes — small crimped-edged rounds with smaller round on top (secured with a little brush of egg white); diamonds; small cottage loaves; or cut in small rounds with plain cutter, mould into balls and flatten, pressing a piece of blanched almond or piece of glacé cherry on each. Arrange on rice paper or oiled paper on a baking tin, brush lightly with white of egg and bake in a very moderate oven (275° F. or Regulo 1) sufficient to deepen the yellow colour a little, but not browning. Time will vary depending on oven temperature, but will be about 25 min.

SAGE AND ONION STUFFING

1 lb. onions, 4 tablespoonfuls breadcrumbs, 2 oz. butter or good dripping, 1 dessertspoonful finely chopped sage or 1 teaspoonful powdered sage, salt and pepper.

Cut the onions into slices, cover them with cold water, bring to the boil, cook for about 5 min., then strain and drain well. Melt the butter or dripping in a stewpan, and fry the onions for about 15 min. without browning. Add the crumbs, sage and seasoning, mix well and use.

SALAD DRESSING, BOILED

1 egg, 2 tablespoonfuls plain flour, ¾ pint milk, 2 oz. butter, 4 table-spoonfuls malt vinegar, 2 tablespoonfuls tarragon vinegar, salt and pepper to taste, 1 level teaspoonful dry mustard.

Mix the dry ingredients together, add the egg beaten with the milk, and cook, stirring all the time in the top of a double boiler, until the mixture begins to thicken.

Strain and when cool, beat in the vinegars gradually. Bottle and keep in a cool place.

SALAD DRESSING WITH EVAPORATED MILK

1/2 tin unsweetened evaporated milk, 1/2 teaspoonful dry mustard, 1 tablespoonful tarragon vinegar, 1 egg yolk, salt and pepper, malt vinegar to taste.

Stir the egg yolk and the evaporated milk together until they are perfectly blended, add the dry mustard, salt and pepper, then stir in the tarragon vinegar. Beat together thoroughly, add malt vinegar to taste.

SALLY LUNNS (TEA CAKES)

12 oz. plain flour, good pinch salt, 1/2 oz. yeast, 2 oz. butter or margarine, 1/3 pint milk, 1 level dessertspoonful caster sugar, 1 egg, sugar and water glaze.

Sieve flour and salt into a warmed bowl, making well in middle. Crumble yeast into a basin and mix with sugar until liquid. Melt fat in saucepan, add milk. When both are tepid, add to yeast, mixing well. Pour into middle of flour and add well beaten egg. Mix gradually with flour, then beat with the hand or a wooden spoon, if preferred. Cover bowl with a clean cloth and leave in warm place to rise, about 45 min. Turn dough out on to floured board and knead lightly for several minutes. Divide into two portions and place one in each of two warm greased 5 in. cake tins. Set tins in warm place until dough has risen again to top of tins, about 15—20 min. Bake in a hot oven (425° F. or Regulo 7) for about 15—20 min. Draw from oven and brush tops at once with sugar glaze made by mixing 1 tablespoonful sugar with 1 tablespoonful milk. Return tins to the oven for a moment for the glaze to dry.

SALMI OF GAME

Remains of cooked game, or freshly roasted and slightly underdone game, salad oil, 1 onion, 1 oz. flour, 1 teacupful stock, pepper and salt, 2 or 3 chopped mushrooms, small glass red wine, small bouquet garni, croûtons of bread.

Cut meat into neat portions, removing any skin and bones. Simmer these trimmings in water for stock. Heat about a tablespoonful oil and fry chopped onion until soft. Add sifted flour and mix well. Stir and cook for several minutes, then add stock gradually, mixing briskly. Add herbs, mushrooms, seasonings and red wine. Simmer together for 10—15 min. Add pieces of game and make these piping hot only. Arrange portions of game on shaped croûtons of bread and spoon sauce over.

SALMON, BOILED

For serving cold

About 3 lb. middle cut of salmon, 2 quarts cold water, 1 teacupful sliced carrots and onions, 1 dessertspoonful salt, 2 large sprigs parsley, 1 bay leaf, 5 or 6 peppercorns, 4 cloves, juice of 1 small lemon.

Wash fish without scaling and place in pan with flavourings and water. Bring to the boil lower heat and simmer for 10 min. Draw pan away from heat and leave fish in cooking water until quite cold before removing from pan. Arrange on serving dish and garnish with cucumber in overlapping slices down centre of fish and a piping of savoury butter for decoration.

Serve with a bowl of mayonnaise.

For serving hot
3 lb. middle cut of salmon, flavourings as in previous recipe, water to cover well.

Put salmon and flavourings into a pan and cover well with water, previously made hot, but not boiling. Cover and bring contents of pan gently to the boil. Simmer gently, allowing 10 min. to the lb. (8 min. for tail end of salmon) and 10 min. over. Dish up and serve with small boiled buttered potatoes, sprinkled with parsley, and with green peas, using a little crimped cucumber for garnish. May be served with a sauce such as Hollandaise, and quarters of lemon.

SALMON AND CUCUMBER WITH DEVILLED EGGS

3 lb. middle cut of salmon, 3 pints cold water, 2 or 3 sprigs parsley, 1 bay leaf, 1 teacupful sliced carrots, 1 medium-size onion, sliced, 1/2 teaspoonful peppercorns, slice of lemon from 1/2 lemon and remaining juice, 1 dessertspoonful salt, 1/2 cucumber thinly sliced, 4 hard-cooked eggs, mayonnaise, little made mustard, paprika.

Wash fish without scaling and place in pan with water, which should cover — add more if necessary. Put in herbs, vegetables, slice of lemon and juice, peppercorns and salt. Cover and bring slowly to the boil. Simmer gently for 12 min., then draw pan from heat and put in a cool place until contents of pan are cold. Lift out fish, draining well, and place on lettuce-lined serving dish.

Shell eggs and cut in halves. Remove yolks and mash well. Blend with a little mayonnaise, lemon juice and made mustard to taste, adding salt as required. Fill egg yolk cases with mixture and garnish with half-slice of cucumber on each. Arrange stuffed eggs round salmon and decorate along the top of the fish with two lines of cucumber in overlapping thin slices. Serve with mayonnaise sauce.

SANDWICH FILLINGS

1. Anchovy fillets, boned, chopped and blended with cooked potato and lemon juice.
2. Asparagus tips moistened with half-whipped cream or with mayonnaise.
3. Banana and walnut butter — ripe banana mashed and blended with an equal amount of butter, a few drops lemon juice and chopped walnuts as liked.
4. Cooked chicken and ham minced and moistened with mayonnaise.
5. Cucumber, finely sliced and dressed with half-whipped cream with sprigs of watercress. If preferred, mayonnaise can be used instead of cream.
6. Dessert apple, grated and blended with cream cheese, moistened with a little lemon juice or salad cream.
7. Chopped egg and anchovy fillets, moistened with mayonnaise.

8. Chopped egg and grated carrot (equal quantities) moistened with mayonnaise.
9. Fish roe (cod, caviare, etc.) moistened with lemon juice and mayonnaise, garnished cress.
10. Frankfurters (sliced) with fried onions and moistened with French mustard.
11. Ham and Cheshire cheese thinly sliced in both cases, moistened with mustard sauce.
12. Lobster (chopped) with chopped egg and cress, moistened with mayonnaise.
13. Olives (green or stuffed) chopped and added to peanut butter.
14. Peanut butter, mashed banana and lemon cheese.
15. Chopped shrimps, chopped watercress, moistened with mayonnaise.

SAUCES

Allemande Sauce (Sauce Allemande)	Norman Sauce (Sauce Normande)
Béarnaise Sauce	Orange Sauce
Béchamel Sauce	Parsley Sauce
Brown Butter Sauce	Piquant Sauce (Sauce Piquante)
Chaud-Froid Sauce	Robert Sauce (Sauce Robert)
Espagnole Sauce	Sabayor (or Sabayon) Sauce
Hollandaise Sauce	Tartare Sauce (Sauce Tartare)
Mousseline Sauce	Velouté Sauce
	White Sauce

Allemande Sauce (Sauce Allemande)

3/4 pint white stock, 1 1/2 oz. butter, 1 oz. flour, 2 egg yolks, 1 tablespoonful cream, 1 teaspoonful lemon juice, nutmeg, salt and pepper.

Melt butter in saucepan, add flour, stir and cook for a minute or two without browning. Add stock, bring to boil, stirring all the time. Now cook very slowly until sauce is smooth and has thickened. Take saucepan from stove, stir in beaten egg yolks, cream and seasonings. Continue to cook without boiling for a few minutes longer, then add lemon juice just before serving.

Béarnaise Sauce

2 shallots, few leaves tarragon, 1/4 pint French wine vinegar, 3 yolks of eggs, 1/2 teaspoonful mignonette pepper, salt, 2 tablespoonfuls Béchamel sauce (below), 2 oz. butter, 1 small teaspoonful chopped parsley, few leaves tarragon, finely chopped.

Put shallots, finely chopped, into a pan with a few leaves of tarragon, the vinegar, and cover with lid. Cook until well reduced. Then cool a little and stir in Béchamel sauce and egg yolks. Season with salt and pepper and whisk briskly over heat until sauce thickens, adding butter in tiny pieces until absorbed. Do not allow to reach boiling point. When ready, strain sauce into another pan. Re-heat carefully and sprinkle in chopped herbs.

To serve with beef, veal, etc.

Béchamel Sauce

1/2 pint milk or milk and white stock of meat, fish or vegetables, according to requirements, 1/2 small peeled onion, 6 peppercorns, 1/2 bayleaf, small piece of mace, 1 oz. butter, 1 oz. flour, salt, pepper, pinch of mixed dried herbs.

Simmer the milk or milk and stock with the onion, flavourings and herbs for 15 min. Melt the butter and mix with the flour. Strain the boiling liquid gradually into this roux until well blended. Boil very gently, stirring all the time. Season to taste with salt and pepper. On no account allow lumps to develop. If they do, strain through a very fine strainer.

Brown Butter Sauce

4 oz. butter, 1 tablespoonful chopped parsley, 2 tablespoonfuls vinegar, pepper and salt.
Cook butter in pan until it browns, then add other ingredients to taste. Simmer 1 min., then serve.

Chaud-Froid Sauce

1/2 pint Béchamel sauce (see recipe), 1/2 pint aspic jelly, 1/2 oz. powdered gelatine, 2 tablespoonfuls cream, few drops lemon juice.
Make aspic jelly and dissolve the gelatine in this. Stir in Béchamel sauce over heat until mixture boils. Add lemon juice, then strain. When cool stir in cream and use as required. If required tinted pink or green, add a few drops carmine colouring to the Béchamel sauce, or a little spinach juice.

A brown Chaud-froid sauce may be made by substituting a brown sauce for the Béchamel and adding tomato sauce for flavouring.

Espagnole Sauce (Spanish Sauce)

3 pints stock, 1 oz. raw lean ham or bacon, 1 1/2 oz. butter, 1 heaped tablespoonful plain flour, small bouquet garni, 1/2 teacupful tomato pulp (sieved), 2 tablespoonfuls sherry (or extra sieved tomato pulp), 1 small carrot, 1 small onion, 3 peppercorns, 1 clove, 1 or 2 mushrooms, pepper and salt.

Melt butter in pan and add chopped ham. Fry for a few minutes to soften well, then add herbs, chopped or sliced vegetables and spices. Stir together for 5 min. over heat, then add sieved flour and stir until browned. Add stock, tomato, pulp, etc. and bring to boil. Leave simmering for 1 hr. Remove fat, strain, re-heat and serve.

Hollandaise Sauce

1/4 pint white sauce (or Béchamel sauce), 1/4 pint white stock, juice of 1/2 lemon, 2 egg yolks, 1 oz. butter, pepper and salt.
Make white sauce and whilst hot, stir in stock and egg yolks. Blend smoothly over heat, simmering for a few minutes, without allowing mixtures to boil. Stir in lemon juice and butter in small pieces. Season to taste, then strain.

Mousseline Sauce (Sweet)

3 egg yolks and 2 whites, 2 tablespoonfuls cream, 2 dessertspoonfuls caster sugar, 1 tablespoonful sherry, maraschino syrup or a fruit syrup.
Whisk whites of eggs to break up well, then add yolks and whisk together. (Any 'germ' of eggs should first be removed.) Add cream, sugar and sherry or syrup and mix well. Place bowl over simmering water and whisk until sauce is smooth and creamy.

Norman Sauce (Sauce Normande)

2 oz. butter, 1 oz. plain flour, 1/2 pint milk, 1/4 pint fish stock, 2 yolks of eggs, seasonings, lemon juice.

Melt half the butter and stir in sifted flour and seasonings. Cook for several minutes, stirring with wooden spoon. Draw pan from heat and add fish stock and milk gradually. Simmer and stir for 10 min., then draw pan once again from heat. Beat egg yolks with 1 teaspoonful milk and add to sauce. Add remaining butter in small pieces and stir over low heat altogether. Add lemon juice last, then strain if necessary. This sauce is served with fish.

Orange Sauce

1 bitter orange, ¹/₂ pint Espagnole sauce, ¹/₂ pint stock, 1 teaspoonful lemon juice, 3 tablespoonfuls port wine, pepper and salt to taste.

Halve the orange and extract juice. Finely shred about one half the rind and boil these shreds in water for several minutes to soften them. Put half the orange juice into a pan with the stock, lemon juice and Espagnole sauce. Reduce to one half of original quantity by boiling without lid. Strain into another pan and add remaining ingredients, including shreds of orange and remaining juice. Adjust seasoning to taste, bring to the boil and skim. Serve with duck, goose, etc.

Parsley Sauce

1 pint white sauce (see Béchamel), 2 tablespoonfuls very finely chopped fresh parsley.

Stir the parsley into the sauce immediately before serving, in order that the parsley may remain very green and retain all its flavour. When serving parsley sauce with fish, one or two teaspoonfuls of vinegar may be added to give a piquant flavour.

If dried parsley has to be used for want of fresh, pour 2—3 tablespoonfuls of boiling water over it and allow it to stand for ¹/₂ hr., then strain off the water before adding it to the sauce.

Piquant Sauce

1. *1 medium chopped onion, 2 oz. butter, 1 oz. flour, salt, pepper, 2 tablespoonfuls wine vinegar, 1 wineglassful dry red wine, 1 wineglassful hot water, 3—4 minced gherkins.*

Cook the finely chopped onion in the butter until lightly browned, stir in the flour until well blended, add the hot water and vinegar, stirring well all the time, then add the wine.

Simmer for 5 min. Strain and add the gherkins before serving.

2. A good piquant sauce can be made by adding 1 teaspoonful mustard and a tablespoonful vinegar to ¹/₂ pint of white or parsley sauce.

3. *¹/₄ pint vinegar, 1 level teaspoonful dry mustard, 1 tablespoonful demerara sugar, 1 tablespoonfuls redcurrant jelly.*

Heat the vinegar, dissolve the sugar and jelly in it, beat in the mustard.

Robert Sauce

¹/₂ pint brown sauce, 1 small onion, ³/₄ oz. butter, 1 teaspoonful made mustard, 2 tablespoonfuls white wine or vinegar, pinch of sugar.

Peel and grate onion. Fry in melted butter until soft without colouring. Stir in mustard, wine (or vinegar) and sugar and simmer gently until reduced by one half. Add the brown sauce and simmer together for 6—7 min. Strain before serving.

Sabayor, or Sabayon, Sauce

2 egg yolks, 1 tablespoonful caster sugar, 4 tablespoonfuls rum, 4 tablespoonfuls cream.

Put egg yolks, sugar, rum and cream into top compartment of double saucepan. Whisk steadily for about 15 min. until mixture thickens. May also be made with wine or milk instead of rum.

Tartare Sauce

1. *¹/₂ pint mayonnaise, 1 teaspoonful dry mustard, little vinegar, 2 tablespoonfuls finely chopped or minced pickled gherkins, or chopped capers.*

Moisten dry mustard with sufficient vinegar (from pickles if possible) to make a thin cream. Stir gradually into mayonnaise.

2. *¹/₂ pint mayonnaise, 1 teaspoonful each finely chopped tarragon and chervil, 1 teaspoonful each finely chopped chives and capers, 1 tablespoonful finely chopped gherkins.*

Stir prepared ingredients together.

Velouté Sauce

1 oz. butter, ³/₄ oz. flour, ¹/₂ pint light stock (veal or chicken), seasonings, squeeze of lemon juice.

Melt butter and stir in sifted flour and seasonings. Cook over low heat for several minutes without browning. Draw pan from heat and stir in stock gradually. Return pan to heat and cook and stir in stock gradually. Return pan to heat and cook and stir until sauce boils. Simmer for 7 or 8 min. and add lemon juice. Strain before using.

This sauce is improved by the addition of 1—2 tablespoonfuls cream, or the yolk of an egg mixed well with 1—2 tablespoonfuls milk.

White Sauce (Simple)

1 oz. butter or margarine, 1 oz. plain flour, ¹/₂ pint liquid (milk or equal parts milk and stock), seasonings, little lemon juice.

Melt fat and stir in sifted flour. Stir with wooden spoon until mixture is clotted in middle of pan. Add liquid gradually, mixing and stirring until smooth and creamy. Cook over very moderate heat for 6 or 7 min. Adjust seasonings to taste, adding a squeeze of lemon juice.

SAUERKRAUT

Pale cabbages, large thick slice of bread, preferably from the bottom of a large cottage loaf, salt, water.

Discard coarse outer leaves of cabbage or cabbages, and slice remainder thinly, about ¹/₄ in. ribbons. Put into a tub or deep bowl and press down firmly with slice of bread on top. Cover with a brine (using about 3 rounded tablespoonfuls salt to the pint of water) until cabbage and bread are submerged. Cover container with a clean cloth and leave in a warm place for 4—5 days.

German Style

Pale cabbages, salt, peppercorns, caraway seeds.

Prepare and shred cabbages as in previous recipe. Wash shreds well and shake free of superfluous moisture. Pack into a suitable container — preferably a wooden tub — with a good sprinkling of salt, a few peppercorns and caraway seeds between each layer. Sprinkle again with salt and cover top with cleaned coarse outer leaves of cabbages. Place an old clean cloth over the top and press down with a large flat platter that fits inside tub. Place a weight on the platter. Leave for 3 weeks in all, but once a week remove covers, press down the cabbage and skim off top liquid. Replace with 1/4 pint warm water and sprinkle again with salt, using about 2 tablespoonfuls.

To Use

Wash as much sauerkraut as required and drain. Put into a saucepan with stock to cover. Simmer for about 2 hr. Brown a grated onion in butter. Sprinkle in a teaspoonful or so sifted flour, and continue frying until flour is also brown. Add to sauerkraut, mix well and simmer again together for several minutes before serving. Sometimes, 1 or 2 raw potatoes are grated into the pan with the sauerkraut whilst cooking.

SCALLOPS

To cook on shell

Remove from shell. Clean shell, grease with butter and sprinkle with breadcrumbs. Replace soft flesh, add seasonings and a sprinkle of lemon juice. Mask with a tablespoonful of flavoured white sauce, sprinkle with tiny pieces of butter and crumbs, then bake in hot oven until browned on top. Serve with quarters of lemon. If liked, cook two on one shell.

Au Gratin

Clean scallops, allowing two per portion. Place in buttered ovenproof dish, sprinkle with pepper and salt and a little grated outer rind of lemon. Add a layer of grated fresh breadcrumbs and pour in sufficient beaten eggs and milk (2 to the pint of milk) to cover. Bake in moderate oven (350° F. or Regulo 4—5) until custard is set, i. e. about 30 min. Sprinkle with freshly chopped parsley and serve with brown bread and butter.

Stewed

Cook in milk for 25—30 min. and serve as a garnish.

SCONES

Plain

8 oz. flour, good pinch salt, 1 level teaspoonful cream of tartar, 1/2 teaspoonful (also level) bicarbonate of soda, 1 heaped teaspoonful caster sugar, 2 oz. butter, margarine or cooking fat, 1/4 pint milk to bind.

Sift powdered ingredients into a bowl. Add sugar and rub in fat finely. Mix to a soft dough with milk. Roll out lightly on flour-dredged pastry board — 1/2 in. thick for oven baking, thinner for cooking on a girdle stone. For oven-baking, brush over rounds with beaten egg or milk; for cooking on girdle stone prick rounds with a fork.

Bake in a hot oven about 15 min. Split and spread with butter. Eat hot.

If cooking mixture on a girdle stone, brown lightly on both sides.

If sour milk is used for mixing, use equal quantities (half-teaspoonful) cream of tartar and bicarbonate of soda.

If preferred, use 2 rounded teaspoonfuls baking powder instead of cream of tartar and bicarbonate of soda.

Wholemeal scones

As for plain scones, but using equal parts wholemeal and white flours. If liked, cut into triangles.

Fruit scones

As for plain scones, but adding 2 oz. cleaned dried fruit and mixing well with other dry ingredients before moistening with milk.

Spiced scones

As for plain scones, but adding 1/2 teaspoonful mixed sweet spices when sifting flour, etc. If liked, stir in a dessertspoonful honey or golden syrup to milk before moistening dry ingredients.

SCOTCH MUTTON BROTH

1 1/2 lb. neck mutton, 2 quarts water, 1 breakfastcupful diced carrots, 2 leeks, 1 small turnip, diced, 2 tablespoonfuls barley, 2 tablespoonfuls dried green peas, 1 stalk celery, 1/2 firm cabbage or savoy, shredded. 1 onion, pepper and salt, 1 dessertspoonful chopped parsley.

Soak peas (after washing) overnight. Put into saucepan with meat and water. Bring to the boil and skim. Wash leeks well and chop into short pieces. Add with diced vegetables, sliced onion, chopped celery and shredded cabbage, barley and seasonings to taste. Simmer gently for about 2 hr. Sprinkle in parsley before serving. The meat is usually served as a separate course, with parsley or caper sauce.

SEA BREAM

Cook as shad, fresh haddocks, codling and such like.

SEA-KALE

Cook as celery.

Sea-Kale with Cream Sauce

1 lb. sea-kale, 1 oz. butter, 3/4 oz. flour, pepper and salt, 1 tablespoonful cream, 1/4 pint water in which sea-kale is cooked, little milk.

Cook sea-kale in salted water until tender. When vegetable is almost tender, prepare sauce by melting butter in pan and stirring in sifted flour and seasonings. Mix until clotted, then add about 1/4 pint vegetable water, gradually, mixing briskly and using milk to make a smooth consistency. Stir and cook for several minutes, then add cream, mix well without further cooking. Strain vegetables, place in heated dish and pour sauce over.

SEED CAKE

8 oz. self-raising flour, 4 oz. margarine, 4 oz. granulated sugar, 1 oz. caraway seeds, 2 oz. finely minced candied peel, 2 eggs, 1 dessertspoonful golden syrup, warm milk.

Cream together the fat, sugar and syrup until very light and fluffy. Beat in each egg separately until thoroughly blended. Stir in the seeds, and peel, fold in the flour, adding a dessertspoonful of warm milk as required to make a soft dough. A dough containing syrup should not be as soft as one without.

Put the dough into a lined 7 in. cake tin, smooth the top with a milky spoon and bake at Regulo 3 or 350⁰ F. for about 1¹/₂ hr.

SEMOLINA PUDDING

1 pint milk, 1¹/₂ oz. semolina, pinch salt, 1 level tablespoonful sugar, 1 egg (optional).

Heat milk in saucepan. When milk is almost boiling sprinkle in semolina, stirring until mixture thickens. Simmer for 7 min., then stir in sugar and salt. If adding egg, draw pan from heat and cool a little first. When mixed, transfer to buttered baking dish. If liked, sprinkle with grated nutmeg. Bake on the middle shelf of a moderate oven at 350⁰ F. or Regulo 4 for 25—30 min. until lightly browned on top.

SHALLOTS, PICKLED

Shallots, vinegar; to each quart vinegar allow: ¹/₄ oz. each allspice, cloves, blade mace, a few peppercorns, 1 dessertspoonful sugar, 2 in. stick cinnamon, salt as required.

Peel shallots and put into a bowl. Sprinkle well with salt and leave overnight. Then rinse well and dry. Pack shallots into jar. Meanwhile, put vinegar and spices, etc., into a pan, cover and bring to boiling point. Set aside for about 2 hr., still covered. Strain over shallots to cover well. Tie down securely.

SHEEP'S BRAINS

Stewed

4 sheep's brains, salt, pepper, vinegar, 1 or 2 small onions, 2 sprigs parsley, sprig thyme, thin strip outer rind lemon, 4 thin streaky rashers bacon.

Wash and soak brains in salted water for an hour. Remove skin, etc., and put brains into a saucepan with seasonings and 1 teaspoonful vinegar. Add boiling water to cover and simmer for about 10 min. Arrange rashers of bacon in another saucepan and put par-cooked brains on top. Add thinly sliced onions, herbs and lemon rind. Strain in sufficient stock to cover. Simmer, covered, for about 30 min.

Fried

4 sheep's brains or 2 calves' brains, fritter batter (see recipe), fat for frying, few sprigs parsley.

Prepare and par-cook brains as if for braising (see below), then cut in slices. Dip each slice into fritter batter and cook in smoking hot fat or oil until golden brown.

Serve with a garnish of fried parsley.

Braised

4 sheep's brains, or 2 calves' brains, pepper and salt, a dozen or so shallots or tiny onions, stock, 4 oz. button mushrooms, about 1¹/₂ oz. butter or margarine, 1 tablespoonful flour, butter, bacon fat or oil for frying.

Wash and prepare brains as if for stewing (see above). Remove skin etc. and place in saucepan with stock, a dash of vinegar and seasonings to taste. Simmer for about 10 min., then remove. Meanwhile, peel and slice onions and fry in hot fat or oil until golden. Stir in sifted flour, mixing well, then add stock gradually to make a smooth creamy consistency. Cook for several minutes, then add brains, sliced mushrooms and any extra seasoning required. Cover and simmer in a low oven for about 25 min.

SHEEP'S HEAD, BOILED

1 sheep's head, 2 carrots, 2 onions, 1 small piece turnip, few peppercorns, 1 bay leaf, 2 strips celery, pepper and salt, 1 oz. butter, 1 oz. flour, chopped parsley.

Split and clean head. Remove brains and cook separately. Soak head in salted water for about 1 hr. Then place head in large saucepan with cold water to cover. Bring contents of pan to the boil, then strain and rinse head. Return this again to the pan, add prepared vegetables, seasonings and bay leaf, and add boiling water to cover. Replace lid and simmer gently for about 2 hr. Then lift halves of head from pan and separate the meat from the bones. Cut meat into neat pieces. Skin and slice tongue. Place meat on a hot dish with vegetables round. Make a sauce — melt the butter and stir in the flour, mixing well. Cook for 2 or 3 min., then draw pan from heat and gradually work in sufficient stock to make a smooth and creamy consistency. Cook for 7—8 min., then add 1 tablespoonful chopped parsley. Pour a little over meat etc. and serve remainder in sauceboat.

SHEEP'S HEARTS, BAKED

As many sheep's hearts as required, veal forcemeat, 1 streaky rasher bacon for each heart, pepper and salt, dripping.

Wash hearts thoroughly, removing pipes. Cut down inside division of each heart to make room for stuffing, which may be omitted, if preferred.

Dust hearts with pepper and salt and wrap a rasher of bacon round each. Place in a pan with an ounce or two of dripping. Cover with greaseproof paper or aluminium foil, and roast in moderate oven at 350° F. or Regulo 5, basting at intervals for about 1¼ hr. Remove covering, dredge with flour and baste again. Continue baking uncovered for a further 10 min.

SHEEP'S TONGUES WITH SPINACH

6 sheep's tongues, bouquet garni, 1 carrot, 1 onion stuck with 3 cloves, 2 strips celery when in season, or a little celery salt, ½ lemon, pepper and salt, 1 oz. butter, 1 oz. flour, chopped parsley, ¼ pint milk, about 2 lb. spinach, nutmeg.

Soak tongues in salted water for 2 hr. Put with herbs and vegetables into a pan and cover with water. Add seasonings to taste, cover and simmer until tongues are tender — about 2 hr. Remove tongues from pan and remove skin and any root bones. Meantime, spinach can be cooked in the water left on the leaves after washing well. Drain and season to taste, adding a little grated nutmeg to taste. Have ready a hot dish for the spinach and arrange tongues on top. Make a sauce by melting butter and stirring sifted flour and mixing well. Add about ¼ pint stock from pan gradually, then milk, and cook together por 7—8 min. Adjust seasoning to taste and add a good squeeze of lemon juice. Sprinkle in a little parsley. Spoon some of the sauce over the tongues, handing remaining sauce separately from sauceboat.

SHEEP'S TROTTERS

These are usually bought partially cooked.

Plain

Wash and scrape if necessary. Stew gently in water to cover, containing a few flavouring vegetables and a bayleaf also. Cook for about 3 hr. Use stock for soup or jelly-making.

Dressed

When cooked and cold, cut meat from trotters and chop neatly. Sprinkle with chopped parsley and serve with a French dressing — or sprinkle with oil and vinegar, with seasoning to taste.

SHERBET POWDER

1/2 lb. loaf sugar, 2—3 lemons, 2 oz. tartaric acid, 4 oz. bicarbonate of soda.

Rub the pieces of sugar over the lemons until all the outer yellow rind has been rubbed away, using extra lemons, if necessary, to colour sugar well. Then crush sugar to a powder and mix with the tartaric acid and bicarbonate of soda. Put into dry bottle and cork tightly. A teaspoonful in a glass of cold water makes a refreshing summer drink.

SHERBET, PEACH

8 peaches, 4 lemons, 3 quarts water, sugar as required.

Skin peaches, halve and remove stones. Crack stones, remove kernels and chop these finely. Chop peaches into small pieces and add with chopped kernels to water. Add juice from lemons and sweeten well. Leave on ice for several hours, then strain before using. Add a teaspoonful sherbet powder to a glass of peach sherbet for a cooling drink, or use as otherwise required.

SHERBET, RASPBERRY OR STRAWBERRY

2 lb. raspberries or strawberries, 3 tablespoonfuls fresh lemon juice, 1 tablespoonful orange flower water, 3 pints water, 1 1/4 lb. caster sugar.

Crush fruit, add flavourings and water. Stir in sugar until dissolved. Leave 8 hr. Strain through muslin, squeezing well, then set on ice until required.

SHREWSBURY BISCUITS

8 oz. flour, 4 oz. butter, 5 oz. caster sugar, 1/2 teaspoonful powdered cinnamon, 1 egg.

Sift flour with cinnamon. Add sugar, mix well, then rub in butter finely. Bind with beaten egg to a dough. Knead lightly on a flour and sugar-dredged pastry-board. Roll out thinly and cut into rounds with tart cutter. Arrange on a lightly floured tin and bake in a moderate oven for about 15 min. Leave on tin to cool, when the biscuits should be crisp and short. Store in airtight tin.

SHRIMPS

To Cook

Put into boiling salted water and cook for 5—6 min. They change colour when cooked — do not over-cook.

Potted

1 pint shelled shrimps, 3 oz. butter, 1 blade powdered mace, few grains cayenne, pinch nutmeg (optional).

Melt butter in pan, add shrimps and flavourings and make hot together without boiling. Put into small pots or cartons. When cold pour a little melted butter over each to seal.

SILVERSIDE, BOILED

Hot

1 joint (4—5 lb.) silverside, fresh from pickle, flavouring vegetables (2 onions, 3 carrots, small piece turnip, 1 stick celery, small bunch parsley, 1 blade mace).

Rinse meat and place in pan with flavourings and water to cover. Adjust lid — which should be close fitting — and bring contents of pan slowly to the boil. Simmer very gently for up to 4 hr., testing with skewer for tenderness after 3½ hr. Small dumplings are usually served with hot boiled silverside, and these are added about 30 min. before dishing up. Place meat on warmed dish, with dumplings round. Sprinkle dumplings with chopped parsley. Serve vegetables separately. If the flavouring vegetables are served, skim these out of cooking pan when tender, and re-heat before dishing up joint.

Cold

Remove meat from pan when tender, draining well. Remove any bones and trim. Press into a round cake-tin and cover with weighted plate until cold. Garnish when serving with sprigs of watercress and wedges of tomatoes.

SIMNEL CAKE

1. *6 oz. margarine, 6 oz. granulated sugar, 3 eggs, 12 oz. self-raising flour, 2 oz. finely minced candied peel, ¾ lb. mixed sultanas and currants, well washed and dried, 1 tablespoonful golden syrup, ½ level teaspoonful mixed spice, strained juice of 1 lemon and grated rind of ½, warm milk as required.*

Cream the fat and sugar together until they are very light and soft in texture and almost white. Beat the eggs lightly together, put aside about a tablespoonful for glazing the top later.

Beat the rest of the eggs gradually into the fat and sugar mixture until you have a thick, yellow cream.

Stir in the fruit, peel, lemon juice, rind and spice. Fold in the sifted flour lightly and gently, until it is all blended with the wet ingredients, but do not beat it any more. Mix the golden syrup with ¼ cupful of warm milk and with it mix the cake dough to a creamy texture that will drop easily from the mixing spoon. Put half the dough into an 8 or 9 in. cake tin lined with greaseproof paper, and smooth it evenly. Press a ½ in. thick layer of marzipan (see recipe) on the dough and cover with the rest of the dough. Smooth evenly on top. Pre-heat the oven for 20 min. at Regulo 3 or 350° F. and bake at that temperature for 1¾—2 hr. Turn out on to a cake cooling wire and leave until cold.

2. *8 oz. butter or margarine, 8 oz. caster sugar, 4 eggs, 9 oz. plain flour, 1/2 teaspoonful bicarbonate of soda, good pinch salt, grated rinds 1/2 lemon and 1/2 orange, 8 oz. currants, 8 oz. sultanas, 4 oz. glacé cherries, 2 oz. chopped mixed candied peel, 1/2 small teaspoonful mixed spice, little milk.*

Prepare a 9 in. cake tin by greasing and double lining with greaseproof paper.

Cream butter until soft. Add sugar and beat together until mixture is light. Add beaten eggs one at a time, adding a little sifted flour and salt (also spice) after each. Fold in half the sifted flour and fruit etc. (including grated rinds). Dissolve soda in about a tablespoonful of milk and stir into mixture, distributing well. Add remaining flour and fruit etc. and again mix well. Put into prepared tin, spreading level to sides, with slight hollow in middle. Place in moderate oven and reduce heat to 325⁰ F. (very moderate) and bake for about 4 hr., or until richly browned and when warmed a skewer pushed into centre of cake comes out clean. Remove cake from oven and leave in tin for about 10—15 min. before turning out on wire tray.

When cold, decorate in traditional style. For example, the cake can be cut through, making two layers, the cut surfaces being brushed with sieved jam, then sandwiched together with a layer of marzipan paste. Coat sides and top edges of cake with marzipan paste, giving the top edges a neat pattern — or an arrangement of overlapping 'leaves' of paste, fixing securely with a little sieved jam or white of egg. Fill top centre of cake with a pool of glacé icing in a delicate green shade. When dry, set tiny fluffy chicks on the surface round a nest of confectionery speckled eggs.

SKATE

To boil

Clean and remove skin. Put into a pan with sufficient salted warm water to cover, and simmer gently for about 30 min., or until fish can be easily separated from the bone. Drain well and serve with a caper or shrimp sauce.

To fry

Clean, skin and cut into portions. Marinate in vinegar to cover, with seasonings and chopped onion. After 1—1 1/2 hr., drain fish well and dust with seasoned flour, or coat with egg and crumbs. Fry in hot fat (shallow or deep) until portions of fish are nicely browned on both sides. Garnish with parsley and serve with lemon.

SLY CAKES, CORNISH

1/2 lb. flaky pastry, 3 oz. cleaned currants, 1 1/2 oz. finely chopped peel, 1/2 teaspoonful grated outer rind of lemon, 1 dessertspoonful brown sugar, little mixed sweet spice.

Roll out pastry to an oblong and cut in half. Mix fruit, peel, sugar and spice with grated lemon rind and spread over one portion of pastry. Cover with the other portion of pastry and press lightly with rolling pin to join, so that currants show through paste 'slyly'. Cut into shapes, brush each sparingly with water and dredge with castor sugar. Bake in a hot oven at 450⁰ F. or Regulo 8 for 15—20 min.

SMELTS, FRIED

Smelts, flour, seasonings, egg and crumbs for coating, fat or oil for frying.

To prepare for cooking, cut just below the gills, making a small slit with kitchen scissors. Gently press out intestines, running the fingers along the fish from the tail end. Rinse and dry.

Toss fish lightly in seasoned flour, then coat with egg and crumbs and fry in smoking hot fat or oil until golden brown. Serve with quarters of lemon, garnishing with parsley.

SNOW EGGS

1 pint milk, small piece cinnamon, 1 strip of thinly pared outer rind of lemon, pinch salt, 3 eggs, 1½ oz. sugar, 1 or 2 glacé cherries, cut in thin slices, small piece angelica, cut into small pieces.

Heat milk with flavourings to simmering point. Draw pan from heat and remove the solid flavourings (lemon rind and cinnamon), leaving milk to cool a *little*.

Separate eggs and whisk whites with pinch of salt until stiff and peaky. With a warmed spoon or 2 spoons drop egg-shaped pieces into the hot flavoured milk. Return pan to low heat and poach gently until 'eggs' are firm. Skim out on to a dish. Whisk yolks of eggs with sugar and stir into hot, but not boiling, milk. Stir over low heat until mixture thickens smoothly. Pour round 'eggs' in dish and leave for a short while before decorating with rings of cherries and chopped angelica. Serve hot or cold.

SOLE AU GRATIN, STUFFED

1 large sole, 1 tablespoonful each breadcrumbs, chopped mushrooms, 1 teaspoonful grated shallot or small onion, 1 small rasher bacon, grilled until crisp then chopped finely, pepper and salt, good squeeze lemon juice, 2 tablespoonfuls white wine, 2 tablespoonfuls good stock from fish trimmings, butter.

Skin and trim fish, removing head and fins, then make a cut down centre of one side with point of sharp knife. Run blade close to bone away from centre to sides of fish, making two 'pockets'.

Mix breadcrumbs, mushrooms, shallot, chopped parsley and bacon with seasonings and lemon juice. Sprinkle half of this mixture at bottom of generously buttered ovenproof shallow dish. Place on top and fill pockets with remaining stuffing ingredients. Dust with seasonings, sprinkle with a few extra crumbs and add one or two extra pieces of butter on top. Pour wine and stock round fish, cover with greaseproof paper and place in moderate oven at 350⁰ F or Regulo 5 for 15 min. Remove paper, and continue baking for a further 10—12 min.

SOLE AU VIN BLANC

4 fillets of sole, lemon juice, ½ pint white wine, fish stock from trimmings, or water, 1 oz. butter, 1 level tablespoonful flour, pepper and salt, paprika.

Season fillets of sole and sprinkle with lemon juice. Roll up neatly from thick end and arrange on a buttered fireproof dish. Pour in wine, stock or water, cover with greaseproof paper and bake in moderate oven at

350° F. or Regulo 5 for about 15 min. Meanwhile, melt butter and stir in flour. Cook for a moment or two, stirring, and when fish is cooked, add liquor gradually, mixing briskly. Cook for several minutes and adjust seasoning to taste. Pour sauce over fillets and garnish with a dusting of paprika or with chopped parsley.

SOLE BONNE FEMME

3 oz. butter, 4 fillets, 6 oz. mushrooms, 2 shallots, 1 packed teaspoonful chopped parsley, 1 small teaspoonful salt, pepper, 1/4 pint fish stock (from simmered fish bones and trimmings), 2 tablespoonfuls dry white wine, 1 tablespoonful creamy white sauce, 1 tablespoonful whipped cream.

Melt 2 oz. butter in a pan and add the chopped mushrooms, chopped shallots and parsley. Mix well, then add fillets of fish seasoned with salt and pepper. Add the fish stock and wine, and simmer slowly for about 10 min., when fish should be cooked but still quite intact. Transfer the fillets to a fireproof serving dish and keep hot. Reduce cooking liquor by simmering uncovered until about a third of its original quantity. Add remaining butter in pieces and adjust seasoning to taste. Just before serving the fish, add cream to the sauce and pour over fish. Set dish under hot grill to brown lightly.

SOLE VERONIQUE

Ingredients and method of cooking as above, but arrange peeled grapes round the fish before lightly browning under grill.

SOLE, TURBANS OF

4 fillets of sole, pepper and salt, lemon juice, 4 medium-large tomatoes, butter, breadcrumbs, paprika.

Dust fillets of sole with pepper and salt. Sprinkle with lemon juice and roll up from thick end. Cut a thick slice from each tomato and scoop out watery pulp. Dust inside each with pepper and salt. Fit a 'turban' into each and sprinkle with breadcrumbs. Dot with pieces of butter and arrange on a buttered baking dish. Cover with greased paper and bake in moderately hot oven for 15 min. Remove paper and raise heat to brown tops of turbans for a further 5 min.
Serve 'turbans' in a bed of creamed potatoes, dusting tops with paprika.

SOUFFLE

Basic recipe, baked
4 eggs (3 yolks and 4 whites), 1 oz. butter, 1 oz. plain flour, 1/4 pint milk.
Prepare a soufflé mould. This is a round, deep, straight-sided ovenproof mould (fireproof glass or china) about 7 in. diameter × 2½ in. deep. Tie round the outside a deep band of folded greaseproof paper extending about 2 in. above rim of mould. Brush with melted butter inside mould.
Melt butter in saucepan and add sifted flour and a pinch of salt. Stir over heat with wooden spoon until mixture is blended. Work in milk gradually, mixing until smooth, then cook for several minutes. Set aside to cool a little, then add egg yolks one by one, beating well after each. If flavouring ingredients are to be added — say about 3 oz. grated

cheese, 4 oz. flaked fish or chopped mushrooms, etc. — now is the time
to add them. Whisk egg whites stiffly and fold into mixture, without
beating. Pour at once into prepared mould and run the point of a
teaspoon quickly round top about an inch in from the edge (to give the
soufflé a 'top hat' effect), then set at once in a moderate oven at 350° F.
or Regulo 5 for about 35 min. Serve at once.

Chocolate Soufflé

Make up basic ingredients (see recipe for soufflé) and before adding
whites of eggs stir in 1 heaped tablespoonful caster sugar and 2 oz.
sweetened plain chocolate melted with a little cold milk. Mix well
before folding in whites of eggs. Proceed as indicated.

Lemon Soufflé

Make up basic ingredients (see recipe for soufflé) and before adding
whites of eggs, stir in 1 oz. fine caster sugar and grated outer rind of
1 small, or half large, lemon. Fold in egg whites and proceed as
indicated.

Steamed Soufflés

Prepare ingredients as in previous recipes. Place soufflé mixture in top
compartment of steamer over boiling water. Place a round of oiled or
buttered double greaseproof paper over top of mould to cover. Steam
for 1 hr. Remove and leave for a minute to shrink. Have ready a hot
dish and turn out soufflé. If a sweet soufflé, serve with a fruit syrup
sauce. If a savoury soufflé, serve with a little sauce piquante, if liked.

SPONGE FINGERS OR DROPS

*2 eggs, 2¹/₂ oz. caster sugar, 2¹/₂ oz. self-raising flour, few drops
flavouring essence.*

Grease sponge moulds with lard and dredge with mixture of flour and
castor sugar.
   Whisk eggs and sugar in basin over steam from gently simmering
water until mixture thickens, up to 10 min. Fold in sifted flour. Half-fill
moulds with mixture, then dredge lightly with sifted flour and caster
sugar. Bake in hot oven at 450° F. or Regulo 8 for about 8—9 min.

SPONGE SANDWICH, FATLESS

*2 large eggs, ³/₄ teacupful caster sugar, 1 teacupful self-raising flour,
pinch salt, flavouring to taste, 1 tablespoonful warm water, jam or butter
cream for filling.*

Separate eggs. Whisk white first, add yolks and flavouring and whisk
well together, over steam from gently simmering water. When mixture
is tepid, fold in sifted flour and salt, then water. Divide between two
greased and floured 7 in. sandwich tins. Bake in hot oven at 450° F. or
Regulo 8 for about 10 min., or until firm to the touch.

STOCK

First stock

*1 lb. each fresh beef and bone (usually shin of beef), 2 quarts cold water,
1 strip celery (or ¹/₂ teaspoonful celery seeds), 1 medium-size carrot,
1 small piece turnip, 1 medium-size onion, small bunch herbs — 2 sprigs
parsley, 1 sprig thyme and 1 bayleaf, tied together — 1 teaspoonful salt*

Cut up meat and chop bones into convenient pieces for pot. If stock is intended for clear soups (consommés) remove marrow from bones, which would cause a slight cloudiness. Put meat and bones into pot with water. Cover and bring slowly to the boil. Remove scum. Continue simmering for 2 hr. Then add vegetables and salt. Cover and continue simmering for a further hr. Strain into a large bowl and leave until cold. Remove any fat that forms on the surface.

Second or household stock

To make this, add cold water to remaining cooked meat and bones, etc., covering well. Simmer for 1—2 hr. If further cooked bones and vegetables are added, use extra water proportionately. with salt and herbs as above, and cook longer. Strain and proceed as for first stock.

STRAWBERRY BAVARIAN

1 pint packet strawberry jelly, 1/4 pint double cream, 1 oz. caster sugar, 1/2 lb. strawberries.

Dissolve jelly tablet or crystals in 1/2 pint boiling water, then add a further 1/4 pint cold water. Set aside a few of the strawberries of even size, and put remainder through sieve. Add to jelly with sugar and mix well. When cool and showing signs of thickening, fold in whipped cream. Divide between sundae glasses and decorate with selected strawberries.

STRAWBERRY JAM, WHOLE

4 lb. small, firm strawberries, 4 lb. preserving sugar, 2 level teaspoonfuls citric acid or 1/2 pint concentrated redcurrant juice.

To make the juice, simmer redcurrants until reduced to a pulp and strain. Return juice to pan and boil until reduced by one-third.

Put the hulled strawberries into a large bowl with the sugar sprinkled between fruit and leave for 12 hr.

Turn into the preserving pan with the redcurrant juice if used, or with the acid, simmer very slowly, stirring frequently to prevent burning.

When a little juice has run, bring slowly to the boil and boil gently until a little jam will set when tested. Stir constantly, but avoid crushing the berries while doing so. When a set is obtained, leave the jam in the pan to cool a little, for if potted too hot, the berries will all rise to the top. While potting, stir the jam several times to ensure that the berries are equally distributed.

STRAWBERRY SHORTCAKE

8 oz. plain flour, 2 small teaspoonfuls baking powder, pinch salt, 2 oz. caster sugar, 2 oz. butter, 1 egg, little milk, grated rind of lemon (about 1/2 teaspoonful), fresh ripe strawberries, caster sugar, whipped cream.

Sift flour with powdered ingredients, add lemon rind, and rub in butter. Mix with beaten egg and milk to make a soft scone dough. Divide between two greased and lined sandwich tins and bake in a moderately hot oven for about 25 min.

Cool cakes on a wire tray.

Put cakes together with a layer of whipped cream and sliced fruit between, dredged thickly with sugar. Spread top of sandwich with a layer of cream and decorate with whole fruit. Dredge with more sugar before serving.

STUFFINGS (FORCEMEAT)

Sausage meat and celery

3 breakfastcupfuls breadcrumbs, 3 tablespoonfuls grated onion, 2 dessertspoonfuls finely chopped parsley, 1 teaspoonful salt, 1 level teaspoonful crushed dried herbs, 1 lb. sausage meat, 1½ teacupfuls finely chopped crisp white celery, little stock or beaten egg and milk for binding.

Mix ingredients together. If stuffing is used for stuffing poultry, add the fried and minced liver of bird or birds, and use giblet stock instead of egg and milk for moistening.

Mushroom and bacon stuffing

1 small teacupful chopped mushrooms, 1 teacupful breadcrumbs, ¼ teaspoonful celery salt (or 1 tablespoonful chopped celery heart), 1 dessertspoonful chopped parsley, 1 teaspoonful grated onion, 1 teaspoonful salt, 1 teaspoonful dried herbs, crushed, 1 oz. butter, melted, pepper to taste, ½ teacupful good stock, or beaten egg to mix.

Mix all ingredients well, and use as required.

SUMMER PUDDING

Line a plain mould or basin with slices of crustless stale bread about ½ in. thick. Fill up with soft fruits in season — blackcurrants, loganberries, blackberries, etc. — previously stewed in the minimum of water with sugar to taste. Pour boiling fruit into lined mould and cover with thick slice or slices of bread. Stand mould on a soup plate and cover with a weighted plate. Leave until next day, then turn out and serve with sauce or custard.

SWEETBREADS

Preparation

Soak in cold water for 15 min. Blanch and cook in boiling salted water for 5 min.

To keep sweetbreads light, now put into cold water, for about 20 min. Use as required.

Braised sweetbreads

2 calves' sweetbread, little fat bacon, 2 breakfastcupfuls diced mixed flavouring vegetables (onion, carrots, piece turnip, celery), 1 teaspoonful mixed spices, tied in piece scalded muslin, small bouquet garni, 1 pint good stock.

Press prepared sweetbreads between two plates and leave for at least 1 hr. Prepare vegetables and place in casserole, then cover with boiling stock. Lay sweetbreads on top. Cover and cook gently in oven for about 1 hr. Remove lid, dot sweetbreads with tiny pieces of fat bacon and return dish to oven until lightly browned. Remove sweetbreads to heated serving dish, surround with diced vegetables — adding some freshly cooked green peas — and pour liquor from dish over.

Fried sweetbreads

Prepare sweetbreads as usual.

Simmer in light stock for about 1 hr. When cold cut into thick slices, coat with egg and crumbs, and fry in shallow or deep fat. Drain well and serve with fried parsley as edible garnish, and vegetables in season.

SWISS APPLE PUDDING

1¹/₂ lb. apples, ¹/₄ pint water, rind and juice of 1 lemon, 4 oz. sugar, slices of bread and butter.

Stew the prepared apples with the water and finely pared outer rind of lemon and the juice. When apples are pulped, remove lemon rind. Have ready a buttered pie-dish and fill with layers of bread and butter, sugar and apples, finishing with a layer of bread and butter, butter side up. Sprinkle generously with sugar and bake in a moderate oven at 350⁰ F. or Regulo 4 for about 30 min. until golden brown on top. Serve with custard.

SWISS BUNS OR FINGERS

Sweetened bread dough, sugar syrup, icing (white or pink).

Divide dough into small pieces. For buns, mould into balls and flatten with the hand. For fingers, shape into rolls. When proved (risen), bake in hot oven at 450⁰ F. or Regulo 7 for about 10—15 min. Brush with sugar syrup and leave until cold. When cold, ice tops.

SWISS ROLL WITH JAM

2 eggs, 4 oz. caster sugar, 3 oz. self-raising flour, pinch salt, 1 dessert-spoonful warm water, few drops flavouring essence or finely grated rind ¹/₂ lemon or 1 orange, jam.

Cream egg yolks and sugar until thick and white. Add warm water and flavouring, then whisk again well. Fold in sifted flour and salt, mixing without beating, then add sifted whites of eggs, blending without beating. Spread over surface of greased and lined oblong sandwich tin. Bake in hot oven 8—10 min. or until just firm to the touch. Turn out on to sugar-dredged paper or clean cloth. If edges have crisped, trim quickly. Spread quickly with warmed jam and roll up. Place, join side down, on wire tray to cool.

SWISS ROLL, FATLESS

2 large eggs, 4 oz. caster sugar, 1 teacupful self-raising flour, pinch salt, 1 tablespoonful warm water, grated rind ¹/₂ lemon or 1 orange or few drops flavouring essence, jam.

Cream egg yolks and sugar until thick and lighter in colour. Add warm water and flavouring and whisk again well. Fold in sifted flour and salt, followed by stiffly whisked egg whites. Spread mixture over surface of greased and lined oblong Swiss roll tin. Bake in hot oven 8—10 min. or until firm to the touch.

Turn out of tin on to sugar-dredged paper and roll up with paper between. When partially cool, carefully unroll, spread with warmed jam, and re-roll without paper, dredging again with fine caster sugar. Place, join side down, on wire rack to cool.

TARTARE SAUCE

See *Sauces.*

TIPSY CAKE

1 thick sponge round, 1 teacupful sherry, 1 pint thick custard, apricot jam, blanched, split and lightly roasted almonds, cream.

Split sponge cake into three layers and put together again with apricot jam. Place in a glass dish and pour sherry over. Leave steeping for a short while until sherry is absorbed.

When custard (sweetened) is cool, whisk to make fluid and smooth, and spoon over soaked cake, covering completely. Stick roasted splinters of almonds in all over and decorate with whipped cream.

A tipsy cake more typical in appearance is made with a sponge cake baked in a tall tin, which calls for a little more sherry for soaking the extra layers of sponge cake sandwiched together with jam.

TOAD IN THE HOLE

1 lb. sausages, 1 pint pancake batter with seasonings to taste.

Heat sausages in hot oven (pricking them first) in large baking tin until fat runs. Pour pancake batter over and return tin to oven. Bake for about 50 min., or until batter is well risen and a rich golden brown colour. Cut into portions and serve without delay.

TOMATO CHUTNEY, RED

5 lb. ripe tomatoes (firm but not soft), ¹/₂ lb. shallots, 1 oz. mustard seed, ¹/₂ oz. whole allspice, ¹/₂ lb. sugar, 1 tablespoonful salt, ¹/₂ teaspoonful pepper, 1 pint vinegar.

Wipe tomatoes and place on baking tin in moderate oven for about 10 min., or until skins split. Remove tin from oven. Strip skins from tomatoes, chop and place in pan with minced shallots. Tie mustard seed and allspice in piece of muslin and heat together until simmering. Simmer gently for 30 min., then add sugar, seasonings and vinegar. Stir until sugar is dissolved, then continue cooking gently until chutney becomes thick. Remove bag of spices and pour chutney into wide-necked bottles or jars. Cover closely.

TOMATO SAUCE, RED

5 lb. red tomatoes, 3 shallots, 1 dessertspoonful salt, 1 oz. sugar, pinch cayenne pepper, ¹/₂ teaspoonful paprika, ¹/₂ pint spiced vinegar.

Wash tomatoes and place in baking tin in moderate oven until skins split and water runs a little. Remove skins and put tomatoes in pan with minced shallots. Simmer together until tomatoes are pulped. Rub contents of pan through sieve and return purée to pan. Add sugar, seasonings and vinegar. Stir over low heat until sugar is dissolved, then continue simmering until sauce is smooth and creamy. Whilst cooking, taste and adjust seasonings as required. When cooked, pour into heated wide-necked bottles and cork down at once.

TOMATO SOUP

2 lb. fresh ripe tomatoes, small ham bone or a few smaller bacon bones, 1 oz. butter, flavouring vegetables (1 onion, 1 carrot, small piece turnip, 1 strip celery or ¹/₄ teaspoonful celery seed), bouquet garni, 12 peppercorns, small blade of mace, salt and pepper to taste, 1 teaspoonful sugar, 3 pints stock.

Wipe and slice tomatoes. Melt butter and fry chopped vegetables until soft without browning. Put these ingredients into a pan with stock, etc., cover and simmer gently for about 2 hr. Remove bunch of herbs and rub soup through a sieve. Thicken with about 1 dessertspoonful cornflour mixed to a thin cream with milk. Cook for several minutes. Add a little cream if liked.

TRIFLE

Sponge cakes, jam, ratafias or macaroon biscuits, sherry or fruit syrup, 3/4 pint fairly thick custard, 1/4 pint double cream, decorations (ratafias, glacé cherries, angelica, blanched and roasted strips of almonds).

Slice the sponge cakes and put together again with jam. Arrange these in a glass dish and add sufficient sherry or fruit syrup to soak well, adding some broken macaroons or ratafias and mixing in, together with a few chopped glacé cherries and chopped angelica. Make a thick custard with custard powder or eggs and milk, sweetening and flavouring to taste. When cool, pour over contents of dish. Leave for an hour or two, then decorate surface with whipped cream and spike with strips of almonds all over. Make a centre piece with a few cherries and stalks and leaves of angelica.

TRIPE, UNDRESSED, TO PREPARE

Wash well in several waters, then scrape all over. Trim away all discoloured parts, also fat. Put into a deep pan, cover with cold water and bring to boiling point. Drain well. Repeat this process — if necessary 2 or 3 times — until tripe smells quite wholesome. Then put again into a pan, cover with water and heat slowly, simmering for about 8 hr., when it should be tender. Use as required.

TRIPE AND ONIONS

1 1/2 lb. dressed tripe, 2 large onions, 1 pint milk and water, pepper and salt, 1 tablespoonful plain flour, chopped parsley.

Blanch tripe and peeled and thickly sliced onions. Drain well. Cut tripe into strips or squares. Put with sliced onions into milk and water, adding seasonings to taste. Cover and simmer gently for 2 1/2 hrs. when tripe should be tender. (If liked, cook in the oven, heating milk and water before pouring over tripe, etc.) Mix flour with a little extra milk and stir into cooked tripe. Mix well and simmer for several minutes longer. Sprinkle in a teaspoonful or so of chopped parsley and serve.

TROUT, GRILLED

3 or 4 medium sized trout, butter or salad oil, lemon juice, pepper and salt, watercress.

Clean fish and dry well. Score across with a sharp knife, making about 3 clean cuts, then repeat on the other side. Dust well with pepper and salt in the cuts and brush over with butter or oil and place under hot grill to brown nicely on both sides (5—10 min. on each side, depending on size of fish). Serve on a hot dish garnished with watercress. Squeeze a little lemon juice over each fish, and serve with quarters of freshly cut lemon.

TROUT EN PAPILLOTE

4—6 medium-small trout, 2 oz. butter, pepper and salt, lemon juice, 1 dessertspoonful finely chopped chives and parsley mixed, 3—4 tablespoonfuls breadcrumbs, 1 tablespoonful chopped mushrooms, 1 yolk of egg, oil.

Wash, clean and dry fish. Prepare a stuffing with the breadcrumbs, herbs and mushrooms, moistening with lemon juice, yolk of egg and seasonings to taste. Divide between each fish, filling neatly. Generously butter 6 squares of greaseproof paper, sufficiently large to enclose fish completely with ends tucked in securely. Brush over outside with oil and place 'parcels' on a greased tin. Bake in a moderate oven, turning once, for 15—20 min. May be served wrapped, or unwrapped with juices poured over, with parsley garnish.

TROUT POACHED WITH GREEN SAUCE

6 medium sized trout, 1 pint water, $^1/_4$ pint white wine, juice of 1 lemon, small bunch parsley, 1 dessertspoonful salt, 1 small teacupful mayonnaise, 1 tablespoonful each finely chopped chives and parsley, $^1/_2$ teacupful finely chopped spinach and watercress, 1 shallot or small onion, grated, or its extracted juice.

Trim the fish and draw. Rinse and wipe. Place in a large shallow pan and cover with liquids — wine, lemon juice, herbs (bunch parsley), salt and water. Cover with lid, or piece of double greaseproof paper (buttered) and heat slowly to simmering point. Continue simmering for 12—15 min. Remove cover and leave fish to cool in liquor. Then lift out, draining well, on to doyley-lined serving dish and garnish with lemon and with sprigs of parsley.

To make sauce, put mayonnaise into a bowl and add chopped or minced herbs and onion flavouring. Mix well and serve.

TRUFFLE CAKES

4 oz. cake crumbs, 4 oz. ground almonds, 4 oz. plain chocolate, $^1/_2$ oz. butter, 1 or 2 teaspoonfuls warmed apricot jam, little rum, few drops vanilla or almond essence, about 4 oz. melted chocolate for coating and chocolate 'rice' or 'vermicelli' to decorate, sweet cases.

Rub cake through wire sieve and mix with ground almonds. Warm chopped chocolate and butter together until melted, then stir in cake crumbs, etc., and flavourings. Add a little sieved apricot jam to make a workable paste. Divide into small pieces. With cocoa-dredged fingers mould to round balls and leave on waxed paper to set. Melt the other quantity of chocolate and use to coat balls, rolling them afterwards in chocolate grains. Place in paper cups.

TURKISH COFFEE

Use pulverised, not ground, coffee. Allow 1 dessertspoonful coffee to 2 tablespoonfuls water. Place over high heat so that contents of pan boil almost at once, then serve into small cups — without straining — and serve without milk. Sugar to taste.

TURKISH DELIGHT (RAHAT LAKOUM)

1 lb. lump sugar, $^1/_4$ pint water, juice of 1 lemon or 1 tablespoonful juice, red colouring, $^1/_2$ oz. powdered gelatine, 2 tablespoonfuls sifted icing sugar, 1 level tablespoonful cornflour.

Soak gelatine in half the water. Put remainder of water into a pan over heat, add sugar and stir until sugar is dissolved and syrup is boiling. Add softened gelatine to pan and stir until dissolved in the syrup.

Simmer for 20 min. before adding lemon juice. Have ready two small rinsed tins. Pour half the mixture into one tin. Add 1 or 2 drops red colouring and some rose water to remainder, mix well and pour into the other tin. The tins should be small enough for Turkish delight to be an inch thick. When cold, cut in cubes and coat with sifted icing sugar and cornflour mixed.

TURTLE SOUP FROM DRIED TURTLE

1—2 lb. knuckle of veal, about 1 lb. shin of beef, 1/4 lb. dried turtle, 1 bacon bone (about 1/2 lb.) flavouring vegetables (1 or 2 onions, 1 or 2 carrots, 2 strips celery), small bouquet garni, 3 quarts water, pepper, salt, few grains cayenne pepper, 1 dessertspoonful lemon juice, 2 oz. butter, 2 oz. cornflour or arrowroot.

Put the dried turtle into warm water about 4 days before making soup. Soak until turtle is swollen and fairly soft, i. e. about 3 days, changing the water every day. Early on the fourth day, proced to make soup. Cut up the other meat into fairly small pieces, and chop any bones to a convenient size. Put these ingredients into a pan with the water. Add turtle tied in a piece of scalded muslin. Heat slowly and skim well. Simmer for about 8 hr., adding extra water — about 1 1/2 pints at the end of this time. Now add the chopped prepared vegetables and herbs. Bring again to simmering point and continue simmering for a further 3—4 hr. Put contents of pan through a sieve and leave liquor to get cold. Untie turtle and cut up into very small pieces. When soup is cold, skim fat from the top. Then make thickening — melt butter in a saucepan and heat until slightly browned. Moisten cornflour with a little stock and stir in butter, mixing smoothly. Add to stock with other seasonings, pieces of turtle and lemon juice. Make piping hot, cooking 8 min.

VANILLA CREAM

1/2 pint fairly thick sweetened custard made with custard powder or with eggs and milk, 1/2 pint double cream, vanilla flavouring, 3/4 oz. powdered gelatine, 2 tablespoonfuls water, 2 or 3 tablespoonfuls dissolved lemon jelly, few cherries sliced to look like rings.

Make custard, stir well and cover with greaseproof paper until cool, stirring at intervals to keep fairly fluid.

Whip cream. Add water to gelatine and stand container in hot water until gelatine is dissolved. Stir into still warm custard, mixing well and adding a few drops vanilla to taste.

Prepare mould and spoon in a thin layer of lemon jelly to cover bottom. When almost set arrange rings of cherries on top in a neat design. Spoon any remaining jelly over each ring, setting it firmly in place. When jelly is firm, blend the cold custard and whipped cream, and fill mould.

Other creams can be made with other flavourings and decorations. If liked, a rich custard can be made by using 3 egg yolks and 1 white of egg to 1/2 pint milk, adding sugar to sweeten well (about 1 1/2 oz.) and flavouring.

VEAL BROTH

3 lb. knuckle of veal or neck of veal, 2 quarts water, 2 strips celery, 2 onions, 3 oz. rice, pepper and salt, small bunch mixed herbs.

Put meat into saucepan. Add water and washed rice. Bring to the boil and skim well. Add peeled, whole onions and celery sticks cut in two pieces. Season well, cover and cook gently for about 3 hr. (Stir occasionally to keep rice moving.)

Sometimes an egg is beaten and put into the soup tureen before pouring soup slowly in, at the same time stirring well.

VEAL, FRICASSEE OF

1. *1½ lb. fillet or knuckle of veal, 1 onion, a strip of lemon peel, a sprig of parsley, 8 peppercorns, salt, ½ pint milk, 2 oz. flour, 1 oz. margarine, 1 pint of veal broth, from the stewed veal.*

Cut the veal into neat pieces about 4 in. long, and 2 in. wide, or a little larger if liked.

Put into a saucepan with the onion, lemon peel, peppercorns, parsley and salt. Cover well with warm water. Bring to the boil, remove all scum, then simmer gently for 2 hr.

Strain the liquid, melt the margarine in a saucepan, and stir in the flour. It must not brown as this is a very white stew.

Gradually stir in the milk, previously brought to the boil, when well blended, add the veal broth. Cook and stir until the sauce is creamy and thick. Put back the meat and heat well through.

Dish up and serve with lemon slices. If liked, wash a dozen tiny pearl onions from a jar of cocktail onions, and add 2—3 min. before dishing up the sauce.

2. *1 lb. veal, 1 small onion, ¼ lb. button mushrooms, bouquet garni (sprig thyme, parsley and small bayleaf), pepper and salt, ½ pint white sauce (using some of the veal stock), 1 tablespoonful cream (top milk), small teaspoonful lemon juice.*

Trim meat and cut into neat pieces. Put them into a saucepan with cover with water. Bring to boiling point and skim. Add sliced onion and mushrooms, herbs and seasonings to taste. Cover and simmer until meat is tender — about 1 hr. Strain stock from meat, using some of this when making the sauce. Add cream and lemon juice to sauce and make very hot without boiling. Return veal to pan and reheat in the sauce. Serve on a heated serving dish with grilled bacon rolls, and slices of lemon. Sometimes crisp sippets of fried bread are also served with this dish. Garnish with sprigs of parsley, or chopped parsley.

VEAL AND HAM PIE

8 oz. veal, 3 oz. ham or bacon, ¼ pint light stock (from veal bones, preferably), pepper, salt, pinch powdered dried herbs, 1 teaspoonful chopped fresh parsley, raised pie dough made with 8 oz. flour and 2 oz. lard or butter, with pinch salt, and about ¾ teacupful hot water (see recipe).

Cut veal and ham or bacon into small pieces. Mix with seasonings. Make hot water pastry. Set aside one-third for covering pie, and keep it warm meanwhile. Line a tin or shape with main portion of dough. Fill up with meat, etc., and add about 1 tablespoonful stock. Moisten top edges of pastry and roll out remaining piece of pastry for covering, pressing edges firmly together. Make a hole in middle of cover, and decorate pie edges with tines of a fork. Brush over with beaten egg and bake in a hot oven for about 1 hr. When cooked, fill up with jellied stock.

Pork meat can be substituted for veal.

VEGETABLES, BOTTLING OF

Under no circumstances should vegetables be bottled by the methods outlined for bottling fruit.

It is recommended that a pressure-cooker be used as follows.

Choose only fresh young vegetables for bottling and process as soon after gathering as possible.

Wash vegetables thoroughly, scrubbing root vegetables to remove all trace of soil and rinsing several times.

After washing, trimming or peeling, all vegetables must be blanched. This is done by plunging them into boiling water for the times given in the table below, then dropping them into cold water. This process shrinks the vegetables, sets their colour and facilitates handling.

Drain well before packing into jars.

Vegetables are processed in brine, i. e. water to which 1 oz. salt per quart has been added. Boil before using.

Processing vegetables

1. Prepare the jars as for bottling fruit.
2. Pack blanched vegetables into clean, warm jars, leaving 1/4 in. head space. Do not pack tightly or press down.
3. Twist bottles from side to side to expel air bubbles.
4. Fill with hot brine to cover vegetables well.
5. Adjust screw tops, or clip tops. Screw top jars should be turned as far as possible, then given a quarter turn back.
6. Have ready pressure cooker with trivet in place, and pour in 1 1/2 pints *hot* water and add a tablespoonful vinegar or lemon juice.
7. Place jars on trivet, seeing that they do not touch each other or the sides of the pan.
8. Fix cover and turn heat to medium and wait until the steam flows freely from centre vent.
9. Lower heat and steam for 5—7 min.
10. Put on 10 lb. pressure control and on low heat bring to pressure, maintaining this at a steady pace. Any fluctuation during processing will cause a loss of liquid from the jars.
11. When processing time is up, turn off heat and leave cooker to reduce pressure at room temperature. Do not reduce with cold water — a sudden cooling will crack the jars.
12. After at least 10 min., remove pressure control and cover, lift out jars on to a wooden or papercovered surface. Leave to cool. With screw top jars, lift out one at a time and tighten screw bands immediately.
13. When cold, test seals. Label and store away in a cool, dark place.

Time Table for Bottling Vegetables

Vegetables	Preparation	Min. to blanch in boiling water	Min. at 10 lb. pressure
Asparagus	Wash, trim off scales, cut in even lengths, pack upright.	2—3	40
Broad Beans	Pod	5	55
French Beans	Wash, string if necessary, cut off ends, pack whole.	3	35
Runner Beans	Wash, string and slice.	5	40
Beetroot	Cut off top. Blanch before slicing or dicing	15—20	40
Carrots	Wash, scrape, slice or dice, leave whole	10	45
Celery	Wash, cut in even lengths	6	40
Mushrooms	Cut off most of stalk. Wash and peel, sprinkle with pepper and salt. Pre-cook in moderate oven until liquid has been extracted. Pack in hot jars, cover with own juice.		40
Green peas	Shell, wash and grade	2—3	50
Potatoes, new	Scrape and wash	5	50

The finished product may appear to have lost much of its brine, but this will not interfere with the keeping quality.

If on opening bottled vegetables, contents do not look or smell wholesome, discard them at once.

VELOUTE SAUCE
See *Sauces.*

VICTORIA SPONGE LAYER CAKE
2 large eggs (2¹/₂ oz. each), 4 oz. butter or margarine, 4 oz. caster sugar, 5 oz. self-raising flour (or plain flour and 1 level teaspoonful baking powder), ¹/₂ teaspoonful vanilla essence, 2 tablespoonfuls warm water.

Cream fat well. Add sugar and beat together until soft and light. Add well whisked eggs gradually, then fold in sifted flour, adding water and flavouring essence. Divide mixture between two greased and floured 7 in. diameter sandwich tins. Bake in moderate oven for about 35 min., or until firm to the touch in the middle.

When cake layers are cool, sandwich together with butter cream, lemon cheese or jam. Dust top of sandwich with icing sugar.

VINEGAR, GARLIC
1 oz. minced garlic cloves, 1 pint vinegar.
Proceed as for shallot vinegar.

VINEGAR, SHALLOT

2 oz. minced shallots, 1 pint vinegar.

Put minced shallots into a glass preserving jar and fill to the brim with vinegar. Seal with patent closure and leave steeping for about 10 days, shaking jar occasionally. Then strain and pour into bottles. Cork down and use as required.

VINEGAR, SPICED (FOR PICKLING)

1 quart vinegar, ¹/₄ oz. blade mace, ¹/₄ oz. stick cinnamon, 8 pepper-corns, ¹/₄ oz. allspice, ¹/₄ oz. cloves.

Tie spices loosely in a piece of muslin and put with vinegar into a pan. Cover pan and heat vinegar slowly to boiling point. Simmer for 5—6 min. Draw pan from heat and leave, still covered, until vinegar is coolish — about 2 hr. Remove bag of spices. The vinegar is then ready to use.

VINEGAR, TARRAGON

Chopped tarragon leaves, vinegar.

Put tarragon leaves into a glass preserving jar and cover with vinegar. Proceed as for shallot vinegar.

WAFFLES, SWEET

4 tablespoonfuls plain flour, 1 large egg, 1 teaspoonful caster sugar, 1 teaspoonful baking powder, ¹/₄ pint milk, pinch salt, 2 oz. butter or margarine, olive oil as required.

Sift powdered ingredients together. Separate egg and add yolk to flour etc. Mix well, adding milk gradually, then melted fat. Beat well. When ready to use, fold in stiffly whisked egg white.

Before using waffle iron, make it hot, turning it once so that both sides are heated. Open out iron flat and pour in a small teaspoonful olive oil. Close iron and make oil hot, turning it over so that oil penetrates the sections. Allow to cool, then reheat iron when required and pour 1 tablespoonful batter mixture over each division. Close iron and bake both sides.

Waffles are cooked when no steam escapes and there is an aroma like a cooked cake.

WAFFLES, SAVOURY

Omit sugar but above ingredients and increase salt to a level half-teaspoonful. Proceed as in previous recipe.

WALNUTS, PICKLED

Green walnuts, brine (1 lb. salt to 1 gallon water), spiced vinegar.

Walnuts should be green and easily pierced with a needle. Discard any that are hard. Cover with brine and leave for 1 week. Drain off brine and cover again with a fresh brine. Leave steeping for 2 weeks. Then drain walnuts, rinse and dry well. Spread out on trays and leave until exposure to air turns them black, which should take about a day. Pack into jars and cover well with hot spiced vinegar, filling to top of jars. Seal when cold and leave for at least 6 weeks before using.

WATERCRESS AND POTATO SOUP

¹/₄ lb. watercress, 1¹/₂ lb. potatoes after peeling, ¹/₂ lb. onions, 2 pints stock or water, 1 oz. butter, salt, 2 tomatoes, plenty of pepper, nutmeg to taste, ¹/₂ pint milk.

Wash watercress, removing any coarse stems. Peel onions. Slice potatoes thickly and put into pan with stock and butter, also sliced onions. Cook until pulped, then rub through sieve. Reheat, adding milk, pepper and salt to taste. Add nutmeg, tasting until of required flavour. Scald, skin and chop tomatoes, and add these with watercress, finely chopped.

WELSH PANCAKES

¹/₂ pint pancake batter (see recipe), 2 oz. cleaned and picked currants, caster sugar, lard for frying.

Heat pan and add a nut of lard. When smoking hot, pour in just sufficient pancake batter to thinly cover surface of pan. Sprinkle in a few of the currants whilst still liquid. Cook until underside of pancake is golden brown. Turn and brown the other side. Roll up — lacy-looking surface outwards — and repeat until mixture and currants have been used up. Pile on a doyley-lined dish and dredge with caster sugar. Serve at once.

Sometimes these pancakes are made just a little thicker than the usual variety, allowing sufficient batter to absorb the currants, so that the fruit is enclosed when the pancake is turned.

WELSH RAREBIT

2 rounds of hot buttered toast, 4 oz. Cheddar cheese, 2 tablespoonfuls beer or milk, 1 saltspoonful made mustard, tiny pinch cayenne, nut of butter.

Grate cheese finely and put into a saucepan with liquid, mustard, cayenne and butter. Stir over heat until mixture is blended smoothly. Spread over buttered toast and serve quickly.

To vary, stir in a yolk of egg to mixture before spreading: add a teaspoonful sifted flour to mixture and a little more beer or milk and cook a little longer before spreading. To improve the appearance, sprinkle extra grated cheese over toast etc. and slip under hot grill to brown slightly.

Buck rarebit

Make rarebit as above and add a poached egg to each round of toast before serving.

WEST RIDING PUDDING

6 oz. short or rough puff pastry, 2 tablespoonfuls jam, 2 eggs, 5 oz. self-raising flour (or plain flour and ¹/₂ teaspoonful baking powder), 4 oz. butter (or margarine), 4 oz. fine caster sugar, grated rind ¹/₂ lemon.

Roll out pastry thinly and line a pie dish at the sides with a strip reaching top of dish. Decorate top edges of dish with cut-outs of pastry — leaves, diamonds, etc. Spread jam at bottom of dish to cover. Cream butter well, add sugar and lemon rind, and beat together until soft and light. Add well-beaten eggs gradually, then fold in sifted dry ingredients without beating. Cover jam with mixture and place dish in moderate oven at 350° F. or Regulo 4 for about 1 hr. or until mixture is firm to the touch. Dust with powdered sugar and serve.

WHALEMEAT

To fry

Whalemeat, cut into portion-size steaks, pepper and salt, oil, vinegar or lemon juice, 1 small onion chopped, butter for frying.

Marinate the whalemeat steaks in above ingredients, leaving for at least an hour before cooking. Wipe meat and place in pan containing hot melted butter, and fry for 7—10 min. on each side, depending on thickness of steaks.

Top each portion with a pat of maître d'hôtel butter (see recipe) and serve with watercress garnish.

To grill

Prepare as for frying, and brush over with melted butter before placing under hot grill and cooking on both sides.

To casserole

Whalemeat, cut into strips, 2 oz. butter or margarine, pepper and salt, 1 small onion, 2 oz. mushrooms, 1 tin vegetable or meat broth (or bouillon cube dissolved in water).

Fry the strips of whalemeat in fat (after preparing as in previous recipes), adding chopped onion. Cook together for 10 min. Add sliced mushrooms, seasonings and stock. Cover and cook in slow oven for about 1½ hr. Thicken liquor. Dish up meat, cover with liquor, and serve with vegetables in season.

WHITEBAIT

Whitebait, lightly seasoned flour (½ teaspoonful salt and good shake of pepper to every tablespoonful plain flour), oil or fat for deep frying.

Put seasoned flour on a cloth and add a good handful cleaned and dried fresh whitebait. Pick up corners of cloth and shake to coat the little fish well. Put the fish into a wire mesh basket and shake to remove surplus flour, then lower into smoking hot oil or fat, and cook until crisp. Turn on to a hot dish and repeat the process with remaining whitebait. When a large quantity must be cooked, return all the fish to the mesh basket and reheat oil or fat to smoking point. Plunge basket in and cook for a few seconds. Drain well and heap on to dish. Border with wedges of freshly cut lemon, and serve with brown bread and butter.

If properly fried, the whitebait should be separate and crisp. To ensure this, flour the fish quickly and fry as soon after as possible, making sure the fat is sufficiently hot first.

WHITING, STUFFED

2 large whiting, parsley sauce, 1 teacupful freshly rubbed crumbs, 1 tablespoonful chopped fresh parsley, 1 small teaspoonful mixed dried herbs, grated rind and juice of ½ lemon, 1 egg, pepper and salt, 1½ oz. bacon dripping or butter, few brown breadcrumbs.

Clean fish and remove eyes. Dry fish and prepare the stuffing — mixing crumbs, herbs, lemon flavouring, seasonings and moistening with half the beaten egg and half the melted dripping or butter. Divide between the two fish, filling the head also. Make secure by sewing flaps of skin with needle and thread. Curl tail of each fish round and put through the eyes. Brush over with remaining beaten egg and sprinkle with brown breadcrumbs. Place prepared fish in a baking tin greased with remaining fat. Bake in a hot even at 425⁰ F. or Regulo 7 for about 20 min. Transfer fish to hot dish and serve with parsley sauce.

WIENER SCHNITZEL (VIENNA SCHNITZEL)

Thin slices of veal, pepper, salt, flour, 1 egg, breadcrumbs, butter.

Pound the fillets until very thin, then coat with seasoned flour. Brush over with beaten egg and coat closely with breadcrumbs, shaking off any loose ones.

Fry on both sides quickly in butter. Serve very hot with a watercress or cucumber salad.

Sometimes schnitzels are served with a poached egg on top. For garnish, capers, chopped olives, chopped egg white or sliced gherkins are used, varying according to the custom of the country in which they are served.

WINE BISCUITS

6 oz. flour, 4 oz. butter or margarine, 3 oz. castor sugar, little sherry, 1 yolk of egg.

Sieve flour, add sugar and rub in fat with finger-tips. Alternatively, beat fat and sugar together and work in sifted flour. Mix to a firm dough with egg yolk beaten with a tablespoonful sherry. Knead until smooth, then roll out thinly. Prick dough all over, then cut into shapes. Some of the shapes can be brushed with white of egg and sprinkled with finely chopped almonds or decorated with pieces of glacé cherries and angelica.

Bake in moderately hot oven at 375⁰ F. or Regulo 5 for about 12 min. until shapes are firm and golden.

YORKSHIRE TEA CAKES

1. *12 oz. plain flour, 1 oz. butter, 1/2 oz. yeast, pinch salt, 1/3 pint milk, 1 egg, sugar glaze.*

Sieve flour into a warm bowl, and make a well in the middle. Melt butter in saucepan and add milk. When mixed and tepid stir into yeast which has been crumbled and mixed to a liquid with a pinch of salt. Pour into middle of flour and add well beaten egg. Mix well for several minutes. Divide into 2 or 3 portions. Knead each in warm place for about 30 min. Bake in a hot oven at 425⁰ F. or Regulo 7 for about 20—25 min. Draw tins from oven, brush with sugar and milk glaze (1 tablespoonful each mixed until sugar has melted) and return to oven for a moment to dry.

2. *1 lb. flour, 1 small teaspoonful salt, 1 oz. yeast, 3 tablespoonfuls warm water, 1¹/₂ oz. lard, warm milk, 1 teaspoonful caster sugar, 4 oz. currants, 1 oz. peel.*

Sieve flour and salt into a bowl and make well in middle. Cream yeast with sugar and add warm water gradually. Pour into middle of flour mixing in a little flour to make a thin batter. Cover and leave for 20 min. Melt lard and add 3 tablespoonfuls boiling water. Make up to 1/2 pint with milk. Mix all together adding fruit and peel.

Knead well. Cut into six pieces, moulding each into a ball. Flatten with rolling pin and prick with a fork. Set to prove for 1/2 hr., then bake in hot oven about 20 min. Glaze as above.

YULE LOG CAKE

1 Swiss roll (see recipe), about 6 oz. chocolate butter cream (see recipe), little white glacé icing (see recipe), small log-shaped piece of marzipan (see recipe).

Cut a slanting slice from one end of Swiss roll. Spread all over with chocolate butter icing — quite thickly. Set marzipan log in place, also coated with chocolate butter cream, then mark with prongs of a fork to resemble the bark of a tree trunk. Pipe a little white glacé icing at the slanting end to imitate the rings of a sawn log, using the writing nozzle of an icing syringe. Set a toy robin on the smaller jutting-out piece of coated marzipan. Alternatively, decorate with a sprig of holly or mistletoe.

ZABAIONE (ZABAGLIONE)

3 egg yolks, 1 1/2 oz. fine caster sugar, 1/4 pint Marsala, Madeira, or Tarragona wine.

1. Put the yolks of eggs and sugar into a basin and whisk together until mixture is very light in colour and foamy. Add wine and mix well. Transfer mixture to a saucepan over heat, and whisk briskly until it commences to rise, but it must not boil. Serve in glasses with a spoon for eating.

2. To vary use 2 generous tablespoonfuls clear honey instead of sugar with egg yolks, and whisk until thick in top compartment of double saucepan over boiling water. Add wine gradually and flavour with a dash of cinnamon. Whisk well before serving.

PART III

KITCHEN LAYOUT AND EQUIPMENT

APPLE CORER. A small knife with a blade curved deeply from side to side. It is thrust into the apple, and a single turn removes the core.

BAKING SHEET. See BAKING TINS.

BAKING TINS. This also covers tins for roasting meat, of which one or two should always be included in your kitchen equipment. A 'trivet' on which a joint can be placed in the tin to allow the heat to get at it on all sides should go with these.

The number of baking tins proper which you will require depends entirely on your personal needs. A good working minimum would be two cake tins (the kind with a removable floor which can be slid out of the tin with the finished cake on it is recommended), a set of bun tins, two sandwich tins and one for tarts and flans. A plain baking sheet is also very useful. With these should go such accessories as a wire cake tray, a set of pastry cutters, and perhaps a 'sleeve', which last is not used strictly for baking but for steaming puddings.

BOILER. In large kitchens the hot-water boiler is often in the same unit as the stove. Some modern solid-fuel cookers incorporate a water-heating system. Nowadays, owing to the expense of keeping a fire burning continuously to heat water, many people have adopted alternative methods such as geysers operated by gas or electricity, or immersion heaters.

BOTTLE-OPENER. For removing caps from bottles. Most can openers incorporate one, but a separate opener is often useful in the kitchen.

BOWLS. See CROCKERY; WASHING-UP EQUIPMENT.

BREADBIN. If bread has to be kept longer than a day or two, it is best to have it in a large, airy bin with a close-fitting lid, kept in a cool place to prevent the bread drying out and hardening.

BREAD-KNIFE. See KNIVES.

BUN TINS. See BAKING TINS.

BUTTER PATS. Other devices beside the traditional grooved wooden bats are available nowadays for shaping butter into neat balls or pats. One in common use consists simply of a metal ring with a scalloped edge, rather like a pastry cutter.

CAKE TINS. See BAKING TINS.

CAKE TRAY. See BAKING TINS.

CAN OPENER. The opener with a toothed wheel operated by turning a handle is much simpler and easier to use than the old-fashioned kind, and has another advantage in the fact that just before it has completed its circuit of the top of the can, the lid twists automatically so that it can be caught and bent out of the way before it falls into the contents. However, for certain kinds of tin without a rim it is awkward or impossible to use, and it is a good idea to invest in one of each.

CARVING KNIFE. See KNIVES.

CASSEROLE. See CROCKERY.

CHOPPER. See CLEAVER.

CLEAVER. A proper butcher's cleaver is often very handy when it comes to jointing rabbit, for example. But it is even more dangerous than most things in the kitchen, and should be carefully kept from children.

COFFEE-GRINDER. Undoubtedly the best coffee is made from freshly roasted and ground coffee-beans. While some shops sell fresh-ground coffee, many do not, and in order to obtain the best possible flavour one should grind as much as one needs for each brew. A coffee-grinder is a small mill, having a crank like a horizontal mincing machine; most types can be adjustted to give fine, medium or coarse coffee.

COFFEE PERCOLATOR. Probably the most convenient way of making coffee, though there are several methods. A percolator consists of a tall (usually aluminium) pot with a spout and handle, inside which is placed a perforated container which holds the coffee over the water. A tube running up the centre siphons boiling water from the bottom of the percolator over the coffee in the container.

COLANDER. A sort of perforated metal basket with a firm-standing base and a handle at either side. Its main use is for washing vegetables and other foods, rinsing salads, and so on. A small colander can also sometimes serve the double purpose of a steamer, but this is not to be recommended if it can be avoided.

COOKERS. See STOVES.

CORKSCREW. Never be without one in the kitchen. The best kind has a wide handle and a screw which is shaped, rather than merely twisted into a spiral. Cheap, inferior corkscrews tend to break the cork. Always insert the screw so that it runs down the middle, not the side, of the cork, and watch for it to emerge at the bottom. Don't turn it too far before pulling the cork, otherwise flakes of cork will break off the bottom and drop into the contents of the bottle.

CROCKERY. Kitchen crockery can be separated into two kinds: that which is actually used in cooking — i. e. put into the oven — and that used only for preparing food.

Mixing bowls, jugs, plates and such miscellaneous items as jelly moulds belong to the latter category. The choice of size for your mixing bowls depends on the number of people you expect to cook for, but two at least, of different sizes, should be available. Jugs serve many purposes besides merely pouring, and three, again of different sizes, are recommended. Plates for kitchen use should be large rather than small, and have shallow but definite rims for such purposes as flouring meat before frying.

Ovenware may be in earthenware or heatproof glass; a round and an oval casserole and a set of four pudding-basins in graduated sizes (which can of course also be used for other jobs) are a good minimum basis to work on.

Miscellaneous items such as jelly moulds depend entirely on your individual needs. A large serving-dish on which (for example) a bird can be stuffed will often be found useful.

CUPBOARDS. Plenty of cupboard space is essential in a kitchen. If possible, there should be separate storage for every category of food — perishable foods should have their own space, as should aromatic foods and spices, dry goods like rice and flour, and so on. It is a good idea to go through your cupboards at regular intervals, making sure there is no taint or dirt in them which might spoil what is kept there.

CUTLERY. The cutlery you use in your kitchen is best made of good-quality stainless steel, since many of the foods prepared with it would tarnish ordinary metals. Make sure that the handles are attached firmly, since there are few things more infuriating than to have the equipment you are using come to pieces in your hand. For guidance in selecting the type of cutlery you will need, see under the individual items, e. g. knives, forks, spoons, etc.

CUTLET BAT. A wooden bat used for beating cutlets, steaks, etc., to tenderise them.

DEEP-FREEZE. A cold-storage cabinet in which frozen food can be kept for months without deterioration. Generally speaking, however, this is not really necessary when so many grocers now have their own frozen-food cabinets. Frozen foods can be kept for some time near the evaporator in an ordinary refrigerator.

DISHCLOTHS. See WASHING-UP EQUIPMENT.

DISHMOP. See WASHING-UP EQUIPMENT.

DOUBLE BOILER. See POTS AND PANS.

DRAINING-BOARD. See SINK.

DRAWERS. Organise your drawer space, like everything else in the kitchen, so that you can at once lay your hand on what you want. Partitioning the inside of the drawers is the best method. Knives should be kept in a drawer of their own, preferably with slotted holders for those on which it is essential to keep a good edge such as the carving knife.

If your drawers are in a table, make sure you line them with washable plastic or something else which can be kept clean by wiping over, for often something from the table-top falls or spills into the drawer, even in the best-regulated kitchens.

EGG-CUPS. At least one plain egg-cup, with a medium, not deep, bowl, should he handy in the kitchen, for in some recipes quantities occasionally include measurements by the egg-cupful.

EGG SEPARATOR. Some people have difficulty in getting the knack of separating an egg-white from the yolk. A simple device is available, consisting merely of a small metal bowl with a slot in the side, which retains the yolk and allows the white to run out.

EGG-SLICER. A slotted metal plate with a dip in the centre, and a frame across which wires are stretched, hinged together. The hard-boiled egg is placed in the centre of the slotted plate, the wires forced down through it, and it is cut instantly into several slices.

EGG WHISK. See WHISK.

FLOOR. The floor of a kitchen *must* be easily kept clean. Tiles are found in many old-fashioned kitchens, and they have their advantages, though they tend to be cold. Plastic tiles are probably the most convenient material. Linoleum tends to absorb damp and unless of exceptionally good quality wears quickly in a busy kitchen. A good idea if you have a 'damp patch' — e. g. under the sink, or around the saucepan rack — is to put down a mat of foamed plastic which holds drips like a sponge and can simply be wrung out and rinsed in the sink after use.

FLOUR DREDGER. Flour should always be sifted before use. An ordinary wire strainer will serve the purpose, the flour being rubbed through it with a wooden spoon. But proper flour dredgers are obtainable, and are of course specially intended for their job.

FORKS. Three forks should always have a place in your kitchen: a large and a small fork of the ordinary four-tined variety, and a two-pronged fork with a bone, ivory or plastic handle for use as well in turning roasts and other food as in carving.

FRYING PAN. See POTS AND PANS.

FUNNEL. A small metal funnel is very handy in the kitchen, for pouring stock into meat pies, for returning cooking oil to a bottle, and for many other purposes.

GARBAGE BIN. It cannot be over-emphasised that kitchen rubbish and waste should be disposed of quickly, for it makes a breeding-ground for flies and disease germs. A pedal-operated bin with a lid is ideal for putting garbage in before it is taken to the dustbins, and can now be obtained in gaily coloured plastic as well as in the traditional enamelled metal finish.

GARLIC PRESS. Garlic, which is almost the essence of cooking in many places on the Continent, is not to everyone's taste. But for those who like it, small presses can be purchased for extracting the juice and flavour.

GRATER. A round or square device formed of sheet metal punched with holes and slits. Invaluable for grating cheese, shredding vegetables, making breadcrumbs, and so on. There are several graded sizes on the one grater, including one for nutmeg, and there is usually also a sharp-edged slit used for making onion rings.

GRILL. Essentially a rack on which food is placed to cook under or in front of a fire or red-hot plate, together with a pan to catch the juices and fat which fall from the food.

ICING SET. This can be used for other things besides decorating cakes. It consists of a forcing bag (nowadays usually made of polythene) or a small metal tube with a piston sliding in it, to which nozzles of different shapes can be attached.

JELLY MOULD. See CROCKERY.

JUGS. See CROCKERY.

KETTLE. There are two main points to think of when selecting a kettle: first, whether it is the right size for your purposes, and second, whether it is designed for the type of stove you are going to use it on. A kettle designed for use on a gas stove is not necessarily suitable to use on a solid fuel range, for instance.

An electric kettle is a convenient and portable means of having hot water ready to hand, and modern types if properly looked after will give long and trouble-free service.

KITCHEN PLANNING. The kitchen, perhaps more than any other room in the house, repays careful thought before laying it out. There are two major principles to bear in mind: the first is to make the most economical use of the space you have, and the second to arrange the layout so that as little energy as possible is wasted in unnecessary walking. It is a sign of bad design if, for instance, you have to walk right across the kitchen from the vegetable storage rack or bin to the sink, back again to get a scraper for the vegetables, back again for a saucepan, and back again to put them on the stove. Organise the kitchen so that everything you are likely to need at one time is within convenient reach. If your kitchen is square or nearly so, it is fatal to put a table right in the middle of the floor; it is amazing how much this increases the distances you have to walk.

Ventilation and lighting must also be taken into account. Allow no draughts which might, for example, cause a cake to drop when you glance into the oven, but equally make sure that kitchen smells have no chance to hang about in the air. If you have to strain your eyes to look into the oven, or to read a Regulo marking, your lighting is poorly arranged and should be changed.

Modern kitchen planning is undertaken with great care, and there are publications and articles on the subject which will repay study.

KNIVES. There are many different types of kitchen knife; each is — or should be — properly designed for a special job, but a complete list of all the possible varieties would be extremely long. The following selection should be enough for most family needs.

Carving knife. The knife used by chefs for slicing a joint has a straight, rather narrow blade with a rounded end. Since, if you have only one carving knife, you will want it to do several different jobs, probably the best general-purpose type has a sharp-pointed tip, very useful in jointing poultry and rabbit as well as for ordinary carving.

Bread-knife. This should have a fairly long blade, a handle you can grip securely, and a serrated (saw-tooth) edge. It should not be used for anything else but its proper purpose.

Vegetable knife. A small knife with a blade 3—5 in. long, usually with a curved and pointed tip and sometimes with a serrated edge, made of stainless steel.

Cook's knife. A pointed knife used for cutting and chopping food.

Palette knife. This is not used for cutting, but for lifting and turning food during cooking; its blade is long and flexible.

In addition, two or three old table knives are useful to keep in the kitchen, and it should be remembered that scissors can be used for many cutting jobs.

LADLE. See SPOONS.

LEMON SQUEEZER. This is a cone-shaped device with a raised rim for catching juice. Halved lemons, oranges and so on are pressed down over the cone, around which is a ring of small teeth to catch pips and prevent them falling into the juice.

MASHER. This consists of a perforated metal plate mounted on a handle, and is useful not only for mashing potatoes and other vegetables, but for such tasks as beating steak to soften it in the absence of a proper cutlet bat.

MEASURE. Some form of graduated measure is essential. A jug is the most convenient kind in many respects. It should be marked in fluid ounces up to a pint or a quart, and in cubic centimetres as well for choice.

MINCER. A mincing machine should be simple to take apart and put together, and it is advisable when buying one to check whether spare parts are easily available. Always be sure to mount it firmly when in use; if you have to set it on the edge of a wooden table, put strips of wood or metal between the clamp and the table to prevent damage.

MIXER. Though costly, these electrically-driven all-purpose devices are genuinely labour-saving and a great boon to the busy housewife. Most models incorporate a variety of 'heads' for mixing, blending, chopping and other tasks. Small, less expensive hand-held types are obtainable.

NUTCRACKERS. These should be of steel for preference. Between the arms are two or more compartments, the larger for walnuts, brazils, etc., the smaller for hazels and almonds.

OMELETTE PAN. See POTS AND PANS.

OVENWARE. See CROCKERY.

PALETTE KNIFE. See KNIVES.

PASTRY BOARD. This should be large rather than small, very smooth, and of a material not likely to split or break. A marble-topped table is better than a board for flaky and puff pastry, but when more than one job is being carried on at a time, a board is really necessary.

PASTRY CUTTERS. See BAKING TINS.

PEPPER-MILL. Freshly-ground black pepper has a more delicate flavour than commercially-ground white. A few turns of the pepper-mill — a small cylindrical device into which the peppercorns are put — suffices to grind enough to flavour most dishes.

PERCOLATOR. See COFFEE PERCOLATOR.

PLATES. See CROCKERY.

POACHING PAN. See POTS AND PANS.

POTATO PEELER. See VEGETABLE SCRAPER.

POTATO RICER. This consists of a perforated metal container in which the potatoes or other vegetables are placed, and a flat metal plate which is forced into the container by means of a handle. It is quick and simple to use, but not really essential.

POTS AND PANS. At least four saucepans of assorted sizes are advisable for family cooking. As well as these a double boiler is useful, and perhaps a steamer, though it is possible to obtain a sort of rack which fits inside an ordinary saucepan and which serves for steaming food over a little water in the bottom. A poaching pan is a shallow, wide saucepan with a frame holding the small individual bowls into which eggs are broken for cooking.
An 8-in. frying pan is large enough for most purposes; choose one in heavy metal, because it heats more evenly. In addition to the general-purpose frying pan, many people like to keep another small pan exclusively for omelettes and perhaps pancakes.

PRESSURE COOKER. This extremely useful device operates through raising the pressure of the steam generated inside it from a little boiling water. The increase in pressure and temperature speeds up the cooking process of anything placed within it. Full instructions and guidance on use and care of the cooker are given when one is purchased. Its speed and economy often recommend it to busy people.

RACKS. These are often better than shelves or bins for storing. As well as plate racks, there are vegetable racks consisting of tiers of baskets which are clean and convenient, washing-up racks which stand on the draining-board and keep the crockery and cutlery safe while you finish your job, and many others which can be seen at any good hardware shop.

REFRIGERATOR. While not quite indispensable in the modern kitchen, the refrigerator is nearly so. It provides a reliable means of storing perishable foods, and modern types should give years of valuable service. The interior of a refrigerator is not actually below freezing point, except near the evaporator, but the temperature is low enough greatly to increase the length of time for which food can be kept.

ROLLING PIN. Hard wood is probably the best material for a rolling pin, but its essential function can if necessary be carried out with a clean bottle or something similar.

RUBBISH DISPOSAL. See GARBAGE BIN.

SALAD SERVERS. A set of salad servers consists of a large spoon and fork made of either wood or plastic. They can often be obtained to match the bowl in which your salads are served.

SAUCEPANS. See POTS AND PANS.

SCALES. Kitchen scales must be accurate, and one thing to make certain of before you buy is that the pan should sit firmly on its stand. There are two types to be considered: the spring balance, with a dial to register the weight, and the older kind with small metal weights. The latter is often preferred for its greater precision, but the weights have a great attraction for small children and are in consequence often mislaid when one needs them immediately.

SCISSORS. Kitchen scissors are quite invaluable. They are used for cutting vegetables up, jointing and chopping meat, trimming salad vegetables, and many other purposes, while on several types the handles are adapted to be used as a bottle-opener, a tack-hammer, a screw-driver and for other miscellaneous purposes.

SCOURERS. See WASHING-UP EQUIPMENT.

SHARPENING KNIVES. See STEEL.

SIEVE. See STRAINER.

SINK. Where possible, the height of the sink should be chosen to suit your needs, since bending down over it is extremely tiring. It should be large enough for washing-up and any laundry you may do; a length of 18 in. is usually enough. If possible, there should be two draining-boards, one on each side, and a splash-back will help to prevent dampness in the wall behind.

Fitting the taps with 'swirlers' (q. v.) makes rinsing down the sink much easier.

SKEWERS. Two or three wood or metal skewers should always be kept handy.

SLICE. A slice is not used for cutting! It is a flat perforated metal plate mounted on a handle, used for removing food from frying fat.

SPOONS. Both metal and wooden spoons should have a place in your kitchen. Wooden spoons are best for mixing and stirring; they should be of a hard, durable wood and should always be dried out carefully after use.

Of the ordinary metal spoons, at least three — a teaspoon, a dessertspoon and a tablespoon — are absolutely essential in the kitchen. They are not only used for stirring and tasting, but for measuring. If possible, a set of measuring spoons should be purchased and saved for this job alone.

A perforated spoon is extremely useful for removing food from boiling water, for example, and for many other purposes, and a ladle is much safer and more convenient than an old cup as a means of taking liquids out of saucepans on the stove. Another specialised spoon is a basting spoon, having a very shallow bowl for use when roasting meat.

STEAMER. See POTS AND PANS.

STEEL. The traditional round steel bar used for sharpening carving knives is still an excellent method of keeping an edge on a blade. However, the technique of using one properly calls for a little practice, and simple sharpening devices which put the edge on in two or three passes can be obtained.

STEEL WOOL. See WASHING-UP EQUIPMENT.

STORAGE SPACE. See CUPBOARDS; DRAWERS; RACKS.

STOVES. The centre-piece of any kitchen is of course its stove. Many different types are available, and dealers and your local gas and electricity showrooms are always ready to help you choose. Here we will only list a few of the advantages of each type.

Gas cookers. These have several advantages; they heat rapidly, and equally their heat can be reduced quickly also. The fact that the flame gives a rough visual control of temperature appeals to people who like to cook using their own judgment. Modern gas cookers are carefully designed to be simple in operation.

Electric cookers. These are extremely clean and efficient in use, and many modern devices such as automatic time switches and quick-boiling rings are fitted to the latest models. Great care also goes into the design of these stoves.

Solid-fuel cookers. Most of the old objections to these — particularly the fact that solid fuel is dirty to handle — have been eliminated in the up-to-date stoves. An advantage of cooking with one of these is that the kitchen is always warm in winter so long as the stove is in operation. Some models incorporate water-heating boilers.

Oil stoves. While not really ideal for large families or for a per-manent installation, cooking with oil is often an idea which might be considered when investment in an alternative method of cooking is not practicable.

STRAINER. At least one of these baskets of fine wire mesh is an absolute necessity in your kitchen, not only for draining water from boiled foods, but for sifting flour in the absence of a proper flour-dredger, for running cold water over boiled rice to separate the grains, and many other purposes.

SWIRLER. The name given to a tube of flexible plastic or rubber to be attached to a tap over the sink so that the jet from it comes out in a smooth flow and can be directed anywhere it is required.

TABLE. Better than a table for most jobs in the kitchen is a wall-counter, made of enamelled steel with cupboard space underneath, but since this may be out of reach, there are several things to bear in mind when choosing a kitchen table.

It should be tough and durable; it should be firm; the top should be wide enough for your needs and it should stand steadily under all kinds of stress, such as the operation of a mincer. Above all, it must be easy to clean.

A marble top is ideal for most purposes; if only wood can be obtained, it is worth covering it with a durable plastic or some other such material, especially if it has to do duty for serving meals as well.

Be careful not to site your table where it gets in the way every time you cross the room.

TEA-TOWELS. See WASHING-UP EQUIPMENT.

TIMER. Some means of reminding you that what you have in the oven is now due for attention is extremely valuable in the kitchen, especially to a harassed mother! Proper kitchen timers are available, but your ordinary alarm clock is a good stopgap.

TIN OPENER. See CAN OPENER.

TONGS. Extremely useful in the kitchen, there are several kinds available. Narrow-ended tongs shaped like giant sugar-tongs are invaluable for turning food under the grill or potatoes roasting around a joint. The larger kind with perforated bawl-shaped grips are useful for lifting food from boiling water and for many other jobs.

VEGETABLE KNIFE. See KNIVES.

VEGETABLE SCRAPER. There is now a device on the market which consists of a rubber tube to be attached to the tap over the sink, having on the end a small round grater through which the water flows. There is also an attachment for removing eyes from potatoes while scraping them. It is definitely superior to the ordinary method of scraping vegetables with a knife, because the grater reduces all the skin to a fine pulp which is washed away as scraping proceeds.

WASHING-UP EQUIPMENT. The first essential is a bowl large enough to hold everything you will want to wash up at any one time. The modern polythene plastic type is recommended, since it is flexible and not likely to break things put into it. Better than a dishcloth for wiping over the dirty crockery is a small mop with a handle which can be rinsed out afterwards and hung up to dry.

For the stains and crust which will not come off with a mop, plastic pot-scourers are very good, though for some really difficult crusts such as the kind left by burnt milk steel wool is necessary. For cleaning out the crevices in the handles of saucepans and elsewhere stiff-bristled brushes, many with renewable heads, can be obtained.

While crockery is waiting to be dried it may be put into a rack, where it will be safer than if it is only piled on the draining board.

Two or three drying-up cloths should be in use at any one time: the ones not in your hand should be drying out ready for exchange when the one actually being used is too damp to go on. These cloths should never be allowed to become greasy or dirty, and should never be used for anything but the washing-up unless they are thoroughly washed immediately afterwards.

WATER-HEATER. See BOILER; STOVES (Solid-fuel cookers).

WHISK. Though one can do one's whisking with a fork, a whisk specially designed for the task ensures a better blend for less effort. There are several sorts of whisk; perhaps the best consists of two blades mounted on a handle and turned in opposite directions with a cogwheel driven by a small crank. Another efficient type is operated by pumping the handle up and down.

WOODEN SPOON. See SPOONS.

PART IV

A GUIDE TO WINES

ALGERIAN WINE. For more than a hundred years now, the French influence in Algeria has ensured that wine-growing in the area is in accordance with the great French tradition. For this reason, Algeria produces some of the best wines grown anywhere outside Europe.

Unfortunately, most Algerian wine is mixed and shipped in bulk, which destroys its individuality to a great extent. Nonetheless, they are well worth investigation.

APERITIF. A drink taken before and perhaps also with the opening course of a meal. In the broadest sense, therefore, a glass of tomato or fruit juice taken in this way is an apéritif. But the term is generally confined to a glass of wine or a cocktail. The recommended apéritif wines are medium to dry sherry, tawny and white port (chilled in summer), Madeira; Vermouth should also be mentioned, either the sweet or dry making a good apéritif.

ARMAGNAC. A fine French liqueur brandy.

AUSTRALIAN WINES. With due respect to the wine-growers 'down under', it can scarcely be said that their wines offer serious competition to European ones, for, while their quality has undoubtedly improved of late years and in many cases reached a good standard, Australia has nothing to offer comparable to the great wines of the Continent.

BARSAC. A white Bordeaux.

BEAUJOLAIS. A red Burgundy.

BEAUNE. A famous red Burgundy.

BORDEAUX. One of the famous wine-growing areas of France. Red Bordeaux is often called claret (q. v.) in this country. White Bordeaux may be served, generally speaking, wherever a dry white wine is recommended.

BRITISH WINES. At one time, some centuries ago, quite a lot of good wine was apparently grown in Britain. Indeed, recently vine-growing experiments carried out in Kent have shown that the chalky soil so suitable for hops can actually produce grapes of fair quality, and there is some hope that, if the idea takes hold, we may once again see native wines fit to stand up to their Continental cousins. Until that day, however, it is as well to steer clear of so-called 'British wines' which are doctored, fortified and added to — in effect, undergo manufacturing processes that deprive their wine basis of those qualities a connoisseur regards as essential.

BURGUNDY. Burgundy is one of the great wine-growing districts of France. Red Burgundy is recommended as a table wine with game, goose, duck, most meat dishes, and so on. White Burgundy (a dryish wine) goes well with shellfish, oysters, fish in general, white meat such as cold chicken, salads, and so forth.

CAKE. An old tradition is the taking of a glass of wine and a slice of cake at mid-morning. Madeira cake gets its name from the fact that Madeira was the wine most often chosen for this snack. A full sherry or a tawny port is also a good match.

CANARY. A wine from the Canary Islands, similar to Madeira.

CELLAR. A wine cellar need not necessarily be a cellar. It can be anywhere where you can store wine safely, but it must be cool, clean, and well ventilated. Damp is as fatal as heat. If you intend to set up a cellar (which need not be elaborate) ask your wine merchant's advice regarding those wines which will improve with aging; rack the bottles on their sides. Concentrate at first on wines of known quality; as you go on you will find yourself becoming more and more knowledgeable.

CHABLIS. A white wine from the Yonne basin in Lower Burgundy.

CHAMPAGNE. The most famous wine in the world. It is often said, 'Champagne goes with everything', and indeed a meal accompanied all through its courses by different kinds of champagne is regarded as a connoisseur's dream. But there is not *just* 'champagne': all champagnes are produced by a special process which gives body, flavour and sparkle, but there are extra-dry *(brut)*, dry, semi-dry and sweet types, as well as pink champagne and the vintage champagnes in which the special qualities of a particular year are preserved.

The appellation 'champagne' is jealously guarded by French law, and provided your bottle bears the words 'champagne, Produce of France' on the label, and has 'champagne' stamped on the cork, you know you have the real article.

Champagne is the celebration wine *par excellence*. See SERVING WINE for details of its presentation.

CHATEAUNEUF-DU-PAPE. A famous red wine from Provence.

CHEESE. Wine and cheese are old friends. A full-bodied vintage red wine is a wonderful partner for good cheese, and port with the cheese course at the end of a meal is a favourite combination. Wine-tasters often use a bit of bread and cheese to clear their palates before the 'rite' commences.

CHIANTI. A dry red wine from Tuscany in Italy; it can be served wherever a dry red wine is recommended, but especially with Italian food, of course.

CHICKEN. A medium red wine is recommended — perhaps a Burgundy or Bordeaux.

CLARET. The English name for red Bordeaux. It goes well with roast chicken, game, goose, duck, and most meat dishes.

COGNAC. A brandy distilled from the wines of the Cognac district in France, and certainly the best-known brandy in the world. It should be served — either at the conclusion of a meal or as a drink on its own — in a small balloon or tulip glass. Warm the glass a little with your hand before drinking, and inhale the aroma to appreciate it to the full.

COMMANDARIA. A heavy, rather sweet wine from Cyprus.

CUP. A traditional party drink, especially in summer. Use claret as a basis for a red wine cup, hock or Moselle for a white one.

CYPRUS WINES. Commandaria (q. v.) is one of these. There are Cyprus sherries available, but they are not to be compared, of course, with the real thing.

DESSERTS. Serve with these champagne, sparkling or natural sweet wines, e. g. Sauternes.

DUCK. With this, a medium to full red wine.

EMPIRE WINES. Australian and South African wines are the best-known. They are referred to under their own headings.

ENTRE-DEUX-MERS. A White Bordeaux table wine.

ENTRÉES. A light dry white wine, a *vin rosé* or a light claret is recommended.

FOIE GRAS. With this luxury dish, a luxury wine: the finest red and sweet white wines.

FRENCH WINES. Here is a list of the most famous wine-growing districts of France: Alsace, Anjou, Bordeaux, Burgundy, Côtes du Rhône, Champagne. In addition, almost every area of the country seems to have its own table wines — the *vin ordinaire* of the region — whose only disadvantage is often that it is overshadowed by a still better neighbour.

FRUIT. Dry champagne, or fine sweet wines, make a good match.

GAME. A medium to full red wine with this.

GERMAN WINES. Hock and Moselle are probably the best known German wines.

GOOSE. A medium to full red wine with this.

GRAVES. A Bordeaux wine, both white and red.

HERMITAGE. A fine wine from the Rhône valley.

HOCK. A dry white German wine, which comes in the traditional tall, slender bottle. May accompany anything with which a dry white wine is suggested.

HORS D'OEUVRES. Generally speaking, it is a shame to waste wine on anything which is dressed with vinegar. But otherwise, a good idea is to continue the sherry or Madeira which you have been serving as an apéritif (q. v. and accompany the hors d'œuvres with it.

HUNGARIAN WINE. Tokay (q. v.) is about the only Hungarian wine at all well known in Britain.

ICE. Never, under any circumstances whatever, insult a wine by putting lumps of ice in it! If the wine is directed to be served chilled (see SERVING WINE) stand the bottle in a bucket of ice, or put it where a cold tap can run over the base for several minutes. *Don't* put ice in the glasses.

ICES. A sweet white wine, such as a Sauternes, is a very good accompaniment.

ITALIAN WINES. Probably the most famous Italian wine is Chianti (q. v.), but Italy is a great wine-growing country, and such names as Valpolicella are esteemed by connoisseurs.

LOBSTER. Dry white wines and champagne go with this.

MACON. A red Burgundy.

MADEIRA. A wine from the Island of Madeira, very popular in Britain many years ago and now enjoying a return to favour. (See CAKE). It is suggested as an apéritif (q. v.), with soup or hors d'œuvres, and by itself with a mid-morning snack.

MALAGA. A Spanish white wine.

'*MARRYING*'. The perfect harmonisation of wine with food has much in common with the perfect harmony of a happily-married couple; neither must disagree or quarrel with the other. The ideal, when serving wine with food, is to ensure that each course is accompanied by the most suitable wine. Even if you are giving a small dinner-party of (say) six people, since you will need more than a single bottle of wine for it, take care to select two or more different wines according to your proposed menu. Throughout this section of the book, it will be found that combinations which connoisseurs recommend as particularly suitable are listed under individual headings.

MARSALA. A Sicilian wine, heavy and rather sweet.

MEAT. A full-bodied red wine is the right accompaniment for equally full-flavoured meats, such as roast, game, venison and so on. A medium red wine goes well with poultry, white meats such as veal, and other similar dishes. A *rosé* often suits the latter well, also. But with meat more perhaps than with anything else, the selection of wine is dependent on individual taste.

MÉDOC. A red Bordeaux.

MONBAZILLAC. A famous sweet white French wine.

MOSELLE. A dry white German wine, recommended wherever a wine of this kind is suggested, e. g. with fish, shellfish, oysters, cold dishes, salads, etc.

MULLED WINE. This is wine heated through with spices and flavourings, a wonderful heartening drink for winter. There are many recommended techniques: one can of course mull wine in a saucepan, but traditional methods include the use of a 'boot', a sort of foot-shaped container with one end pointed for thrusting into the hot embers of an open fire, and the use of a red-hot poker thrust into the wine. This latter method has mainly the virtue of a spectacle — the accomplished 'muller' will dust the ash from the poker with his bare hand before inserting it in the wine — for it destroys the bouquet.

A full red wine such as a Burgundy is best for mulling; the choice of spices and flavourings can be altered to suit your own tastes, but there are dozens of accepted recipes.

NUTS. Port and nuts are a traditional after-dinner combination.

OPENING WINE. Use the corkscrew with care. Insert it delicately down the middle of the cork (it is therefore necessary to begin pushing the end of the screw in slightly off-centre, so that the vertical axis of the screw eventually does pass down the middle). If you let the screw scrape down the side of the neck, it will break the cork. Watch it carefully as you come to the bottom of the cork; when the base of the cork bulges, stop turning and start pulling — otherwise fragments of cork will break away and fall into the wine.

Draw the cork with a single steady pull, if necessary grasping the bottle between your knees. A fine old wine may have a sediment, in which case decant it, leaving the sediment at the bottom. Most table wines of the cheaper sort are good to the bottom of the bottle. An old wine should be drunk the day — better yet, the evening — it is opened, but a young ordinary table wine will keep for a day or two if re-corked with care. Sherry and port, of course, keep for several days, and are perhaps better decanted.

When you have opened your bottle, pour out a little into a glass and taste it. You may have the ill-luck to chance across a poorly stoppered bottle, or one which is 'corked' and spoiled. Set it aside and take it back to your wine merchant; he will almost certainly be glad to re-place it.

OYSTERS. For a luxury food, a luxury wine. Dry champagne is excellent. But any good dry white wine can be served with oysters.

PINOT. An Alsatian wine.

PORT. A full-bodied wine, red, tawny or white, which comes from the Douro region of Portugal, not far from Oporto. It is a wine which has long been popular in Britain, and indeed its designation is protected by British law. Ruby (red) port is dark in colour and medium sweet; tawny is lighter in colour, owing to being kept in cask longer, and white is made from white grapes. All these have the same rather high strength.

It is recommended for serving as an apéritif (q. v.), for which tawny and white port may be chilled, and as a dessert wine with nuts or after-dinner coffee. It also goes with a mid-morning snack (see CAKE).

Many mixed drinks use a basis of port. e. g. the well-known port and lemon. A drink said to be popular in the port region itself, where the local wine of course is a standard drink, is port made into a long drink with soda-water.

POULTRY. A medium to full red wine with this: roughly speaking, the darker the meat and the fuller the flavour, the fuller the accompanying wine. Thus for chicken a medium wine, or even a *rosé*, for duck and goose a full one.

RHINE WINES. See GERMAN WINES.

RIESLING. An Alsatian wine. A similar wine from Yugoslavia (Yugoslav Riesling) can be obtained and is to be recommended.

ROASTS. See MEAT.

ROUSSILLON. A region of France known for its natural, sweet wines.

SALADS. A dry white wine may be used to go with these, but it is well to bear in mind that vinegar and wine are natural enemies, and if the dressing is very sharp or acid it will destroy your enjoyment of the wine altogether. It is probably advisable in such a case to postpone the wine until the next course, and drink water for the moment!

SAINT-EMILION. A red Bordeaux.

SALMON. Dry white or first-class sweet white wines are the recommended accompaniment.

SAUTERNES. A sweet white Bordeaux, very highly regarded.

SERVING WINES. Part of the enjoyment of having wine with a meal is derived from the pleasure one has in serving it, and it is as well to master the following fairly simple rules in order to make the most of your wine.

As regards actually getting the wine out of the bottle, see OPENING WINE. But there is much more to be borne in mind than simply un-corking. There is a way of getting the best out of every wine you serve, and it is a pity not to make use of it.

Champagne, the queen of wines, should be served cool but not cold. It is commonly thought that it should appear at table in a bucket of ice. This is regarded as an error, for if the wine is too sharply chilled its fine bouquet cannot escape. A bucket of water with a few lumps of ice in it is the recommended method; but cooling can be accomplished either by using the refrigerator (with maximum caution!) or simply by wrapping the bottle in a damp cloth and standing it in a draught for some time. 44° to 48° F. is the recommended temperature. If champagne is served too warm, it loses its lightness and sparkle.

When it comes to uncorking champagne, avoid the wasteful violence of the removal that shoots the cork across the room and spills a quantity of wine all over the carpet. Ease the cork free very slowly, holding the bottle slightly away from the vertical, and you will find your bottle stays full. Wipe round the neck with a clean cloth before pouring.

As for the best glass to use: a slender and deep one is the best, not the commonly-used shallow glass with a wide bowl on a stem. Give the bubbles some distance to rise, and the sparkle will remain longer, and with it the crisp lightness which is the appeal of the wine. A tulip glass, or what is known as a *demi-ballon,* is advised.

Pour the wine into the glass, holding the bottle at the base, as though you were pouring a bottle of stout — and trying to avoid a 'head' on it — an unworthy comparison, but apt, for the wine should not be allowed to fall for more than the minimum possible distance. It should flow, not run, into the glass, preferably down the side. Only half-fill the glasses; the wine goes flat rapidly once it is out of the bottle.

Finally, if you are going to use a swizzle-stick or 'mosser' in your champagne, all we can say is you might as well have bought an ordinary wine. Whisking the wine destroys in a moment those unique qualities which its growers and cellarers have spent years in developing.

White Wines and Vins Rosés should also be served cold. Dry wines are best at about 45⁰ to 50⁰ F., sweet at 40⁰ F. This counteracts the slight tendency of sweet white wines to be cloying. Do *not* put ice into the glasses. It is a counsel of perfection to chill the glasses also before serving.

Sparkling White Wines should be treated in the same way as both the above — in other words, they should be cooled because they are white, and they should be poured with care because they are sparkling. The crispness imparted to them by their effervescence is destroyed, as is champagne's, by careless pouring and long standing in a glass.

Red Wines, in general, should be served at room temperature, clarets at say 60⁰ to 64⁰, Burgundy very slightly less warm. Red wines may be opened up to a quarter of an hour before drinking, to let them 'breathe'; this brings up the aroma and heightens the pleasure of drinking them.

All Wines are best served in half-full glasses.

Glasses do not have the over-riding importance some people give to them. A table wine will taste equally good from wine-glasses, or from small, clean, highly-polished tumblers. A fine wine with a notable bouquet should be honoured with a suitable glass, as recommended above under champagne, but there is a good reason for this — the shape and curvature and depth of the glass are all calculated to bring out the best qualities in the wine. It is unnecessary fuss to serve a good but ordinary wine in the same elaborate manner as a superbly good one.

Finally, remember to match your wine carefully to your food, and you will have mastered the basic rules of wine serving.

SHELLFISH. Hock, Moselle, white Burgundy, Graves — and the inevitable champagne! — all such white wines go excellently with shellfish.

SHERRY. The real sherry comes from Spain; the name is derived from Xeres (modern Jerez). The name is now also applied to wines of a similar type produced in other countries, especially Cyprus, South Africa and Australia.

Essentially, sherry is a full but not heavy wine. It is rather to be drunk for its own sake than as an accompaniment to food. As an apéritif (q. v.) a dry sherry really has no rival: it is particularly suitable when good wines are to go with the subsequent meal, for it does not affect the ability of the palate to appreciate them. Cocktails and heavier wines may sometimes have an altogether disastrous effect in this respect.

There are several qualities of sherry, broadly sweet, medium, medium-dry, dry and very dry. The medium and medium-dry are the most popular kinds, but some people maintain that they like a sherry 'so dry you can practically shake it out of the bottle like dust'!

As well as being taken as an apéritif, sherry may be continued with the hors d'œuvres or soup, particularly with clear soup. A full medium sherry also goes well with a mid-morning snack (see CAKE).

Certain South African sherries obtainable nowadays are of a quality one can respect, and indeed some of the various wines of sherry type which are marketed under the name have a character of their own. But they are not really sherry. Still, this fact need not prevent one from enjoying the best of them on their own merits.

SOLE. Dry white or first-class sweet white wines should be served with this.

SOUP. A common practice, especially with clear soup, is to continue the wine served as an apéritif — dry or medium-dry sherry, dry Madeira, for instance — until the end of this sourse. With a thick soup, it is better to go on at once to a proper table wine, usually the white wine which will be served with the fish course, or the light red which is to go with the meat, poultry or whatever of that nature is on the menu.

SOUTH AFRICAN WINES. Certain South African sherries have merit. See EMPIRE WINES.

SPANISH WINES. Sherry, of course, is indisputably the best-known Spanish wine. But all around the Mediterranean shores of Europe, from Spain to Greece, the countries have wines of their own which we may not encounter in Britain because they do not retain their qualities during shipment.

SWEET COURSES. With these, champagne, sparkling or natural sweet white wines, such as Sauternes.

TABLE WINE. Any wine primarily intended as an accompaniment to food, from the *vin ordinaire* of France, which one orders in a French restaurant as readily (or perhaps more so) as one asks for a jug of water in England, to the outstanding vintage wines served at banquets on the grand scale. In general, they are not full or heavy; full wines like port and sherry are taken on their own or with snacks which serve rather to set off the wine, instead of the wine setting off the food.

TASTING. The business of tasting wine is taken very seriously indeed by the connoisseur; it is often described as a 'rite', and in fact the solemnity with which a tasting is conducted by experts has something of the quality of a religious service. Of course, it is not for most people to acquire the knowledge and skill in tasting required for the task, nor are most people fortunate enough to make the acquaintance of the wines these experts hold almost in awe, on which has been lavished the skill and care of cellarers often for many years. But it is as well to know something of the techniques employed, for even at one's own table one's enjoyment can be heightened and one's purchases of wine better appreciated, if one knows how to make the most of their appearance, their aroma and their flavour.

The first and most important requirement is to clear the palate, as they say — that is, to make sure the sense of taste is not dulled. A little bread and cheese is good for this; fatal are smoking or the eating of sweets immediately beforehand. Even the drinking of water is forbidden by many experts.

The wine to be tasted is poured into a glass of the appropriate shape, not filling it more than half full. The bouquet will then gather in the empty half. Hold it up to the light to examine it for colour, clarity and 'brilliance'.

Hold the glass in the cupped hand, turning it slowly; the warmth and movement helps to increase the fragrance.

Inhale this fragrance; after that, and only after that, taste it in small sips retaining the wine in the mouth for long enough for the full delicacy of the flavour to make itself felt.

Of course, all this carefulness is wasted without the knowledge to use it; therefore, if you decide you want to know more about wine, get to know the distinguished wines gradually.

TOKAY. A wine of Hungarian origin.

TRAMINER. An Alsatian wine.

TURBOT. Dry white wine or first-class sweet white wine is served with this.

VENISON. A full-bodied red wine for this; if the venison is prepared elaborately, then the wine should be correspondingly fine.

VERMOUTH. Made on a basis of wine flavoured with herbs and sweetened to a greater or lesser degree. There are two well-known varieties, Italian and French; they are served either plain, as an apéritif (q. v.), or with spirits (e. g. 'gin and It') as cocktails.

VIN ROSÉ. Intermediate in colour and to some extent in nature between red and white. This wine is of a translucent pale reddish colour, and though it should be served cold like a white wine, it goes well with those dishes with which a light red wine may be served.

VINTAGE YEARS. Strictly speaking, there is a vintage, or gathering of the grapes and making of wine, every year in a vineyard. But it is customary to refer to those years in which the wine is of especially good quality as 'vintage years'. Since most wines deteriorate after many years' storage, many vintage years are lost to us today, but whenever a superlative crop arises we can look forward to enjoying wines which may come to be equally good.

For most table wines the best recent years were: 1943, 1945, 1947, 1948, 1949, 1952, 1953, 1955. For port: 1942, 1945, 1947, 1948, 1950, 1955.

My Own Recipes

My Own Recipes